Britain, Australia and the Bomb

Also by Lorna Arnold

BRITAIN AND THE H-BOMB

WINDSCALE 1957

Also by Mark Smith

NATO ENLARGEMENT DURING THE COLD WAR

Britain, Australia and the Bomb

The Nuclear Tests and Their Aftermath

Second Edition

Lorna Arnold
Official Historian

and

Mark Smith
Programme Director for Defence and Security,
Wilton Park, West Sussex

First published 2006 by
PALGRAVE MACMILLAN
Houndmills, Basingstoke, Hampshire RG21 6XS and
175 Fifth Avenue, New York, N.Y. 10010
Companies and representatives throughout the world.

PALGRAVE MACMILLAN is the global academic imprint of the Palgrave
Macmillan division of St. Martin's Press, LLC and of Palgrave Macmillan Ltd.
Macmillan® is a registered trademark in the United States, United Kingdom
and other countries. Palgrave is a registered trademark in the European
Union and other countries.

ISBN-13: 978–1–4039–2101–7 hardback
ISBN-10: 1–4039–2101–6 hardback
ISBN-13: 978–1–4039–2102–4 paperback
ISBN-10: 1–4039–2102–4 paperback

This book is printed on paper suitable for recycling and made from fully
managed and sustained forest sources.

A catalogue record for this book is available from the British Library.

Library of Congress Cataloging-in-Publication Data

Arnold, Lorna.
    Britain, Australia and the bomb : the nuclear tests and their aftermath /
Lorna Arnold and Mark Smith. – 2nd ed.
        p. cm.
    Rev. ed. of: A very special relationship. 1987.
    Includes bibliographical references and index.
    ISBN-13: 978–1–4039–2101–7 (cloth)
    ISBN-10: 1–4039–2101–6 (cloth)
      1. Nuclear weapons – Testing. 2. Great Britain – Military relations –
Australia. 3. Australia – Military relations – Great Britain. I. Smith, Mark,
1965 July 1– II. Title.

U264.A77 2006
355.8'251190941—dc22   2006050312

10 9 8 7 6 5 4 3 2 1
15 14 13 12 11 10 09 08 07 06

Printed and bound in Great Britain by
Antony Rowe Ltd, Chippenham and Eastbourne

Contents

List of Tables, Figures and Maps

Tables

Figures

Maps

List of Photographs

Photographs 10–13 are reproduced by kind permission of The National Archives.

Foreword

Those of us who have sat at the controls of a V-bomber, ready to carry a British nuclear bomb to targets behind the Iron Curtain, had little insight at the time into the complexity and ingenuity that had made our independent deterrent possible. Lorna Arnold, assisted in this new edition by Mark Smith, has brought us the technical, political and practical problems which faced the architects of Britain's nuclear weapons programme. When US cooperation ceased in 1946, the postwar British government might have decided to concentrate its meagre resources on the welfare state. That both the Attlee and Churchill governments pressed on, first with atomic and then with thermonuclear weapon developments demonstrated the political importance attached to nuclear weapons and great power status at that time.

This book tells the human story behind those decisions, and what that meant in terms of turning policy into a working device. The generous cooperation from Australia harps back to an age when the dangers from atmospheric nuclear tests were less well understood. The Aboriginals also paid a particular price to their way of life. Nevertheless, it is a story of scientific achievement and organisational mastery. Arranging complex tests on the other side of the world, which involved thousands of people and new engineering and physics, was all done without e-mail, satellite communications or desktop computers. Britain and Australia cooperated in an astonishingly successful project. The development of the thermonuclear H-bomb was done in a much shorter timescale than the United States or the Soviet Union had managed.

This history appears at an important time in the continuing story of nuclear weapons. In the UK, discussion has started about the future of the British deterrent, which is now much smaller in number than during the Cold War. It is also less independent than the early days. There is less attachment to the arguments of the 1940s about world power status, but concerns remain about the continuing need for a deterrent against possible threats from emerging nuclear powers. States such as Iran, North Korea and others, which perhaps aspire to nuclear weapon status, face many of the hurdles which are detailed in these pages. Before commentators or politicians talk glibly about the easy development of nuclear weapons, they would do well to read this book.

The determination of politicians, scientists, military and officials in the immediate postwar years made it possible for Britain to have an independent nuclear deterrent. I have no doubt that it contributed to the strategic uncertainty, which kept a nuclear war at bay through the Cold War. This book is a fitting tribute to them.

Air Marshal the Lord Garden KCB

Preface

This book recalls a unique and probably unrepeatable fifteen-year partnership, of historic importance to both Australia and Britain. Between 1952 and 1957 British scientists and engineers, thanks to extraordinary Australian generosity, carried out twelve atmospheric atomic explosions on Australian territory, with invaluable help from the host nation. After these trials ended in 1957, smaller weapons experiments continued until 1962. These Australian trials enabled Britain to develop atomic bombs. Though they did not include hydrogen bomb tests, they also played an essential part in the development of the British megaton devices tested at Christmas Island in 1957–8.

Between 1945 and 1963 (the year of the Partial Test Ban Treaty) the US and the Soviet Union conducted hundreds of atmospheric nuclear tests, as the nuclear arms race began. Some trials were very large, releasing huge quantities of radioactivity into the environment. In this context, the much smaller British programme (21 tests in all) looks insignificant. But it was highly effective in establishing Britain as a nuclear power and securing the Anglo-American nuclear relationship, which for over 40 years has been at the core of British foreign and defence policy. This could not have come to pass without indispensable Australian aid, which was so freely given.

This story should not be forgotten. Why a new edition of a book published in 1987, and out of print for many years? There are two reasons. First, the subject matter is still of considerable interest. Controversies surrounding it recurrently appear in the media, and in political discourse in Australia and the UK. However, since 1987 no other book on the subject has appeared. Second, new information has appeared, in both Australia and the UK, enabling the story to be brought up to date.

Therefore, it is now opportune to review and update the story. We are now able to follow through the story of the Maralinga Range after 1987, particularly the clean-up of the range. Moreover, further epidemiological studies have been undertaken and published on the health of test participants. Finally, a greater range of declassified material is now available compared to 1987, which makes possible some amplification of some scientific and technical content.

This combination of factors meant that a second edition was both necessary and desirable. A central part in making this possible was played by Professor John Simpson OBE, of the Mountbatten Centre for International Studies (MCIS) at the University of Southampton, who has over forty years' experience of researching British nuclear history. After consultations with the Ministry of Defence, owners of the copyright to the original edition, it was decided to conduct the research for the new edition at MCIS, with John Simpson acting as supervisor and peer reviewer for the new material. MCIS was an especially congenial and appropriate home, since it is also running a major research project on British nuclear history 1952–73, funded by the AHRC.

Some parts of the story did not require rewriting. Others did. Some have been augmented by new material which we felt would amplify and enrich the existing text. In particular, the release of official documents since 1987 has enabled us to explain better the interrelationship of certain Australian and Christmas Island tests, and present an outline of the 1952–8 British tests as a coherent programme. Consequently, the technical and strategic purpose of each test is now discussed in more detail, and a short chapter on the Christmas Island thermonuclear tests in *Operation Grapple* has been added. The recent reports on the effects of testing on participants and on the environment that have been released in the UK and Australia are also discussed in additional chapters. The bibliography and the references have also been brought up to date. We hope that this new edition will throw light on a history about which little published information has been available, but which has been the subject of much myth, misinformation and misinterpretation.

* * *

Our thanks are due to all those who have helped us in preparation of this new edition: John Baylis, Brian Jamison, Ken Johnston, Peter Jones, Gerry Kendall, Glynn Libberton, Chris Maddock, Mike McTaggart, Richard Moore, Kate Pyne and John Simpson.

List of Abbreviations

AAEC	Australian Atomic Energy Commission
ACAE	The Anderson Committee
AE(O)	Atomic Energy Organization
AERE	Atomic Energy Research Establishment
AHPR	Australian health physics representative
AIRAC	Australian Ionizing Radiation Advisory Council
ANU	Australian National University
ARC	Agricultural Research Council
ARDU	Australian Radiation Detection Unit
ARL	Australian Radiation Laboratory
ASIO	Australian Security Intelligence Organization
AWTC	Atomic Weapons Tests Committee
AWTSC	Atomic Weapons Tests Safety Committee
BNTVA	British Nuclear Test Veterans Association
CAE	Controller, Atomic Energy
CAW	Controller of Atomic Weapons
CBL	convective boundary layer
CDEE	Chemical Defence Experimental Establishment
CEA	Commissariat à l'Energie Atomique
CND	Campaign for Nuclear Disarmament
CPAE	Controller of Production (Atomic Energy)
CSAR	Chief Superintendent Armaments Research
CSHER	Chief Superintendent High Explosives Research
CSIRO	Commonwealth Scientific and Industrial Research Organization
CXRL	Commonwealth X-Ray and Radium Laboratory
DAWRE	Director Atomic Weapons Research Establishment
DGAW	Director General of Atomic Weapons
DPC	Defence Policy Committee
DRPC	Defence Research Policy Committee
GHD	Gutteridge, Haskins and Davey
HER	High Explosives Research
ICBM	intercontinental ballistic missile
ICRP	International Commission on Radiological Protection
IF	Indoctrinee Force
ISV	in situ vitrification

LRWE	Long Range Weapons Establishment
MARSU	Maralinga Range Support Unit
MARTAC	Maralinga Rehabilitation Technical Advisory Committee
MBWP	Monte Bello Working Party
MEP	Maralinga Experimental Programme
MM	multiple myeloma
MoD	Ministry of Defence
MPD	maximum permissible dose
MPL	maximum permissible levels
MRC	Medical Research Council
NATO	North Atlantic Treaty Organization
NRAC	National Radiation Advisory Committee
NRPB	National Radiological Protection Board
NZNTVA	New Zealand Nuclear Test Veterans Association
OAW	Operational Use of Atomic Weapons
PIPPA	plutonium-producing power reactor
PTBT	Partial Test Ban Treaty
RAAF	Royal Australian Air Force
RAF	Royal Air Force
RAN	Royal Australian Navy
RDU	radiation detection unit
RE	Royal Engineers
R-EVCA	Radiation-Exposed Veterans Compensation Act
RES	reticuloendothelial system
RN	Royal Navy
SAGW	surface-to-air guided missile
SMR	standard mortality rate
SRCA	Safety, Rehabilitation and Compensation Act
TAG	Technical Assessment Group
UK	United Kingdom
UKAEA	UK Atomic Energy Authority
UKMOSS(A)	United Kingdom Ministry of Supply Staff
UNSCEAR	United Nations Scientific Committee on the Effects of Atomic Radiation
US	United States
USAEC	United States Atomic Energy Commission
USAF	United States Air Force
VEA	Veterans Entitlement Act

1
Atomic Policies and Policymakers

Origins

Why, and how, did Britain decide at the end of the Second World War to develop her own atomic weapons?[1] The origins of the decision go back to 1939, the year that saw both the outbreak of the war and scientific discoveries that were to lead to the atomic bombs that ended it.

During 1939 it was found that when neutrons – uncharged particles from the nucleus of an atom – bombarded atoms of uranium, not only were fission fragments and an immense amount of energy released, but also some spare neutrons which could then split other uranium atoms so that a chain reaction was possible, releasing more and more energy. It was only two days before war broke out in September that the great Danish physicist Niels Bohr, with an American colleague, J. A. Wheeler, published the theory that gave understanding of uranium fission. That is, the basic scientific knowledge was openly available to the whole world.

Scientists in several countries had seen during 1939 that uranium fission might be a source of heat and power far beyond anything ever known. It also seemed that it might provide an explosive of unprecedented power. If so, would German scientists be able to develop it for Hitler? Bohr's paper made this seem unlikely, as it showed that fission is much more likely to occur in one kind of uranium atom – the fissile isotope uranium-235 – than in uranium-238 atoms. But natural uranium consists mainly of uranium-238 (99.3 per cent), with only 0.7 per cent uranium-235, and a chain reaction can be achieved in natural uranium only if the neutrons are slowed down (or moderated) to increase their chances of hitting the fissile uranium-235 atoms. Slow neutrons, however, cannot produce the tremendously fast reaction required for an atomic explosion. Scientists who realized that the fast neutron was necessary for an atomic bomb thought it

1

would be possible only by using pure uranium-235; they did not think a bomb feasible, therefore, since the task of separating uranium-235 from the slightly heavier but chemically identical uranium-238 would be impossible. So although physicists in Britain and America continued with uranium research – which might prove very important in the long run – they did not see it as a contribution to winning the war. Britain had other more urgent wartime projects, such as radar research, and the United States did not enter the war until December 1941, when Japan attacked Pearl Harbor.

In the spring of 1940 there came a turning point. Two physicists in Birmingham, England – Rudolf Peierls, a refugee from Germany, and Otto Frisch, a refugee from Austria – wrote a memorandum that showed that a lump of uranium-235 of about 5 kg would give the prodigiously fast reaction needed for an atomic explosion equivalent to several thousand tons of dynamite. The memorandum then suggested an industrial method for separating uranium-235. It drew attention to the radiation hazards such a bomb would create. Finally, it emphasized the strategic and moral implications.

As a result of the Frisch–Peierls memorandum, a scientific committee, codenamed the Maud Committee, was set up.[2] Soon after, as France fell, two French scientists, Hans von Halban and Lew Kowarski, escaped to England. They came from a Paris-based team that had been the first to report early in 1939 the possibility of achieving a slow chain reaction in ordinary, natural uranium. Even though scientists believed by 1940 that this slow reaction would be useless for a bomb, it held out the hope of nuclear power. The two French physicists carried with them the total world stock of heavy water which they had brought from Norway; this was the best known and most efficient moderator for slowing down neutrons. The French scientists settled at the Cavendish Laboratory in Cambridge, and here two of their colleagues predicted that in the course of slow chain reactions in ordinary, unseparated uranium a new element almost completely unknown in nature would be formed, which would behave like uranium-235 and would be usable for bombs. This was the element later called plutonium.

The Maud Committee, fearful of possible German progress, worked with frantic haste. In the summer of 1941, it presented to the British government a brilliant and comprehensive report showing the possibility of an atomic bomb – certainly with uranium-235 and possibly with plutonium – and described the processes and plant required. It even estimated the cost. A copy of the report was taken to the still neutral United States where groups of scientists were, rather desultorily, studying bomb possibilities. It was only after they received the Maud Report that the Americans took the project seriously and, even before Pearl Harbor, launched what was to be the huge Manhattan Project.

The British government meanwhile immediately set up an organization with the codename *Tube Alloys*. Clearly, the project would mean an enormous industrial effort. Was it possible to build the plant in beleaguered Britain, which was under enemy air attack and short of manpower and materials? British scientists and politicians decided that the first pilot plants ought to be built in Britain, and later full-scale plants in North America, preferably in Canada with American help. But the project had such vast implications that there was a fear of transferring all the work from Britain to the United States, which was still neutral and might become isolationist after the war as it done after the 1914–18 war.

At the end of 1941, the British were ahead and the United States suggested a joint project. But the proposal was treated with cool condescension; the British wanted exchanges of information, and no more. By the summer of 1942 Americans had forged ahead very fast. The British, still struggling to build a few pilot units for a uranium separation plant, now wished to be partners in the American project, but they were too late and were not wanted; even the exchange of information ceased. The British were desperate: they realized that the atomic bomb would be the key to national power in the postwar world, and they also had great hopes of peaceful nuclear energy, but they could not make progress alone and were cut off from knowledge of the American project.

After great efforts, Winston Churchill eventually persuaded Franklin D. Roosevelt to sign the Quebec Agreement in August 1943.[3] It enabled the British to participate in the Manhattan Project, and also set up arrangements for joint exploitation and purchase of uranium supplies. There were two other important provisions: first, that neither side would use the bomb without the other's consent; and second, that neither would communicate any atomic information to third parties except by mutual consent. After the Quebec Agreement, nearly all the British scientists working on uranium-235 or on fast neutrons for bombs joined the US project; most went to Los Alamos, the atomic bomb laboratory in New Mexico. The British contribution to the Manhattan Project, though on a very small scale, was of high quality and of key importance in some crucial areas of research, so that again it hastened the completion of the bombs.

Meanwhile, the French and British scientists at Cambridge engaged in slow neutron work had been moved to Canada where a joint research establishment was set up, and after the Quebec Agreement the Americans underwrote the project, which was directed by the British scientist, John Cockcroft.[4]

When the war ended, there was almost no doubt in the mind of British politicians and scientists that Britain must have her own nuclear programme. It was a flexible and open-ended programme, to carry out research 'covering all uses of atomic energy' and to produce fissile material in sufficient quantity to enable Britain to develop a programme 'for the use of atomic energy as circumstances may require'.[5] At first this did not mean atomic bombs, for there were hopes that international control of atomic energy might be established; but the Atomic Energy Commission of the new United Nations Organization, set up in January 1946, failed and was wound up in May 1948.[6] However, it was generally assumed that Britain would make atomic bombs, and the engineers given the task of constructing reactors to produce plutonium had been told that it was for bombs, to be made with utmost urgency in the vital interests of the nation. A very secret decision to make atomic bombs was taken by ministers in January 1947 – it was not disclosed to Parliament until May 1948 – and from this time an independent nuclear deterrent became a cornerstone of British government policy.[7] It was endorsed by both the major political parties (except for a twelve-month interval, 1960–61) and supported by the majority of the public; there was little criticism or questioning before 1954 and no substantial organized opposition until the Campaign for Nuclear Disarmament (CND) was founded at the beginning of 1958.

What were the reasons underlying the 1945 and 1947 decisions? There were strategic grounds; there were considerations of status; and there was Britain's relationship with the United States.

Strategic reasons

Strategic ideas about atomic weapons were very general at first. In 1945, shortly before the atomic bombing of Japan, an advisory committee of British scientists (at least two of whom later strongly opposed the British weapons programme) concluded that the only answer to an atomic bomb was to be prepared to use it in retaliation – i.e. deterrence.

The 1947 decision was not made in response to an immediate military threat. It was based, rather, on an intuitive feeling that Britain must possess this climacteric weapon. It was seen as a manifestation of the scientific and technological strength on which Britain must depend. At the end of the war, it must be remembered, though there were American occupying forces in Germany and Austria, there was no formal commitment on the part of the United States to defend Britain or Western Europe and no 'nuclear umbrella'. NATO was not set up until 1949.

Even in the closing stages of the war some people, notably Churchill, had become increasingly apprehensive about a postwar Soviet threat. But for a while after the end of the war no immediate danger to the peace of the world seemed very likely. However, by early 1948 the developing Cold War made the military threat much closer and more menacing. A Communist regime was established in Czechoslovakia in February 1948; in June the Soviet blockade of Berlin began, and lasted nearly a year; the three-year Korean War broke out in June 1950. In September 1950 the Labour government undertook a general rearmament programme.

Status

The second reason for Britain's decision to possess nuclear weapons was her belief in her great power status. Her wartime achievement, without which Germany would probably have been victorious, and her crucial atomic role masked her changed status in the world. There were indeed two superpowers: the United States, with its atomic monopoly and economic might; and the Soviet Union, which became the second nuclear power with its first atomic test in 1949 – fully three years before Britain's. This was a shattering blow to Britain, which had expected to be second in the field. But although Britain was not a superpower, she was, amidst the devastation of other European countries, a great power only one step below the superpowers. If, in the new atomic age, she did not make atomic bombs she would, to quote Lord Cherwell, Churchill's friend and scientific adviser, 'rank with other European nations who have to make do with conventional weapons'. 'If we are unable to make the bomb ourselves', he wrote, 'and have to rely entirely on the United States for this vital weapon, we shall sink to the rank of a second-class nation, only permitted to supply auxiliary troops, like the native levies who were allowed small arms but not artillery'.[8] Atomic weapons seemed to guarantee continuing great power status for Britain. Hardly anyone except Sir Henry Tizard, then chief scientific adviser to the Ministry of Defence, questioned this view. In 1949 he wrote, 'we persist in regarding ourselves as a great power ... we are *not* a great power and never will be again. We are a great nation but if we continue to behave like a great power we shall soon cease to be a great nation. Let us take warning from the fate of the great powers of the past and not burst ourselves with pride (see Aesop's fable of the frog)'.[9]

The Anglo-American relationship

The partnership embodied in the 1943 Quebec Agreement had been reaffirmed by Churchill and Roosevelt in another agreement signed in September 1944 at Hyde Park (Roosevelt's country home in New York State).[10] It said *inter alia* that full Anglo-American collaboration in developing atomic energy for civil and military purposes would continue after the war 'unless and until terminated by joint agreement'. But after Roosevelt's death, the agreement proved to be worthless, as no one in the US Administration knew about it. Yet another agreement, proposing 'full and effective collaboration' in atomic energy, was made in November 1945 in Washington by Harry Truman, Clement Attlee and Mackenzie King, the Canadian premier.[11] But in a few months these agreements were swept aside when, in August 1946, the US Congress passed the Atomic Energy Act (the McMahon Act), which prohibited the passing of classified atomic information to any foreign country, including Britain, and imposed the severest penalties, including the death penalty. At one blow it ended the Anglo-American cooperation of the Quebec, Hyde Park and Washington agreements of 1943, 1944 and 1945. Only one area of partnership remained: the arrangements set up by the Quebec Agreement for the joint procurement and allocation of uranium, the indispensable raw material of atomic energy.

The McMahon Act meant that Britain must develop her atomic project on her own, without American help. Despite forebodings in Whitehall, this was not a serious obstacle to the building of the original atomic plants and a simple Nagasaki-type bomb. The withdrawal of Anglo-American atomic collaboration, however, was of the utmost political and strategic concern to Britain and of great technological importance for more advanced weapons.

While the British atomic energy project developed independently, successive British governments strove ceaselessly in the next twelve years to regain the Anglo-American atomic partnership. There were hopeful moves and disappointing failures. In 1948, a secret arrangement – the *modus vivendi* – was made which offered some scientific and technical collaboration.[12] But it amounted to very little and entailed the surrender of the clause in the Quebec Agreement which provided that neither country would use the atomic bomb without the consent of the other. (A right to consent before atomic bombs were used from British bases was regained in 1951, but did not apply to any use of bombs from overseas bases.)

There was, however, one concession to Britain's Commonwealth ties. The Quebec Agreement had forbidden the passing of any atomic information to third parties, but now the *modus vivendi* made provision for 'areas of cooperation between members of the British Commonwealth'.

The nine areas specified included health and safety, detection of distant nuclear explosions, survey methods for uranium and treatment of uranium ores, and research reactors. It was this annex to the *modus vivendi* that from January 1948 governed the supply of information by Britain to Australia.

The next initiative came at the end of 1949. So far Britain had simply wanted an independent deterrent and a full exchange of information with the Americans, but the vastly increased American technological lead (and the Soviet test detected in August 1949) made much closer collaboration desirable. Talks began in Washington in late 1949, but broke down in January 1950 after the arrest for espionage of Klaus Fuchs, the German-born, British-naturalized scientist at Harwell who had worked at Los Alamos during the war.[13]

There was a slight advance in cooperation in 1955 when an amendment to the McMahon Act permitted further limited exchanges of information. But the breakthrough did not come until 1958. Before then the Americans were not particularly impressed by what Britain had to offer as a partner. While Britain was beginning to acquire atomic bombs, the United States and the Soviet Union were already acquiring the infinitely more powerful thermonuclear bomb. Only a month after the first British atomic test in October 1952, the Americans exploded the world's first thermonuclear device, and the Russians tested a thermonuclear bomb nine months later. One US senator, asked for his views on atomic cooperation with Britain, said 'We would be trading a horse for a rabbit'.[14]

The Churchill government decided in June 1954 that Britain, too, must have thermonuclear weapons. A new programme of weapon development began which resulted, in the short space of three years, in a series of high-yield weapon tests in the Pacific. By 1958, the success of the British independent nuclear weapons programme had been demonstrated in Australia and at Christmas and Malden Islands in the Pacific. Moreover in 1956 Britain had opened Calder Hall, the first land-based nuclear power plant on an industrial scale in the world. All this convinced the United States that Britain was a worthwhile partner with a valuable contribution to make. After the necessary amendments to the McMahon Act, a bilateral agreement, this time in treaty form, on 'Co-operation on the Uses of Atomic Energy for Mutual Defence Purposes', was concluded in July 1958.[15] It included exchanges of technical information and weapon designs, and a further agreement in 1959 extended the exchanges to fissile materials; later, nuclear weapon test facilities were shared – the first joint test was in Nevada in March 1962 – and the United States agreed to supply missiles to Britain, who was to fabricate her own warheads. After twelve years of enforced independence, a new era of nuclear interdependence began. It had been one of the main objectives of successive British governments and its pursuit had overridden all other such relationships whether with European or Commonwealth countries.

Organizations and men

The Attlee organization

Who made these atomic decisions, who advised on them and who were the men who carried them out?[16]

In the Attlee government the crucial decisions were taken, not by full Cabinet, but by a small and active ministerial committee known as Gen 75 – called by Attlee 'the Atom Bomb Committee'. Because of its exceptional secrecy, its decisions were not even reported to the Cabinet. A still smaller group of ministers, Gen 163, took the decision in January 1947 to make an atomic bomb. The Prime Minister, Lord President of the Council and Foreign Secretary were in both these groups; the Chancellor of the Exchequer was on Gen 75 only; and the Minister of Defence and the Dominions Secretary were on Gen 163 only. In February 1947, a proper ministerial committee – the AE(M) Committee – was set up to handle policy questions requiring the consideration of ministers, under the chairmanship of the Prime Minister, but it met infrequently and Gen meetings, variously numbered, were still used to deal with the highest matters of policy.

The other ministerial committee that discussed atomic energy was the Defence Committee, also under the Prime Minister's chairmanship, but it was not kept regularly informed on the atomic project and took no decisions on the programme until 1950, when it had to deal with important questions of priority between atomic and other weapons.

So atomic policy was made, under the especially close direction of the Prime Minister, by small ministerial groups with varying membership, but an almost constant inner core – the Prime Minister himself, the Foreign Secretary and the Minister of Supply, who was departmentally responsible but who had much less influence on policy than Bevin.

Ministers were at first advised on policy by a committee of Service and official representatives (the Anderson Committee – ACAE) chaired, for the sake of continuity, by Sir John Anderson, an Independent MP who had been the Cabinet minister in charge of atomic energy in the wartime coalition government and who now sat on the Front Bench of the Conservative Opposition. These strange arrangements never worked well, and the ACAE was disbanded in 1947. A new official committee, the AE(O), was set up in late 1946 and became very hardworking and effective after Roger Makins (later Lord Sherfield) took the chair early in 1947 on returning from the Embassy in Washington, where he had dealt with atomic energy matters. He had unrivalled experience of Anglo-American relationships in atomic energy, and the connection was maintained when he became Ambassador in Washington (1952–56) and, later, chairman of the UK Atomic Energy Authority (1960–64).

On the Defence side, the Ministry of Defence was created in October 1946, and in January 1947 a scientific adviser, Sir Henry Tizard, was appointed and a Defence Research Policy Committee (DRPC) was set up. It was to advise the Minister of Defence and the Chiefs of Staff on defence science policy, but was forbidden to encroach on the territory of the ACAE and was starved of information until after the ACAE was wound up. Then the DRPC was allowed an atomic energy sub-committee.

The minister departmentally responsible for atomic energy was the Minister of Supply, in whose vast department atomic energy was placed by the 1946 Atomic Energy Act. The ministry provided a ready-made infrastructure for the new project, and there it remained until mid-1954 when, as we shall see, the UKAEA was formed.

Britain was unusual in not creating at once a new, single-purpose organization to accommodate this new project. The Americans had set up the United States Atomic Energy Commission (USAEC), the French had set up the Commissariat à l'Energie Atomique (CEA), and other nations followed suit. Britain alone poured new wine into old bottles. There were some advantages, but the results did not look logical or tidy.

Within the Ministry Lord Portal, the impressive ex-Chief of the Air Staff, was appointed to head the atomic energy project, aided by a small staff of civil servants, some with experience of *Tube Alloys*. He was responsible to the Prime Minister and tended to bypass his departmental minister. His special strengths were the weight he carried with the Americans and his influence with the Chiefs of Staff and the Service departments. At first he was Controller of Production (Atomic Energy) (CPAE), but in 1950 became Controller, Atomic Energy (CAE) with his jurisdiction extended to include the research establishment at Harwell, under Cockcroft, and the weapons establishment under William Penney, as well as the industrial organization under Christopher Hinton, which had the task of producing fissile material.[17]

When Lord Portal retired in 1951 he was succeeded by the much less weighty but amiable General Sir Frederick Morgan.[18] He remained in the CAE post until 1954, and after the Atomic Energy Authority was formed he continued in the Ministry of Supply as Controller of Atomic Weapons (CAW). When he retired in 1956 the post became DGAW (Director General of Atomic Weapons) and was occupied by officials who were birds of passage.

Of the three separate parts of the project – Cockcroft's research establishment at Harwell, Hinton's industrial complex based at Risley, Lancashire, and the weapons establishment under Penney – only the third concerns us here. It had a small, highly secret staff, drawn in 1947 from the Armaments Research Department of the Ministry of Supply, of which Penney had been appointed Chief Superintendent (CSAR), with responsibility for conventional weapons research of all kinds, at the beginning of 1946. The atomic weapons project was given the designation 'High Explosives Research' (HER) and Penney became CSHER. The work was located first at Fort Halstead, Kent and later, from 1950, at Aldermaston, Berkshire.

Reorganization under the Conservatives

When the Churchill government took office in October 1951, Lord Cherwell was appointed Paymaster General. Soon a Prime Minister's directive – a bizarre document, as Margaret Gowing calls it – divided responsibility for atomic energy between the Paymaster General and the Minister of Supply (who was statutorily responsible under the 1946 Atomic Energy Act).[19] The demarcation of functions was confused and the scope for misunderstanding and conflict almost limitless, especially with two such forceful characters as Cherwell and Duncan Sandys, who was the Minister of Supply from 1951 to late 1954. Morgan observed that when one (or both) was abroad there was peace, but when they returned to London warfare was resumed.

Cherwell was determined to reorganize the atomic project radically and remove it from the Ministry of Supply and indeed from the Civil Service. He was convinced that 'the dead hand of the Civil Service' was responsible for the fact that the Soviet Union had beaten Britain by three years to its first bomb test.[20] He wanted an entirely new kind of body, an atomic energy commission funded by a Treasury grant-in-aid, but with the freedom and flexibility of private industry. Churchill was reluctant to agree to a change, at least until after the first atomic test, but eventually, in 1953, a committee was set up to make recommendations on the form of the new organization. It led to the UKAEA Act of July 1954 and the creation of the UK Atomic Energy Authority – an upheaval that added to the burdens of the project leaders.

The new Authority took over the functions, staff, laboratories and plant of the old Ministry of Supply atomic project. On weapons there was a complicated demarcation system. The Ministry of Supply retained responsibility for development and production of all nuclear warheads and arranged contracts with the Authority for fissile material; it was also responsible for the overall planning, organization and conduct of major trials and arrangements for running the range in Australia. This allocation of responsibility for trials was laid down by the AE(O) in May 1954 and confirmed a year later.[21] Coordination within Whitehall was effected by an atomic weapon tests executive committee (called variously, according to the trial in hand, Mosex, Buffalex or Antex). As for policy on tests, this continued to be handled by committees much as before, and a high-level official committee on nuclear test policy was not set up until 1957.[22]

The scientific conduct of the trials was the task of Aldermaston, where there was a small but effective trials planning staff with experience going back to the *Hurricane* and *Totem* trials. The Service departments set up their own internal organization for dealing with trials; the Air Ministry needed an especially strong one. But after 1954 the Ministry of Supply, although it had overall responsibility for trials, only had a minute staff to handle them. Under the CAW (later, the DGAW) the Director of Atomic Weapons (Trials) was a genial and hardworking retired naval officer, Captain F. B. (Frankie) Lloyd, RN. He had a total staff of two junior officials, neither of them a scientist. He pointed out the various weaknesses of the whole organization and the inadequacy of his own tiny directorate, but little seems to have changed by the time he retired in 1960, when the Ministry of Supply was wound up and its atomic weapons functions passed to the Ministry of Aviation.[23] By then the major trials had ceased, though the Maralinga range was still very much in use for minor trials.

The men

Of the British politicians who made the nuclear decisions, and the officials and scientists who advised them on policy and implemented it, only a few can be mentioned here. Because of the central importance of nuclear policy all Prime Ministers from Clement Attlee to Harold Macmillan were deeply involved. Attlee initiated and fostered the programme, and also the arrangements with Robert Menzies, the Prime Minister of Australia, for the first test in the Monte Bello Islands in 1952.

The *Hurricane* plans were carried through by the Churchill government, which took office in October 1951. Churchill, who retained from the war his powerful interest in atomic energy (and an obsession with the old Quebec and Hyde Park agreements), paid detailed attention to *Hurricane*, even taking the chair himself at planning meetings. The Australian connection was strengthened by the friendly relationship between Churchill and the conservative and anglophile Menzies. Until Churchill retired in April 1955 he dominated defence policy. Events developed rapidly, with the first and second weapon trials, the decision in 1954 to make a British hydrogen bomb, the launching of the first civil nuclear power programme in 1955 and the establishment of a permanent range in Australia. There was also the beginning of an intense debate on fallout and Churchill responded quickly to parliamentary and public anxiety by setting up in 1955 a Medical Research Council enquiry into radiation hazards.

Anthony Eden, who followed Churchill in April 1955, bore the full brunt of the fallout debate, and during the first half of 1956 agonized and temporized over the decision to approve the high-yield nuclear explosions (the first *Grapple* series) in the Pacific in 1957. He also had to face growing national and international opposition to weapon tests, increasing Australian sensitivity, uncertainties about the future of testing and the difficult stop-go international discussion that finally led to a test moratorium in late 1958. But before then he had resigned because of ill-health and had been succeeded, in January 1957, by Harold Macmillan.

Macmillan, who had briefly (1954–55) been Minister of Defence, was perhaps the most deeply engaged of all in atomic affairs. His premiership of nearly five years began with a major change of defence policy, enunciated in the Defence White Paper of April 1957, and with the first series of weapon tests in the Pacific, which gave Britain a thermonuclear weapon capability.[24] His period of office saw the continuation of the fallout controversy; the birth of CND; and the beginning and end of a three-year moratorium on tests by the three nuclear powers.

His talks with General Eisenhower in October 1957, and their joint Washington Declaration, opened a new era in Anglo-American atomic relations and led directly to the 1958 bilateral agreement on nuclear defence. Under Macmillan's administration interdependence flourished; strong practical links were forged, and the Polaris Sales Agreement was made in April 1963. At the same time, international disarmament negotiations progressed, even if slowly. The Partial Test Ban Treaty, which banned atmospheric weapon tests, was concluded and came into force in October 1963, just as Macmillan resigned the premiership.

Of Churchill's ministers the most influential was Lord Cherwell, his friend and scientific adviser for many years, a member of his wartime

Cabinet, and Paymaster General in his 1951–55 administration. Cherwell was a distinguished scientist as well as a Conservative politician. His involvement with atomic energy went back to the Maud Committee and, through membership of a technical committee, he had retained an official position in atomic matters throughout the Attlee years. The connection continued, and until his death in 1957 he was a board member of the UKAEA, which he had created almost single-handed. Of the three Ministers of Supply who were statutorily responsible for atomic energy from 1946 to 1954 when the UKAEA was set up, only Duncan Sandys left a lasting impression. Nor did successive Ministers of Defence – there were three between 1954 and 1957 – until Sandys. He was an exceptionally forceful, energetic and hardworking minister, but abrasive in personality. His three years as Minister of Supply were frustrated by the conditions imposed by the Prime Minister's directive and by conflicts with Cherwell. It was also a crucial period of action: Hurricane, Totem, plans for Maralinga – Sandys had doubts about the wisdom of a permanent range – and the formation of the Atomic Energy Authority which he strongly and openly opposed. At the Ministry of Defence from January 1957 to October 1959 he was responsible for the 1957 Defence White Paper, written in a few weeks largely by himself, which based defence policy more firmly than ever on nuclear deterrence and announced the end of conscription in 1960. It was elaborated by the 1958 and 1959 White Papers.[25] Of the administrators and scientists who advised ministers and implemented the nuclear weapon policies, Portal and Makins have already been mentioned. The latter was influential especially in the Anglo-American context. So too was the first chairman and chief executive of the Authority, Sir Edwin (later Lord) Plowden. He was at the heart of policymaking in Whitehall and played a vital part in achieving the 1958 bilateral agreement.

The defence policy was dependent on the work of hundreds of scientists, engineers and technicians engaged in research, producing fissile material and other special materials, and designing, fabricating and testing nuclear devices and weapons. They came together from many sources, some returning from the Manhattan Project or from Canada, some from radar research, some from other defence research establishments, some from the universities.

The man who was recognized as indispensable to the weapon programme was William Penney. He had become assistant professor of mathematics at Imperial College at the early age of 27; during the war he worked for the Home Office on the effects of high explosives, and for the Admiralty on the effects of waves on the transportable Mulberry harbours used in the Allied invasion of Europe. In 1944 he went to Los Alamos, and became a key member of its staff. He was one of the two official Britons (the other was Group Captain Leonard Cheshire VC) in the observer plane in the Nagasaki bombing raid of 9 August 1945, and in 1946 was invited to take part in the US bomb tests at Bikini Atoll. The Americans made several unsuccessful attempts to persuade him to work in the United States. 'He is our chief (indeed our only real) expert in the construction of the bomb and I do not know what we should do without him', Cherwell wrote to Churchill. 'He played an outstanding part in designing the original American bombs at Los Alamos in the war and participated in the first tests. The Americans admit frankly that they would give a great deal to get him back. But on an appeal to his patriotism he gave up the offer of a very attractive professorship and came into government service. He is not always tactful but his heart is in the right place. He now runs the bomb production establishment ... and is responsible for the whole of the scientific side of the Australian test operation'.[26]

'Penney's mathematical skill', Margaret Gowing writes, 'had the elegance, simplicity of approach and intuitive understanding that build a great reputation'. His pre-war academic work had also given him an interdisciplinary approach, and he had an outstanding ability to find practical solutions to problems. He had, besides, a gift of communication, and of simple and lucid explanation of scientific matters to the uninitiated, whether politicians, servicemen of all ranks or radio audiences. He got on extremely well with the Americans and with the Australians, because they both found him entirely honest and unaffected.

Who were the men who worked with him?[27] He had much greater difficulties of recruitment than did the already well-known Cockcroft at Harwell. A top-secret weapons establishment was less appealing. There had to be tight security restrictions; deadlines were inexorable; the work was often difficult and dangerous; the scientists could not publish their results as Harwell staff were comparatively free to do; and some potential recruits had conscientious objections, or a strong distaste for weapons.[28] The weapons group was always short of staff, sometimes desperately so. Few of the returning Manhattan Project scientists, even those from Los Alamos, joined the weapons work. Most of Penney's men, therefore, were extracted from defence research establishments. His senior scientists were generally older than those in Cockcroft's or even Hinton's organizations, and were highly experienced in their various fields. They were joined by a few wartime recruits, including some clever young academics. For reasons of space, only a few of the weaponeers can be mentioned here, but they included R. Pilgrim, an expert in blast measurement who had been at the 1946 US test with Penney and who played a central part in trials planning operations; G. L. Hopkin, metallurgist; L. C. Tyte, W. J. Challens, C. A. Adams and I. Maddock, who were experts in electronics and instrumentation; E. H. Mott and W. J. Moyce, explosives experts; D. E. Barnes and G. C. Dale, health and safety specialists; D. T. Lewis, chemist; J. Corner, mathematical physicist; and Frank Morgan, radio-chemist, the only Harwell scientist who agreed to transfer to Penney's staff.

One other man, who was not a scientist, must be mentioned here. In 1950 Admiral P. Brooking, a retired naval officer, was appointed as Penney's deputy to give him some relief from administration. Later, in 1954, the Chief of the Royal Naval Scientific Service, William (later Sir William) Cook succeeded him, with special responsibility for managing the hydrogen bomb programme. The schedule was very tight, and he was a highly efficient and hard-driving organizer. But in 1958 he was promoted and moved from the weapons post in a major UKAEA reorganization.

Penney himself was more and more in demand to advise on disarmament, test limitation and test ban negotiations, and by the time the major trials came to an end he was spending much of his time in Whitehall or Geneva. Then in 1959 he moved from Aldermaston to Harwell, as UKAEA board member for scientific research, and his responsibilities for nuclear weapons passed to a newly appointed member for weapons research, Air Chief Marshal Sir Claude Pelly. In 1961 Penney became Deputy Chairman, and in 1964 Chairman, of the UKAEA.

The British public

What about the British people on whose behalf all this was done and who paid for it in their taxes? It is sometimes thought that there was from the beginning opposition to atomic weapons. But there was no controversy when the atomic bomb decision was disclosed in the House of Commons in May 1948. There was no opposition on party lines; the Labour Party (except briefly in 1960–61) officially supported the policy, though some Labour MPs attacked nuclear weapon tests from 1954 onwards, when anxiety about fallout flared up all over the world. Later, many individual Labour MPs were to become supporters of CND. This was launched at the beginning of 1958, grew very rapidly and recruited many well-known names, including the philosopher Bertrand Russell, who in 1961, at the age of 89, went to prison for demonstrating against nuclear weapons; yet in 1947, when the United States still had a nuclear monopoly, even he had advocated using the threat of preventive war to compel the Soviet Union to accept an American plan for international control of atomic energy.[29] Even when the nuclear issues, especially weapon tests, were being hotly debated, public opinion polls showed remarkably steady support for – or at least acquiescence to – government nuclear policy. It was against this background that the British weapon tests were planned and carried out.

2
Why Australia?

Why not an American range?

With no wide open spaces like the arid regions of New Mexico and Nevada, the British had to look overseas for a test site. They needed a large, uninhabited area, in a friendly country, where they would have logistical support and local facilities. Ideally, they would have liked to use an established American range; the benefits and economies were obvious, although there would be some disadvantages. In the winter of 1949–50, high-level atomic negotiations in Washington offered the hope of renewed Anglo-American collaboration, including an integrated weapons programme, but in February, as we have seen, they broke down after the arrest for espionage of the German-born Harwell physicist, Klaus Fuchs.

Nevertheless, it still seemed that weapon-testing facilities might be obtained through the US military authorities, who were encouraging, and in the summer of 1950 an official request to use the range at Eniwetok in the Pacific was made to the US Chiefs of Staff.[1] But no reply came, and in September the British Chiefs of Staff recommended to the Prime Minister a site suggested by the Admiralty – the Monte Bello islands, a small uninhabited group of islands off the north-west coast of Australia, 'the coast of coral and pearl'. Here a British ship, prophetically named the *Tryal*, had been wrecked in 1622 – the first documented contact with Australia.

Attlee promptly sent a message to the Australian Premier, Robert Menzies. In it he proposed Eniwetok; a reply from the Americans was still awaited, but meanwhile he hoped that the Australian government would approve in principle a British weapon test on Australian territory and would agree to a survey of the Monte Bello islands.[2] Menzies quickly assented and in November 1950, after a somewhat curt refusal from the US Chiefs of Staff, a small survey party went to Australia and reported on the Monte Bello site in January 1951.[3]

Meanwhile, Penney had been looking at alternative possibilities in Canada.[4] Provisional plans for an integrated Anglo-Canadian effort were drawn up and the site requirements were defined. These included a detonation area, a temporary camp site at least 10 miles upwind and a base camp with laboratories, workshops, etc., at least 25 miles upwind. The site would have to be isolated, with no human habitation within 100 miles downwind. Prevailing winds should blow contamination over the sea, but clear of shipping. The site should be large enough to accommodate the detonation of about a dozen weapons over several years; since each explosion would cause severe contamination over a radius of about 500 yards, each detonation would have to be at least 3 miles from the previous one.

Seven sites in Canada were investigated, and one, near Churchill on the west coast of Hudson Bay, seemed suitable from the technical point of view, except that the sea was too shallow for ships to be used near the shore.

Attlee and Menzies discussed the subject again when the latter visited London in January 1951. Then, in March, Attlee wrote to say that Britain would not wait any longer for the American test site, and would be most grateful both for permission to use the Monte Bello islands in October 1952, and for Australian help in preparing and carrying out the trial. The explosion, he said, would contaminate at least some of the islands with radioactivity, and for about three years the area would be unfit for habitation or even for visits by the pearl fishers who occasionally went there. Menzies agreed to a detailed survey of the islands.

An Australian general election was pending, but as soon as the Menzies government was re-elected in May 1951, formal agreement to the test was received from Canberra.[5] However, British ministers had decided to make one more approach to the Americans, while keeping the Australian option open, and June 1951 was set as the deadline for a final decision. But it was August when the American Secretary of State replied; although he refused the British request for Eniwetok because of the McMahon Act (see Chapter 1), he offered alternative proposals for a joint test in Nevada. Penney flew to Washington for urgent consultations, which convinced him that from his point of view a satisfactory test in Nevada was possible.

However the general opinion, including that of the Chiefs of Staff, was that the test should be in Australia (see Map 1). There would be considerable political advantage in showing, as Emanuel Shinwell, the Minister of Defence, said, that Britain was not merely a satellite of the United States. The Nevada conditions were very restrictive and would make all the British results available to the Americans without reciprocity, whereas if the British had an independent programme they would control their own operations and would acquire knowledge of their own which could be used to negotiate with the Americans. Independence, it was argued, would be invaluable, and the costs would be little greater and not in dollars. Penney had already forecast the need for a dozen explosions and the British needed a test site that could be relied on; previous atomic experience had led them to be wary of reliance on the United States, and the Nevada option would be a gamble as the Americans might later 'turn off the tap and leave us helpless'. The Canadian possibility had already been abandoned, and if the Australian option was also abandoned it would probably be for good. There were other objections to the American site for Britain's first test. 'In the lamentable event of the bomb failing to detonate', said Cherwell, 'we should look very foolish indeed' – and in full view of all the American newspapers.[6] Most

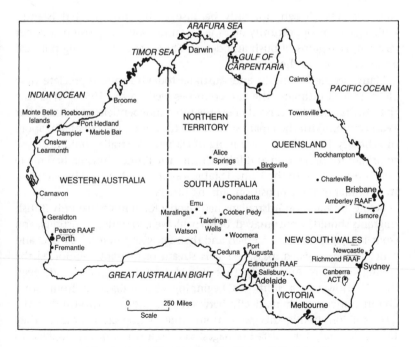

Map 1   Australia, showing the Monte Bello islands

importantly, Nevada would not provide the shallow underwater test that the Admiralty especially wanted; it was essential to know the effects if atomic bombs in enemy ships were exploded in British ports.

A decision was further delayed by a general election, which brought Churchill and a Conservative government to power in October 1951. Finally, in December 1951, ministers confirmed the Australian site, with only ten months to go before the trial, codenamed *Hurricane*. The choice was decisive. As Penney wrote three months later: 'If the Australians are not willing to let us do further trials in Australia, I do not know where we should go'.[7]

Meanwhile, active planning had begun over a year earlier,[8] since stores – including, for instance, 150 miles of cable for communications – would take months to procure and the first ships of the *Hurricane* flotilla would have to sail from England in February 1952 if the test was to be in October that year. If not, a whole year would be lost since favourable weather conditions seemed likely only in September and October.

Political pros and cons

Australia was chosen not only because of her uninhabited islands, which gave the opportunity of a shallow underwater explosion, and her vast empty regions of bush and desert. There were also strong political arguments for the choice.

Many people in Britain and Australia today cannot appreciate how close, indeed intimate, the two countries were in the 1950s.[9] It is true that Australia had necessarily become more independent of Britain after Pearl Harbor. With the Japanese thrust to the South, the fall of Singapore in February 1942 and the bombing of Darwin, Australia could not look to Britain for protection and John Curtin, the Prime Minister, had made an historic appeal to the United States – an action deplored by Menzies, then Leader of the Opposition, among others.

Before the war most Australians had taken it for granted that only British migrants should be encouraged, or even allowed, to settle in Australia, and from 1946 British ex-servicemen and their families had received free, and other Britons assisted, passages. This stream of migrants reinforced the feeling of many Australians that Britain was their motherland, even 'home'. However, a shift was beginning as immigration from other countries increased dramatically: between 1947 and 1970 two-thirds of the 21/2 million immigrants were from other European countries; they too could apply for assisted passages. The population nearly doubled to 13 million, of whom fewer and fewer had British links or antecedents.

Trading patterns also changed. In the 1950s, Britain was still Australia's most important trading partner and British investment in Australia was greater than that of all the other countries of the world put together. But trade with the United States and Japan was growing, and by the 1960s Japan was far and away Australia's main trading partner. Nevertheless, the announcement in 1961 of Britain's intention to join the Common Market, heralding a major change in Britain's trading allegiance, shattered many Australians. The loosening of the Commonwealth bonds was signified in 1973 by the changes in British nationality laws. Hitherto British and Australian passports had been interchangeable. Now they were separate, and Australian passports no longer bore the words 'British subject'.

In 1950, the Cold War turned into a fighting war in the Far East, not Europe, and Australia was deeply involved as her forces fought again in Korea and Malaya. In 1949 Menzies had become Prime Minister; strongly pro-British, he had intense feelings of loyalty to the British Commonwealth. He firmly believed that Australia must play her part in the common defence of the free world and that, although in defence matters generally Australia had tended to turn to the United States, there was still scope for Anglo-Australian defence co-operation. This was already being demonstrated at Woomera, the range stretching 1,250 miles across the coast of Western Australia which was used for testing and developing guided missiles and long-range weapons. This joint project (named after an Aboriginal weapon, a throwing-stick used to launch spears) began very soon after the end of the war, and was in operation by 1950. Britain was producing all the weapons for testing and supplying much of the equipment and scientific personnel, whereas Australia, at a cost of some £10 million a year, provided all the support as well as some scientists and engineers. A partnership in weapon testing was therefore not unprecedented, and use of her territory and resources to help the British nuclear deterrent was seen as part of Australia's defence contribution.

Australia was especially interested after the war in the industrial development of atomic energy, seemingly so important to a country thought to have no indigenous oil and little coal. (Exploration was to change this, as Australia proved to be very rich in coal as well as uranium, but so far has not found a nuclear power programme worthwhile.) She was determined to keep abreast of atomic research and development, and hoped for Commonwealth collaborative project led by Britain. However, at the Conference of Dominion Prime Ministers in May 1946 the only collaboration offered was limited to a few places for Australian research fellows at Harwell, and help in finding and developing uranium supplies. In 1947, Australia and New Zealand asked for information about Gleep, the low-energy research reactor at Harwell, but no agreement was reached. One of the stumbling blocks was that the Americans were known to be dubious about Australian security, and in 1948 one unnamed critic was said to have alleged that 'no Australian, from the Prime Minister down, can be trusted not to be careless or worse'.[10] In fact, their security arrangements during the weapon tests were to be highly effective.

The British thought hard during 1947 about a coordinated Commonwealth programme, but because of the Quebec Agreement (see Chapter 1) could do nothing without consulting the United States. It was decided to seek Canada's views first, and then those of the United States. The Canadian authorities were so emphatic that full cooperation with the United States must take priority over all other objectives that the idea of a Commonwealth programme was abandoned. As we saw, the *modus vivendi* of 1948 made special provision for information to be given to British Commonwealth countries, but only in strictly defined areas.

By 1951, Australia was interested in beginning a nuclear power programme and naturally hoped for British help. The proposal was discussed when Menzies was in London in January 1951; he was told that under existing rules it would be a classified project, that American and Canadian agreement would be needed before Britain could help, and that they would be very exacting about security. After his visit, he and Attlee exchanged telegrams about the promising uranium prospects at Radium Hill in South Australia, and Attlee reaffirmed Britain's desire to help with the nuclear power project, but again pointed out the limitations imposed by the tripartite agreements.

The supply of uranium was in the early postwar years expected to be the limiting factor in atomic development. Then reserves were found in Australia at Radium Hill and at Rum Jungle in the Northern Territories, and by 1951 it was clear that Radium Hill would produce important supplies of ore. But Britain could not accept Australia's offer of joint development because the time did not seem opportune to seek American agreement to the sharing of classified information with her. So in 1952 Australia invited a US mission to examine all their uranium occurrences; paradoxically it was then the Americans who brought the British into the negotiations, and successful deals were made between Australia and the Combined Development Agency (the tripartite body set up by the Quebec Agreement to obtain and allocate supplies of uranium ore).

British desire to cooperate with Australia was genuine, but largely frustrated by existing commitments to the United States – in the Quebec

Agreement and later the *modus vivendi* – and by American distrust of Australian security to which the British were hypersensitive.[11] The overwhelming desire for a renewed Anglo-American partnership, and the fear of spoiling the chances of achieving it, inhibited all Britain's other relationships in the Commonwealth and Europe. The Americans themselves lacked these inhibitions and tended to be more forthcoming with the Australians than they would allow the British to be. Britain's inability to help the Australians, except to a quite minor extent, was the more open to criticism because of her dependence on Australia for a site for *Hurricane* and almost certainly for further trials.[12]

In spite of the disappointments and frustrations over technical cooperation, the Australians showed great generosity over *Hurricane* even when the British were in an agony of indecision over whether to go ahead with the Monte Bello plan or accept the belated Nevada offer in September 1951. They collaborated wholeheartedly, and the Services gave indispensable, and free, assistance in support of the test.

The risks in these uninhabited islands seemed negligible; there was little or no hostile public opinion in Australia – rather, some pride in an historic occasion. However, the Australian government was well aware that it could not abrogate its sovereign rights and duties; if secret and hazardous operations were to be carried out in its territories by another nation – however close a friend – it had at least to know what was happening and to exert some real control. It was responsible for the safety of its own people and land; it had to decide how far it could accept general assurances of safety from the British, and what information it needed in order to examine them critically and in detail. It had to answer to its own Parliament and public opinion, and eventually to face a general election. It had too to answer for its expenditure in money and resources; not a large consideration for *Hurricane*, but more onerous later.

The British, constrained by both the agreements with the United States and their unquenchable hopes of renewed Anglo-American partnership, were very inhibited in providing information to the Australians. They had, moreover, developed a general feeling that the fewer the people who knew Britain's weapon secrets the better – whether in the United States or the rest of the world. If the British felt they could not give even the Australians information about nuclear reactors, it was still more impossible to tell them anything about atomic bombs, and information about a test could reveal secret weapons data. What did the Australian authorities, who were not intending to develop atomic weapons themselves, need to know for their own purposes? How much could they be told without disclosing highly classified data and violating obligations to the United States?

For both countries there were administrative complications. Unlike the United States, which was carrying out huge test programmes in its own country or in American Trust territories in the Pacific, Britain would be operating on the soil of another sovereign state. This was bound to be complicated, even though the arrangements were surprisingly informal at first. Proposals for tests had to be approved by British ministers and then submitted for Australian approval, and each one had to be processed through two government machines. The British had to work out with Australian colleagues 12,000 miles away the details of complex operations that involved several government departments and all the armed services of both nations. Nothing could be said officially in either country without coordination; every announcement, speech or answer to a Parliamentary Question in either country had to be discussed, agreed and synchronized. Public relations involved the Australian press and public, as well as the British. Press stories in one country might be, and sometimes were, picked up instantly in the other.

The political relationship between Britain and Australia in the postwar decade-and-a-half is reflected in the fact that these curbs on the transmission of information to the Australians about explosions in their own country – equivalent to thousands of tons of TNT and releasing large quantities of radioactive fission products – were regarded as reasonable by the British government and acceptable by the Australian government.

Politicians and scientists

'The last of the Queen's Men'[13]

Menzies towered over Australian politics throughout the whole period of weapon tests. A most able and experienced politician – he had held many ministerial offices since entering Parliament in 1928 and had been Prime Minister from 1939 to 1941 – he became Prime Minister again in 1949 at the head of a Liberal/Country Party coalition government and retained office for seventeen years until he retired in 1966. To some he was an urbane, far-seeing world statesman, to others he seemed an arrogant and unscrupulous reactionary, but all agreed on his ability.[14] An extreme anglophile, he was the last of a long line of Australian Prime Ministers who felt that London was the centre of the world.[15] He was loaded with honours by 'the motherland'; a Privy Councillor, a Companion of Honour and, in 1963, a Knight of the exclusive Order of the Thistle, he succeeded Churchill in 1965 as Lord Warden of the Cinque Ports, an honorary office of immense prestige.

Menzies was the presiding genius of the Anglo-Australian special relationship. His support, and that of his government, for the British atomic weapon test programme were crucial, as Australian public opinion became more and more restive. If he had lost power, it was probable that a Labour government under Dr Evatt would have put an end to the tests. The British were well aware of how much they owed Menzies, and how much they depended on his personal support and his continuation in office. An Australian song of the time might have been written for them:[16]

But we might lose our Menzies; wherever would we be
If Menzies means as much to you as Menzies means to me?

The Australian minister in charge of atomic energy matters, including the British weapon tests and the permanent proving ground at Maralinga, was, until 1958, Howard (later Sir Howard) Beale. He gave the British programme his enthusiastic support, sometimes in difficult circumstances. The major trials were over by the time he moved to Washington, where he achieved considerable success as Australian ambassador.

The scientists

The scientists in Australia with knowledge and experience of atomic energy nearly all had close links with Britain and British scientists, and at least two – E. W. Titterton and J. P. Baxter – came from England to posts in Australia after the war; Titterton to the Australian National University in Canberra (ANU) and Baxter to the University of New South Wales. There was, as we have seen, no distinction at that time between British and Australian nationality and no separate passports. Three Australian-born scientists – Oliphant, Martin and Eddy – had been in the Cavendish Laboratory at Cambridge under the great Ernest Rutherford. Some – Mark Oliphant, Phillip Baxter and Ernest Titterton – had worked in *Tube Alloys* and the Manhattan Project.

Four scientists require special mention here; three because of their parts in the British atomic weapon test programme, and one because of his conspicuous absence from the stage. The missing actor was M. L. E. (later Sir Mark) Oliphant, Director of the Research School of Physical Sciences in the Australian National University – which he helped to found – in Canberra. He was born and educated in Adelaide and went to Cambridge University in 1927. In 1935 he was Rutherford's assistant director of research at the Cavendish. In 1937 he became Professor of Physics at Birmingham University, where Frisch and Peierls wrote their famous memorandum showing that an atomic bomb was possible.

Oliphant was a member of the Maud Committee and in 1943 joined the Manhattan Project. For his outstanding contribution, General Groves, the head of the Project, put forward his name, and his only, in 1946 for the Congressional Medal of Freedom with Gold Palm. This is the highest honour the United States can bestow on a foreigner.[17] However, it was not then Australian government policy to permit foreign decorations for Australians, and Oliphant did not receive the award. If he had, the subsequent story would have been very different. He did not know about it until 1980.

After returning in 1950 to Australia and the ANU, he was made chairman of an industrial atomic energy policy committee. Yet this most distinguished nuclear physicist was not invited to advise on the tests by the Australian government. The omission was due to an absurd event in 1951 when he was to attend a scientific conference in Chicago but was unable to obtain an American visa. He was not accused of communist connections or subversive activities, and the security authorities, in the United States and Australia, had nothing against him. He had never, he said, knowingly transgressed security rules. If he had done so, the highly security-minded Groves would certainly not have recommended him for any honours. But the McCarthy era was in full swing and Oliphant was a victim of innuendo and political smear, labelled 'inadmissible', 'a do-gooder', 'one of the boys who monkey around with pinkos'.[18] The visa affair, despite Oliphant's friendly personal relationship with Menzies, immediately and powerfully affected the attitude of both the Australian and British governments because of their sensitivity to American reactions. If his participation in atomic energy affairs might, however unreasonably, have unfortunate repercussions in Washington, he had to be excluded.[19]

The question of Australian observers at the first weapon test in October 1952 did not arise until early 1952. Canadian scientists were to participate; as we saw in Chapter 1, Canada, as a signatory of the tripartite agreements, was in a different position from other Commonwealth countries. The Australians asked about their own scientists. Penney wanted to invite two or three, and one from New Zealand, and he was anxious also to borrow Titterton from ANU, not as an observer but as a telemetry expert. Lord Cherwell, the British minister responsible for atomic energy policy, was asked to authorize this. His prime concern was that the presence of Australian scientists might give the Americans an unfavourable impression of British security arrangements. However, if the problem was frankly explained to Menzies, and he felt that some

Australian scientists should attend, Cherwell would be prepared to accept Titterton, and two junior technicians might also be accepted.

The Australians were understandably dissatisfied; after all, the British were using their territory and were dependent on them. Eventually the British authorities invited the Australian Defence scientific adviser, Professor L. H. Martin, as well as Titterton; later, W. A. S. Butement was included. Accommodation was scarce, and all of them would not only observe but make themselves useful. After the visa incident, Cherwell and the British government would never have agreed to invite Oliphant for fear of American reactions, and about the same time the Australian government itself reconstituted its Atomic Energy Policy Committee in order to exclude him from discussions even of peaceful applications of atomic energy.[20] So, contrary to public expectations, Oliphant was not invited to *Hurricane* or any of the subsequent tests, and the Australian government did not ask him to serve on its Atomic Weapons Tests Safety Committee (AWTSC). If asked, he might well have refused; he hated scientific secrecy and, as he wrote to a friend, 'That is why I dropped right out of the military business when I came back to Australia'.[21]

Thus the Australian scientists present at the 1952 trials were Martin, Butement and Titterton. In 1955 they all became members of the AWTSC, together with Eddy, Baxter and, later, L. J. Dwyer. Eddy – head of the Commonwealth X-Ray and Radium Laboratory (CXRL) – died shortly after the *Mosaic* trial in 1956, and the new head of CXRL, J. E. S. Stevens, took his place on the committee. J. P. (later Sir Phillip) Baxter was a British chemist from ICI who had worked on *Tube Alloys* and the Manhattan Project, took a chair in chemical engineering at the University of New South Wales in 1949 and later became chairman of the Australian Atomic Energy Commission. However, he played little or no part in the AWTSC. Dwyer, head of the Australian Commonwealth Bureau of Meteorology, was soon appointed to the AWTSC – wisely in view of the crucial importance of meteorology in the trials – and was a very active member.

L. H. (Sir Leslie) Martin – another Cavendish Laboratory man – was Professor of Physics at Melbourne University, and the government's Defence scientific adviser from 1948 to 1960. He was responsible for the setting up, none too soon, of a safety committee (AWTSC), which he chaired until 1957, and he was present at many of the trials. After 1957 he withdrew from the AWTSC and proposed its reorganization, but was active in advising the Department of Defence and the Australian government on the British minor trials at Maralinga (see Chapter 10).

Alan Butement, who was Chief Scientist at the Department for Supply, was born in New Zealand and educated first in Australia and then in England, where he worked for nearly twenty years in an Admiralty experimental establishment and in the British Ministry of Supply. During the war he was engaged in radar research. In 1947 he returned to Australia to help set up the Long Range Weapons Establishment (LRWE) of which the Woomera range is a part, and became its first chief superintendent. Then, in 1949, he was appointed to the Department for Supply, which was responsible for atomic energy matters, including the tests. Besides being on the AWTSC and present at most of the trials, he was very actively involved in exploration for weapon test sites, and in the business of getting them established. It was he who named the greater desert area chosen for the permanent range Maralinga, an Aboriginal word meaning field of thunder.

Also most influential was E. W. (later Sir Ernest) Titterton, though unlike Martin and Butement he did not have a departmental base. He was Professor of Physics at ANU. He had been Oliphant's first research student at Birmingham University, had worked there with Otto Frisch, and then had been one of the group under Oliphant that developed the cavity magnetron, which revolutionized radar and changed the course of the war. In 1943 he went to the Manhattan Project and remained at Los Alamos until 1947, becoming head of the Electronics Division there. He was a senior member of the Timing Group at *Trinity*, the first atomic test at Alamogordo in July 1945, and was an adviser on instrumentation at the American *Crossroads* trial at Bikini Atoll in 1946 – where, as the anonymous 'voice of Abraham', he gave the countdown and detonation orders.[22] After leaving Los Alamos, he spent the next three years at Harwell. Penney badly needed Titterton's experience and special scientific skills, and he tried hard but unsuccessfully to attract him to the weapons establishment. In 1950 Oliphant offered his old student a chair at ANU, and Titterton (though he had been tempted to return to the United States) accepted and migrated to Australia.

In view of Titterton's unique expertise, it was natural that Penney, who had so much wanted him on his staff, should be anxious at least to borrow him as a telemetry expert at *Hurricane*. It was in that capacity, rather than as an observer for the Australian government, that Titterton took part. He attended all the major trials – after 1955 as a member of the AWTSC – and when the AWTSC was reconstituted as a three-man committee he became chairman. He had a knowledge of atomic weapons and an experience of weapon testing since 1945 that few scientists in the world, and no other Australian scientist, had. But, as a very new Australian with close British ties and a Los Alamos background, his position was bound to be seen by many as an ambiguous one.

3
Hurricane – 1952[1]

Planning

Cross Roads, the American test at Bikini Atoll in the Pacific in 1946, was a gigantic scientific experiment some 5,000 miles from the US mainland: 150 aircraft and over 200 ships had been employed, and 42,000 men had taken part. It was difficult to carry out these complex operations at a great distance; *Hurricane* was such an operation, but British resources were scanty and plans modest. Dr L. C. Tyte, the technical director of *Hurricane*, and his small planning group in HER[2] at Fort Halstead, Kent (the main atomic weapons establishment before the Aldermaston site was developed) estimated the manpower requirements at 245 scientists and scientific assistants and 100 industrials, but the number of scientists who eventually carried out the trial was only 100.

Tyte's group prepared a 'trial book' on every aspect of the HER part of *Hurricane*. They ordered instruments and stores, planned the scientific operations and safety measures in meticulous detail, selected and trained people, organized teams and allocated duties.

Though the atomic explosion was the purpose of the enterprise, HER's plan was part of a bigger overall operation, involving several British and Australian government departments and all the armed services of both countries. A coordinating committee called the *Hurricane* Executive, representing all the UK interests under Admiralty chairmanship, was formed in March 1951 and soon afterwards Rear Admiral A. D. Torlesse was appointed as task force commander. In Australia a *Hurricane* Panel was set up in July 1951 to coordinate action there. It was chaired by the Deputy Chief of Naval Staff and comprised representatives of the three Services, the Department of Defence and the security authorities.

The British Navy, already overstretched, had a challenging task. Five suitable ships had to be designated and specially fitted out in complete secrecy and with no time to spare; ship conversions were done at Birkenhead, Chatham and the Clyde. An aircraft carrier, HMS *Campania* (a Second World War conversion from a banana trade merchantman), after completing her duties in the 1951 Festival of Britain, was to serve as flagship and headquarters of the whole expedition. Two landing ships, HMS *Zeebrugge* and *Narvik*, were to transport a detachment of Royal Engineers and their heavy civil engineering equipment, and on arrival in the Monte Bellos, *Zeebrugge* was to move to act as a laboratory for the radio-chemists. Another landing ship, HMS *Tracker*, would be the health control ship and health physics laboratory. An old River Class frigate, UMS *Plym*, which would transport the armed test weapon, was secretly designated as the target vessel, destined to be destroyed in the explosion; *Plym* had to be fitted with an elaborately equipped weapon room in which the device could be safely detonated by remote control.

This flotilla was to transport civilian scientists, Army personnel and large quantities of stores of all kinds. It would be a long voyage – up to eight weeks for *Campania* and *Plym*, which would have to go round Cape, not through the Suez Canal. The Royal Navy was to take the opportunity of showing the flag, making formal calls at various ports *en route*. The length of the voyage would allow scientists more time polish their plans, but most unfortunately the opportunity was not taken to organize joint planning meetings on board between the scientists and the Naval Staff.

Once arrived in the Monte Bellos (see Map 2), the flotilla would have to provide completely for all the *Hurricane* personnel, as well as its own, crews, for some twelve weeks on a group of bare and inhospitable islands with no resources of any kind, not even fresh water. Besides food and shelter, transport would be needed. It would be much more complicated carrying out the test in these small, scattered islands than on a single island or on the mainland, for scientists would have to commute from ship to shore and from island to island in order to set up and maintain their equipment: batteries, cameras, blast gauges, seismographs, calorimeters, thermometers, ionization chambers, air samplers, and so on. This traffic meant constant boat work, with a frequent boat service to take scientists to their scattered workplaces and return them at night to camp or ship so that no one was left marooned on an outlying island. The Royal Navy also had helicopters available.

Hurricane was primarily a naval operation, but the work of the other Services was of the greatest importance. By the time of *Hurricane* there

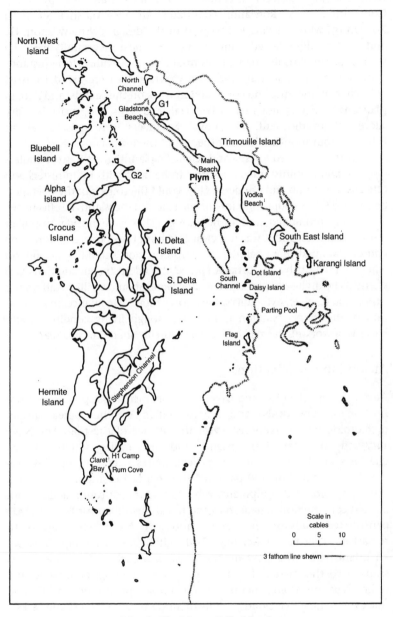

North West
Island

North
Channel

Gladstone
Beach

G1

Trimouille Island

Bluebell
Island

G2

Main
Beach
Plym

Vodka
Beach

Alpha
Island

Crocus
Island

N. Delta
Island

South East Island

Karangi Island

Dot Island

South
Channel

Daisy Island

S. Delta
Island

Parting Pool

Flag
Island

Stephenson Channel

Hermite
Island

Claret
Bay

H1 Camp

Rum Cove

Scale in
cables

0   5   10

3 fathom line shewn

Map 2   The Monte Bello islands

were ten RAF officers attached to Penney's staff, led by Wing Commander J. S. Rowlands GC (later Air Vice-Marshal Sir John Rowlands), who was closely involved in the design of the weapon. He and his carefully selected team collaborated most successfully with the scientists. The RAF also had an essential role in providing long-distance communications and transport. Army personnel were asked to assist with civil engineering and construction work on the islands, and a small planning staff was attached to Fort Halstead. This, too, proved a very successful arrangement. The Royal Engineers were due to sail in February, four months ahead of the rest of the flotilla.

Apart from detailed logistic and scientific planning, there were endless political and administrative questions to be dealt with by ministers and officials in London and Canberra. How could the secrecy of the operation be ensured? How could entry into an area around the islands be effectively, and legally, prohibited, and for how long? (They were outside Australian territorial waters, and it was not clear to whom they belonged, as no one had ever wanted them before.) What information should be given, and when, to the British and Australian press? Should Australian and Canadian scientists be invited to participate? They were. Should civilian staff on the expedition be given extra duty allowances or special insurance, in recognition of the long separation from home, rough living conditions, and hazards of working in small boats in a reputedly shark-infested sea?

Australian participation

Australia was asked for, and gave, generous logistic support. The Royal Australian Navy (RAN) and the Australian Weather Bureau began meteorological observations a year in advance of the trial. The Navy surveyed and charted the islands and surrounding waters, marked channels, laid buoys and moorings, ferried passengers and supplies, provided a weather ship, and patrolled the area before and after the trial. The Army provided equipment, vehicles and transit camp facilities. An airfield construction squadron of the Royal Australian Air Force (RAAF) constructed roads on the islands, and with Navy help – and with remarkable speed and efficiency – laid a vitally important pipeline from an inland river to a jetty on the coast, from where fresh water was shipped to the islands. It was to carry out radiological surveys, and under separate arrangements collect samples of airborne debris and track the radioactive cloud. The RAAF undertook various flying tasks – courier services and passenger transport; security patrols and coastal monitoring by Dakotas; and air sampling by Lincoln aircraft.

As discussed earlier, a few Canadian scientists were to participate in the test, but the question of Australian scientists was apparently, but most surprisingly, not discussed until February 1952. In April, at Penney's personal request, as we have seen, the Australian government was asked if E. W. Titterton might take part as a telemetry expert. Two junior Australian scientists were also requested, one to join the health physics group, and at the same time laboratory facilities for the British radio-chemists were asked for.

These arrangements did not please the Australian authorities, who thought they should have senior representatives present as observers. It was not until September that the question was resolved by an invitation to Professor L. H. Martin, the Defence Scientific Adviser, and W. A. S. Butement, the chief scientist at the Department of Supply, as well as to Titterton.

Safety

The safety of the Australian mainland

By the time the flotilla was to sail, it was impossible to keep *Hurricane* a secret any longer and in February 1952, after much discussion of the precise wording, a joint announcement was made by the two governments:

> In the course of this year the United Kingdom government intend to test an atomic weapon produced in the United Kingdom. In close cooperation with the government of the Commonwealth of Australia, the test will take place at a site in Australia. It will be conducted in conditions which will ensure that there will be no danger whatever from radioactivity to the health of people and animals in the Commonwealth.

Radiation safety had been a paramount consideration for Penney and his staff in planning the trial. Though this was the first British test, the scientists had available both theoretical knowledge and practical experience of atomic weapon tests and weapon effects. British scientists, including Penney, had participated in the US trial in New Mexico in July 1945, and six had been present at Bikini Atoll in June 1946. They also had a substantial handbook, *The Effects of Atomic Weapons*, which the Americans had published in 1950. It contained a mass of up-to-date information on the nature of atomic explosions; the characteristics of air, surface, underground and underwater bursts; the significance of local, or early, fallout and long-range fallout; blast, radiation and thermal damage; properties of radiation; the clinical syndrome of radiation sickness; genetic effects of radiation; radiation monitoring instruments; decontamination procedures; and methods of protection.

The British scientists knew that the shallow underwater explosion of a 'nominal' atomic bomb – about 20 kilotons – would create a fireball that would rise high into the atmosphere carrying a column of water and spray as well as fission products and other bomb constituents, together with many tons of steel, some of which had been vaporized, perhaps 1,000–10,000 tons of sand and 10,000–100,000 tons of water. Because of the great weight of water drawn up in the plume, the fallout would be precipitated quickly and within a few thousand yards from the point of detonation; most of the radioactivity would be dispersed in the water around the islands and would not be intense, except close the explosion centre and for a short time after firing. The fallout hazard was therefore expected to be very localized, with little if any risk of contaminating the Australian mainland – 47 miles to the south-east at the nearest point – unless the wind was blowing from the islands towards it. Meteorology was crucial to safety.

In the autumn of 1951 HER staff prepared a report on the meteorological and safety aspects of *Hurricane*, and especially the safety of communities on the mainland. The coastal region, it noted, was arid but subject to occasional tropical storms, and 100–150 miles inland a range of hills rose to 3,000 feet. In this area, within 150 miles from the islands, were several townships, four airfields and about 20 homesteads.

The authors of *The Effects of Atomic Weapons* had recognized that serious radioactive hazards might be caused downwind of a surface explosion, but early fallout in inhabited areas had been little studied and no relevant standards existed. The International Commission on Radiological Protection (ICRP) – an independent scientific body first set up in 1928, and reconstituted in 1950 to deal with postwar radiation protection matters – had recently recommended exposure limits for radiation workers, but had not yet dealt with non-occupational standards. (It did not do so until 1958.) It was also considering occupational limits for ingested and inhaled radioactive substances; the British Medical Research Council (MRC) had tentatively suggested a limit 100 times lower for the general population.

The HER scientists argued that if the ICRP pronounced it safe – that is, involving a risk that was small compared to the other hazards of life – for a radiation worker to receive an exposure of 0. roentgen (r) a week for all his working life – perhaps for 40 years – then an integrated dose of 2 r, equivalent to one month's occupational dose, was reasonable for other people as what was probably a once-for-all exposure. Calculating the fallout that, in the most unfavourable conditions, could reach the mainland, and the external and internal radiation doses it could give rise to, the HER report concluded that there was a risk of exceeding the safe levels if the wind was blowing from any direction between west and north-east (through north), especially if the winds were fairly uniform at different heights.

To avoid this, firing criteria had to be correct and weather forecasting reliable. The meteorologists would have to work with the scientists responsible for theoretical predictions. The latter, knowing the design and estimated yield of the weapon, could calculate the probable height of the cloud, the probable size and distribution of fallout particles in different parts of the cloud and in its stem, and their rate of fall. From these data, combined with the meteorologists' forecasts of wind directions and speeds at various altitudes, it would be possible to predict fallout patterns and advise the trial director and task force commander when conditions were favourable or unfavourable for firing.

Wind directions and speed usually vary considerably at different altitudes, and two years' observation of wind frequency during October on the west coast of Australia showed that, at altitudes of 6,000 ft and 10,000 ft, 83 per cent of the winds would carry the cloud over the mainland, but winds at 3000 ft would do so less frequently. Out of the ten days in October when other conditions (such as tides) were suitable, there would probably not be more than three days when the wind would blow the cloud away from the mainland; in some years, perhaps six or eight days; in some years, perhaps none. Firing opportunities might therefore be infrequent, but *Hurricane* was deemed to be of such vital importance that these odds were acceptable even though a long wait might be necessary.

Meteorological forecasting for *Hurricane* was to be based on routine weather forecasts from Canberra and special information from the Australian weather ship and the RAAF stations at Pearce, Onslow and Port Hedland. Once all was ready and the standby period had begun, D-1 (the day before the firing) would be decided on the basis of regular and frequent forecasts. Detailed preparations would then be put in hand and, if forecasts continued favourable, D-day would be declared and everyone would take up his allotted position. D-day itself would be declared only if meteorological conditions were right, the sea was calm enough for the boats and the technical requirements could all be fulfilled; if the wind changed or some unforeseen hitch occurred, the firing might have to be cancelled and a new date set for D-1. The firing criteria designed to protect the mainland, the ships and H1 (the main island site) defined acceptable speeds and directions of mean winds at surface level, at heights up to 5,000 ft and at heights up to 30,000 ft. No air up to 5000 ft should reach the mainland from the site of the explosion within ten hours; this would allow time for the comparatively heavy particles of fallout carried by low-level winds to be deposited in the sea. After final meteorological observations, if the task force commander, jointly with the scientific director, decided that the firing should proceed, countdown would begin.

Post-firing precautions were to include high-level flights over the coast to measure atmospheric radioactivity and a radiological survey of the Australian coastline from Onslow to Broome by Harwell scientists in low-flying RAAF aircraft fitted with sensitive detectors. If the low-level air survey indicated any need for it, a ground survey would also be carried out using jeeps. However, provided the firing took place in the meteorological conditions specified, the planners were confident that there was no risk of significant deposition of radioactivity on the mainland. On this the Australian authorities had to rely on the categorical assurances given by the British, as they did not have technical information about the test.

Safety of trial personnel

Safety distances were calculated that would give assurance that no one was in danger from the explosion itself – whether from blast, heat or initial radiation – and all the trials personnel would be upwind of detonation and at least 6 miles (10 km) away. The main hazard would be immediately after the explosion, especially to those who, during the so-called 're-entry phase', were to make sorties to the contaminated lagoon and islands to collect instruments and samples.

The ICRP had, as we have seen, recommended a weekly limit of 0.5 r, which it considered adequate to protect radiation workers routinely exposed to radiation. Penney approached the MRC for advice, and suggested radiation standards which his staff had discussed with J. F. Loutit, the Australian-born MRC radiobiologist, and with W. G. Marley, Harwell's chief radiological expert, who had been at Los Alamos. An MRC panel – after studying the proposals in the light of ICRP recommendations, clinical experience and published American data – endorsed three maximum permissible levels (MPL) of external gamma radiation during the trial.[3]

The first limit was the 'normal working rate', a low rate for continuous exposure over a period of normal working; this was 0.1 r a day for gamma radiation (equivalent to 0.06 r to important organs). The second, the 'lower integrated dose' of 3 r (gamma), was allowed only if necessary to ensure smooth working, and with the radiological safety officer's permission. Anyone receiving a dose at this limit would not be exposed to radiation again during the operation. The third, the 'higher integrated dose' of 10 r (gamma), was for use in cases of extreme urgency in order to recover vital records that might otherwise be lost; it required the express approval of the task force commander (who would be advised by the scientific director and the health physics adviser). Anyone exposed at this limit would be withdrawn from radiation work for a year.

The 0.1 r exposure level for a working day was the same as the existing ICRP occupational limit, and though a 3 r integrated limit was not in the 1950 ICRP recommendations, it was adopted by the ICRP in 1958 (when 3 r in 13 weeks replaced the weekly limit for radiation workers).

These levels, which the MRC panel considered to be innocuous – or at the worst to carry negligible risks – were then authorized by the Chief Medical Officer of the Ministry of Supply. He added certain requirements about film badges, exposure records, respirators and protective clothing. The Ministry passed the information to the Admiralty, War Office and Air Ministry for agreement, and the radiation standards were embodied in *Hurricane* plans and *Hurricane* trial orders, together with detailed safety rules and procedures. These MPLs referred to external, not internal, radiation; the latter was not considered a hazard for *Hurricane* personnel, as respirators and protective clothing would be worn for operations into areas where radioactive material might be inhaled.

The British scientists were aware that these standards were similar to those used in trials in America. The US limit in 1950 was 0.1 r in one day, or in special cases up to 3 r in one day if approved by the top radiological officer; the person exposed then received no more radiation for 30 days. Exposures above 3 r required permission from the task force commander, but no upper limit was specified. In 1952 and again in 1953 the Americans altered their rules somewhat, limiting exposures whenever possible to r in 10 weeks and 3.9 r in 13 weeks (the length of the respective test periods).

The *Hurricane* scientists gave much thought to safety. Their calculations were based on 'worst-case' assumptions and allowed, they felt, ample safety margins. They were confident that, given reliable forecasting by the meteorologists, no public hazard would arise. They also had grounds for confidence in the safety of *Hurricane* personnel, and in the event no doses over 5 r were recorded.

The prohibited area

With *Hurricane* in view, the Australian Parliament rapidly passed the Defence (Special Undertakings) Act 1952, which went through all its stages between 4 and 6 June. It declared that, for reasons of security and the safety of shipping, an area within a radius of 40 miles of the Monte Bello islands was a prohibited zone. There were some doubts in Britain about the Act, because it implied Australian sovereignty over a considerable extent of the high seas outside territorial waters, and so might create an unfortunate precedent. The British proposed that, following the American example, the two governments should issue a joint warning nearer the date of the test. The declaration of a danger area would be based purely on safety considerations and would not imply sovereignty. To seaward, a safe distance of 100 miles was necessary, but this distance was reduced in sectors south of Monte Bello to avoid including a part of the Australian mainland, since firing would not be permitted in conditions that might allow fallout to contaminate it. The terms of the warning were agreed; it was promulgated on 8 August through the usual channels used for warning shipping and aircraft of all nations, and safety patrols by Australian ships and aircraft were arranged.

The expedition

The voyage out to Australia was not the prolonged rest cure that the British scientists had been promised by one senior official in Whitehall. There was much practical work to be done – checking, re-packing and stowing stores, calibrating pressure gauges, building and testing electronic equipment and so on – and much further planning, for there would be little spare time after reaching the islands. Regular meetings of the team leaders were held on board, but without some of the senior scientists (who were coming later by air) and without the Naval staff. Also unfortunate, though inevitable, was the absence of Australian scientists and Service staffs, who did not meet the *Hurricane* party until it reached Fremantle.

For some, the voyage was nightmarish. Conditions on board were overcrowded and extremely uncomfortable, especially in hot weather. In certain winds the *Campania*'s ventilation system distributed fumes from the engine room into some of the cabins, making them almost uninhabitable. Seasickness afflicted most of the scientists at some time. Tensions frequently arose, especially on board the *Campania*, between the Naval officers, with their formal and disciplined tradition, and the boffins, with their easygoing manners and unconventional dress, and their habit of discarding jackets and ties in tropical heat. The 'passengers' were often in the way while shipboard routines went on around them. Where were they to go while the ship was scrubbed over? Where should they sunbathe if not on the quarter deck or the gun platforms?

With professional naval precision, *Campania* anchored on 8 August, exactly on schedule, in the so-called 'parting pool' east of the Monte Bello lagoon. The lagoon was encircled by numerous tiny islands – with such nostalgic names as Crocus, Primrose, Gardenia and Bluebell – and four larger ones, North West Island, Hermite, Trimouille and Alpha. The scientific party found good roads and jetties and excellent buildings prepared for them by the Army, assisted by the Royal Australian Air Force. 'Truly the RE are magnificent', Tyte enthused, and so too were the Australians. On-site preparations began with all speed. Probably the busiest team was the telemetry and communications group – responsible for the electronic firing system and for the network of communications and controls linking the ships and field sites – under Ieuan (later Sir Ieuan) Maddock.

The main site – the only one that would be occupied at the time of the explosion – was H1, on Hermite Island (see Map 2 above). Here there were excellent laboratories containing the control room from which the weapon in *Plym* would be fired, and all the apparatus that would monitor the firing circuit, inspect the state of the telemetry equipment throughout the islands, and receive and record multiplication-rate observations. Here too were the generators, and the area for charging the all-important batteries that would provide power for field equipment.

The main photographic stations were to be on Hermite, Alpha Island and North West Island. The remotely controlled, high-speed cameras would operate at speeds up to 8,000 frames per second, to show the development of the fireball, the water column, the cloud and other visual effects. Ultra-high-speed cameras at H1 would photograph early self-luminous stages of the explosion.

Most of the sites to be used for investigating blast and thermal effects were on Trimouille. At hundreds of points there and adjacent islands gauges of many different types were placed: blast gauges, diaphragm gauges, seismographic gauges and hollow containers (including 200 empty petrol cans, used so effectively by Penney at the 1946 Bikini test). Air-sampling equipment, made from modified vacuum cleaner units, was set up. Thermometers and calorimeters, and samples of special paints and clothing materials to show the effects of heat from the explosion, were placed at selected points.

At many points on the four main islands, the Radiations Hazards Division sited ionization chambers, of high and low sensitivity, complete with amplifiers and pen recorders and protected in shock-proof cylindrical structures. Some were connected by telemetry to the ship, HMS *Tracker*.

A small MRC team under Dr W. J. H. Butterfield was to study the effects of radioactive deposition on plants and to measure the uptake of fission products, especially iodine and strontium.[4] Other investigations included the effect of blast on structures and on aircraft, the protection, of food from contamination, the decontamination of ships under service conditions and the radioactive hazard to ships from a 'base surge' should it occur. (In the event it did not.)

Two serious problems soon appeared. It had been intended that most of the scientists would live on the base ship, *Campania*, going to and from the islands at morning and night, with only a few men occasionally having to camp ashore. However, the survey party had underestimated the effects of weather and tides. *Campania* could not enter the shallow waters of the lagoon and had to be anchored in the Parting Pool, but the pinnaces could not tie up alongside her at night there and had to be moored many miles away. For the scientists, this placed impossible restrictions on the length of the working day. Worse still, the small boats could not work in the Parting Pool in rough weather: soon after arriving, the scientists were confined to the base ship for three days. Even in good weather the swell in the Parting Pool made it a hazardous business to transfer between *Campania* and small craft tied up alongside, especially for landlubbers wearing the army boots issued for the rough terrain of the Islands. Most of the scientists therefore had to live ashore during the week, and the Navy quickly improvised two big tented camps, on Hermite and Trimouille. Despite complaints about the food and trouble with flies and termites, the arrangement was reasonably successful, and the Naval officers were no doubt as glad to have the scientists out of their way as the scientists were to be free from shipboard constraints.

The second big problem was the boat service. Travelling times proved to be nearly twice those estimated in the boat plans, and even the journeys between *Campania* and *Plym* often took $2\frac{1}{2}$–3 hours. The transport craft were too few and often broke down. The crews were perhaps the most overworked members of the expedition, but for all their efforts the scientists lost much valuable working time waiting about for long overdue boats. Incredibly, Tyte said, the success of the whole expensive operation hung on the 'thin red line of 3 or 4 LCMs'.[5] There were other thin red lines. The operation was hampered by many shortages and deficiencies – electric generators, VHF radio – telephone links which proved defective (taxi sets had fortunately been brought and they saved the situation), vehicles, duplicating equipment used for issuing instructions, and staff. The expedition carried no spare men, and it was lucky that there were no serious accidents or illness. One junior assistant was responsible for maintaining all the batteries on which much of the field equipment on the islands depended – 'no batteries, no trial' – and when he proved unsuitable, a replacement was hard to find.

All was ready for scientific rehearsals on 12 and 13 September and a full rehearsal on 18 September. Staff movements were planned in detail, boat schedules drafted and mustering lists prepared, for everyone and everything had to be in exactly the right place at the right time. From the time when assembly of the weapon began, all non-essential staff had to be at least 5 miles from ground zero, and by H-hour all ships, and nearly all personnel, had to be at least 10 miles south (i.e. upwind) of the target vessel. A few key staff would be stationed at H1 on Hermite Island, about 7 miles south-south-west of the explosion.

The radioactive core of the device arrived in a Sunderland flying boat on 18 September, in time for the rehearsal. On 22 September, Penney arrived, relaxed and confident, a powerful boost to morale. After reviewing the situation, he hoped that 1 October might be D–1 day, but cancellations were always possible because of the weather and there might be several successive D–1 days, with all the attendant problems of maintaining equipment and fully charged batteries in a state of readiness in the many scattered sites.

On the morning of 2 October, D–1 was announced. Scientists were busy inspecting and testing their equipment until they were evacuated from all the islands, except Hermite. There they passed a cold and windy night in the camp at H1, tired and tense after five years' strain and stress and gruelling hard work. Just after midnight, work began in the weapon room in HMS *Plym*, berthed off the western shore of' Trimouille; after finally setting the arming switch, the last two men made the rough return journey from *Plym* to H1 before dawn. Soon the camp was aroused, and D-day had begun.

After final meteorological observations, the task force commander and scientific director decided that the trial should proceed. The wind was from the south, so that all the early fallout would be carried north over the Indian Ocean. At 09:15 hrs (local time) Maddock began countdown to zero. Three seconds after zero, men running out of the buildings at H1 saw a huge water column rising rapidly, in complete symmetry and utter silence. Nothing visible remained of *Plym*. Thirty seconds after zero a faint tremor appeared to emerge from the ground, followed almost instantaneously by the crash of the blast wave.

Soon after the detonation, Penney sent a personal cable to Lord Cherwell and Duncan Sandys, the two atomic energy ministers:

> We have records in all-important scientific experiments. We have fully met our guarantee to the Australians that no harmful contamination will be deposited on the mainland. All contamination went northwards and will stay there for at least another 10 hours. It is possible that no contamination whatever will reach mainland. The dispersion is already sufficient to eliminate all danger from fallout now taking place.
>
> The meteorological conditions were extraordinarily fortunate for us and I am sure that no estimate of the power of the bomb can be made from photographs from the mainland. I think that we can rest assured that no significant dust samples can be collected by foreigners. We alone will know the power and efficiency of our weapon.
>
> The reasons why the top of the cloud did not go above 15,000 ft were first that the air was very dry and second that there was a strong inversion at 15,000 ft. The ball of fire evaporated the water spout but even so the cloud was not saturated. Consequently there was no regaining of latent heat from condensation as the cloud lifted and the cloud stopped at the inversion. The blast wind raised a great sandstorm and this observation alone in my opinion justifies the expectation that the weapon efficiency was up to my predictions.
>
> The heat flash was intense but of short duration. It caused widespread fires in the vegetation over Trimouille. These fires are now dying away 8 hours after the burst. The contamination is intense on land north of Point Zero but is slight south of Point Zero. Our telemetry safety monitors are giving 10 r per hour 5 hours after burst at 1 mile due north. Our monitor further north is reading 3,000, but we distrust this. All scientific work is proceeding smoothly and everybody is in good heart.

Twenty minutes after detonation, the men who had been at H1 left for much-needed rest and sleep on board *Campania*.

Meanwhile, aboard *Tracker* preparations were being made for controlling re-entry into the radioactive areas to take samples and collect records and instruments. All the men entering contaminated areas had to pass through the health control in *Tracker*, to be briefed and issued with film badges and protective clothing; and each party was accompanied by a health escort. On return they were undressed, monitored and, where necessary, decontaminated. On a few occasions up to five showers were needed. The sorties were very exhausting in the hot weather, especially in the brown protective clothing (white was worn for later trials). The resulting thermal stress was near the limits of tolerance for some men, who lost 2–4 litres of sweat in four hours, and up to 7 kg in weight; one of the effects of dehydration was extreme nervous irritability.

In certain cases where respirators had been thought unnecessary, urine analysis revealed minute traces of radioactivity, which were soon eliminated. As the radioactivity must have been inhaled, the need for respirators, and their effectiveness, were both demonstrated. On some of the later sorties, after the levels of contamination had been reduced by radioactive decay, protective clothing and respirators were dispensed with, since thermal stress had become a greater hazard than radioactivity.

Re-entry sorties and recovery of the records continued, interrupted by some very bad weather and gale force winds, until 23 October. After the hardships and difficulties of the previous three months, and the stress of the past two or three years, tensions found release in some splendid parties in the wardroom of *Campania*, where much liquor was drunk and some unprintable songs were sung by scientists and Naval officers in hearty unison.

The flotilla sailed from the islands on 31 October, and most of the scientists left the ship at Fremantle and were flown home by the RAF. Meanwhile, an Australian unit of 18 men from the three Services, under an RAAF squadron leader who had taken part in *Hurricane*, was established on Trimouille to carry out training in radiological health and safety and to undertake security duties after the task force departed. The British health team provided radiation detection equipment and other stores, and a detailed brief on residual radiation hazards to the unit, which remained in the Monte Bellos until 16 December. Then, apart from periodic inspection and security patrols by HMAS *Hawkesbury*, and a British scientific survey in November 1953, the islands were deserted again until preparations began for *Operation Mosaic* in 1956.

'This important experiment'

Churchill sent Menzies a message of thanks and a report on the operation, and made a statement to the House of Commons, on 22 October:

> The object of the test was to investigate the effects of an atomic explosion in a harbour. The weapon was accordingly placed in HMS *Plym*, a frigate of 1,450 tons which was anchored in the Monte Bello

Islands. Conditions were favourable and care was taken to wait for southerly winds so as to avoid the possibility of any significant concentration of radioactive particles spreading over the Australian mainland. Specimen studies of importance to Civil Defence and to the armed services were erected at various distances. Instruments were set up to record the effect of contamination, blast, heat flash, gamma-ray flash and other factors of interest.

The weapon was exploded in the morning of 3 October. Thousands of tons of water and of mud and rock from the sea bottom were thrown many thousands of feet into the air and a high tidal wave was caused. The effects of blast and radioactive contamination extended over a wide area ...

Very soon after the explosion, two naval officers undertook the danger task of flying helicopters over the heavily contaminated lagoon where *Plym* had lain. This was in order to take samples of the water so that its radioactivity could be measured. After a longer interval, scientists and service personnel in protective clothing entered the contaminated areas to examine the effects and to recover records.

Technical descriptions of the performance of the bomb cannot of course be given. It may however be said that the weapon behaved exactly as expected and forecast in many precise details by Dr W. G. Penney, whose services were of the highest order. Scientific observations and measurements show that the weapon does not contradict the natural expectation that progress in this sphere would be continued ...

The explosion caused no casualties to the personnel of the expedition. No animals were used in the test. Apart from some local rats which were killed, no mammals were seen in the affected area and such birds as there were had mostly been frightened away by the earlier preparations.

Churchill emphasized the British government's great indebtedness to Australia: not only had the Australian Commonwealth allowed the use of their territory for the test but all branches of their government – and particularly the Navy, Army and Air Force – had given most valuable help in the preparation and execution of 'this important experiment'. He warmly congratulated all concerned in producing the first British atomic weapon on 'the successful outcome of this historic episode', and in conclusion complimented Attlee and the Opposition on initiating it.

How safe was *Hurricane*?

Safety of the mainland

How well did the *Hurricane* safety measures work? The islands themselves were, as expected, heavily contaminated at some points and
remained so for a time. The survey in November 1953 found them still
highly radioactive in places, but it was possible to use certain areas again
in 1956. There seems to have been negligible radioactivity on the
Australian mainland. Twenty-four hours after the explosion, the coastline was surveyed by Harwell scientists using very sensitive detectors
aboard Dakota aircraft, which flew along the coast from Broome to a
height of 500 ft – a very bumpy, airsick flight of 4–5 hours in turbulent
conditions. As no radioactivity was detected, it was decided that no
ground survey was necessary. Eight hours later, high-level flights
detected a localized concentration of radioactivity in the atmosphere at
an altitude of 10,000 ft but hardly any at 8,000 ft.

Air samples were taken 200 miles from ground zero, at a height of
8,000–10,000 ft, by Lincoln aircraft of the RAAF, about six hours after
the explosion. Some of the samples were analysed in a Melbourne
University laboratory by a team of four Harwell radio-chemists. Others
were flown back to England for analysis.

Later there would be a network of over 80 fixed monitoring to detect and
measure fallout on the Australian continent; there was no such monitoring
in 1952. It was an essential part of the *Hurricane* plan that there should be
no fallout on the mainland. But though the cloud containing the radioactive debris went safely out to sea after the explosion, hours later light
evening breezes blowing onshore brought back some radioactivity and a
secondary cloud crossed Australia from west to east. In the next week, very
low levels of radioactivity were detected by two of the scientists from
Harwell in rainwater samples from three places, one of them Brisbane.

The public health impact on the Australian population of fallout from
all the major trials was recently estimated by two Australian scientists[6]
using all the available data and considering all the known pathways – by
external radiation, and by internal radiation from ingesting radioactivity in food or water or inhaling airborne radioactivity. Since monitoring
results were not available for *Hurricane*, they used data from the 1956
and 1957 trials, taking account of wind trajectories and such factors as
the comparative yields of the various detonations. Their resulting estimate of the collective dose equivalent to the Australian population from
Hurricane was 110 man-sieverts (11,000 man-rems) a figure that, they
said, might be too low by a factor of 2 or might be 10 times too high.

Safety of test personnel

Of the 1,518 *Hurricane* personnel issued with film badges, 1,263 received no exposure above the measurable threshold, and only 14 received more than 0.5 r during the whole operation; 0.5 r it will be remembered, was the normal weekly limit. No doses over 5 r were recorded. These figures compare favourably with the exposures of radiation workers at the time, for whom the ICRP limit was then 0.5 r a week (i.e. 25 r a year) continuously for a working lifetime.

The RAAF had not issued radiation dosimeters and film badges to its Lincoln aircrews and no special precautions had been taken. When the Air Ministry had made enquiries two years previously, Harwell's chief radiological officer, W. G. Marley, had advised them that aircraft should avoid flying through the visible cloud after an atomic explosion, but that once the visible cloud had dispersed there would be no danger. (This view seems to be in line with American conclusions in the 1950 edition of *The Effects of Atomic Weapons*, though these relate to an air burst, not an underwater burst.) The *Hurricane* Executive had informed the Australian authorities that the radioactive hazard to aircrews in flying through the cloud would be negligible and that there would be no risk of the aircraft becoming contaminated. Later experience (see Chapter 4) showed this view to be mistaken, but calculations made after *Totem* indicated that the radioactivity levels at *Hurricane* and the radiation doses to Lincoln aircraft and crews were only a fraction of those at *Totem*, and were considered to be of no medical significance.

What did *Hurricane* achieve?

Hurricane had been a close-run thing, and could easily have failed. The plutonium was ready only just in time. The boats and vehicles were only just sufficient. There was no margin for illness or injuries, and if a few men had gone sick, the trial could have been seriously hampered. If the weather had been unfavourable on 3 October, there would only have been one other opportunity, on 23 October, before the task force was due to sail for home. Thanks to immensely hard work in Britain and in Australia – by scientists, engineers, servicemen, boat crews and all concerned – and also thanks to a fair share of luck with the weather, *Hurricane* was a success.

For the scientists, it was the climax of a period of intense work; 'our first eruption', as one of them, well read in Milton, called it. It was also the beginning of a new period of research and development. It confirmed that their design worked, and that they had the makings of a nominal – i.e. about 20-kiloton – plutonium bomb, similar to the Nagasaki bomb, but with many advantages over the bombs which the Americans were making in 1946 when collaboration had ceased.[7] The scientists learnt a great deal from *Hurricane*, and the next two years saw dozens of scientific reports on all aspects of the trial. There were new data on shallow underwater nuclear explosions and hence on the possible effect of shipborne nuclear bombs in ports and harbours, a defence problem that had much exercised the British authorities. Data were provided for military and civil defence authorities on the effects of blast on various types of buildings, equipment and materials. Useful biological information was gained – though no animal experiments were done – by catching and examining local fish and animals and collecting vegetation for analysis. Much was learnt about radioactivity from local fallout, about protective clothing and about decontamination methods. The operation also yielded valuable administrative lessons (not always applied in later tests) about the need for sufficient time and staff for planning, and for closer coordination between the various elements involved; about the dangers of underestimating the resources required; about the inadvisability of sending the main scientific party by sea; and about public relations. All these lessons were summed up in a report by Captain Pat Cooper, a retired Naval officer who acted as a liaison officer, and technical aide to Penney.

To the world, *Hurricane* marked Britain's entry into the ranks of atomic powers alongside the United States and Russia. It did not, however, mean that Britain had an operational nuclear weapon: they had the art but not the article (the device tested at Monte Bello was by no means a service weapon; one scientist described it as a 'lash-up'). Even when 'weaponized', significant numbers could not be available for several years, and the V-bombers, the intended delivery vehicles, were not yet in production. The triumphant announcement that the test had been successfully carried out did not mean what the public perhaps understood. The British press generally reacted with chauvinistic pride but considerable inaccuracy, making flattering assumptions that the bomb could have been tested earlier but had been delayed for the sake of major improvements; that it was much more powerful than any American bomb; that it was much smaller, and that it had been tested in a guided missile. In some quarters, however, the press greeted the test with modified rapture; if not a waste of resources, it was a regrettable necessity due to the failure to integrate Anglo-American defence, or was an expensive demonstration designed to secure American cooperation.[8]

Before *Hurricane*, in March 1952, Churchill had expressed the opinion that the outcome of the test was of supreme importance because it would put Britain in a far better position to secure the full cooperation of the United States, which was essential to the success of a strategic air plan in war. He saw the test as establishing 'equality', thus enabling Britain not only to exchange scientific and technical information more freely with the Americans, but also to initiate joint consultations on targets and methods of attack. But the Americans – with their first thermonuclear test only a month away – were not particularly impressed. Dr Solandt, of the Canadian Defence Research Board, who was in Washington just after *Hurricane*, found there a feeling that the British weapon programme was merely a propaganda effort to interest the US authorities. By 1958, thanks partly to further tests in Australia, the position was to be very different.

4
Totem – 1953[1]

The plan for *Totem*

Before *Hurricane* it was already clear that more tests would be needed, but none was expected before 1954. However, after *Hurricane* Sir William Penney (he had been knighted after *Hurricane*) decided another two tests were necessary to answer some important questions. The purpose of the tests was to resolve some urgent questions surrounding fissile material production, as well as to assess the performance of weapons currently under development.[2]

As part of their 1952 appraisal of global strategy, the Chiefs of Staff had asked for a doubling of plutonium output for the nuclear weapons programme. This had been approved by the government, and two new plutonium-producing power reactors (PIPPAs[3]) were to be built for that purpose at Calder Hall, adjacent to Windscale. Unlike the original Windscale piles, the PIPPAs would produce electricity as well as plutonium. As net producers of electricity, they had great cost-benefit attractions.

These dual-use advantages had to be balanced, though, by the need to produce a sufficient amount of weapons-usable plutonium. The dilemma centred on the irradiation time: how long the uranium fuel could be left in the reactor. Leaving the fuel for longer periods meant that the burn-up of uranium was increased, which produced more fissile material and thereby made a cheaper product. However, this same process meant that plutonium from the Calder Hall reactors would have a higher proportion of plutonium-240 than that from the Windscale piles and this presented problems for weapons design. Pu-240 is subject to spontaneous fission, thereby producing neutrons which could start the weapon's atomic reaction too soon. Whilst there would still be an explosion, plutonium from Calder Hall was expected to generate a smaller yield for a given amount of plutonium than would be the case using material from the Windscale piles.

Consequently, it was necessary to determine the level of Pu-240 that could be tolerated whilst still obtaining the optimum yield for a design. The weapon scientists had set the proportion conservatively, but on the basis of an unproven theory. Nor did they have complete confidence in their theory of yield versus quantity of Pu-240. The *Hurricane* device had given about the expected nominal yield – approximately 25 kilotons – but gave no information about the effects of increased Pu-240 levels in reducing yields. The plan for the two *Totem* tests, then, was to try two isotopic levels of Pu-240 in order to obtain a clearer picture.

In December 1952, Penney sought and obtained ministerial approval for two test explosions for this purpose. The aim was summarized for the Cabinet Committee as 'to establish certain minimum characteristics of the fissile material suitable for use in atomic weapons, in order that the existing piles may be operated, [and] any future nuclear reactors for the production of fissile material may be designed, to secure the maximum output and the lowest cost which is consistent with the efficiency of the weapons'.[4] The operation was later codenamed *Totem*, and Cherwell remarked dryly that 'anything up the pole would be appropriate'.[5] The test was to be in October 1953 and, as for *Hurricane*, the planners would be pressed for time.[6]

Monte Bello was out of the question; the Navy could not mount another expedition in the time available. Penney fully understood the difficulties and knew that the great distance to Australia was a serious logistical handicap. The *Totem* tests would be smaller and simpler than *Hurricane*, and what was needed was a test site where the logistics would be much easier. But the use of an American range was still impossible, the timescale did not permit another worldwide search, and nowhere nearer than Australia seemed feasible.

On his way to *Hurricane* in October 1952, Penney had called secretly at the Woomera rocket range in South Australia, and he and Butement had visited a potential test site – identified as X200 but soon given the name Emu Field – which the Australians had found in the desert 300 miles north-west of Woomera (see Map 3).[7] Penney proposed that the new trial should be mounted there, and in December 1952 Churchill asked Menzies to approve the use of this site. The safety problem, his note said, had been carefully investigated. Full assurances could be given to the Australian government, and the UK government would be glad to arrange for Penney to go through the calculations with Professors Martin and Titterton. Further, the test would be carried out only when

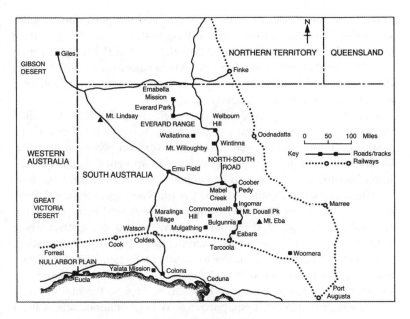

Map 3   The Emu/Maralinga area

the Australian authorities were satisfied that the necessary weather conditions were met.[8]

Penney told the high-level Atomic Energy Official Committee that in his opinion the Australians had been 'reasonably content' with the way in which the British had carried out *Hurricane* without telling them very much about it. But *Hurricane* had been an island test. *Totem* would be conducted on the mainland and consequently Australians would want to know much more about it. Besides the details to be supplied to Martin and Titterton about contamination, he suggested that he should orally tell them and one or two specially cleared high-ranking officials to be nominated by the Australian government about certain general principles of the weapon, including the implosion-compression principle. This information would probably have to be disclosed to Butement, who was in charge of Woomera. It was intended, Penney said, to ask for some Australian Army officers to help in the radiological survey teams. This would give them valuable military experience and would reduce the number of men who would have to be sent out from the United Kingdom. They would obtain information about radioactive contamination, but only from low-yield weapons. To prevent them from underrating the British military weapon, they should be told that the object of *Totem* was to compare the efficiency of two low-powered weapons and to settle 'controversial design information'. Failing that, they might at least be told that the test was to determine how the yield of the weapon varied with the weight of plutonium. These views were passed on to Lord Cherwell. Only the last of these suggestions was accepted, and the information was confined to radiological safety.

Menzies quickly approved the Emu Field proposal. The Australian Department of Supply assumed responsibility and set up a *Totem* Panel. Australian troops immediately began construction work on the site. Meanwhile, the British had set up an interdepartmental committee, the *Totem* Executive (or Totex), and had appointed a trial planner, L. C. Tyte, who had been scientific superintendent at *Hurricane*, and a technical director, C. A. Adams. In May 1953, however, Tyte moved to a post at the National Coal Board. Staff lists were drawn up and the matters where Australian help was to be sought were itemized. Instructor Commander Westwater RN was to be responsible for weather forecasting, as at *Hurricane*, but Australia was to be asked for major meteorological support in personnel and equipment. Construction work was to be kept to the minimum by shipping large trailers ready equipped to serve as laboratories, offices and a health centre.[9] Plans for air sampling would be much the same as for *Hurricane* and the assistance of the RAAF would again be requested.[10]

An Australian liaison mission headed by Brigadier C. L. Lucas, the X200 site commander designate, arrived in England early in February for discussions on the site plan, buildings, water supplies, communications, meteorology, safety, contaminated waste and security. It was soon clear to the British that the worst difficulties would be overland transport and water. The nearest track was 100 miles away and the terrain was difficult; only vehicles with tracks or special wheels could cross the sandy ridges, and 30 miles a day would be good going. Most stores would have to be air-freighted to the site, and in fact Lucas stated that only loads impossible for air transport could be allowed to go over land. This called for a much bigger air transport exercise than had been anticipated, in which the RAAF effort would need to be supplemented by the RAF, and it became necessary to construct an all-weather airstrip at the site.[11] The plan for a village of trailers was now out of the question, as they could not be towed to the site and were too big to airlift; Nissen huts would have to be erected, and the men would have to live in tents. In the event, some 2,500 tons of supplies and equipment were flown in to Emu Field and only 500 tons transported overland.

Water was an equally serious problem and Lucas stated that supplies were insufficient for more than 300 people; the shortage of water suitable for decontamination and for processing film badges would strictly limit the numbers who could work in contaminated areas. This meant that no experiments ancillary to the weapon trial itself could be included unless they were exceptionally important. Despite this, the Operational Report written after the tests was critical of the late introduction of new experiments, such as a flash propagation project that had been brought in at the end of April, and recommended that a firm deadline, beyond which no further projects would be accepted, should be established in future.[12]

It was agreed that 45 Australian servicemen, including some of the naval personnel who had been at *Hurricane*, would take part. Twenty of them would have a course of radiological training to ensure that they took proper precautions, and this training might be considerably extended. Squadron Leader Thomas, who had been at *Hurricane* and in the post-trial unit at Monte Bello, would be available and would play a key role.

Though the nearest inhabited area was about 110 miles from Emu Field, a region to the north that was used by Aboriginals for hunting was only about 50 miles away. An Australian official had been specially appointed by the Australian authorities to deal with native affairs and to look after the interests of the neighbouring Aboriginals, and nine (later seven) Commonwealth government officers were given the task of ensuring that none strayed into the prohibited area. It was emphasized by Totex that contaminated materials on the range must be disposed of in such a way that the Aboriginals would not be endangered by their characteristic ingenuity in salvaging and using material discarded by white people.[13]

The basic timetable for the trial was agreed with the Lucas mission. All equipment, except the weapons, was to be shipped early in June, to reach Adelaide by late July. A great deal of this equipment had also been used at *Hurricane*, and in fact it is unlikely that *Totem* could have taken place at all without this recycling of equipment.[14] *Totem* staff were to arrive in Australia by the first week in September, the weapons would follow later in the month, and the trial, consisting of two firings about ten days apart, would take place in October/November.[15]

In March 1953 a British mission led by C. A. Adams, the *Totem* technical director, paid a two-week return visit to Australia. The prospect they found was daunting. The area was flat, with clumps of saltbush and occasional mulga and she oaks, and dead wood. The land surface was a compact mixture of sand and stone, with an underlying fine red dust that impregnated their clothes. There was little water. The weather was hot – 105° F during a large part of the day – but chilly at night. Clothing to cover the whole body, including a bush hat and a veil, were said to be necessary for protection; bush flies, unless constantly brushed away, settled on hands, face, arms and shirt in a thick black mass. Bush fires might be troublesome. The airlift problem would be extremely difficult, and they noted that the question of the possible long-term effects of radioactive contamination, which might be carried long distances and precipitated by rainfall, had not been resolved.[16]

The British government sent the Australian government an invitation for Australian scientists (expected to be Martin, Titterton and Butement) to be present at *Totem*. Meanwhile Penney's staff was preparing a safety brief, and in May they completed and despatched to Australia an appreciation of the *Totem* airborne hazard. This report (numbered A32) predicted the fallout for a 5-kiloton device but was capable of adjustment to the higher figure of probable maximum yield, for both shots, of 10 kilotons. The mechanism of the rise of the mushroom cloud and the distribution of contamination at various levels was not yet understood in detail, but it was certain that a large amount of material would be thrown up into the air – the vaporized 'gadget', the 100 ft steel tower it was to be mounted on, fission products from the explosion, and sand from the ground. As the fireball cooled, the vaporized material would condense into small particles, together with some of the fission products. Other fission products would adhere to, and contaminate, the particles drawn up from the ground as the mushroom cloud rose. Once in the air, the particles would be dispersed by the wind and eventually fall to earth. If the contamination they caused was severe enough, it could be a health hazard – from external radiation (by fission products deposited on the ground or on the person), or from internal radiation (due to contaminated air, food or water). The body could tolerate some radiation, according to A32, but above a certain level there would be a threat to health. Permissible contamination levels, the paper continued, had already been laid down for *Hurricane* by the MRC, on the basis of ICRP recommendations. To determine safe distances and safe firing conditions, these permissible levels had to be related to the expected contamination on the ground, and this depended on wind conditions. The fallout deposited downwind would steadily decrease with distance; moreover, the further the particles were carried before they fell to the ground the less dangerous the contamination would be because of dispersion and radioactive decay.

If the wind blew steadily at 20 miles an hour and in the same direction at all levels, the fallout would be along the line of the wind, spreading outwards by atmospheric turbulence as the distance increased. To either side of the central line, the intensity would fall off rapidly. In such conditions, from a 5-kiloton explosion, contamination outside a 50-mile radius could exceed a 'zero risk level' only in a narrow sector, extending 120 miles from ground zero. This sector would be an area of 'slight risk'. For a 10-kiloton burst the corresponding distances would be 70 miles and 170 miles.

Neither a 'zero risk level' nor a 'slight risk level' was mentioned in the ICRP recommendations. They were proposed by Aldermaston, and were derived secondary limits that referred to levels of deposited radioactivity, not to maximum permissible doses of radiation. The Aldermaston health physicists defined the 'slight risk level' as 'that quantity of fission products which may cause some slight temporary sickness to a small number of people who have a low threshold sensitivity to radiation'. This level was derived from the maximum amount of external gamma radiation that could be tolerated with the previously defined 'slight risk'. At that time, this level was taken by most scientists as 25 r (250 mSv), and therefore this was the standard adopted for the 'slight risk level'.

'Zero risk level' they defined as 'that quantity of fission products which will cause no measurable effect on the body'. ICRP gave 0.3 r (3 mSv) as the maximum permissible dose (MPD) of external gamma radiation that might be received weekly over a lifetime; from this the authors of A32 argued that, for zero risk, 3 r (30 mSv; ten times the weekly limit) ought not to be exceeded in any ten-week period.

These basic limits continued to be used almost throughout the Australian atomic weapon trials, though the secondary limits were revised at intervals. Corresponding limits were also set for beta radiation, and for internal radiation by the different exposure pathways. The variations in levels of surface radioactivity set for later trials were not variations in the MPD but in the quantity of radioactivity that it was calculated could give rise to such exposures.

The conditions for firing set out in A32 were intended to be such that there was nobody in a fallout area where the surface radioactivity was above 'zero risk level'. These conditions were comparable to those derived from the published results of test firings in the United States, where more than 20 atomic weapons or devices had by this time been exploded at the proving ground in Nevada, but the British calculations were more conservative. A32 recommended two practical limitations on firing the *Totem* rounds. First, to protect the base camp, firing should not take place if the mean wind up to a height of 10,000 ft was between 100° and 130° Secondly, if – improbably – wind direction was constant with height the zero risk zone for a 5-kiloton detonation might be as far as

120 miles from ground zero. In that case, to safeguard the nearest homesteads and Aboriginal hunting grounds 100 or so miles away, firing should not take place if the predicted wind was 190° or between 218° and 246°.

The Australian scientists had several questions on A32, especially about the predicted height of the cloud. In June, Titterton had an opportunity to visit England and was able to discuss A32, and the trial generally, with Penney and his staff. After this, and some correspondence with Aldermaston, Martin and Titterton informed the Australian Prime Minister in June that they were satisfied that no injury to health would result from the effects of the proposed explosions.[17]

In July 1953 Totex – the *Totem* Executive in London – issued the following instructions to the trials staff:

Firing will occur only if

(a) the mean wind from surface to any level below 10,000 ft does not lie between 330° to 130°through north
(b) it is forecast that no rain will fall within 12 hours, nearer than 200 miles downwind.

Firing conditions for *Totem* 2, if necessary, can be slightly less stringent because we do not this time have to preserve a clean firing site for an immediately following trial ...[18]

The test preparations had of course been conducted in the greatest secrecy, and early site operations had been publicly described as tests of pilot-less bombs at the Woomera rocket range. The announcement of the test's true purpose was not made until 24 June, four days after a British newspaper had run a story that 'Britain's biggest ever atom bomb' would be tested at Woomera in 1954. The story was wrong about both the size of the explosion and the date of the test, but inched closer to the truth in its claim that the test was designed to make the maximum use of plutonium in the weapon.[19] The joint announcement by Britain and Australia that a weapon test would be conducted at Woomera was followed on 31 July by an announcement of the dates for the tests. Britain had initially insisted that the tests should be attended only by those with a direct responsibility in the operation, and had resisted suggestions for some press coverage. However, the June announcement seems to have prompted steadily increasing demands from the media, especially in Australia, for some coverage to be permitted. In September, Sandys visited Australia and bowed to the pressure.

At a press conference, Prime Minister Menzies announced that one aircraft would be provided for representatives of the press to attend the test. They would be screened from the explosion until a 'go' signal from Penney, upon which the screen would be let down and photographs of the mushroom cloud would be permitted for a designated time.[20]

Operation *Totem* – Round 1

The main scientific party flew to Australia on 17 August and began preparations both for firing the first *Totem* round at T1 and for a series of minor component trials – codenamed *Kittens* – which was also to be conducted at Emu Field (see Chapter 10). Preliminary *Totem* rehearsals took place on 24 and 27 September, and the first device arrived by air on 26 September.

When Penney flew in on 29 September the first *Kitten* test had already been successfully carried out and the *Totem* teams were nearly ready for a full-scale rehearsal. There were 158 British staff there, and 17 Australians. Five Australian officers were in the radiation hazards group, which totalled 35 and was much the largest group; six Australians were in the meteorological team; Titterton and four others made up a neutron detection group; one Australian officer took part in the small 'target response' programme for the investigation of weapon effects. In addition, the air-sampling and cloud-tracking programme was a major RAAF contribution (see below). Logistically, the whole operation was entirely dependent on the RAF and the aircraft that provided a freight and passenger service between Woomera and Emu Field.

On 30 September a party of VIPs, including Lord Cherwell and Mr Butement, visited the site, and Butement remained for some days after the rest had left. After a full-scale rehearsal on 1 October, standby began on 7 October, but was cancelled almost immediately because of bad weather. Captain Frank Lloyd RN, a senior Ministry of Supply official, described conditions in a letter home:

> Life here is fun provided one always has a return ticket. A temperature range of 50° to 60° per 24 hours plus a very dry air is most bracing. The food is good, the beer is plentiful and the only thing we really lack is fresh water. The dust is the devil ... The Australians under Lucas have done a first class job over here ... all Bill's staff are in great heart ...[21]

The weather had been hot and blustery, but on 8 October the rain began. D-1 was declared on Monday 12 October, but had to be cancelled. Penney cabled to London:

> Rain stopped play. Unseasonable weather continues to provide easterly winds which endanger camp and have given us dark clouds and considerable rain. We are doing everything possible to reduce time between the two explosions and will certainly regain a few of the lost days. My policy is to wait until conditions are entirely satisfactory, Press and VIPs notwithstanding, and not to fire on a Sunday.[22]

D-1 was declared again on 14 October, a party of press representatives and VIPs flew in from Adelaide, and this time conditions held good. The first round was fired at 7 am on 15 October (local time), about an hour after sunrise. The cloud rose to 10,000 ft, extending upwards to 15,000 ft. The explosion was more powerful than expected, and at 10 kilotons was the maximum adopted for fallout and safety calculations. Penney cabled Cherwell and Sandys that 3 kilotons were radiated as heat, and 7 kilotons as blast.[23]

The cloud was tracked for two-and-a-half days.[24] It preserved its identity to a remarkable extent and was clearly visible as a cloud even after 24 hours. It was reported later that owing to the very stable atmospheric conditions, the cloud did not diffuse rapidly but was stretched in the direction of motion. It therefore produced a narrow band of radioactivity on the ground underneath its path. Penney noted that due to the lack of air turbulence this contamination contour was 20 times as long as it was wide in places, and unlike any seen hitherto.[25]

Preliminary reports of the fallout pattern on the ground, from airborne surveys extending to a distance of 400 miles, were passed to Penney over the next few days. The reports showed that the sideways dispersion effects of wind shear and turbulence on the radioactive dust in the cloud and stem were less than expected. However, the level of radiation off-range was said to be within the 'no risk' specification. Two years later, however, the calibration of the instruments used for the airborne radiological survey was reviewed, and the contamination levels were reassessed; the fallout at Wallatinna, a homestead to the northeast, was corrected to a level about half-way between 'zero risk' and 'slight risk'.[26]

Other questions about the fallout from the *Totem* shots and its possible health effects are discussed later in this chapter.

Operation *Totem* – Round 2

Immediately after the first round, Butement went off with a small reconnaissance party, which was joined by Penney and J. T. Tomblin, Adams' deputy, to look at another possible test site in the South Australian bush. They returned to Emu Field a few days later, in readiness for the second *Totem* round, T2. Meanwhile the *Kittens* series proceeded without a hitch, until the fifth and final experiment on 17 October (see Chapter 10).[27]

At T2, as at T1, the device was mounted on a steel tower. Preparations were delayed by more bad weather, an unpleasant combination of rain, gusty winds and sandstorms. The weather improved on 24 October, and the next day standby was declared.[28] Penney called a technical meeting of scientists in the evening to review the predictions of fallout patterns and to make certain that favourable conditions would hold good for firing early next day. He was joined by Titterton, two Australian meteorologists, two British meteorologists and three other British scientists. Penney and his staff estimated the probable maximum yield at 10 kilotons, the most likely yield at 2–3 kilotons, and the absolute minimum at 1/4 kiloton. Westwater, the senior British meteorologist, estimated the cloud heights for these yields at 14,000 ft, 12,000 ft and 5,000 ft, respectively. Corner, the scientist in charge of theoretical predictions, calculated that for a 10-kiloton burst, even with winds of 100 miles an hour, the zero risk level would be 100 miles from ground zero; winds of this speed were not expected, and the distance would be less with lower wind speeds. Results of air surveys appeared to indicate that the ground contamination levels from the T1 shot were about four times lower than had been predicted, and to confirm that the theoretical predictions had (as intended) been based on very pessimistic, worst-case, assumptions. This view was in fact erroneous, since, as we have seen, it was later found that the method used to interpret the air survey data gave ground contamination levels lower than they actually were by a factor of three.

At the meeting on 24 October, the meteorologists said that the wind was likely to carry the cloud from T2 to the south-east. The nearest populations were at Tarcoola and Woomera, 200 and 300 miles away, respectively; there seemed to be a wide safety margin. Asked whether rain might fall through the cloud and bring down fallout before it left the mainland, one of the Australian meteorologists assured the meeting that there was no risk of rainfall. The cloud would go up into a hot, dry, mass of air which could not produce rain; then it would take some 50 hours to leave the mainland, and before it could be overtaken by a moist, westerly air stream it would be too dispersed to present any hazard. It was agreed that the meteorological conditions likely to prevail for T2 satisfied the criteria accepted by Martin and Titterton, and that the safety factor was probably four times greater than previously believed.

The meeting then discussed possible reactions if the cloud was seen by members of the public. Apparently, the cloud from T1 had been seen from Oodnadatta, probably from an aircraft. It was agreed that if there were any press questions about the cloud, the answer could be that it might have been a rain cloud. This ad hoc meeting was 'off-side' in making such a suggestion, as the responsibility for dealing with the press lay with Captain Lloyd, who was present at *Totem* but who was not at the meeting. However, nothing more was heard of a *Totem* cloud until the 'black mist' stories of 1980 (see below).

On the morning of 27 October, weather conditions held good and T2 was fired at 7 am (local time). Penney reported to ministers – that is, to Cherwell and Sandys:[29]

> T2 gave us a miserable night but went off on time with highly satisfactory wind conditions. My estimate from seeing explosions and comparing ground fused areas of two bursts from the air is that the yield of T2 was between 12 and 18 kilotons. [It was in fact 8 kilotons.] This high yield proved superiority of intuition over maths, since our calculated yield was 2 or 3 kilotons. Extremely important consequences to our whole atomic energy programme ... Top of cloud about 25,000 ft and bottom at 20,000. Stem torn shreds before our eyes, and fanned out into quadrant between south and east. Cloud rapidly dispersing. Started moving towards Point 60 miles north of Woomera but will swing towards east and then north of east.

The weather turned hot and sultry and, by the evening of 27 October, a heavy storm broke, which continued intermittently all night. It did not, however, affect the *Totem* 2 cloud, which by this time was far away and well dispersed. Dismantling and packing began the next day, 28 October, in cold damp weather, and the site was practically closed down by 2 November. A force of Australian officers arrived, to be given a course in health control and guarding contaminated areas; on 6 November responsibility for the site was transferred from *Totem* staff to the Australian authorities in the person of Squadron Leader Thomas RAAF, who had taken over after *Hurricane* in 1952. By 12 November, all the *Totem* staff had left Emu Field.[30]

Two experiments

The Centurion tank

The timetable and the difficult conditions at Emu Field limited ancillary investigations very severely.[31] Two experiments, however, were carried out. One was on the effects of the explosion on a Centurion tank with a simulated tank crew. The tank, provided by the Australian Army, was placed at about 250 yards from ground zero. Two hours before the explosion, it was left with its hatch closed, its engines running and the brakes off; the crew was represented by roughly fashioned dummies, each with two film badges. The prompt radiation dose to the crew would have been sufficient to cause radiation sickness in a few hours and death within a day or so,[32] but damage to the tank was much less than expected; immediately after the explosion its main engine was still running. It had not caught fire, although all external textile had disappeared and the front surfaces had a sandblasted look to them. It was driven from the test site under its own power. After examination it was test-driven over very rough terrain without difficulty, and was pronounced battle-worthy.[33]

Operation Hot Box

A second experiment was an Air Ministry operation codenamed *Hot Box*. In February the *Totem* Executive had approved a proposal that an RAF aircraft should fly into the mushroom cloud within a few minutes of the detonation. This flight was not part of the trial proper, nor part of the air-sampling or radiological survey programmes, but was a separate experiment planned by the Air Ministry.[34] They wanted to take advantage of *Totem* to investigate aircrew safety, behaviour of aircraft and aircraft contamination in conditions of nuclear warfare.

The origin of *Operation Hot Box* goes back to 1948, when Squadron Leader D. A. Wilson, a consultant in radiology to the RAF, was attached to the Health Physics Division at Harwell. There, in 1949, he was shown some papers written by Fuchs, the Harwell physicist, which concluded that aircraft would be unable to operate anywhere in the vicinity of a nuclear explosion for some days. These papers had apparently been influential in the United States as well as in the British Air Ministry. Wilson was not convinced, and found errors in the calculations. He was also convinced that it was important for flight crews to possess information on the behaviour of aircraft passing through an atomic cloud, and for ground crews to know the level of contamination to be expected.

This information demanded practical experiments, and Wilson proposed to the Chief of the Air Staff and the RAF medical authorities that, when British atomic tests began, the opportunity should be taken of exploring the potential hazards to flying personnel. As *Hurricane* was unsuitable for this experiment, it was postponed until *Totem*. A specially prepared Canberra, equipped with precise instrumentation, was loaned to Wilson (now a Group Captain) at the beginning of 1953 and the air-crew was assembled – Wilson himself as observer, a young RAF medical officer, Squadron Leader Geoffrey Dhenin GM, as pilot, and a volunteer (ex-Pathfinder) navigator, Wing Commander E. W. Anderson. At least two of the aircrew were well versed in radiation hazards, and they had planned *Hot Box* for months. 'It was', Wilson testified to the Royal Commission nearly thirty years later, 'in no sense a *Boys' Own Paper* type of exercise. It was a serious scientific experiment'.[35] *Hot Box* was the first experiment its kind, and produced results which were of value to the US Air Force as well as the RAF. In fact, *Hot Box* would set operations param-eters for a sortie by Canberra aircraft using atomic bombs. The *Hot Box* Canberra, incidentally, collected air samples for Frank Morgan, the radio-chemist responsible for weapons diagnostics – the study of the performance of the weapon by radiochemical methods.

The aircraft entered the cloud six minutes after the detonation (the cloud by this time was 2,000 yards wide), passed through it, and then made short runs above and below it. The thickness of the cloud forced the pilot to switch on the aircraft lights, and there was much turbu-lence. Wing Commander Anderson, writing for the aviation journal *The Aeroplane* shortly after *Hot Box*, described the experience in vivid terms:

> The cloud looked reasonably peaceful by now as if it had stopped developing, but common sense could not quite overcome a qualm at the last moment and a feeling as if of flying into a brick wall. Then everything outside the aircraft went brown and we started to joggle about. For a few seconds it was like riding over cobblestones in an oxtail-soup fog and then, suddenly, the sky was blue again and, a moment later, the cobblestones changed to smooth macadam.[36]

After landing the three officers showered, changed their clothing, and were monitored and medically examined. Analysis of blood and urine samples showed no trace of fission products. Their film badges and dosimeters – two films, and two dosimeters to each man – gave high readings. The films indicated exposures of about 10–15 r (100–150 mSv) and the dosimeters gave readings of about 20 r (200 mSv); however, film badges are generally more reliable, as quartz fibre dosimeters behave erratically in rough conditions, and altitude and turbulence could have accounted for the discrepancy.

Because the dose recorded by the film badges was close to the maximum permitted by the Ministry of Supply (21 r (210 mSv) over a six-week period) and because the Air Ministry's essential requirements had been fulfilled, the second sortie, after T2, was cancelled at the insistence of Penney and Adams. All three RAF officers were ready and keen to go again, but accepted the common sense of the decision. Instead, sampling rockets were used at T2, but surface winds prevented them entering the cloud as planned. Wilson watched from the ground, and could not resist mentioning in his report that the failure of the Jindiviks (unmanned aircraft, designed for use as target drones) only showed 'how useful it might have been had we been airborne, standing-by, at the time'.[37]

The exposures registered for Wilson and his colleagues were the largest recorded at *Totem*. Most (83 per cent) of the recorded exposures were less than 0.3 r (3mSv) in a week.[38]

Contaminated aircraft

Besides their routine transport, communications and patrol duties British and Australian aircraft had several different air survey and air sampling tasks. The radiological surveys were for safety purposes: to detect and chart fallout more rapidly and extensively than ground surveys could do alone, and to track the radioactive cloud – by instruments when it was no longer visible – until it had dispersed or had left the Australian continent. Other flights were for weapons diagnostic purposes: aircraft were required to collect air samples early, but at some distance from ground zero; radiochemical analysis of the samples was used to provide essential data on the performance and yield of the weapon.

Yet other aircraft collected later air samples, at varying distances up to 2,000 miles from ground zero, for scientific intelligence purposes. This was an independent and especially secret programme directed by Harwell and was based on their experience of monitoring foreign weapon tests by collecting long-distance samples. It was hoped to improve the efficiency of these monitoring methods by studying the results from British tests where the weapon information was known instead of unknown. The RAAF undertook these flights and made a very substantial contribution to this programme; at *Totem*, two squadrons of Lincoln aircraft and over 160 ground and air staff were involved.

Two days after *Totem* 1 a radiation hazards officer from Emu Field, who was visiting Woomera, checked the exterior of the *Hot Box* Canberra, which had been washed and scrubbed sufficiently to reduce the surface radioactivity to 'active service' standards. He found it still very contaminated in places, and when the *Totem* 2 flight was cancelled he began further work on it. He also advised the RAAF to suspend work on the Lincolns which had been on long-distance air-sampling sorties. Aircrews returning from their sorties had reported that their cloud-tracking instruments had gone off scale, and the station had called on Group Captain Wilson, of the *Hot Box* crew, for help. He, in fact, knew nothing about this intelligence programme, which was being controlled by a Harwell scientist based at Salisbury, near Adelaide. Wilson checked the aircraft interiors, and estimated the radiation exposures of the aircrews – who had no film badges although one pilot happened to have a dosimeter. As a medical radiologist Wilson was able to assure the station commander that no one had received a significant exposure. Nevertheless the RAAF were understandably annoyed and worried because they had had no warning of radioactive hazards on these operations because the British, from their previous experience of intelligence flights, had expected none. There was a flurry of activity and some strong feelings, and Wilson immediately took an opportunity to visit Melbourne and call on the Director-General of Medical Services, RAAF, to explain the situation to him.

Meanwhile another radiation safety officer arrived at Woomera equipped to set up a health control system. A laboratory-style 'active area' with physical barriers was not feasible, but the precautions were explained to everyone, and service discipline and supervision, he reported, ensured that they were strictly observed. Two of the Lincolns were found to be substantially contaminated and three slightly; unlike the more streamlined Canberras, their exterior seemed almost designed to trap contamination.

A similar control was set up at Amberley. Nine Lincolns there were contaminated. The only significant risk was to the ground crews; one man was reported to have spent three hours climbing over the wings of a recently landed aircraft, and he had worn the same overalls for two more days before the contamination was realized. Measurements made on the overalls suggested at the time a total dose of 3–5 r, but it was later assessed to be much lower.

Other RAAF Lincolns operating from Richmond, near Sydney, also became contaminated, but full precautions were taken promptly thanks to the US Air Force. There were USAF aircraft based at Richmond and it had been agreed long before *Totem* that two B29s should take part in the long-distance sampling after T1 and T2. The B29s were 'flying met labs' and the crews were well protected against radiation hazards. They were surprised and shocked by the extent of contamination of the Lincolns and by the lack of safety measures, and they lent the RAAF monitoring instruments and instructed them fully on what to do. As a further precaution, it was arranged for all civil aircraft in the eastern part of Australia to be subjected to height restrictions after T2, although in the event this was not necessary.[39]

The lack of foresight about the radiological protection of aircraft and men involved in the air-sampling programme was undoubtedly a serious deficiency. Separate control of the programme by Harwell, the failure to coordinate in the planning stages, the inadequate Harwell presence on the spot and the extreme secrecy all contributed to it. So did the belief that conditions would be like those of the British aircraft collecting samples over the Atlantic, and the misleading advice given to the Air Ministry in 1950 (see Chapter 3). Yet another factor was the unexpected meteorological conditions, which produced little wind to dissipate the cloud to the predicted extent. Fortunately, no one is assessed as having had a severe radiation dose. Moreover the position was put right before T2, thanks to the USAF and *Hot Box*.

Some *Totem* lessons

The two *Totem* shots, besides giving information on the plutonium-240 question, taught the scientists a great deal in the next two or three years about the conduct of trials and, in particular, about early fallout. The data were derived from two sources: ground and airborne surveys. The monitoring stations that were later set up all over the Australian continent did not exist at the time of *Totem*. After *Totem* 1, ground surveys had been carried out up to 10 miles from ground zero; after *Totem* 2, up to four miles. Altogether 4,400 measurements had been recorded. Aerial surveys had been made by aircraft fitted with sensitive radiation-detecting instruments and flying at 500 ft over the fallout area. They had made over 80 traverses, up to 400 miles from ground zero. Aerial surveys were valuable because they could cover large distances very quickly; ground surveys were more limited in their range, and exposed the surveyors to radiation above the normal working limit. However, there were problems with using data from airborne surveys: partly because of errors and uncertainties in the interpretation of aerial readings in terms of actual ground contamination: partly because of navigational problems and difficulties of maintaining a constant altitude when flying low in turbulent conditions.

After extensive analysis and re-analysis of the *Totem* data, it had become clear by 1956 that, because of the very unusual meteorological conditions, the early fallout from the first shot had been about twice that from the second and had provided an ideal demonstration of the validity of a 'no-shear' dispersion model. It was clear too that post-event analysis did not support the belief that the A32 methods of predicting contamination were safely pessimistic, partly because it had underestimated the proportion of the radioactive content of the cloud that would remain in the stem.[40] Nevertheless, because the conversions from radiation exposure values to 'zero risk' and 'slight risk' levels of surface radioactivity contained very conservative assumptions, A32 allowed for a considerable margin of error. Detailed studies of the *Totem* data were put to good use in the development of new and improved predictive methods to succeed A32.

Totem experience also provided administrative and organizational lessons, summed up by Captain Pat Cooper, who had commented on *Hurricane*. Generally the operations, he said, had proceeded smoothly, but in future the air-sampling operations should be integrated more fully into the trial plan and controlled more closely by the headquarters organization. The main difference in organization between *Hurricane* and *Totem* was that the former was run like a military operation, with a naval task force commander in overall control, and a scientific director responsible for the scientific aspects. *Totem* had no task force commander, and the scientific director had a most demanding scientific job to do without having to coordinate and control so many disparate groups. (In any case a civilian could not have been placed in immediate command of the British and Australian military elements.) The scientific group had operated very successfully, but a more extensive headquarters control was needed, embracing both the scientific and supporting forces and providing communications, transport and all the technical services for the whole operation.

The timetable had been desperately tight, as the *Totem* Executive had realized, and in a trial so hurriedly prepared as *Totem* and planned by different groups of people 12,000 miles apart, full mutual understanding was impossible. There had been occasional clashes of strong and sometimes discordant personalities, but cooperation had been admirable. The RAAF stations had made an outstanding contribution. Woomera had been invaluable as railhead, transit camp, rest station, control headquarters for the Lincolns and Dakotas, and home for *Totem* administrative and signals staff. Operation *Totem* had been a technical success, said Cooper, thanks to the excellent spirit of the scientific groups and to the effective Australian support 'given willingly and enthusiastically by all concerned from top to bottom'.

Enthusiasm for the joint partnership was expressed at greater length by the Australian Minister for Supply. Understandably, while paying tribute to British achievements, he found it desirable to emphasize or even overemphasize the part played by Australia. All Australians, he said, had cause to feel proud of their country's contribution, especially the planning and construction work done at Emu Field in the face of incredible difficulties and the great skill and professional ability of the RAAF pilots and crews. 'Although only a small nation', he concluded 'we have given eloquent proof of our ability and willingness to take major part in the defence of the freedom of mankind'.[41]

Totem in retrospect

After the *Totem* shots, the ground contamination by fission products seemed slight, apart from a narrow corridor downwind of the tower sites. This fallout, however, proved to be very different from what was expected, consisting of quite large particles that were not readily picked up by passing vehicles or blown about by the wind. On windy days, columns of dust extended several hundred feet into the air, but the radioactivity of the dust did not appear to be very high. Fallout had contaminated an unmanned photographic site on the eastern side of Emu Field, and this fact may have started the rumour that the camp was abandoned and never used again because of contamination.[42] *Totem* was indeed the only major trial to take place there, but as we have seen, Butement and Penney were reconnoitring another site even before the second shot. Emu Field would have been quite unsuitable for a permanent test site; its disadvantages were so daunting that it is surprising it was used at all. But then the *Totem* operation had been considered especially urgent.

A network of fallout monitoring stations was to be set up across Australia in 1955, but there was no such system at the time of *Totem*. The Australian scientists Wise and Moroney, in their 1985 appraisal of the public health impact of fallout from the British atomic tests, made estimates for *Hurricane* and *Totem* based on all the available information, re-examined in the light of more recent knowledge on the behaviour of fallout and pathways of exposure. They calculated the total Australian population dose from T1 as 70 man-sieverts (7,000 man-rems) that is, one-tenth of the total from all twelve atomic tests from 1952 to 1957. That from T2 they calculated as 60 man-sieverts (6,000 man-rems).

When the Australian Royal Commission came to consider the *Totem* tests, three issues remained outstanding, more than 30 years after the operation. The first was the question of radiological dosage for the Aboriginal population, the second and third were both concerned with the T1 shot: specifically whether it should have been fired when it was, and the incident known as the black mist.

Radiation exposure and the Aboriginal population

The Royal Commission concluded that radiological procedures for the *Totem* tests were, on the whole, 'well planned and executed', and the levels of contamination that A32 had defined as 'zero risk' and 'slight risk' were reasonable in view of the standards of the time. However, it also found that these risk levels were calibrated for the 'people living in houses and wearing clothes and shoes'; the standards therefore failed to account for the higher levels of exposure among peoples living outdoors without shoes and little clothing. Consequently, the Commission concluded that 'there was a failure at the *Totem* trials to consider adequately the distinctive lifestyle of Aborigines and, as a consequence, their special vulnerability to fallout'. This conclusion was accepted by the British Submission, and in fact was acknowledged at the time. The successor document to A32, which was implemented in time for the next round of tests in *Operation Mosaic*, contained an Appendix that took into account the exposure levels for 'unclothed people living in semi-primitive conditions'.

The firing of T1

A second area of controversy was the decision to go ahead with the firing of T1 on 15 October. With winds blowing from between 211° and 240°, the decision complied with the Totex directive. It can be argued, however, that it did not meet the A32 criteria. A32, it will be remembered, advised against firing when the wind was at 190° or between 218° and 246° if the wind direct was 'constant with height', but did not define the term. Is a wind structure varying over an arc of 23° – or at most 29° – to be considered 'constant with height' or not? If it is, T1 did not conform to A32; if not, it did.

The Royal Commission concluded that T1 had been in breach of the A32 criteria, which had stated that a 5-kiloton explosion had the potential to exceed the 'zero risk' level in nearby inhabited areas if there was very low wind shear. As we saw earlier, the explosion was 10 kilotons and wind shear was very low indeed. Ronald Siddons of Aldermaston calculated in his testimony to the Commission that A32 had underestimated fallout levels by a factor of three, and that fallout in the Wallatina and Welbourn Hill levels had exceeded the levels set in A32. The British Submission concurred that contamination levels had been underestimated, although it none the less insisted that the assumptions of A32 were reasonable at the time and that the 'slight risk' did not come near inhabited areas.

Both the Commission and the British Submission therefore concurred that T1 should not have been fired when it was. The lingering dispute was concerned with the information on which the decision to fire was taken. Was it *knowingly* made in conditions that were unsatisfactory? Some nuclear weapons scientists, as well as others, have since said that it was a mistake to fire at the time, and Penney admitted as much to the Royal Commission. However, he also pointed out that this was a judgement made with hindsight. Information available to the trials staff after the explosion should not be confused with information available to them beforehand. Predictions of the movement of the cloud in the hours following the explosion were made by the *Totem* meteorologists on the basis of information – from a network of weather stations – that was several hours old by the time the firing decision was made. At the pre-firing conference the senior British meteorologist, Commander Westwater RN, was apparently satisfied that conditions were suitable, but there is no documentation (pre-firing conferences were not usually minuted). The scientists who had to carry out the downwind monitoring of the fallout were expecting a much wider plume, and were astonished by the narrowness of the plume as their surveys developed.[43]

Penney, as we have seen, was determined to wait for entirely satisfactory predicted conditions. It was his firm policy never to proceed if anyone at the pre-firing conference had the slightest reservation. Moreover, the agreement between Britain and Australia stipulated explicitly that 'the test would only be carried out when the Australian authorities were satisfied that the necessary weather conditions were met'.[44] In short, the Australian participants had an effective veto over firing. This does not mean that the T1 decision was valid, but it does mean that everyone present, including the Australian scientists and the meteorologists, was satisfied at the time the decision was taken. Possibly the meteorologists overestimated the effect of wind shear and atmospheric turbulence. Possibly the forecasts of the wind shear acting on the cloud as it moved during the first few hours indicated greater deviation than was actually measured at the site, within minutes of the explosion, and contained in Westwater's report. No complete and convincing explanation of the T1 firing exists, but neither is there anything to suggest that the decision was taken in conditions on which anyone had any reason for doubts at the time.

The black mist

Twenty-seven years after Totem, the T1 cloud reappeared when a story about a 'black mist' became current in Australia. (An Australian anthropologist, Professor Annette Hamilton, had heard it ten years earlier.) After a broadcast about the nuclear weapon tests, an Aboriginal named Mr Yami Lester told a member of the Central Australian Aboriginal Congress about an event during his boyhood at Wallatinna Station, near the opal mining town of Coober Pedy. The date was uncertain; Aboriginals have no systematic method of dating, but probably few people could exactly date incidents in their childhood after 30 years. About seven o'clock on this particular morning, Lester said, there was a big bang and everybody in the campsite woke up asking what it was. Some time later – perhaps the next day – they saw a black, greasy, shiny smoke rolling up to them through the mulga (the Australian scrub or bush). It had a very strong smell, and it stayed around for a while. Later, he said, people began to be ill, and some, he thought, might have died. The symptoms were sore eyes, sickness and diarrhoea. He himself became blind in one eye, and wholly blind a few years later; an eye specialist told him that his blindness was due to glaucoma and measles.

Other varying reports of 'a rolling black smoke or mist', 'a reddish cloud', 'blackish smoke settling all day on the trees ... as an oily dust', and a 'big coiling cloud-like thing like a dust storm' came from other places in the region, in particular from Welbourn Hill station. There was much public and media interest in Australia, and an account appeared in 1982 in a book by Adrian Tame and F. P. J. Robotham.[45] The Australian Ionizing Radiation Advisory Council was asked to investigate, and in 1983 its conclusions were published in a general report on the atomic tests (AIRAC No. 9). AIRAC was somewhat sceptical, but concluded that if the black mist had been caused by any of the tests it must have been by *Totem*, as Wallatinna was much nearer to Emu Field than to the range at Maralinga where the 1956 and 1957 tests took place. T1 was more likely than T2 because of its unusual fallout pattern due to low wind shear and low turbulence, and the trajectory of the cloud must have passed fairly close to Wallatinna. However, measurements made by ground surveys at the time had shown that, even immediately under the centre of the plume and at a distance of only ten miles from ground zero, the radiation dose would have been too small to cause acute illness. Wallatinna was 107 miles from ground zero, and there were no local features to cause a 'hot spot' there. Doses sufficient to cause radiation sickness therefore seemed most unlikely – AIRAC calculated the highest as in the range 0.1–1.0 r (1–10 mSv) – and the probability of long-term damage to health was extremely low.

In 1983 the story reached the British press. On 3 May an article in *The Observer* reported allegations that some Aboriginals had been exposed to airborne debris from the British atomic test at Emu Field on 15 October 1953, and had suffered short- and long-term heath damage. Scientists at Aldermaston decided that the black mist stories, even if they seemed unlikely, ought to be further investigated, and they asked the Meteorological Office to collaborate in a study based on all the meteorological and radiological data from *Totem* and employing the latest knowledge and computing techniques. The joint study, using twelve variants of a basic mathematical model, was completed in 1984. It concluded that the sites at Wallatinna and Welbourn Hill did receive fallout from the test on 15 October 1953; that debris drawn into the convective boundary layer (CBL) – the layer of air close to the earth's surface – could have been sufficiently concentrated to be visible to observers; and that it might have had an appearance similar to that described. (However, the descriptions varied considerably, especially as to the colour of the cloud – black, grey, white, blue or reddish.) Nevertheless the highest possible lifetime radiation doses that could be deduced from any of the mathematical models used in the study were 100–120 mSv (10–12 r) or more realistically 10–15 mSv (1–1.5 r). Neither could have had adverse health effects in the short term, and the long-term carcinogenic risk was insignificant – about 1 in 10,000, but probably lower. This view of the health impact of T1 was similar to AIRAC's, though reached by an entirely different method.

AIRAC reviewed its 1983 findings in 1985. It continued to prefer observed data from corrected (or normalized) aerial survey results to estimates based on hypothetical models. But it, too, was still satisfied that any radiation dose received at Wallatinna (where the highest fallout occurred) was most unlikely to have exceeded the annual limit then allowable, and certainly could not have caused acute radiation sickness. It also seemed improbable that a black mist attributable to a single test could have extended to all the sites, besides Wallatinna and Welbourn Hill, from which 'black mist' stories had come.

However, the number of stories and the similarities between them mean that there is little doubt that some form of unusual cloud or mist was seen by a number of people during the *Totem* tests. The 1985 Royal Commission and the British Submission concurred on this, and further concluded that this phenomenon was almost certainly the T1 cloud, which, due to the unusual wind conditions, was clearly visible for at least 24 hours after detonation. There was simply little else that could have caused such an effect. Consequently, it followed that those in the vicinity might have been subjected to fallout. Again, the Commission and the British Submission, in their different ways, concurred that this was, at the least, a probability. The Royal Commission stated that it 'believes that Aboriginal people experienced radioactive fallout from T1 in the form of a black mist or cloud', while the British Submission was more tentative: 'The visible phenomena would have been a dark and unusual cloud, perhaps associated with a light deposit of fine dust'. The question of whether the dust caused the immediate symptoms described by witnesses, and the blindness of Yami Lester, was more difficult. The British Submission, taking into account its own radiological findings and those of AIRAC, concluded that the fallout was not sufficiently radioactive to cause short-term radiation sickness. The Commission was unable to reach a decision.

To summarize, the controversies over the *Totem* tests centred mostly on T1, and in particular the decision to fire. Despite the sometimes antagonistic tone of the Royal Commission hearings, some clear areas of consensus emerged during the 1980s. It was accepted that the radiological contamination criteria failed adequately to take account of the likely exposure for Aborigines, that the contamination levels exceeded those laid down in A32, and that T1 ought not to have been fired when it was. The last of these was in fact the source of most of the problems. The black mist and the higher levels of contamination were consequences of the unusually low wind conditions at T1, and dispute has remained over how far this could realistically have been taken into account at the time. The lack of explicit records of the decision make this a difficult issue, but it should be pointed out that there is also a lack of any recorded dissent about the decision. Penney's policy was not to fire in the presence of dissent and it must therefore be assumed that none existed. Consequently, it is reasonable to conclude that no one at T1 saw fit to give anything other than the go-ahead.

5
A Pregnant Pause: 1953–56

After *Totem* there was a pregnant pause before the next major British trial in the Australian spring of 1956, but international nuclear testing continued apace. Meanwhile, the United States carried out 23 more tests, making 65 since the end of the war. These included their second thermonuclear explosion at Bikini Atoll on 1 March 1954; the first had been in October 1952.[1] During the same period Russia had exploded at least seven nuclear weapons, including one in the megaton range. For Britain, the $2\frac{1}{2}$ years between *Totem* and the next trials saw important changes in the context of its nuclear test programme. First, it was decided that atomic kiloton weapons would no longer be the primary deterrent, and that Britain must therefore follow the US and Soviet Union and develop megaton and thermonuclear weapons. Second, an international moratorium or ban on testing began to look like a genuine possibility. And third, the domestic political setting of testing policy shifted, as a growing anti-nuclear constituency and increasing public concerns over fallout made themselves felt. These three factors combined to create a different context by the time of the 1956 tests.

The British H-bomb decision

Within a month of *Hurricane*, the US had successfully tested the world's first thermonuclear device. Britain, in contrast, had only just acquired an atomic capability, and it would be some time yet before that was translated into an operational capacity. With the colossal power of thermonuclear weapons representing the nuclear future, Britain was suddenly back to square one in its hopes for renewed Anglo-American nuclear collaboration, which were thought (correctly) to lie in demonstrating comparable nuclear technological capabilities.

Churchill was fully aware of the size of the gap that had suddenly opened up between Britain and the US: 'the difference between the hydrogen bomb and the atomic bomb,' he told Sir John Colville, 'is greater than that between the atomic bomb and the bow-and-arrow'.[2] This was something of an overstatement, but it was undeniable that thermonuclear weapons created significant new problems for British nuclear strategy, with its twin aims of influencing US policy and deterring the Soviet Union. The first of these aims was at the heart of a growing concern that Washington's new-found, but surely temporary, technological advantage might tempt it into a dangerously confrontational policy towards the Soviet Union in the short window before both sides had thermonuclear weapons.[3] The best, and perhaps only, way in which Britain might check such adventurism would be if it were to have a thermonuclear strategic capability of its own, which would give it a role and thereby a voice in US nuclear strategic planning.

A second concern was a growing awareness that, when the Soviet Union *did* acquire a thermonuclear weapon, the implications of mutual superpower vulnerability were potentially disturbing. These implications were succinctly summarized by the Air Defence subcommittee: 'when New York is vulnerable to retaliation, the USA will not use her strategic weapon in defence of London'.[4] That apprehension was to dog NATO's nuclear policy for the rest of the Cold War, and in fact helped prompt French withdrawal from the Alliance military structure in the 1960s. The latter option would be unthinkable for Britain, of course, and so the only alternative seemed to be for the UK to have a deterrent capability of its own. The atomic bomb would be insufficient; in the thermonuclear age, it was widely held that the only deterrent to a megaton weapon was another megaton weapon.

Consequently, the principles of 'deterrence in concert' *and* independent deterrence both dictated that Britain must develop megaton bombs. However, the technical and financial implications inherent in such a decision gave pause for thought. In February 1953 Churchill asked Cherwell to investigate the possibility of a British H-bomb and its likely costs. His report, which arrived two months later, noted some practical problems attendant on an H-bomb project, including the fact that the UK's current bomber fleet would probably not be able to carry the weapon, and some uncertainties over the exact nature of the materials involved in true thermonuclear weapons. Cherwell's overall conclusion, however, was upbeat: 'we think we know how to make an H-bomb'.[5] Technical realities, however, suggested that this was a premature judgement.

Penney had been collecting what he called 'certain snippets of information' from the US, in order to allow joint evaluation of the Soviet nuclear test programme. By January 1954, these, when added to Britain's own work on thermonuclear weapons, were sufficient for the British scientists to have an idea of the principal features of H-bombs. Two distinct types had been identified. The first was a fission weapon supplemented with thermonuclear material (more usually referred to as a 'boosted bomb'), the second a thermonuclear bomb in which most of the yield came from thermonuclear reactions. Penney, however, still felt that 'a vital part is missing'.[6]

Cherwell and Penney differed about the technological problems that had to be overcome in order for a thermonuclear weapon to be produced, but they shared a confidence that it *could* be done, and at bearable cost. Cockroft concurred: 'Thermonuclear weapons are undoubtedly simpler to make than scientists thought ... The weapon is comparatively cheap and easy to make'.[7] This consensus, despite the fact that the scientists at Aldermaston were still uncertain how a thermonuclear weapon worked, was implicit in a report by the Working Party on the Operational Use of Atomic Weapons (OAW) that was presented to the Chiefs of Staff on 2 June 1954.

The report, based on a paper submitted by Penney, identified three main problems in producing H-bombs: procurement of materials, finding scientific and technical staff, and testing facilities. The OAW considered that there were now only three choices for British policy: press ahead with atomic weapons and leave thermonuclear weapons to the US; address the problems of procurement, staffing and testing in order to produce a British H-bomb by 1958; or to develop thermonuclear weapons with existing resources and accept long delays.

The Chiefs considered the report, and made their own recommendations to the Defence Policy Committee (DPC). The second of the OAW options was the favoured choice, and this was accepted by the DPC. Indeed, it is hard to see how they could have decided otherwise, given the prevailing strategic and political orthodoxy. The DPC recommended an accelerated H-bomb programme with greater resources and more staff, a decision that Churchill, rather presumptuously, took to indicate that the rest of the Cabinet would follow suit. The Cabinet, however, was resentful at being bypassed in this fashion, and declined to be bounced into rubber-stamping the DPC's decision. Instead, a three-week debate followed the Prime Minister's notification to Cabinet on 7 July of the DPC decision. Questions of cost, the rationale for pursuit of a thermonuclear capability and procurement were discussed at length until, on 27 July, it was finally agreed that the production of thermonuclear weapons would go ahead.

This decision was taken in the greatest secrecy, because it was believed necessary for the public to be given time to become accustomed to the idea of a British thermonuclear bomb, particularly in the wake of the widely publicized effects of the *Castle Bravo* test (see below). Consequently, another six months passed before the H-bomb decision was announced in a Defence White Paper in February 1955.[8] 'We must contribute to the deterrent and to our own defence', it said, 'by building up our own stock of nuclear weapons of all types and by developing the most up to date means of delivery'. It assigned even higher priority to the 'primary deterrent'. Not having her own deterrent force would, it was argued, weaken Britain's prestige and influence in the world, surrender her power to influence American policy, and perhaps imperil her safety. Having the hydrogen bomb would make Britain a world power again. The hydrogen bomb, unlike the atomic bomb, was 'a great leveller', cancelling out the disparity between small countries and large.[9] The entire foundation of human affairs, Churchill told Parliament, was revolutionized by the hydrogen bomb, and with this awesome weapon in their arsenals none of the major powers would dare resort to war. Safety, he predicted, would be 'the sturdy child of terror', and 'survival the twin brother of annihilation.'[10]

Penney and the British weapon scientists now had a three-fold task. They had to build up a stockpile for the RAF of *Blue Danube* bombs based on the device tested at *Hurricane* in 1952. They had to develop and design a range of new and more efficient atomic weapons, to meet Service requirements and to make the most economical use of costly fissile material (weapons-grade plutonium was valued at £40,000 a kilogram in 1956). They had to pursue megaton weapon research, involving boosted fission weapons and true thermonuclear weapons, and carry this through to completion at all speed.

They found themselves working in a changing political climate, worldwide and in Britain. Nuclear weapon testing had not been a matter of controversy until March 1955, but then a tremendous debate was initiated by the consequences of the American *Bravo* H-bomb test at Bikini. Within weeks, public concern in Britain began to grow. For the fledgling anti-nuclear movement, three issues were central: concern over the effects of fallout, the prospects of a test ban, and the possibility of a British thermonuclear weapon. The British government, as we have seen, had already arrived at its decision on the last of these, but the questions of fallout and a test ban had taken on a global prominence.

The fallout debate

On 1 March 1954, during the *Castle* test series, the US detonated the *Bravo* shot, a megaton ground burst. The test site at Bikini was surrounded by a warning area of some 30,000 square miles of ocean within which there might be a hazard to shipping or aircraft at the time of a weapon test. Survey aircraft searching the area in preparation for *Bravo* reported no shipping present; the meteorologists forecast wind directions such that fallout would miss the small group of atolls to the east.

In the vivid phrase of one Los Alamos scientist, the *Bravo* shot 'went like gangbusters'; the yield was nearly 15 megatons – three times the 5–6 megatons expected, and the biggest nuclear explosion the US ever produced.[11] Moreover the winds did not conform to predictions, and fallout was blown over three little islands about 170 miles away in the Marshall Group. The 28 Americans stationed there were quickly evacuated, but the islanders were not rescued immediately. Then it was found that they had been showered with radioactive coral dust, and that most were suffering from radiation sickness and burns.[12] There was no rescue at all for the crew of a Japanese vessel, *Lucky Dragon*, fishing outside the warning area about 72 miles east of Bikini. The boat was heavily contaminated; all the crew became ill and one died after getting home to Japan.[13] The amount of fallout from the shot was huge: far more than should have been expected from a thermonuclear weapon which derived most of its power from the fusion of light elements. A Japanese scientist who analysed fallout from the *Lucky Dragon* concluded, correctly, that the *Bravo* shot had been a three-stage device, consisting of an atomic trigger, lithium deuteride to produce the thermonuclear reaction, and a layer of fissile uranium. The British physicist Dr Joseph Rotblat, in an analysis of such devices, concluded that hydrogen bombs could be made at low cost and with virtually no limitation on size.[14] The correctness of his analysis of the bomb's composition was publicly confirmed soon afterwards by Dr William Libby, a member of the United States Atomic Energy Commission (USAEC).

A reassuring statement on the *Bravo* aftermath – 'the 236 natives all appeared to me to be well and happy' – was made by Lewis Strauss, chairman of USAEC, at a press conference on 31 March. What thoroughly alarmed the American public was a remark that he made during the question period, not about fallout but about the horrific potential of thermonuclear weapons which, he said, could be made 'as large as you wish ... large enough to take out a city ... any city', such as New York.[15]

Strauss's remarks achieved global circulation. In Britain, the Australian nuclear scientist M. L. E. Oliphant made a similar claim when he stated that the *Bravo* shot had been 'a mere baby' in comparison to what could be achieved with thermonuclear weapons.[16] As testing took on an aura of controversy that it had hitherto lacked, the *Daily Mirror* conducted a poll in which 92 per cent voted for an international conference on a test ban; and *The Times* published a leader arguing that, 'It can be stated that all this [i.e. a test ban] has been tried before. Mankind, if it is to survive, can never give up trying. Some day the decisive date for good or ill will come. It is as least worth seeing whether that date was not March 1st'.[17] Elsewhere, calls for a ban were being made by the Church of England Synod in Canterbury, the British Council of Churches, several trade unions and a growing caucus in the Labour Party.

At the heart of concerns was the possible effect of fallout, which had been graphically and publicly demonstrated by the *Lucky Dragon*, but about which very little information was freely available. This meant that worst-case thinking could flourish unchecked, but governments remained acutely aware of the possible consequences of releasing information. The British government, having made a decision to pursue an H-bomb of its own, was particularly conscious of this problem. The GEN 465 committee expressed the dilemma well: if no information was available, 'speculation will err on the side of pessimism, since it is the exaggerated and alarmist statements which attract most attention'. On the other hand, 'the man in the street [is] apt to be more fearful about comparatively mysterious forces like radioactivity than he is about the immediate effects of bomb damage', and in consequence the public might be so alarmed by what the government told them about fallout that 'the government would be handicapped in the pursuit of a policy of nuclear weapon development'.[18]

The first detailed accounts of global and local fallout, and the implications for civil defence, were given unofficially by Dr Ralph E. Lapp in the *Bulletin of Atomic Scientists* in October and November 1954.[19] He revealed that a 15-megaton explosion close to the ground could contaminate an area of 4,000 square miles with lethal radioactivity and 50 super-bombs could 'blanket the entire NE USA in a serious to lethal radioactive fog'. For some months in late 1954 and early 1955 the US government debated whether to release full information about fallout; it was urged to do so by the civil defence authorities, but feared that it would only lead to a demand for the cessation of tests. It finally issued an official report in February 1955, but, a few days before it was published, a further article by Lapp appeared.[20] This estimated that debris from *Bravo* had covered an elliptical area nearly 200 miles long and 50 miles wide, some 8,000 square miles in all; if such a bomb fell on Washington, it said, lethal fallout would cover the entire State of Maryland.

The official report confirmed Lapp's analysis, and admitted that anyone living 160 miles downwind of the explosion would be killed. But the main subject of the official report was global fallout and the worldwide effects of nuclear testing (especially the effects of strontium-90) rather than the danger from nuclear weapons used in war. It stressed that the radiation exposure from all tests so far was only 0.1 r, about 1 per cent of the average radiation exposure per generation from natural background sources. Although testing admittedly created some risks to human health, including genetic health, they were minute compared with the advantages gained for 'the security of the nation and of the free world' – a cost-benefit equation that would not have been universally accepted.

Scientific controversy about fallout and its effects proliferated. Two key reports in the UK investigated its likely effects in the contexts of testing and of nuclear war: the Strath Report of 1955 and the Himsworth Report of 1956.

The Strath Report

In late 1954, an interdepartmental committee was set up to investigate the likely effects of fallout from a thermonuclear attack on the UK. The committee was headed by William Strath, and worked on the basis of a Joint Intelligence Committee assessment of the likely scale of a Soviet attack: 'We believe that the Russians will regard the UK as such a threat that they will aim to render it unusable for a long period, and will not hesitate to destroy great parts of the UK to achieve this aim'.[21] The Strath Report was submitted in March 1955 and made for horrifying reading. Ten ground-burst H-bombs, each of 10-megaton yield, 'would effectively disrupt the life of the country and make normal activity completely impossible'. The fallout from such an attack would 'immobilise considerable areas of the country and force inhabitants to keep under cover for some days and in certain areas for a week or more'. Thousands of square miles of agricultural land would be rendered unusable, as would open water supplies for large parts of the population.

Strath's report was principally concerned with civil defence, but he was fully aware of the implications of his findings for public policy. The H-bomb decision, and the 1955 White Paper that publicized it, put thermonuclear deterrence at the heart of British strategy. The public,

Strath recommended, must 'understand what is involved ... A consistent policy of education is therefore required to acquaint everyone with the effects of the hydrogen bomb, and particularly with the hazard from radioactivity about which people are still largely ignorant.'[22] This entirely sensible recommendation did, however, present the government with a dilemma: how could the necessary public education about the effects of fallout be pursued without heightening the already growing public concern about the effects of testing? The latter issue was the province of the Himsworth Committee.

The Himsworth Committee

As the group led by William Strath came to its appalling conclusions, the Prime Minister responded to parliamentary pressure and public concern and promised a review of the existing scientific evidence on the medical aspects of nuclear-related radiations. The Medical Research Council set up a committee of distinguished scientists and medical men under its secretary, Sir Harold Himsworth. It included experts in radiology, radiobiology, genetics, epidemiology and physics as applied to medicine, and was very varied in outlook as well as in scientific disciplines. Only one member, Sir John Cockcroft, came from the UKAEA. In the US, the President approved a similar study, funded by the Rockefeller Foundation and led by Dr Detlev Bronk, President of the National Academy of Sciences.

The Committee's deliberations took time, and in 1956 the Prime Minister postponed an announcement of *Grapple*, the 1957 megaton trials in the Pacific, in spite of increasing practical difficulties caused by the delay, because he was anxious to include an authoritative assurance from the Himsworth report, and he wanted also to include an undertaking to try to secure international limitation of tests. The Himsworth Committee agreed its report on 24 May 1956 except for one member who was abroad and who, it was thought, might be difficult. However, all the members signed and the report was submitted to the government. Himsworth thought that the consensus of scientific opinion would agree with his committee, but he was not sure what American reactions would be.[23] The report was not, it should be emphasized, a report on nuclear weapon tests or fallout; nor was the committee, as Churchill habitually called it, the 'genetic committee'. It was concerned with both somatic and genetic hazards of nuclear and allied radiations from all sources – natural, medical, industrial and military. But it was its findings on nuclear weapon tests that ministers so anxiously awaited. Would the committee have good news for them? they asked Himsworth. After much discussion in Cabinet and Cabinet committees, it was decided that the Prime Minister should make an announcement on 7 June about plans for *Grapple*, shortly before the publication of the Himsworth report.[24]

The Bronk and Himsworth reports, with impeccable timing, both appeared on 12 June 1956 and came to very similar conclusions. This is not the place to compare them, but a detailed comparison is of great interest.[25] To the immense relief of British ministers, the Himsworth report concluded that existing and foreseeable hazards from external radiation due to fallout from test explosions of nuclear weapons – fired at the existing rate and in the same proportion of different kinds – were negligible.[26] Genetic effects would be insignificant. The Committee's greatest difficulty was in assessing the strontium-90 hazard; there was evidence of a marked increase in the amount of strontium-90 through-out the world, but at present levels no detectable ill effects were to be expected. 'Nevertheless', the committee warned, 'recognising all the inadequacy of our present knowledge, we cannot ignore the possibility that, if the rate of firing increases and particularly if greater numbers of thermonuclear weapons are used, we could, within the lifetime of some now living, be approaching levels at which ill effects might be produced in a small number of the population'.

The report estimated that the population dose from fallout from bombs so far exploded would, in the next 50 years, amount to 0.02–0.04 per cent of the radiation received in the same period from natural radiation sources. It would gradually increase to 1 per cent if firing continued indefinitely at the same rate. The contribution from medical diagnostic X-rays was estimated at perhaps 22 per cent of the natural background. Lord Cherwell read the report 'with much satisfaction', not to say amusement; he found it comic that a medical committee had discovered that medical X-rays caused far more genetic mutations than all the nuclear weapon tests.

Though the committee had originated in public fears about fallout, it had dealt with radiation hazards comprehensively for the first time. Only a few sections of the report were specifically on nuclear weapon tests and they were mainly concerned with global fallout from thermonuclear tests. So, although the report was highly relevant to plans for Britain's first thermonuclear tests in 1957 and to discussions of a possible international test ban, it had little bearing on the kiloton trials in Australia. It gave the British thermonuclear tests a green light, but with a grave warning to proceed with caution.

Both the American and the British reports had a somewhat limited national perspective, but in December 1955 after much pressure from the non-atomic member states, and after months of argument and negotiation about its membership and scope, the United Nations set up a scientific committee on the effects of atomic radiation (UNSCEAR). Its function was not to set standards or recommend what member countries should or should not do; it was to receive, collate, evaluate and publish information on radiation levels and on the effects of radiation on man and his environment. It fulfilled an invaluable role. It had a world outlook and its first report, in 1958, by scientists from 15 different countries, brought together comprehensive data on fallout that could have been collected and compiled by no other means. But this lies well beyond our 1953–56 period.

The test ban issue

On 1 April, in the wake of the *Castle Bravo* explosion and the *Lucky Dragon* tragedy, the Japanese government formally asked the US government to suspend hydrogen bomb tests in the Pacific during the fishing season (November–March), and called for international control of atomic energy and nuclear tests. The next day Jawaharlal Nehru, the Prime Minister of India, urged a standstill agreement by the atomic powers while the United Nations sought a means to ban atomic weapons.

The idea of a moratorium was discussed by the US Secretary of State, J. F. Dulles, and British Foreign Secretary, Anthony Eden, between April and June 1954. At first they saw some merit in it, but then decided not to support it. It was unacceptable to the British government once it had taken the decision to develop and manufacture megaton weapons. In Britain there was a spate of Parliamentary Questions, over 100 Labour MPs signed a motion demanding that all nuclear tests should be stopped, and a full-dress debate was held in the House of Commons on 5 April 1954. On 19 April, Pope Pius XII in his Easter message gave a solemn warning about the pollution of the atmosphere, the land and the oceans.

It seemed probable that sooner or later tests would have to be abandoned, but none of the three nuclear powers wanted to stop unilaterally. If there was to be an agreement to end tests, each nation naturally wanted to secure conditions and timing that would be best – or least disadvantageous – for it. A nation could gain propaganda advantages from proposing a ban on testing when it had completed it own tests.

Britain, as the comparative latecomer, was in the most difficult position of the three powers. Since the United States and the Soviet Union were several years ahead of her in developing both atomic and thermonuclear bombs, she did not want to be obliged to cease testing before she was ready to do so. But nor did she want an arms race that she could ill afford, or to incur international disapproval, especially from Commonwealth countries; besides, parliamentary and public opinion was vociferous enough to worry the government. Then, too, she had to be careful not to show willingness to suspend tests just when the Americans were planning a series; she had to be prepared to 'share the odium'. At the same time the British government could not be sure that it might not find the rug pulled from under its feet by a sudden American test ban initiative.

In April 1955 President Eisenhower wrote to Nikita Khrushchev proposing a test ban; if the two agreed to end tests before Britain had completed what she regarded as her essential programme, she could hardly continue alone. Yet if she had to stop too soon, she would be locked into a position of inferiority. Of course, if radioactive fallout from the tests really was a worldwide danger to health – and on this the scientists were divided – Britain could not support the continuation of tests, but she was nevertheless anxious not to be forced to cut them short before achieving her basic objectives.

Test ban talks began in July 1955, but tests continued; Russia's second thermonuclear test, with a yield of 15 megatons, took place in November 1955, and the Russians then announced on Moscow Radio their willingness to cease further experimental explosions if the United States and Great Britain did the same. This had the effect of sharpening public awareness. Parliamentary pressure on the Eden government – Anthony Eden had just succeeded Churchill as Prime Minister – was increasing, led by former Labour ministers. Eden argued that the Russian offer was not made officially and that it might have appeared in a better light if it had been made before Russia's recent megaton explosion. The British government was ready to discuss these matters at any time, he said, but in any such discussions regard would have to be paid to the number and nature of the tests that each country had already made.[27]

On 3 December, the *Manchester Guardian* published an article that the government took very seriously:

> The Prime Minister has been strangely reserved about H-bomb experiments … On Thursday … he said that Britain would not take the initiative in proposing such a meeting … why ever not? … How long will the competition go on? What may be its price in terms of more people with mental disabilities, more infants with malformed limbs, and more adults who are sterile? … The need is simply to limit large explosions, not to prohibit all nuclear weapons tests of

whatever size ... Why not propose a limit of one explosion each annually? ... Sir Winston Churchill said, it may be recalled, that we must have a British bomb in order to make sure of our voice in shaping Western policy; and regrettable as it may be, one British explosion may be the price of impressing Congress and the Pentagon.

The Prime Minister instructed the Ministry of Defence to consider these ideas urgently, and the reply was prompt.[28] Single detonations were less efficient than a planned series, and limiting them to one a year would make them prohibitively expensive in money and resources. Without some comprehensive scheme of disarmament, which seemed highly unlikely, the preservation of peace depended on maintaining a continuously effective deterrent. The nuclear art was advancing extremely rapidly and it would be against British interests to accept any limitation of tests which would reduce the prospects of maintaining the deterrent and keeping (said the Ministry) ahead of the Russians.

The need for continued testing was argued by two of the most senior ministers, Lord Salisbury (Lord President of the Council, with responsibility for atomic energy policy) and Selwyn Lloyd (Minister of Defence).[29] After the Second World War was ended by the two atomic bombs on Japan, their argument ran, it was clear that a few such bombs – at most of the order of hundreds – would suffice to destroy any country in war. Now, however – they were writing in December 1955 – megaton weapons had entirely altered the situation, because of their immense destructive power and because of the ease and speed with which they could be delivered. To destroy Russia with a stock of a few hundred kiloton weapons would take a very great aircraft effort, over at least a number of days; in this time Russia, by virtue of possessing megaton weapons could certainly destroy her attacker before she was herself put out action by kiloton weapons. It was now clear that a very small number of megaton bombs, perhaps a few tens, would suffice to destroy in war, and a long time thereafter, the economy of any country. Kiloton weapons were no longer, by themselves, a major deterrent. Megaton weapons had become the primary deterrent; the possession of kiloton weapons would constitute a secondary deterrent.

Besides megaton weapons, the ministers said, Britain needed two types of kiloton weapons; one of 10–100-kiloton yield and a tactical weapon of 1–15 kilotons. The second type was more problematic, and full-scale tests were essential. If kiloton tests were now to be prohibited, Britain would be limited to the first type, and to crude, uneconomical and unreliable designs of the second (tactical) type. If megaton tests were to be prohibited, then Britain could not make a megaton weapon. The supply of kiloton and megaton weapons to the Services, they concluded, rested heavily on Britain's ability to continue testing.

In January 1956 the Prime Minister broadcast to the nation:

> You know we are making the H-bomb in this country just as one of the previous governments made the A-bomb. I don't think there's any party difference about that; but we are making it because we believe that the H bomb is the most powerful deterrent to war that exists in the world at the present time ... and so we have to build up the deterrent power. And there I must tell you something else. You cannot prove a bomb until it has been exploded. Nobody can know whether it is effective or not until it has been tested. That is why I have said there should be tests; that is why I have said I couldn't put us in ... the position of inferiority to other countries; but that doesn't mean that I wouldn't like an agreement to limit, or restrict, or regulate tests; I think it would be a very good thing if we could reach one.[30]

The British government believed that political pressure to ban tests might be more manageable if it showed some readiness to consider plans for limitation and regulation of tests. Provided its own position was safeguarded, there would be great propaganda advantages in not leaving all the initiative to Russia and India. However the Ambassador in Washington, Sir Roger Makins, was much disturbed: 'Of the three States making nuclear weapons', he cabled, 'we alone have not tested the megaton weapon and we cannot do so before 1957 ... we have the most to lose from any curtailment of our freedom to conduct nuclear tests, and therefore the most to lose from raising the question of limitation'.[31]

The British at this time were planning two series of atomic tests in 1956, as well as their first H-bomb test in 1957, while the Americans were planning a series in the Pacific in 1956. The British government was most anxious to ensure that the Americans understood the necessity of the 1957 trials, and did not change their attitude as soon as they had completed their own 1956 programme. At the end of January 1956, a British delegation led by the Prime Minister went to Washington for talks. The President and his advisers maintained the view that the regulation of tests was impracticable and that the tests were of the highest military and scientific value. Moreover, high air bursts did not cause the same harmful fallout as ground bursts, because they did not suck large amounts of dirt and debris into the radioactive cloud.[32] It was agreed that, if questioned, the Prime Minister should say that the regulation of nuclear tests had been discussed during these meetings and that the two governments held the firm conviction that, if properly conducted, these tests were not harmful.

The British side continued to argue the advantage of showing some readiness to control or limit tests. They expected a steady build-up of public feeling, not only from the left but from middle-of-the-road opinion and from the Churches, and the British public was inclined to believe there was a real health risk. The American officials disagreed and seemed confident that the two independent reports on biological effects of radiation, being prepared by the Bronk Committee in America and the Himsworth Committee in Britain, would be reassuring even if not conclusive. However Dulles conceded that if it was shown that nuclear tests harmed the human race, the two governments would certainly do something to control them.[33]

This then was the political background to Aldermaston's work from 1953 to 1956. Penney and his scientists were working in an atmosphere compounded equally of extreme urgency and extreme uncertainty. They were under pressure to complete their research and development programme as quickly as possible, to beat the ban on testing – and even perhaps a ban on fissile material production – that seemed inevitable sooner or later. This sense of urgency affected everyone in the project, and prompted the most strenuous efforts from scientists, engineers and industrial workers alike.

A new organization and a new test range

Soon after *Totem* in 1953, there were big organizational changes. As we saw in Chapter 1, the Atomic Energy Authority was set up in 1954, outside the civil service but wholly funded by the Treasury, managed by a chairman and chief executive and a board of full- and part-time members. In this reorganization Penney became Board Member for Weapons Research and Development as well as Director of the Atomic Weapons Research Establishment (DAWRE). Responsibility for nuclear weapons and trials was divided between the new Authority and the Ministry of Supply. One of the first tasks was to establish a permanent proving ground. *Hurricane* and *Totem* had been ad hoc operations, but now the time for improvisation was over and some more settled arrangements were needed. Emu Field was, as we have seen, a very difficult and restrictive site; though the Monte Bello islands were to be used for one more trial, they were not suitable for general use. The search for a permanent proving ground first began in late 1952; that search, and its outcome, are the subject of the next chapter.

6
Maralinga – A Permanent Proving Ground

The search for a range

'I am surveying the world, but particularly Australia', wrote Air Marshal Sir Thomas Elmhirst, the appointed chairman of Totex (the interdepartmental committee responsible for the general planning of the *Totem* trial) in July 1953.[1] In the Admiralty (which had found the Monte Bello islands for *Hurricane*) Captain Le Fanu was also surveying the world, from the Shetlands and the Hebrides to the Bahamas, from Somaliland and West Africa to islands in the Pacific and Indian Oceans. They were both seeking a 'permanent proving ground' for atomic weapons.

When, after *Hurricane*, Sir William Penney visited South Australia in October 1952 to look at possible sites for *Totem*, he had left with the Australians a summary of the conditions that a permanent range would have to satisfy. Though Emu Field provided an immediate answer for *Totem*, it was never considered as a permanent site – it had too many disadvantages – nor were the Monte Bello islands, though they were to be used once more in 1956.

In May 1953 the Chiefs of Staff were advised that a permanent inland site was needed. They asked Elmhirst to look for one, and he wrote to Major-General Stevens, the head of the Australian Atomic Energy Commission (AAEC) and chairman of the *Totem* panel in Melbourne.[2] It was undesirable, he said, to continue with hurriedly prepared and very expensive expeditions to ad hoc sites, well though he thought these improvisations had turned out. He described the ideal site – a 100-mile radius free from human habitation; road and rail communications to a port; an adjacent airstrip; a good water supply; reasonably flat country; a tolerable climate for permanent staff and visiting scientists; not too much rainfall; predictable meteorological conditions, with prevailing winds that would carry fallout away from firing areas. Finally, an island would be excellent for security. The only suitable sites in Australia, Elmhirst thought, were Groote Eylandt, in the Gulf of Carpentaria, and an area somewhere to the north of Emu Field.

Major-General Stevens agreed that hurried preparations like those for *Totem* were 'bad in every way', but the Elmhirst specifications were so exacting that very few, if any, places in the world would meet them all. A site north of Emu Field would be too near cattle stations or the Aboriginal reserve. Groote Eylandt would not do at all: it was densely wooded and a timber company had sought timber concessions; there were no port facilities; there was a population of seven Europeans and 400–600 Aboriginals. An area in South Australia near Port Augusta seemed best, but a permanent site, he warned, should be selected only after most careful investigation.[3]

In September 1953, Penney was authorized to talk to the Australians about the alternative sites they had suggested after an air reconnaissance. At the same time the Chiefs of Staff asked the Ministry of Supply to make further efforts to find somewhere more suitable than South Australia, but, having again 'scrutinized the world', Captain Lloyd of the Ministry of Supply, like Captain Le Fanu, found no acceptable alternative.[4]

Meanwhile, in October 1953, Penney and two of his staff, with Butement, took time off from Emu Field, between *Totem* 1 and *Totem* 2, to visit a remote part of South Australia that had been reconnoitred earlier, first by air and then overland. (A vivid account of the expedition has been published – *Blast the Bush*, by the Australian surveyor, Len Beadell.) It was bush country, but a treeless area of about 100 square miles had been observed, some 50 miles north of the Transcontinental Railway, near a spot marked 'Tietken's Well'. Supplies were dropped here, a camp set up and a runway constructed in only two days, by four men with Land Rovers pulling a length of railway line. Here Penney and Butement landed and were met by a small Australian party, and together they went exploring for three days.

The region was described in an Aldermaston report:

> The Range is just beyond the Nullarbor ('treeless') Plain lying to the north of the shores of the Great Australian Bight. The Plain has thin soil which carries only a mantle of desert pea and knee-high salt-bush. The Plain which covers about 400 × 450 miles bears traces of the sea which once rolled over it – little cliffs, shells, wave marks hundreds of miles inland. Lost in the salt-bush are the bones of the last diprotodons. Occasional blow-holes, like ancient craters, emit a foetid smell ... To

quote Professor J. W. Gregory, 'These long, low, open plains, with their gentle undulations, suggesting the freedom of the sea with the stability of the land, have to many men an unequalled fascination ...'

Beyond the northern limits of the Nullarbor Plain, the country becomes rather more attractive, consisting of low sandhills, thickly covered by mulga and mallee trees. These are up to 20 ft high. As the district has been practically untouched by man ... many trees of great age still stand. In this country, it is a very simple matter to get lost.

Penney described it as 'gently undulating and covered with low salt-bush and occasional sparse patches of mulga which gave it the appearance of English downland'. To the north lay hundreds of miles of uninhabited wooded country and desert. The Australian geologists were confident of finding water by boring, and their confidence was eventually justified. There seemed no danger of the dust-storms that had been so troublesome at Emu Field. The area, identified as X300 but later named 'Maralinga' by Butement, seemed ideal to Penney. It was very different, however, from the Nevada test site, 70 miles from Las Vegas, with its excellent road, rail and air communications with every important military and scientific centre in the United States.[5]

Before returning to Emu Field for T2, he had a detailed discussion about the site with Butement.[6] It covered such matters as water supplies, roads, telephones, range layout and the location of the firing sites, the camp and the airfield. Then Penney said, 'You have told me already where the homesteads are and I see no difficulty in getting firing conditions which will give no danger whatever to the homesteads, but I would like to know what is the position about the Aboriginals'.

There used to be a mission at Ooldea, or a little north of there, Butement told him, but it had been abandoned. There had been a track from Ooldea up to the north, but he understood that it was no longer used, 'except by one or two elderly blacks and then on rare occasions'. There was no need whatever for Aboriginals to use any part of the country round the proposed site; the main Aboriginal reserve to the north was well away from the area and should not present any sort of problem. This sounded very satisfactory to Penney, but he particularly asked that when the Australians submitted a report on the site they should include a statement about the location of the homesteads and about where the Aboriginals were likely to be. The tests, he said, would be fired in meteorological conditions in which the radioactivity would be in the sector between the north and east and would not affect human habitations.[7]

While still in Australia, Penney had talks with the Prime Minister, the Minister for Supply and Major-General Stevens. Menzies, he reported on his return to England, had apparently not realized previously (or had forgotten) that Australia had had no access to the British atomic weapons programme; or indeed, that the British had no access to the US programme. Penney had said that if there were to be further weapon tests in Australia, the British would have to work closely with the Australians, and he would like some integration of effort between the two countries. Since the British would be using Australian facilities and staff, it was only reasonable that some Australians, given security clearance, should receive information about the weapons, and he would welcome Australian scientists into the project in England. Menzies had agreed with these views and Penney believed he would like an invitation on these lines to accompany any request for a permanent, range. In his opinion, the offer should be made without waiting for an Australian request.

In further talks, Penney and Stevens had discussed the possibility that Britain might help the Australians build a reactor, using Australian uranium, to produce plutonium for atomic weapons. Some of the weapons might be returned to Australia. The cost of the scheme would not be great and it would ease Britain's shortage of plutonium. The Australians for their part would assist with the weapon tests. Stevens welcomed some such an arrangement, on the grounds that the Australians were nervous about their whole future position, industrial and military, and would be glad to have help from Britain. But Australian views were not unanimous. When Lord Cherwell (the Minister responsible for atomic energy policy in the Churchill government) visited Australia in October 1953, his proposals on very similar lines were rejected by the Australian Cabinet; it doubted whether Australia could afford to maintain any large-scale atomic project for many years to come. It was therefore decided in Whitehall that proposals for a permanent range should simply be linked with an offer for selected Australian scientists to come to England to familiarize themselves with atomic weapons matters.[8]

Meanwhile the UK High Commissioner in Canberra had passed a list of Penney's requirements to the Australian government. The range must have good road access, an airstrip and fresh water of high purity. It must be large enough to use for up to three bursts a year. Since the contamination around the firing site would extend to a radius of $\frac{1}{2}$ mile and would have to be avoided for three to four years after use, some 20 firing sites would be needed. The camp should be 15–20 miles from the weapon sites, the orientation of camp and weapon sites depending on detailed analysis of meteorological conditions. Weapon sites and observation sites should be as level as possible.

A detailed Australian report produced early in 1954 by Butement recommended the Maralinga site (see Map 4).[9] It was, he said, reasonably flat, and sufficiently large – some 16 miles from east to west, and at least 12 miles north to south. The south edge of the area was about 32 miles north of the Transcontinental Railway between Ooldea and Watson, and 80 miles north of the coast. The range area would encroach slightly on

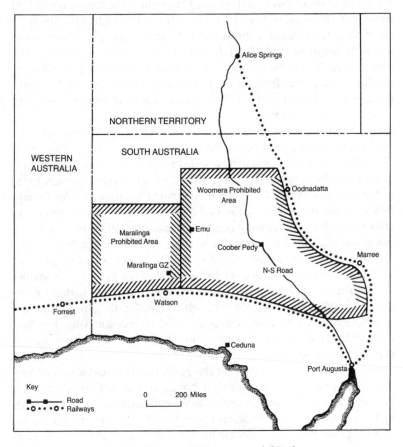

Map 4   Maralinga and Woomera prohibited areas

the northwest corner of an Aboriginal reserve at Ooldea, but the reserve was abandoned. The country was hot and arid, but less so than Emu Field, thanks to night breezes from the sea. The rainfall was higher (as the weaponeers were to discover). Water supplies would be easier than at Emu Field.

The camp would be located on a ridge south-west of the trials area, and the airfield would be further south, on the edge of the Nullarbor Plain. Constructing the range – including roads, a railway siding, an airfield, a camp area with semi-permanent buildings for 350 people, laboratories, workshops, offices, stores and a landline for communications – would cost about £1.9 million. A more westerly area on the Nullarbor Plain, which had also been surveyed, would cost £200,000 more, and was less suitable; alternatively, to improve Emu Field to the standard required would cost much more, say £3.6 million. It would be difficult, Butement concluded, to envisage a site superior to Maralinga. The Aldermaston scientists began to study the fallout considerations assuming that the danger area for contamination could have a radius of 150 miles; as the Transcontinental Railway was well within this distance to the south, firing would not be possible if the wind, at any level, was between 290° and 070° through north.

So far there had been no contact between governments, and the Butement report had not been considered by Australian officials or ministers. There was still much to be decided and agreed before construction could begin but the British Chiefs of Staff were talking of trials in 1955, or the spring of 1956. They wanted an airburst to prove the *Blue Danube* (Mk 1) bomb; the centre section had been exploded as *Totem*, and deliveries to the RAF had already begun in November 1953, but an operational test was obviously desirable as soon as possible, if only to give at leas one aircrew the experience of dropping it. Secondly, the Chiefs of Staff wanted a tower test of a smaller bomb (*Red Beard*) for use by smaller aircraft than the V-bombers. Thirdly, they wanted a detonation underground or at ground surface – of which neither the British nor the Americans then had any experience – in connection with the War Office's draft requirements for an atomic land mine. Finally they wanted various 'effects' experiments.[10]

Since by now it was likely that the government would soon approve the development of the hydrogen bomb, it was not surprising that Penney was worried that his resources were insufficient for atomic trials in 1955 as well as thermonuclear research and development. Moreover, Maralinga would not be suitable for H-bomb tests, and when the time for them came another site would have to be found.[11]

A decision in sight

The technical case for Maralinga seemed clear; the political arguments now began. If Britain was to continue to develop atomic weapons she would need numerous trials over the next decade. The development of any weapon was a continuous process, requiring trials at intervals – to prove operational weapons; to assist in developing new weapons; and to test new ideas arising in the course of development, or completely new ideas. There were also many secondary objectives. All the Services, and also the Civil Defence authorities, wanted information on the effects of different types of explosions on equipment and stores, on structures, on ships, on aircraft and airfields, and on men with or without various kinds of protection. The need for 'target response' tests would remain, even if more information on weapon effects could now be obtained from the Americans, after the extension of technical cooperation under the *modus vivendi*, early in 1954, to include by experimental simulation 'effects of atomic weapons on human beings and their environment'.[12]

Instead of a permanent site, the alternative – which Duncan Sandys, the Minister of Supply, much preferred – was to carry on ad hoc, in the hope of amendments to the McMahon Act which would permit the use of Eniwetok.[13] Politically, it was suggested, *ad hoc* arrangements might also suit the Australians better. But Eniwetok prospects were uncertain; it would cost a great deal, and in dollars; and it was thought that, scientifically, the Americans might prefer independent British tests. A permanent site, it was calculated, would save time, resources and money; it would reduce the length of absence of scientific staff from Britain, and would make possible better living and working conditions. The capital cost of Maralinga – say £2 million – and an estimated expenditure of £750,000 for each test there (excluding the cost of the weapons themselves) looked very attractive if there was to be an extensive trials programme; the cost of *Hurricane* (excluding the weapon and HMS *Plym*) had been some £1.8 million, and the cost of *Totem* (excluding the weapons), £1.325 million.

If the next trials were to be in April/May 1956, the scientists would have to start work at the range in December 1955. Construction would take at least 16 months, and little could be done in January or February (when the shade temperature would average 120 °F and metal tools would be too hot to touch). Work must therefore start by July 1954. Time was pressing, but there had still been no formal approval by British ministers and no approach to the Australian government. A decision seemed unlikely before the Australian General Election on 29 May.

There were three questions for the British to ponder meanwhile. Should the Australians be asked to contribute to the cost of the range? If so, what would they want, by way of cooperation, in return? Lastly, how far could the British go in such cooperation without prejudicing their relations with the Americans?

The first question was not only a matter of money, though the British would welcome Australian financial help. The Woomera range was an example of cost-sharing; at first the Australians had been unforthcoming, but after some wrangling their attitude had completely changed and they became not just 'landlords leasing land' but partners in 'a great scheme of Empire development'. An Australian contribution to the cost of Maralinga would avoid the embarrassment of having a purely UK establishment on Australian territory. On the other hand, it was argued, if the Australians were asked to contribute, they would then want more information. On the second question, Penney thought the Australians would want at least as much information as at *Totem* – no papers, but full information on weapons effects, and opportunities to inspect damage to tanks and other equipment. They would also want to send four or five scientists to Aldermaston.[14]

The third question was referred to Washington.[15] As we have seen, atomic collaboration with Commonwealth countries (other than Canada) was restricted by the tripartite Anglo-American-Canadian wartime and postwar agreements, and was inhibited by Britain's fear of damaging her prospects of a renewed Anglo-American partnership. The British Ambassador, Sir Roger Makins, who had unrivalled experience of Anglo-American atomic negotiations in Washington, queried whether it was intended to seek American approval before giving information to the Australians, or simply to offer the Australians what the British themselves considered their agreements with the Americans would permit. He thought the moment inopportune for broaching the subject with the Americans. In his opinion, divulging information on weapons effects would cause no difficulties; but he could imagine no circumstances in which the Americans would agree that information about design and construction of atomic weapons should be given to Australia; apart from its sensitivity, weapons information must be regarded as being of joint origin. The Foreign Office reasonably thought that the complete postwar break in Anglo-American cooperation on atomic weapons after 1945 might by this time justify a different view. However, if the Australians were not going to have a weapons programme, Makins suggested, there was no reason to give them such information, which the Americans themselves were forbidden by law to pass to other countries.

If the British did so they would 'certainly lose any chance ... of getting information about the manufacture and design of United States weapons'.

At last, in June 1954, ministers agreed to negotiations with the Australian government for the range at Maralinga,[16] though Duncan Sandys, the Minister of Supply, doubted that it would be an economy; it might be obsolete before the savings were recouped. He thought too that the Australian government would have difficulty in getting its public opinion to accept a permanent proving ground; Emu Field had been accepted because *Totem* was a 'one-off job'. It was further argued that if Britain was going to concentrate on hydrogen rather than atomic bombs, the site would be wasted; this would also happen if an international agreement to ban atomic weapons, or tests, was reached, although indeed no such agreement was in sight.[17]

The approach to the Australian government was delayed while a proposal linking it to an agreement on uranium supplies was considered, but telegrams were eventually despatched at the end of July. The High Commissioner wrote to Menzies on 2 August about the range and about proposed trials in April/May 1956. He rehearsed the arguments for a permanent proving ground for atomic weapon trials to be carried out during the next ten years. The choice lay between Emu Field and Maralinga, and the British government would be guided by the Australian government, who could best assess local factors. The experts believed that Maralinga, in suitable meteorological conditions, would provide a sufficient margin for higher-powered bursts than in previous trials, but there was no question of testing hydrogen weapons. Britain would depend on Australia for much help in works and services, and hoped that facilities could be provided as a joint project. The precise apportionment of costs would be for negotiation. (The rumour of a range in Canada was unfounded, the High Commissioner added; in the uninhabited areas the climatic conditions were unsuitable.)[18]

Within a month, the Australian Cabinet approved the proposal in principle, and Menzies replied in October 1955, agreeing to Maralinga as a permanent range.[19] The power of the weapons to be tested, and meteorological conditions for the tests, would have to be agreed beforehand with the Australian government, and there must be no question of testing hydrogen bombs. Australia would contribute the site and provide such assistance as she could. But she was unlikely to make more than a token contribution towards construction, because of other pressures on her Service and civil resources; labour was very scarce in Australia and the RAAF was fully engaged on a big airfield extension programme in

Northern Australia and on construction work in Malaya. Nor would Australia be likely to help financially as the defence budget was already overstretched. A planning team should be sent from Britain as soon as possible; meanwhile Menzies would talk to Sir Thomas Playford, the Premier of South Australia, who was known to have views about the reclamation of the reserve that formed part of the area.[20] The British government thanked Menzies warmly, and deferred questions of finance and defence priorities, perhaps to the Commonwealth Prime Ministers Conference in the New Year.[21]

A warning came from one British official in the Ministry of Supply:

> I am bound to say that I am left with the feeling (perhaps quite unjustified), that there is a blissful unawareness of the fact that public hostility to A tests has increased many fold since our last efforts ... I would urge that someone had better be thinking about what ... to say if they are forced to in response to what may be a torrent of uninformed criticism.[22]

The *Mosaic* repercussions in 1956 would prove him right (see Chapter 7).

The Wilson mission

In November 1954 a mission of six officials and scientists, led by J. M. Wilson, a senior official at the Ministry of Supply, went to Australia for talks in Canberra and Melbourne and a visit to South Australia. Penney commented that it had taken over a year, since his expedition with Butement in 1953, for the British government to ask for Maralinga and the Australian government to agree in principle. (The delays had been mostly in London.) By hindsight, he said, a mission should have gone to Australia in April or May 1954 in anticipation of – but without prejudice to – agreement between the governments.

The Wilson mission returned and reported that the Maralinga site was excellent.[23] The Australians would undertake preparatory work there, but labour thereafter would have to be provided either by a UK Service force of about 700 men, or – more expensively – by a civilian force employed by a contractor and largely imported. Much of the material, including prefabricated buildings and cement, would have to be shipped from the United Kingdom. The range could not possibly be ready by April/May 1956, and the trials should be postponed to September/ October 1956; to achieve even these later dates, the main construction force would have to begin work by 1 June 1955, and the Australians would have to complete preliminary work on the site before it arrived. Whatever the difficulties of providing a Service construction force from the United Kingdom, the timetable must be kept because any delay would hold up important trials programmes in subsequent years.

The Wilson report emphasized that the Australians were much concerned about radioactive contamination, and intended setting up a safety committee of four or five leading scientists to advise the government. It would continue and formalize the arrangements previously made for *Totem* whereby Penney had given information to Martin and Titterton so that they could assess the safety of the tests for themselves.

Finally, the report listed points to be covered in an Anglo-Australian agreement. These included tenure of the site (an initial period of ten years was suggested); compensation for any damage; information to be furnished to the Safety Committee; Australian access to the ranges; safety responsibilities; joint arrangements for publicity; a joint administrative committee; and weapon effects data for Australia.

The Memorandum of Arrangements

The previous understanding between Australia and Britain about trials had been surprisingly informal, based on exchanges of brief personal letters between the Prime Ministers, with no specific agreements on such matters as conditions of occupation, use of the sites, precise allocation of costs, or compensation for damage or injury. The rights and obligations of either side were hardly defined at all. In both countries the organization was ad hoc. With a permanent range under discussion, and perhaps ten years of testing to come, the time for such informality was past.[24] The Australian government, for internal political reasons, had to have a clear understanding of the terms on which the permanent proving ground was to be made available, and in the wake of the Wilson mission Menzies sent a letter outlining an agreement. Its main points were as follows. The period of occupation should be ten years, which might be extended by mutual agreement. H-bomb tests were ruled out. Australian agreement must be obtained before any test was carried out and the Australian authorities must be given enough information to satisfy them on safety. The United Kingdom should be responsible for the safety of the area and people entering it, and be liable for damage to persons or property. The Australian authorities should be fully informed and consulted on planning and progress, and should coordinate and control all administrative activities in Australia in connection with the tests. A joint Anglo-Australian committee should be set up in Australia.

Menzies met Eden, the British Prime Minister, and other ministers to discuss the permanent proving ground during a visit to London in February 1955. They agreed that the main construction work at Maralinga would be undertaken by a UK civil contractor, but Menzies saw no difficulty in having the firing areas built by Australian Service personnel. The Australian Services would also supply men to assist at the tests, but the question of manning the range between trials was deferred.[25]

A draft memorandum of arrangements was sent from London to Canberra in the following month. One clause in particular was certain to cause problems:

The United Kingdom government undertakes to indemnify the Australian government in respect of valid claims, arising outside the prohibited area, through

(a) death or injury of any person resulting directly from any tests carried out, and

(b) damage to property similarly resulting.[26]

The Australians produced a new draft that was approved by a Cabinet Committee on 4 May and sent to London.[27] They wanted an indemnity 'in respect of all valid claims *whatsoever*', for death, injury or damage resulting from the tests, whether inside or outside the prohibited area. They suspected that London did not realize that the prohibited area extended as far as Woomera and contained 3,000–4,000 inhabitants, not counting Aboriginals who might pass through. The Australians would not agree to a British proposal to define a smaller prohibited area; they also urged that any claims by Australians present at the tests, under arrangements made for Australia to provide personnel, should be a British responsibility. Opinion in London was divided. 'If we press the Australians too strongly we shall lose the substance for the shadow', wrote one Ministry of Supply official; the Australians, he said, were becoming restive about the amount of their contribution to such projects, they were in many ways apprehensive about the trials, and it would be increasingly difficult to secure their goodwill and cooperation.[28] But against this view, a grudging Treasury view prevailed; the Australian government inexplicably agreed; and in the final version the British government had no liability for claims from Australian nationals present on the range or at the trials in the course of duty.

The most important features of the agreement (see Appendix A) were the ten-year term; the use of the range rent-free; the prohibition of hydrogen bomb tests; Australian agreement before tests; the provision by the British of information relevant to safety; Australian responsibility for preventing unauthorized entry into the prohibited area (which was defined in an annex); participation by other British Commonwealth nationals in tests; claims for damage or injury; and the control of the project by a joint committee under Australian Department of Supply. chairmanship. The controversial claims question was settled by clause 11, by which the United Kingdom undertook to indemnify the Australian government in respect of all valid claims due to tests carried out on the site (except for claims made by employees or servants of a government other than the UK government – in most but not all cases the Australian government – who were in the prohibited area specifically in connection with the tests).

A financial memorandum attached to the Memorandum of Arrangements stated that Britain would bear most of the costs, except for:

(a) the cost of any target response or other tests done specifically at Australian request;
(b) the expenses of Australian personnel attending trials at the proving ground, at the Australian government's request; and
(c) the cost of providing Australian Service personnel for specific tasks at the proving ground.

These two memoranda comprised the only formal agreement between Britain and Australia on this big and important project.[29] It was concluded more than $3\frac{1}{2}$ years after *Hurricane* – five years after *Hurricane* planning began – and there had been three atomic detonations meanwhile and a fourth was imminent. Although the text was finally agreed in March 1956, in September there had still apparently been no exchange of signatures on the two documents. In the close relationship then existing between the two governments, friendly arrangements, rather than legal contracts, were the order of the day.

Action at last

Aldermaston, while waiting for the two governments, had had to decide how far they could anticipate such an agreement. If all action had been postponed meanwhile, there would have been no hope at all of

completing the range by August 1956. Planning had in fact begun immediately after *Totem*, a draft plan had been ready in December 1953, and
contract action had been taken on many items, especially those requiring
extensive prototype tests (such as weapon towers and recording shelters).

Swift action followed the Wilson mission's report of 6 January 1955.
Within a fortnight, the project had been comprehensively examined,
with Sir Alexander Gibb and Partners as possible consultants, and the
Kwinana Construction Group as possible contractors. Treasury approval
was sought at the end of February and received on 5 March. All the specifications that Aldermaston had been preparing for the past twelve
months, with John Costain Brown Ltd as consultants, were handed over
to Sir Alexander Gibb and Partners, who lost no time in subcontracting
to the Costain Brown drawing offices. In April, representatives of the
consulting engineers and contractors visited Australia, where three
members of the Aldermaston trials planning staff were already at work,
and they were able to exchange ideas very fully on the spot.

On 4 May, Mr Howard Beale, the Australian Minister for Supply,
announced to the Australian press that the British and Australia governments were to join in a huge works project in South Australia costing
£5–6 million. Maralinga would be, he said (inaccurately), 'the Los Alamos
of the British Commonwealth'. He explained that the types of atomic
bombs, developed by Sir William Penney and his brilliant team of scientists, would be tested there, but no hydrogen bombs. The site, selected by
Penney and Butement, had been chosen and planned to combine the
maximum security with 'the completest respect for life, property and
stock', and tests would take place only in meteorological conditions
which would carry radioactive clouds harmlessly away into the desert.
Each test would require the prior approval of the Minister for Supply, no
test would be made until a committee of Australian scientists had satisfied itself that there was no danger, and the Australian Meteorological
Bureau would advise the British team on safe conditions for firing.

The project was, he concluded, 'a challenge to Australian men to
show ... the pioneering spirit of their forefathers' and 'a striking example of inter-Commonwealth cooperation on a grand scale'. 'England has
the bomb and the know-how; we have the open spaces, much technical
skill, and a great willingness to help the Motherland. Between us we
shall help to build the defences of the free world'.

The Maralinga committee

With the new permanent proving ground, new and permanent organizations were necessary in Australia to replace the ad hoc arrangements

and special panels created for *Hurricane* and *Totem*. One was a standing committee, with representatives of all the Australian departments concerned and a British representative from the Ministry of Supply's staff in Australia, UKMOSS(A).[30]

This was the committee required under clause 17 of the Memorandum of Arrangements, 'to consider all matters of joint concern in relation to the establishment and maintenance of the proving ground and to the arrangements for any trials thereon as may be approved from time to time and to advise the responsible departments through their respective representatives'. The functions of the committee were to include 'the coordination of all activities within Australia of the United Kingdom and Australian Government Departments and Authorities, and their agents concerned with the project, and such executive action in matters of joint concern in Australia as may be agreed by the representatives of both parties'.

It was set up at the Australian Prime Minister's request in May 1955, by his Minister for Supply, who had been given this departmental responsibility months before the Memorandum of Arrangements was finally agreed. Though named the Atomic Weapons Tests Committee (AWTC), its first task was to deal with the construction and operation of the range at Maralinga, and it was called the Maralinga Committee until May 1956 when it decided – in view of tests under way on the Monte Bello islands and being planned in the Pacific[31] – to revert to its proper title of the AWTC. It continued work until 1957, when it was replaced by a Maralinga Board of Management with a small executive staff.

During its first year the committee met frequently to deal with preparing and constructing the range – work that was being done under severe difficulties and great pressure to meet the deadline for trials in September/ October 1956. While the AWTC was heavily engaged in progressing the Maralinga construction programme, it was already involved in *Mosaic* and *Buffalo* planning, as well as longer-term questions of administering the Range.

Maralinga would need a permanent staff even between trials, and it was agreed that the range commandant should always be an Australian officer. The Australian government rightly attached the utmost importance to retaining administrative control of the range, as a duty to the Australian people and a necessary indication that Australian sovereignty was being safeguarded. The British concurred, not only because it was right and reasonable, but also because it involved Australia in responsibility for the project and in sharing any criticism.[32] But inevitably the commandant (an Australian Army colonel) had divided responsibilities – to the British staff (or the trials director when present) for the technical operation of the range; to the Department of Supply for the general administration of the range; and to the Service authorities in South Australia for the discipline and administration of Australian forces. The Australian government provided a Service contingent of nearly 200 men during construction at Maralinga and some 370 for the 1956 trials period, and promised between 40 and 50 for care and maintenance between trials. After *Buffalo*, Maralinga arrangements were to be reviewed and considerably altered, as we shall see.

The Atomic Weapons Tests Safety Committee

With the prospect of atomic trials at regular intervals – and especially in the context of worldwide concern about fallout – the Australian government was anxious about radioactive contamination. When the Wilson mission had raised the question of *Kittens* tests, the Australians had asked for full details, and in February 1955 Aldermaston provided a comprehensive report, *The Scope and Radiological Hazards of Kittens 1955*. It was referred to the Australian Department of Defence for Professor Martin's comments. He saw no objection, but suggested some formal arrangement for checking the safety aspects of these and subsequent tests; a safety committee of four or five leading scientists might be considered. An independent study by a small committee would enable the government to reassure the Australian people that they were not being endangered.[33]

The Department of Defence agreed and proposed five names (though it later favoured a committee of three). Of the five, Martin, Titterton and Butement had already been involved in *Hurricane* and *Totem*. The new names were Dr C. E. Eddy, the Director of the Commonwealth X-ray and Radium Laboratory, and Professor J. P. Baxter, member (and later chairman) of the Australian Atomic Energy Commission. Menzies accepted the five names; he believed the committee must include members 'Sufficiently well known to command general confidence as guardians of the public interest' who were not 'in any way to be identified as having an interest in the success of defence atomic experiments'.[34] He doubted if a committee of less than five could meet these requirements, particularly if the Defence Scientific Adviser and the Chief Scientist of the Department of Supply (Martin and Butement) were members.[35]

The list included, in Dr Eddy, one scientist with special expertise in radiological protection; he was responsible nationally for precautions against the radiation hazards of X-ray and radium equipment. Somewhat surprisingly the list had no meteorologist, but L. J. Dwyer, the Director of the Australian Bureau of Meteorology, was later co-opted. As we saw in Chapter 2, Professor Oliphant, Australia's most distinguished nuclear scientist, was not included.[36]

The list of members was sent to London before the AWTSC was formally constituted.[37] All the members, as we also saw in Chapter 2, were well known in British circles. The committee was established in July 1955, and was enjoined, at some length:

(a) to examine the information and other data supplied by the UK government relating to atomic weapons tests from time to time proposed to be carried out in Australia for the purpose of determining whether the safety measures proposed to be taken in relation to such tests are adequate for the prevention of injury to persons or damage to livestock and other property as a result of such tests; and

(b) to advise the Prime Minister, through the Minister for Supply, of the conclusions arrived at by the Committee as a result of such examination, and in particular as to whether and if so what additional, alternative or more extensive safety measures are considered necessary or desirable.

The committee was to have the power to co-opt other persons subject to the prior approval of the Minister for Supply and the UK government.[38] Like the AWTC, it was reorganized in 1957, after *Buffalo*.

Safety regulations

The health physicists at Aldermaston prepared comprehensive radiological safety regulations for everyone concerned with the trials, whether at Maralinga itself, Emu Field, Salisbury, the RAAF airfield at Edinburgh Field which was the main airbase for trials, or anywhere else in Australia. These regulations, which were agreed with the AWTSC, placed responsibility for radiological safety during trials on a health physics adviser to the trials superintendent, appointed by the Director of Aldermaston. In periods between trials, an Australian health physics representative at the range (the AHPR), appointed by the Australian authorities, would take over.

The MPLs for external gamma radiation laid down in *Radiological Safety Regulations, Maralinga* were based on the current (1955) ICRP recommendations, and were:

(a) A normal working rate of not more than 0.3 r a week of radiation.

(b) A lower integrated dose of up to 3 r of gamma radiation.

(c) A higher integrated dose of up to 10 r of gamma radiation.

(d) A special higher integrated dose of not more than 25 r of radiation.

The regulations also set limits for beta and neutron radiation, and internal radiation, and they emphasized that every endeavour must be made to keep the average exposure as low as possible. The lower integrated dose (b) required the express permission of the health control officer and would be given only when necessary for the smooth running of the operation. The higher integrated dose (c) applied only in cases of necessity, in order to recover records and information that might otherwise be lost; it required the personal permission of the trials superintendent, after consultation with the health physics adviser and medical adviser. Anyone receiving either the lower or the higher integrated dose – (b) or (c) – would not be further exposed to radiation until his average weekly exposure, from the start of the operation, was below the normal working rate. The special higher integrated dose, (d), was new since *Hurricane* and *Totem*. It applied only in cases of extreme necessity, and only to personnel not normally exposed to radiation. It required the personal permission of the trials director, with health physics and medical advice as before, and of the AWTSC in the case of Australian personnel. (There is no record that this last provision was ever required.) Anyone receiving a 25 r dose would not be further exposed to radiation for three years.

The regulations also defined non-active and active areas, and classified active areas – BLUE (no special clothing needed), RED (protective clothing to be worn as instructed) and YELLOW (fully protective clothing essential). There were rules about entry to different areas, about film badges and personal monitoring, about laundering and waste disposal, about storage and movement of radioactive materials. They emphasized that officers in charge of any task must ensure that their staff understood the hazards, and must see that the regulations were rigorously observed; Service officers in command of Service units or personnel must see that the regulations, and any other safety instructions, were brought to the notice of their men and were enforced.

Construction of the range

By December 1954 an Australian survey party from the weapons research establishment at Salisbury, near Adelaide, had moved in, first to Maralinga and then to Giles, 600 miles away and 450 miles south-west of Alice Springs. At Giles a new meteorological station[39] was later to be set up to improve weather forecasting for trials; it was of great importance to the trials (as well as to Woomera), and Butement was later reported as saying that without it the Safety Committee would not permit any trial at Maralinga.[40]

The South Australian Department of Mines began boring for water, at first with disappointing results. The Department of Works cleared a site to be used for *Kittens*, built a camp, laboratory and stores, and made roads and tracks, in time for the *Kittens* series in May 1955 – all this in spite of the oppressive summer heat between January and March. Land lines were laid from Port Augusta to Maralinga and communications equipment installed. Emu Field was opened up again as an active station to assist in fallout measurements. The Australian 'token contribution' was proving extraordinarily generous and effective.

The contractors began work at Maralinga in June 1955. There were formidable problems in accommodating some 700 workmen in bush and desert country '500 miles from anywhere'; the medical authorities warned that the construction camp was too crowded; all the water used still had to be transported by rail; supplies were delayed by shipping strikes. Unfortunately, site management was inefficient, and progress reports were so discouraging that the prospects of completion in time for *Buffalo* looked poor. In London, the Minister of Supply and his senior officials held frequent and anxious meetings with the consulting engineers and contractors.

By April 1956 there had been a reorganization, and a complete change of atmosphere on the site was reported. Captain Lloyd of the Ministry of Supply visited Maralinga in May and June, and was impressed by the friendliness and wholehearted cooperation he found there, the excellent work done by the resident engineer who had 'given his utmost', and the new and very efficient range commandant who was about to take over. Despite continuing water problems, and the recent derailment of more than 20 trucks of urgently needed freight, there was a feeling of confidence that the range would be ready in time for *Buffalo* though at greater cost than estimated.

Meanwhile another major trial, *Mosaic*, was in progress in the Monte Bello islands. That is the subject of the next chapter.

7
Mosaic – 1956[1]

The technological and strategic developments described in Chapter 5 were swiftly apparent in *Operation Mosaic*, the first round of tests for three years and the beginning of the most intense period of British weapon trials. With megaton weapons now regarded as a necessity for strategic deterrent purposes, the question of how to produce them became a key preoccupation for British scientists. After the government's thermonuclear weapon decision in the summer of 1954, scientists had expected their first test of such a device to be in 1958, but by early 1955 they hoped to be ready by 1957. However, they lacked essential scientific data that they could obtain only by experiment in a third series of tests.

First steps to megaton weapons

It is important at this stage to emphasize that a megaton weapon is not necessarily the same thing as a thermonuclear weapon: the term 'megaton' refers to the size of the explosion, while 'thermonuclear' refers to the method of producing it. At the time, it was believed that a thermonuclear weapon would produce most of its very large yield by the fusion of light elements. However, it was also considered that the addition of smaller quantities of light elements might significantly boost the yield of a large fission device, although most of the yield would still come from nuclear fission reactions.

The distinction between boosted fission weapons and thermonuclear weapons is a fine one, but should not be overlooked. The linking theme is the use of light elements to produce large explosions. With the *Grapple* thermonuclear trials scheduled for 1957, investigations into the behaviour of light elements in nuclear explosions had taken on a great urgency, and it was this that provided the rationale for the *Mosaic* tests.

At this stage, British thinking about boosted weapons concentrated on the use of a layer of lithium-6 deuteride around the fissile material in a modified atomic warhead.[2] The yield of the warhead would be enhanced by thermonuclear reactions in the lithium deuteride layer. This design was referred to as 'Type A', and the weapon based upon it was given the codename *Green Bamboo*.[3] Morgan noted to the Defence Policy Research Committee in December 1955 that, 'one way or the other experience in the use of lithium deuteride must be obtained in 1956 since upon this experience depends in very great measure the detail of the 1957 trials'.[4]

It was also believed possible that a still larger yield might be produced by using a uranium tamper (a layer of uranium surrounding the fissile material and lithium deuteride). A rumour from the US had suggested that using uranium in this way would increase the yield by 50 per cent on top of the boost given by the lithium deuteride layer.[5] This possibility – and it was no more than that – explains why the original plan to fire a single shot at *Mosaic* was subsequently amended to allow two tests: one with a lead tamper to investigate the boosting effect of lithium deuteride alone, and one with a uranium tamper to assess the effects of that modification.

Such was the rationale for *Mosaic*: the tests would provide important information in developing megaton weapons. As things turned out, by the end of 1955 the Aldermaston scientists had concluded that the boosting methods of the *Green Bamboo* design were not in fact likely to give a significant increase in yield. This conclusion, however, was drawn from calculation rather than empirical data. The growing likelihood of a global moratorium and/or ban on tests put a premium on finding dependable ways to produce megaton weapons quickly, and consequently it was vital to be *sure* that the calculations that this was not a technically feasible route were correct. *Mosaic* was, therefore, an example of negative testing, so to speak, although the test would still have positive value in its demonstration of the behaviour of light elements.

In April 1955 the single scheduled test became two. However, running two tests would use larger quantities of lithium deuteride, a substance hitherto produced in very small amounts. The AEA were having difficulty in producing enough, and for much of 1955 it was uncertain that sufficient quantities would be available in time for *Mosaic*.[6] One possibility was to switch a *Mosaic* shot and the first round scheduled for *Buffalo* (a test of the *Red Beard* warhead). This was not necessary in the end, but as late as February 1956 the possibility was still under consideration.[7]

Like *Totem* before it, *Mosaic* was planned under conditions of great urgency. The first operational statement, when the test was still known as *Giraffe*, is dated March 1955: little more than a year before the operation commenced. This meant little time was available to arrange supplementary experiments, particularly in the light of Captain Cooper's criticisms of the way that preparations for the *Totem* trials had been hampered by repeated addition of new experiments. None the less it was British practice to wring as much information as possible from nuclear tests, since they were such a drain on economic, technical and manpower resources.

One potentially valuable experiment was a study of the precursor shock. This is a wave of air pressure moving ahead of the main blast, which forms under certain conditions in a nuclear explosion and can affect the parameters of the blast wave. As early as August 1954, AWRE was interested in studying the precursor shock, not only because it could lead to 'operational information of major significance', but also because the US was similarly interested, which might in turn be useful in restarting Anglo-American information exchanges.[8]

Unlike the other trials in Australia, *Mosaic* was not accompanied by ancillary investigations of weapons effects and target response.[9] The only ancillary experiments were those carried out for the Admiralty by HMS *Diana*, to obtain scientific data on fallout, and to study the protection of ships passing through nuclear fallout conditions. Maralinga was too far from the sea to permit such experiments, and therefore, as the Admiralty pointed out to Aldermaston, *Mosaic* was the only trial that would afford an opportunity for these experiments (codenamed *Hotshot Foxtrot*) which might very loosely be regarded as a naval counterpart of the RAF's *Operation Hot Box* at *Totem* in 1953.[10]

As noted above, it was vitally important to obtain the information that *Mosaic* would generate by the end of 1956 because this would determine the nature of some of the *Grapple* trials. But Maralinga would not be ready until September or October 1956, and was already booked for a fourth test series, *Buffalo*. Emu Field was unsuitable, and a return to the Monte Bello islands was the only possibility.[11] Captain Cooper had already made a post-*Hurricane* appreciation of the islands as a possible site for further atomic tests. Whether trials could be held there again, he said, depended mainly on whether there was enough room. Contamination would make operations inconvenient, and the areas remaining for use were considerably restricted in size and shape; however, if there was not enough space on land, some equipment might be installed on rafts or barges in the lagoon. Weather and sea conditions were crucial; although the climate was pleasant from April to October, boat work was difficult, and more boats would have to be provided, as well as helicopters. For *Hurricane* the resources deployed had been dangerously small and planning had been very rushed; planning for the next trials could not begin too early.

A British scientific party led by W. N. Saxby of AWRE visited the islands in November 1953 and found them still very contaminated and unlikely to change for ten years or more. They surveyed the islands and redefined the 'slight risk' and 'no risk' areas.[12]

Aldermaston and the Service ministries discussed the matter, especially the best method of approach to the Australian government. The difficulty was how to explain the use of light elements in the proposed trial: as an important step towards testing a megaton weapon? Or as the next step in the development of fission bombs – with added light elements which might give a small, even insignificant, fusion yield but still with a total yield measured only in kilotons? There were elements of both, of course, but political considerations meant that the issues needed to be carefully presented.

It had been agreed that no thermonuclear tests would be carried out in Australia. Although these experiments would not be tests of thermonuclear weapons, there might be difficulties. R. G. Elkington of the British Ministry of Supply noted that the tests would be vital for developing thermonuclear weapons, but that 'the Australians are very sensitive on the question of thermonuclear explosions and it would be inadvisable to lay emphasis on this aspect of the trials'.[13]

This sensitivity was brought to the fore in startling fashion when a UKAEA spokesman was reported in the press as suggesting that 'experiments useful in developing the hydrogen bomb' might be conducted in Australia. An instant response came from Beale, who said, 'A spokesman for the UKAEA – if there is one, which I doubt – has no authority to speak for Australia. I assert categorically, as I have already done more than once, that the Australian government has no intention whatsoever of allowing any hydrogen bomb tests or any experiments connected with them to take place in Australia'.[14]

That no H-bomb tests would be conducted was of course true, but the *Mosaic* trials *were* undeniably connected to the thermonuclear trials.[15] As we shall see, this was not the last time that an inaccurate intervention by the Australian Minister of Supply would complicate matters. Eden cabled Menzies on 16 May, and was frank about the purpose of the trial if vague about its nature:

You know well the importance we attach to speediest development of efficient nuclear weapons and the great part they can play in interests of Commonwealth strategy. Our research and development work is going so well that we hope to carry out certain experiments early in 1956 and to have a full-scale test of thermonuclear weapons in 1957 ... I should like to ask for your help in making arrangements for experiments in early 1956. As you know, Maralinga cannot be ready until September/October of that year, when we are already planning to carry out certain weapon trials. If we can carry out experiments in April 1956 we shall not only save 6 months valuable time in our weapon development programme, but we shall get greater value from Maralinga tests in September/October.

Our people here ... suggested that your agreement should be sought to a programme of two firings in the Monte Bello Islands in April 1956. The experiments would consist of atomic explosions with the inclusion of light elements as a boost. It would of course be made clear in any public announcement that the explosions were atomic and not thermonuclear ... The smaller of the two shots [would] be fired first and if this was completely successful the second and slightly larger shot would not then be fired. Neither would give a yield more than 2½ times greater than in the *Hurricane* operation.[16]

The explosions would be on towers to reduce contamination and fallout would be less than one-fifth that of *Hurricane* bomb.

We should of course ensure that shots would not be exploded unless conditions were such as to involve absolutely no danger to health of people or animals on mainland, and should give your people the same facilities[17] for checking safety measures as they had at previous trials and as they will have at Maralinga.

We should be prepared to bear cost of operation but should be grateful for all such logistic support as Australia could provide ...[18]

Menzies quickly agreed in principle. His reply was very friendly and cooperative, but firm. Australia, he said, would continue to assist within the limits of her resources, but he was in the dark about the logistic support involved. Manpower was short and he was anxious about the cumulative effect on Australia's resources of so many commitments, including her contribution to the strategic reserve for Malaya and the operations at Woomera and Maralinga. He was also concerned about safety:

I notice from your description of the nature of the shots to be fired that each would give a yield considerably greater than in the case of the bomb fired in the *Hurricane* operation. In view of this I ask that the most meticulous care be exercised in the scientific checking of safety measures to ensure the safety of people and animals on the mainland.

Eden assured him that safety measures would be meticulous, that as before the British would welcome discussions on safety checks with the Australian scientists, and also that senior Australian Service officers would be welcome as observers at the test. Resources required for the test would only be about 10 per cent of those used at *Hurricane*. A British party would, as suggested, visit Australia shortly for discussions.

The agreement between Prime Ministers cleared the way for planning. The Monte Bello islands were familiar territory, and the Aldermaston scientists by this time had experience of three tests. But *Mosaic* was unlike previous tests, partly because of its novel purpose, partly because it was the first to take place under the new dispensation. In Britain, as we saw in Chapter 1, the Atomic Energy Authority had been created in 1954 and had taken over Aldermaston; responsibility for weapon trials had been divided between it and the Ministry of Supply's Controllerate of Atomic Weapons, headed by General Morgan. In Australia the AWTSC had been set up in 1955; the Memorandum of Arrangements had been agreed by Australia and Britain, and although it referred specifically to Maralinga, it was tacitly assumed to apply to all weapon trials in Australia. Anglo-Australian relations in respect of trials had thus been put on a more formal basis, with clearly defined rights and obligations, and though the Australians had certainly not struck a hard bargain their position had been strengthened.

Planning the operation

Captain Cooper had said of *Hurricane* that it was a rush job and that more time should be allowed for planning later trials. One argument for the permanent inland range was that it would speed up the programme, since any naval expedition to Australia would need two years' notice. But *Mosaic*, once again, was a Royal Navy operation, and mounted with little time to spare; it was 15 months, not two years, from its conception in February 1955 (as *Operation Giraffe*) to the planned firing dates in 1956. By June 1955, when intergovernmental agreement was reached, only ten months were left; there was much work to do and a long voyage lay ahead. An appreciation in March 1955 by the Aldermaston trials staff had been 'over-optimistic and unrealistic in terms of time and manpower', the Operational Commander said later, and after *Mosaic* he commented that a further three or four months of planning and preparation would have made the task easier and more certain of success. There had been no margin; this theme recurs again and again.

At a preliminary meeting of the Service departments and Aldermaston, on 3 May, it was tentatively decided to place the weapons on towers, one on Trimouille Island, and one on Alpha Island, and to control the firing from the base ship, anchored 15 miles away in the lagoon. The scientific party, it was estimated, would number 35–40 (this proved an underestimate) and an engineering force of about 30 would be needed. A timetable was agreed. The ships would have to be refitted and ready for sea-trials by mid-November; they would have to sail from the United Kingdom by 5 January 1956 and reach the Islands by 7 March; the sites would then have to be prepared by 18 April; the full rehearsal should be not later than 30 April; and the two shots should be fired on 1 and 10 May, weather permitting. Compared with *Hurricane*, there were two time-saving factors; the ships would go through the Suez Canal and not round the Cape, and the scientific party and the main Royal Engineer Force would go to Australia by air instead of by sea – a *Hurricane* lesson well learnt.

In London the Atomic Weapons Trials Executive, under the chairmanship of General Morgan of the Ministry of Supply, was already planning *Operation Buffalo*;[19] its terms of reference were extended to include *Mosaic*, and it became the executive authority in London dealing with all aspects of the operation, sitting as 'Mosex' or Buffalex', according to the agenda. The Royal Navy appointed Captain (later Commodore) Hugh C. Martell RN as Operational Commander in June 1955; C. A. Adams, who had been deputy to Dr Tyte at *Hurricane* and to Sir William Penney at *Totem*, was appointed scientific director, to be assisted overseas by I. Maddock as scientific superintendent. Group Captain S. W. B. Menaul was to command the RAF *Mosaic* Air Task Group.

Captain Martell decided at once that joint planning should be done at Aldermaston – another *Hurricane* lesson well learnt – which resulted in a successful integration of operational and scientific plans and an admirable understanding between the Service and scientific elements throughout the operation. The Operational Commander, besides being in command of all HM ships, was responsible – under the Atomic Weapons Trials Executive – for overall control, planning and execution of the operation, including safety and security. Army, RAF and scientific personnel were to be commanded by senior Army and RAF officers and the scientific superintendent respectively – Lieutenant-Colonel R. N. B. Holmes RE, Group Captain Menaul and I. Maddock. At Aldermaston AWRE planning of the trial was the responsibility of J. T. Tomblin, head of Trials Planning Branch, which was part of the Trials Division under R. Pilgrim. The latter was one of the British scientists who had been at Los Alamos during the war and at Cross Roads in 1946, and he had been invited to visit the Nevada Test Site in 1955.

Planning in Australia

On 22 July 1951, as promised in Eden's message to Menzies, a small mission led by Martell and including Adams and Menaul went to Australia to discuss all aspects of *Mosaic* with the Department of Supply, the Maralinga Committee, the Services, the Bureau of Meteorology and the Australian security staff. Adams gave Butement, as a member of the AWTSC, a broad description of the scope of the operation and the probable yields. He suggested that safety precautions and firing conditions should be governed by the principles in Report A32 (which the Australians already had) and showed him fallout contours for the *Totem* shots – 'nominalized' to 20 kilotons, i.e. redrawn as they would have been if the yields had been 20 kilotons – demonstrating the effects of wind shear and absence of wind shear. They decided to correspond further about safety questions and to meet again early in 1956, and it was agreed that at least two members of the AWTSC would be on board the headquarters ship, HMS *Narvik*, when decisions to fire were taken.

Meteorological plans were discussed with Dwyer, the head of the Bureau of Meteorology. One or two Australian meteorologists, it was agreed, would be attached to the Operational Commander's staff as consultants. A RAN frigate might be stationed to act as a weather reporting ship, and a second weather ship would be necessary to give warning of hurricanes – not infrequent in the area – and willy-willies (whirlwinds) coming from the Timor Sea.[20]

As a counterpart to Mosex, in August the Australians set up the Monte Bello Working Party, under a naval chairman; paradoxically but sensibly, it operated as a sub-committee of the Maralinga Committee. Plans went forward rapidly in Britain and Australia. A revised timetable was agreed, with HMS *Narvik* reaching Fremantle by 11 February instead of 28 February, since Martell and Adams were both worried about Monte Bello weather conditions in April/May and wanted more margin for possible delays in firing.[21] They had every reason to be apprehensive about limited opportunities; the prevailing winds in the area in April and May were westerlies, and the Australian meteorologist, H. R. Philpot, had concluded that in these months the chances were low of winds between 30,000 ft and 50,000 ft blowing into the appropriate sector (i.e. from 270° to 045° through north). Moreover, favourable winds nearly always meant rough weather, which would hamper boat work. A further constraint on firing opportunities was the political ban on Sunday firings.[22]

Menzies asks questions

Eden sent a message to Menzies at the end of August to say that a public announcement of the test could not be delayed, as preparations would soon be too visible to be kept secret:

> I understand that the planning of the Monte Bello test is going ahead and that your government is proposing to send naval vessels to the Islands early next month to begin the laying of the moorings. This raises the question of publicity, to which we have been giving some thought. It seems desirable to issue in the near future a general statement about our plans for tests in 1956 both at Monte Bello and Maralinga. We have therefore prepared a short draft ...

On receiving Eden's original request in May, Menzies had evinced no concern about the nature of the trial or the light elements mentioned. Now he became anxious and wanted a fuller explanation. Some of his officials had gained the impression from Australian scientists that *Mosaic* might be described as a hydrogen bomb test; if this was by any definition true, he and his government would want background material to enable them to deal with questions after the public announcement that the trial was to take place.[23]

A prompt reply to Canberra read: 'Australians can be reassured. An H bomb in normal parlance is a weapon of large yield, that is, in the megaton range, which employs the fusion reaction of light elements on a large scale. The proposed tests are not of this character but are the fission weapons used as vehicles for certain diagnostic and experimental tests'. As for the explanation Menzies wanted, the answer given was:

> The smaller yield weapon is a fission weapon which in order to get scientific data contains small quantities of the light elements used in thermonuclear bombs. The light elements are expected to react but the quantities are so small that the effect on the yield is small. The larger yield weapon is a fission weapon containing somewhat larger quantities of the light elements, but containing no uranium with

which the light elements can react.[24] The behaviour of the light elements will be diagnosed with the help of traces of various materials.

An H-bomb is essentially a bomb in which the major explosion is due to a reaction of considerable amounts of light elements, and the yield is large – in the megaton range. The two rounds at *Mosaic* are of low yield – a few tens of kilotons – and the small amounts of light elements incorporated are solely to investigate the nature of the reaction.[25]

These doubts apparently dispelled, a carefully agreed statement about the forthcoming operation was released simultaneously in the United Kingdom and Australia on 12 September 1955. It explained that rapid progress in the atomic weapons programme made further trials necessary before the range at Maralinga would be ready in late 1956. The Australian government had therefore agreed to the use of the Monte Bello islands for trials in April/May 1956. Fallout on the islands and the nearby sea would be less than that from the *Hurricane* explosion in 1952; there would be no danger to people or livestock on the mainland, and detonation would take place only when the meteorological conditions were fully satisfactory. After this third series at Monte Bello, a fourth would take place at Maralinga later in 1956. None of the tests would exceed a few tens of kilotons in yield, and some would be smaller. The Australian meteorological service would provide meteorological information for both series. As in earlier tests, the decision to fire would be made only after eminent Australian scientists, nominated by the Australian government, had made their own, independent assessments. There had officially been no such procedure at *Hurricane* and *Totem*; however, at least three eminent Australian scientists had been present at both of these trials and had been consulted by Penney when the decisions to fire were being taken.

The Services complete their plans

At Chatham, refitting of HMS *Narvik* began early in July, and she was commissioned on 25 November – thanks, said the Operational Commander, to feverish activity by all dockyard departments working day and night. An already tight timetable was made more difficult by changes of plan and inaccurate briefing due to security restrictions, and most of the officers and crew joined the ship late, but the sailing date was met. One useful change of plan was the decision to use *Narvik* only for operational control and not for scientific activities; in particular, the firing control was to be on Hermite Island, where a camp for eight scientists would be set up. This made more space available on board; even so it was barely adequate and the meteorologists, for example, worked in very cramped conditions. Electronic instrumentation was simplified as a result of the change and scientific sea-trials became unnecessary, with a valuable saving of time. Arrangements for movement of personnel before firing were also made easier.

The ships of Task Force 308, formed for the trials, were in four groups. The first was HMS *Narvik* and HMS *Alert* (loaned by the Commander-in-Chief, Far East). The second group consisted of RAN vessels, HMAS *Fremantle*, HMAS *Junee* and HMAS *Karangi*, and two lighters. In the third group were five Royal Navy destroyers from the Far East and East Indies stations, employed on weather reporting duties. Lastly, HMS *Diana*, a destroyer on special detachment from the Mediterranean Fleet, was to carry out Admiralty-sponsored experiments on fallout.

By the end of December, HMS *Narvik* had completed her refit and trials, had loaded all stores and was ready to sail. A small party of Royal Engineers was on board; the other RE, together with two Aldermaston staff, were to fly to Australia to join HMS *Narvik* at the end of February 1956. The main scientific party would leave London by air on 1 April. Stores were to be carried by HMS *Narvik* and by commercial shipping, but a considerable tonnage had to be sent by air freight.[26]

The RAF air task group, originally formed with the Maralinga trials in mind, was responsible for air communications and transport, safety patrols, long-range meteorological reconnaissance flights over the Timor Sea, the collection of cloud samples, cloud tracking, radiological surveys of the islands and the coastal area, and aerial photography. Twenty-five aircraft were engaged, including three RAAF Neptunes used for safety patrols, and 107 officers and 407 NCOs and men, most of them volunteers. The majority were based at airfields at Pearce and Onslow, but four RAF Shackletons flew daily weather flights from Darwin. Seven specially equipped RAF Canberra bombers were to collect and deliver cloud samples, and to track the radioactive clouds until they were clear of the Australian continent. Five RAF Varsity aircraft were to assist in cloud tracking at lower levels and to carry out low-level radiological surveys. Two Whirlwind helicopters were to provide a ferry service (and air-sea rescue service if needed) and to help the Varsities in low-level surveys. Special air transport between the United Kingdom and Australia and between bases in Australia was provided by four Hastings aircraft.

The air task group had some early difficulties with too little time for planning, late delivery of equipment, aircraft needing modifications and hitches over movement of personnel, but the advance party of 84 officers and men duly moved to RAAF Pearce in January 1956. The main party followed in the second half of March; the travel arrangements were chaotic, but once at Monte Bello all went well. Liaison with the scientific staff and cooperation between the RAF and RAAF were both excellent.[27]

The Army contribution, though less obvious, was outstandingly good. Royal Engineers under Lt.-Col. Holmes worked in intense heat, ten hours a day, seven days a week – reportedly 'cheerfully' – on construction and civil engineering work. This included the erection of aluminium towers for the two weapons. There were difficulties due to bad drilling by the manufacturers, and none of the men were trained erectors – one was a plumber whose hobby was mountaineering – but they did their job admirably.

Meteorology and theoretical predictions

By the end of October the AWTSC had specified a need for two ship-borne weather reporting stations, one 600 miles west and one 600 miles north-west of Monte Bello. As two or even three ships were required to keep one ship on station, the Admiralty suggested that one should be replaced by a wind-finding radar station on Christmas Island (that is, Christmas Island in the Indian Ocean, 190 miles south of Java, *not* the Christmas Island in the Pacific, used for the *Grapple* trials in 1957 and 1958). The AWTSC agreed and the Royal Naval Weather Service set up a station there. On HMS *Narvik* there was to be a meteorological office with two Australian meteorologists, a Royal Navy meteorological officer and six naval ratings. This group would work closely with the scientists in the theoretical predictions group, whose task, before firing, was to correlate the theoretical fallout patterns with the forecasts provided by the meteorologists, and to advise whether the forecast conditions were suitable for firing. After firing, they and the ten meteorologists had to determine the probable position of the cloud, so that the tracking and sampling aircraft could be told where to look for it; it would soon become invisible and would have to be found by means of radiation-sensitive instruments.

The procedures leading up to a decision to fire were carefully defined in the joint Operational Plan:

> The scientific conduct of the trial will be under the control of a scientific superintendent who will notify the operational commander and the scientific director when the groups have completed their

preparations. When Service units have similarly notified the operational commander that they are ready, a standby state will be declared and the decision to fire will be taken when the meteorological forecast is suitable.

During the standby period the operational commander and scientific director will be kept informed of forecasts by the staff meteorological officer. The representatives of the Australian Safety Committee, who will be similarly kept informed by the senior Australian meteorologist, will jointly with the scientific director decide when the forecast shows that firing is permissible in relation to radiological safety. This decision will be given by the scientific director to the operational commander who will authorise final preparations and firing if he is satisfied that all other operational requirements are met.[28]

It is clear from these procedures that the AWTSC representatives had an effective veto on firing.

Health and safety planning

In the Maralinga Safety Regulations, which it had been decided should apply to *Mosaic*, the standards laid down for trials personnel were almost the same as those for *Hurricane* and *Totem*. The difference was that, above the higher integrated dose of 10 r (100 mSv), a 'special higher integrated dose' of 25 r (250 mSv) was permissible in cases of extreme necessity.

As for population exposure limits, it should be remembered that firing was to take place only when the predicted winds would blow the bulk of the fallout away from the mainland and across the ocean, so that no significant radioactive contamination would be expected to reach the Australian population. During September 1955, Aldermaston sent two papers to the AWTSC. The first, entitled 'Safety levels for contamination from fallout from atomic weapons tests', defined two levels for guidance on contamination, A and B, to replace those previously defined in A32 as 'zero risk' and 'slight risk'; these descriptions were dropped because 'slight risk' might be thought to imply an exaggerated possibility of injury. Level A was 'that level which will not cause any observable effect on the body'. Level B was 'that level which could cause a small observable effect, such as slight temporary sickness, in a few people if they had a low threshold sensitivity to radiation'; these hypersensitive people were considered likely to be only a fraction of one per cent of a population.[29]

At their Nevada Test Site the Americans applied a derived limit approximating to level B, but the Aldermaston scientists did not wish to seek Australian agreement to such high level, and they suggested a level between A and B – at 1/2B instead of B. This, they believed, would give only a slight chance (if any) of any physiological effect which, if it occurred, would be temporary and hardly observable. They hoped by accurate fallout forecasts to keep exposures well below this level, but, as a marginal possibility, the half-level seemed reasonable. The AWTSC took some time to consider this suggestion, but then decided that level A should apply to Aboriginals, because they would be less sheltered from radiation exposure by housing, clothes and footwear, and less likely to remove contamination by washing. Half level B could apply to the rest of the Australian population.

The second paper Aldermaston sent to the AWTSC gave upper limits for the yield of the *Mosaic* weapons as 'one and four nominal' (i.e. 20 kilotons and 80 kilotons), and presented the evidence of *Totem* contamination as a guide to estimating probable contamination from *Mosaic* under various meteorological conditions. A third paper was being prepared on the probable frequency of favourable weather, and the meteorological conditions to be laid down for firing, matters which the AWTSC was studying independently. For both Aldermaston and the AWTSC, Adams emphasized, safety must be the paramount consideration and an appropriate safety margin must be allowed, but if an unnecessarily wide margin of safety was required they might wait in vain for an opportunity to fire.[30] This would be a particular problem for the much larger explosion of G2, and even under the British figures it was estimated that there would be only two or three days per month through May and June when conditions would be favourable: a tight window under any circumstances.[31]

Scientific planning

The operation being planned was stripped to its scientific essentials, with no ancillary experiments except the Admiralty exercise to be carried out by HMS *Diana*. Even so, the tasks detailed in the Joint Operational Plan seemed a formidable load for 50 scientists. They were organized in nine groups under Adams, the scientific director, and Maddock, the scientific superintendent, with a small headquarters staff of four. The largest groups were the Radiochemical Group with ten men at RAAF Pearce; the Radiological Health Group with six at Monte Bello and four at RAAF Pearce; and the Electronic Operations Group, with nine at Monte Bello. The other groups were very small; four for weapon assembly, three for weapon functioning, two for theoretical predictions, two for blast measurements and two for photographic measurements (all at Monte Bello), with two decontamination specialists at RAAF Pearce.[32]

Everyone, British and Australian – dockyard workers, servicemen of all ranks and scientists – worked desperately hard to meet the *Mosaic* deadlines. But the whole operation might have been aborted by one item. The fusion reaction which it was the purpose of the trial to investigate depended on the presence of a small quantity of a lithium deuteride. The Atomic Energy Authority's Production Group had no experience of making it – few people in the world had – and was having the utmost difficulty in getting a production process to work. William Cook, Penney's deputy at Aldermaston who had special responsibility for megaton bomb research and development, saw that the whole trials programme might have to be re-phased. 'If the *Mosaic* trial at Monte Bello is delayed until September', he wrote, 'we shall be unable to hold the naval support there without jeopardizing the 1957 trial [i.e. *Grapple*, in the Pacific]. If the trial is delayed this far we propose firing the Monte Bello rounds at Maralinga in the autumn. In view of the large yield of one weapon this can only be done if we fire it on a high tower, much higher than the towers we have provided for *Buffalo*'. In October 1955, he sought, and obtained, approval to order a 300 ft tower, which, he said, would not be wasted if the lithium deuteride was ready after all. It was ready just in time and *Mosaic* went ahead as planned.

Arrival in Australia

Mosaic passed from the planning to the operational phase. The RAF advance party arrived at Pearce on 10 January; HMS *Narvik* had sailed on 29 December and reached Fremantle on 23 February, where the Royal Engineers came aboard. The Australian ships of the task force assembled at Fremantle and soon all were ready to sail to the Monte Bello Islands. But first Commodore Martell met the Monte Bello Working Party (MBWP) to review the situation and discuss outstanding questions. The target dates for the two tests were amended to 16 May and 11 June and the terminal date was agreed as mid-July to avoid overlapping *Mosaic* with the preparations for *Buffalo* at Maralinga.

Meanwhile the Australian Minister for Supply, Howard Beale, had made a public statement about the test, explaining the arrangements made to ensure that firings took place only in satisfactory weather conditions. He described the 'vast network of hundreds of reporting stations' throughout Australia, New Zealand, Indonesia and islands in the Indian Ocean, the Royal Navy's weather ship and weather station at Christmas Island, and the special meteorological flights from Darwin. On the basis of reports from all these sources, and analyses by the Australian Bureau of Meteorology in Perth and Melbourne, forecasts would be jointly compiled on HMS *Narvik* by the British meteorology officer and a senior Australian meteorologist. They would keep both the scientific director and the AWSTC fully informed. Then, after Commodore Martell declared standby, the AWSTC and the scientific director together would decide when the weather pattern showed that firing was permissible. They would tell Commodore Martell of their decision, and he would authorize final preparations and firing if he was satisfied that everything was in order. The problem for the forecasters was to predict the approach of suitable conditions early enough to enable all preparations to be completed, and then to satisfy the AWTSC and the scientific director that the conditions would persist long enough after the firing for the atomic cloud to drift out over the sea and diffuse harmlessly into the atmosphere.[33]

Daily meteorological flights from Darwin began on 2 March. Three days later, delayed by a hurricane, HMS *Narvik* sailed for the islands, and arrived on 8 March. Reconnaissance and construction work began at once, and a camp on Hermite was ready by the end of March; meanwhile, at Onslow, the Royal Australian Navy was building a mainland base camp. The main scientific party reached the islands on 7 April and Adams arrived on 22 April. He missed two very distinguished visitors; on 15 April the First Sea Lord, Earl Mountbatten, and Lady Mountbatten called in at the Monte Bello Islands to see the *Mosaic* expedition.

Operation Mosaic – G1

A tremendous amount had been done before the scientists came, but they had much work to do before the first round (referred to as G1) could be fired. Scientific rehearsals were held on 27 April and 2 May, followed by a full rehearsal on 5 May. Preparations for G1 were complete, except for the fissile material. It was delivered by a special RAF Hastings flight to Onslow. HMS *Alert* collected it on 11 May and assembly of the weapon began next day. On 14 May, the members of the AWTSC reached Monte Bello, and standby began. A small party of VIPs – six Australian Service chiefs – and press representatives arrived to observe the explosion from HMAS *Junee* and *Fremantle*. D-1 was declared on 15 May, the favourable weather conditions held, and on the morning of 16 May G1 was successfully detonated.[34]

Twenty minutes after the explosion the sampling Canberras entered the cloud, and four hours later cloud tracking began. By sunset the seagulls were back, circling the ships. The Radiological Health Group, in a specially fitted motor cutter, surveyed the lagoon, and next day re-entry operations began. On 18 May, HMS *Diana*, after carrying out the Admiralty's fallout experiment, sailed for Singapore.

The AWTSC, after getting results of the mainland surveys, left the Islands – they were to return for G2 – and the chairman, Professor Martin, sent a brief report on G1 to the Prime Minister:[35]

> The requests of the Safety Committee for meteorological predictions of safe firing conditions and for examining the subsequent radioactive fallout by air and sea operations were fully met.
>
> The control of movements of shipping and aircraft worked smoothly. The air search of restricted areas showed with certainty that there was no shipping, other than that associated with the experiment, in the prescribed danger area.
>
> The meteorological predictions were complete and accurate and the operation was carried out without there being any hazard whatsoever to life on the mainland, ships at sea, or to aircraft.
>
> The whole operation proceeded with precision and was a complete success.

Nevertheless it had not been entirely plain sailing. The Australians had thought they were going to do the forecasting, and the methods used by the British and Australian forecasters were greatly at variance. Then, at busy periods, the volume of incoming meteorological information tended to saturate *Narvik's* communication system. Prediction of a possible D-day, Maddock said, was undoubtedly the problem needing most attention since he came to the islands. He had been dismayed by the uncertainties in the wind forecasting; during the rehearsal, wind conditions at the instant of mock-firing were significantly worse than had been predicted at midnight or even in the early morning forecast. Large uncertainties were also likely in forecasting wind forces, and a predicted wind speed of 10 knots might turn out at anything from 5 to 15 knots. For the real firing, fortunately, predictions proved much more reliable, but there seemed to be no solution to the problem of a 16-hour gap between the latest meteorological information used as a basis for the decision to fire and the actual time of firing.

Adams, Maddock and the British meteorologist Matthewman met Dwyer and Philpot in Melbourne a few days later to try to resolve the difficulties; the atmosphere was friendly, but the Australians could not accept the British point of view. The British thought the Australian method of prediction unsatisfactory and unrealistic; since the meteorological conditions they were seeking were very elusive, excessive constraints could make them unattainable. Dwyer made it clear that, for his part, this consideration was secondary to maintaining absolute safety, and he added that public opinion in Australia was strongly opposed to the trials. Adams and Maddock went on to meet the Monte Bello Working Party and the AWTSC. The MBWP was wholeheartedly cooperative; they found the AWTSC extremely reasonable, but acutely conscious of the political atmosphere and possible press and public reactions to any untoward incident.[36]

Martell sent Penney a full, personal, handwritten account promptly after the first detonation.[37]

G1 was fired yesterday after a very successful set of met. forecasts – far more successful than the average practice ones we have had. The only point on which I have regrets is in the concessions I made to ensure the cooperation of the Safety Committee. The question of their seeing anything of the assembly luckily didn't arise, as we went straight into D-1 on the morning after their night arrival. However they asked for a meeting with me in the morning $1\frac{1}{2}$ hours before the decision had to be taken. From their attitude, not only at this meeting but in conversation the previous night, it was clear that they are very perturbed about the Australian political situation, and about the organization and knowledge behind the opposition to atomic tests. Both Martin and Titterton show this apprehension most markedly ... Martin took the attitude that they could not function as a Safety Committee unless they were given more information about the nature of the tests. I therefore said I would repeat and confirm what had already been stated to Mr Menzies and, after an assurance that the information would be treated as [Top Secret] said:

(a) Although the major part of the yield of the explosions would come from fission we had for scientific purposes included a small amount of material to give information on thermonuclear processes.
(b) An increment of yield would result from this inclusion which would be proportionally small.

(c) We would give them predicted fallout patterns for both the probable yield and the maximum figure for safety purposes, and that both these figures would include an allowance for the presence of the thermonuclear material.

... I ought, I think, to have stone-walled on the lines that such information as UK was prepared to give had already been given to Mr Menzies and that they should get their information from him ... However my reaction at the time, with the knowledge of a particularly favourable met. situation coming up, was that it was expedient to repeat to the Prime Minister's committee information that had been given to him ... The risk of a deadlock seemed large at the time ... They particularly wanted to know how they stood in relation to public assurance that this is not a hydrogen bomb and wanted more than a repetition about the range of yields.

There is a background to this, of which you have probably seen the Press reports – trouble with the Seamen's Union over a ship, *Kytra*, which might be within 500 miles of Monte Bello, and protest marches through Perth with placards about Australians becoming guinea pigs. The Safety Committee is on our side, but a bit jittery ...[38]

The results – G1

What did Penney and Cook and the staff at Aldermaston think about G1? It neither elated nor depressed them. Excellent records had been obtained, and the experiment had been technically successful (moreover without American help in measuring the multiplication rate, which Penney had sought in vain). The results agreed pretty well with their calculations and the yield was in the 15–20-kiloton range as expected. But G1 also showed that their more optimistic hopes about the effects of the thermonuclear reaction had not been realized; the effect of the small quantity of lithium deuteride had been slight. In this respect, G1 did not give all the information required and there was no question that G2 would be needed, despite the Prime Minister's expectation. Nevertheless, it did give confidence in the improved performance of the implosion system.

The G1 results immediately affected plans for the larger G2 detonation. It had been intended in G2 to use lead instead of natural uranium which would undergo fission by fast neutrons and might result in a higher yield than that agreed with the AWTSC (i.e. a planned upper limit of

80 kilotons, with 100 kilotons as a conservative basis for safety calculations). However, the results of G1 meant that natural uranium could
safely be used in G2.

The first *Mosaic* shot had been satisfactory. All had gone smoothly and
there had been no delay due to unfavourable weather. But after the
disagreements over meteorology, and the Australian anxieties reported
by Martell, the prelude to the bigger G2 shot was full of suspense.

Operation Mosaic – G2

Scientific rehearsals for G2 were held on 28 and 31 May and a full
rehearsal took place on 4 June. On 6 June the fissile core was delivered
by air to Onslow and was again collected by HMS *Alert*, and assembly of
the G2 weapon began. Standby was declared on 10 June.

Then came the most trying time of the whole operation. The chances
of favourable weather were not good; ever since HMS *Narvik* arrived in
early March there had not been a single day suitable for firing a weapon
like G2. There were now only 30 possible days until 15 July, set as the
terminal date for the operation, since – apart from the approaching
Buffalo trials – *Narvik* had to be home in time to refit for the 1957 *Grapple*
trials in the Pacific. No sooner did the weather look promising than it
suddenly changed, but everything was kept in a constant state of readiness
so that any opportunity could be taken without delay. This meant
continually preparing, moving to action stations – the ships had to be at
least twice as far away from ground zero as for G1 – and then cancelling
when the predicted conditions worsened.

Weather was not the only problem. 'Adams is in considerable
difficulty with the Australian Safety Committee over the firing of G2',
Cook wrote to the Admiralty, 'and he had to be very restrictive about
weather conditions to meet the Safety Committee and so to obtain
agreement to fire'. Adams was very worried that before 15 July there
might be no weather that would satisfy the AWTSC, and he urged that
everything should be done by both the British and Australian governments to make an extension possible, if it should prove necessary. Firing
G2 had by now become so important that Cook acknowledged to the
Admiralty that 'some delay to *Grapple*' would be acceptable if that was
the sacrifice required for the test to be carried out.[39]

The AWTSC must have been the more uneasy because after G1, the
decontamination group had found that aircraft based at Onslow had
measurable radioactive material in their engines and on their undercar-
riages, though radiological surveys by the Varsities had found the

mainland clear of radioactive contamination from the shot. The explanation seemed to be local winds blowing onshore in the evening.[40]

The situation was all the more sensitive as Howard Beale, the Minister for Supply, had mistakenly said in a radio programme that G2 was going to be smaller than G1. Why he said this is a mystery. Butement, in Beale's Department, certainly knew the figures. Yields for G1 and G2 had been given to the AWTSC when Adams visited Australia in mid-July and he had discussed the whole business informally with Martin, Butement and Titterton. If it had not been for Beale's broadcast, a longer danger area than that for G1 would have been declared for G2, but to avoid embarrassing the minister this was not done and no public correction of his mistake was made.[41]

The AWTSC was also pressing Adams for further information about the G2 weapon. Penney was always more inclined than Whitehall to be candid, and he appreciated that Adams was in an awkward situation. Nevertheless he strongly advised against showing the committee any significant weapon details, though he did not object to their seeing the outside of the cabled ball in the centre section. They could be told that the fissile material was at the centre of a large ball of high explosive and that elaborate electronics were necessary 'to get symmetrical squash', but no details of the explosive's configuration or the inner components might be disclosed.

The weather continued unfavourable until 18 June. Then conditions suddenly changed, the wind moderated to 25 knots and wind directions up to 60,000 ft were suitable for firing. D-1 was declared, all was made ready, and ships moved to their stations. At 10.10 am on 19 June Maddock began the countdown. (After having spoken the countdown on three occasions he was known as the 'Count of Monte Bello'.)[42]

At 10.14 am (local time), G2 was detonated. The explosion was spectacular. G1, by comparison, was like a penny squib competing with a Brock's thunderflash, said Martell. Two newspaper photographers who were watching from the mainland wrote, 'We saw the bomb explode. First was the glow of the fireball, then a brilliant orange light suffused the horizon and waned, and immediately the atomic genie rose gracefully into the upper atmosphere. It was a magnificent sight'. The mushroom cloud was seen at Port Hedland 265 miles away, and the 'rumbling blast' of the explosion was felt 280 miles away at Marble Bar.

Tracking of the cloud began at once, but next day, 20 June, the RAF Canberras from Darwin could no longer locate it. It was clear that the cloud had not passed over the mainland at any point – though some radioactive material did – and the Safety Committee decided that further tracking was unnecessary. But that was not to be the last of the G2 cloud.

'Task Force 308 deactivated'

Re-entry sorties began on 20 June, the day after G2, and packing up and re-embarkation began on 22 June. The scientific director and the main scientific party left the islands in HMS *Alert* on 23 June and on the 26th, the rest left with the Royal Engineers in HMAS *Karangi*. From Fremantle they flew back to Britain. Next day HMS *Narvik* sailed for Singapore, well before the terminal date of 15 July, after all the suspense about weather and the possible need for an extension. On Martell's suggestion he and Adams went on a goodwill tour to Onslow, Pearce, Fremantle, Adelaide and Melbourne to meet as many as possible of the people who had helped, and to thank them.

Prefabricated posts shipped to the islands were placed to cover all the possible entrances to contaminated areas, and warning notices were erected in English, Greek, Malay, Chinese and Japanese. *Mosaic* was over, and technically and logistically it had gone very smoothly, in spite of the rushed planning. The troubles of the 1952 Monte Bello expedition were entirely avoided, thanks to good personal relations between Martell and Adams, to joint planning from the outset, to the sensible decision to fly the scientists to Australia to join the expedition, and to the care taken over mutual understanding (for example, a booklet about 'Life on *Narvik*' was given to every civilian on the ship).[43]

Clouds of confusion

Before considering the achievement of the operation and its safety, we must follow the vagaries of the G2 cloud. On the evening of 20 June – the day after the detonation – 'something of a panic' arose when it was mistakenly reported that a dangerous atomic cloud had drifted inland. Beale was entertaining some newspaper editors to dinner at Woomera and while he was making a speech, one of them received a message and immediately left the room; as the message was passed on, others quickly followed. The story had started when a miner in Western Australia got a reading on his Geiger counter that he considered high; deciding that it was due to the nuclear test he told a local journalist, who at once telephoned his newspaper, which in turn alerted its editor at Woomera.

While the newspapermen were pressing Beale for a statement, in Canberra the Cabinet and the Deputy Prime Minister, Sir Arthur Fadden (Menzies was abroad) had heard the story and were frantically trying to find out what was going on. Beale, as the minister responsible, was expected to know; they asked him what the hell he was doing and if he wanted to ruin the government. But the only people who could give him the facts were the AWTSC and the scientists on HMS *Narvik* and, as luck would have it, the radiotelephone was out of order. Meanwhile, someone in Beale's department in Melbourne told him that the Bureau of Meteorology had sent a message to *Narvik* which suggested that the radioactive cloud had crossed the coast. This was not the case, but some material was carried inland by low-altitude winds and some low-level radioactivity was dispersed over the mainland – less than level A.

Beale felt obliged to issue a press statement that night, though he had not been able to obtain authoritative information and its terms had not been agreed with the British as they should have been. He told the press that at altitudes of 5,000–10,000 ft all significant particles of fallout had gone into the sea, but at 18,000–20,000 ft some cloud containing minute particles had drifted inland, although it was now tending to drift back towards the coast. When communications with *Narvik* were restored late that night, Martin informed him that the main cloud was safely over the Arafura Sea, 100 miles away, and that there had never been any danger to the mainland. In the morning Beale therefore gave a further statement to the press, but it was still inaccurate; it was based on what Martin had said, but it implied that the cloud had been overland but had moved out safely to sea again.

That same morning, 21 June, Sir Arthur Fadden told the House of Representatives that the AWTSC had stated that there had been no risk to life or property on land or elsewhere. The Opposition led by Dr Evatt pressed for, and were promised, more information. The AWTSC then had the task of trying to reconcile the conflicting statements. It said that the bulk of the radioactive fallout had been deposited in the sea and the remaining activity had moved as a cloud at a very high altitude over the sea. There had been *no* cloud between 5,000 and 10,000 ft, and activity between 15,000 and 20,000 ft had been very small. On these facts there was no present or future risk to property or life. Ministers were still not entirely satisfied, and Beale sent a further enquiry to the AWTSC asking specifically whether the cloud had drifted over land at any time. The AWTSC reaffirmed that the cloud did not pass over the coast, but added that nevertheless there was a little activity over land, as was normally to be expected. If atmospheric temperature inversions trap some of the rising radioactive material at altitudes where the wind is in a different direction from that determining the path of the main cloud, the trapped material may be blown in other directions. It was not at any time dangerous.

Four days later Sir Arthur Fadden issued a long statement. After describing the behaviour of the light and heavy particles in fallout, he explained that conditions for the G2 test were chosen so that radioactive particles would remain over the sea until the harmful concentrations had fallen out. It was inevitable that small quantities of fine particles would fall in other directions, including some on the Australian mainland; measurements confirmed that there was some deposition but that it was completely harmless. He was satisfied that the whole operation had been carried out without risk and assured the Australian people that, for both governments, safety was the highest consideration. But the Deputy Leader of the Labour Party declared that the next Federal Labour government would vote no money for nuclear tests or for the development of the means of waging nuclear war.

The Australian newspapers gave front-page and sometimes sensational treatment to G2, but editorial comment was generally restrained. The fact was not mentioned – though it was picked up later – that G2 had been much bigger than G1 whereas the minister had said that it would be smaller. There was less tendency to blame Britain than might have been expected, though some press reports did point the finger at her. The Sydney *Morning Herald* considered that pressure to discontinue the tests would be little short of calamitous since it was in Australia's interest for the British Commonwealth to have atomic weapons. The Melbourne *Herald* suggested that the way to reassure the public was for the Safety Committee to publish regular reports about the amount of fallout – as indeed the AWTSC was to do. The Melbourne *Age* wrote of a terrible responsibility resting on the authorities concerned, 'to make sure "charged" clouds do not stray'. *Truth* warned that if one Australian were maimed through any miscalculation in these tests, 'the Australian people will hurl you and all your guilty colleagues into oblivion'. Some Australians remained imperturbable; when a Sydney *Daily Telegraph* reporter telephoned a small north-western town to ask about local reactions, he was told, 'Oh, they're a fairly complacent crowd here. It takes something fairly important or severe to make them take notice'.[44]

The G2 cloud story is instructive. Adams commented later that it was always known that the explosions would cause a small increase in radioactivity; if this had been publicly explained beforehand the outcry could have been avoided. The information had been available in Australia, and in Britain in an unclassified document, which made clear that some radioactivity overland was inevitable. But it had been classified by the Australian authorities – presumably to avoid unnecessary public alarm. This, Adams conceded, was perhaps politically understandable, but with hindsight it was exactly the wrong decision.[45] In all public statements politicians and officials had tried to avoid any mention of contamination; the Australians had asked for the word to be deleted from a pre-*Mosaic* press release drafted by London. This was a classic example of the familiar dilemma of nuclear public relations: candour requires difficult explanations and may mean trouble. Lack of candour may mean even more trouble and require even more difficult explanations later.

Martell complained of a lack of imagination in Whitehall. He doubted if London appreciated the tremendous impact the tests would have on the Australian public, and did not shrink from saying so: 'If it can be imagined that a Commonwealth nation were planning to explode a bomb in the Scilly Isles ... the British public would be howling for information ... A considerable amount of adverse criticism which followed the firing of G2 would have been avoided if the Press had been given more and accurate facts about this second trial'.

Proposals that the press should attend *Mosaic* had not been favoured by the British.[46] From a purely practical point of view, Adams thought that the journalists might get very bored and frustrated cooped up on a small ship waiting for the weather, and with little of interest to see. But British ministers had disliked the idea on principle and had concurred only because the Australians were insistent. The elaborate arrangements made for agreeing and coordinating public statements might have been adequate for press releases issued at leisure in advance of operations; though even as early as March the British Minister of Supply, Reginald Maudling, complained that 'Mr Beale has already made two announcements on his own initiative and without following agreed procedure with us'.[47] There were British breaches of the procedure too. But the G2 affair showed that the arrangements could not cater for the unforeseen or for emergencies in which events moved fast and radio-telephones broke down. The story of the G2 cloud is much more about politics, public relations and communications than it is about safety. Martell described it as 'a striking illustration of what can occur if the Press and therefore the public are insufficiently or inaccurately briefed'.

Whitehall's lack of imagination appears not only at *Mosaic*, where Martell observed it, but generally – in a failure to appreciate either the true extent of Britain's indebtedness or the generosity of Australia's contribution. The Australian government took political risks in accepting the trials on Australian territory, but was astonishingly unexacting. Whitehall for its part was mean at times, showed little awareness of Australian public opinion and was often insensitive to Australian feelings – for instance, about the control of the Maralinga Range, or the preferential position of Canadian scientists at the trials. However, Anglo-Australian relationships at the working level were generally very good and a strong sense of camaraderie developed.

Mosaic in retrospect

G1 and G2 together made essential contributions to Aldermaston's knowledge of the fusion reaction, of the high-energy neutrons it releases, and of the very complex effects of the fissions they produce in natural uranium. The Aldermaston scientists also had to develop improved techniques for measuring the multiplication rate in nuclear explosions and were led to a salutary re-examination of basic questions about yield – its meaning, and its measurement by a variety of methods (radiochemical analysis of debris, ultra high speed photography, and gamma flash and blast measurements). The purpose of *Mosaic*, Penney had said, was 'to confirm that we have not made a fundamental mistake'; it did so and was crucial to the plans for *Grapple*, the megaton bomb tests to be mounted in 1957 in the Pacific.[48]

The Royal Commission was critical of the decision to hold the trials at Monte Bello at all, arguing that the chances of the right weather condi-tions at that time of year were too low for the site to be suitable.[49] *Hurricane* had, of course, been conducted in October, which the Commission noted had then been regarded as the only time at which climactic conditions would be favourable for atomic tests.[50] In response, the British Submission argued that 'it cannot be said to have been unreasonable' to use Monte Bello, since 2–3 days of suitable weather per month was likely.[51]

What are we to make of this issue? A window of 2–3 days a month is, by any objective standards, a very narrow one indeed and would be highly vulnerable to unseasonal or unexpected weather, especially for a large test like G2. We also have seen that the British were recurrently concerned about the very limited opportunities for safe firing, and that G2's firing on 19 June was in fact the first suitable day since March. In this light, the Royal Commission's assessment is justified. However, it can also be said that the British scientists would certainly not have chosen a site with so few opportunities for firing if there had been an acceptable alternative, and the fact is that no such alternative existed. Holding *Mosaic* at Maralinga was not an option because that would clash with the *Buffalo* trials, and testing at Monte Bello in October, as the Commission seemed to favour, was impossible for the same reason.

Mosaic had been conducted under conditions of great urgency, a recurrent theme of British nuclear trials, and consequently conditions were less than ideal. The British were therefore compelled to accept fewer opportunities for safe firing, but that should not be taken to imply that corners were cut on safety.

HMS *Diana*

The destroyer's movements had to be planned so that after the detonations she would be in the right place, at the right distance from ground zero (65 miles for G1 and 130 miles for G2), to receive the required amount of fallout without breaching the safety standards laid down for *Mosaic*; exactly the same radiation rules applied to the crew of HMS *Diana* as to all other participants in the trial. This meant close liaison with the theoretical predictions staff and meteorologists. If the direction or intensity of the fallout was wrongly calculated, HMS *Diana* might either miss the fallout, or receive more than intended. If the predictions were right, and if she was correctly stationed, and if the protective measures ('pre-wetting' and washing down) worked as expected, the radiation exposure to a man on deck would be 12.5 mSv (though no one would be on deck) and the dose below deck would be 3 mSv, the normal weekly working limit. At the worst – supposing fallout was 20 times greater than estimated, protective measures were ineffective and a man actually was on deck – his exposure might be up to 250 mSv (equivalent to the special higher integrated dose).

In the event, *Diana*'s movements were flexibly controlled and she intercepted the fallout, though not without some problems of tracking. The prediction aspects of the experiment were judged to be satisfactory. The intended degree of fallout on the upper deck was achieved, and decontamination procedures were rapid and thorough. No member of the ship's company received a measurable exposure to gamma radiation. The only misfortune was the loss of an unmanned whaler fitted with scientific equipment. *Diana*, on her way to station before G2, was to drop this boat in an area not far from ground zero where fallout was expected to be intense. However, the whaler was lost in bad weather, during one of the many ship movements which occurred between G1 and G2, and it could not be recovered.

How safe was *Mosaic*?

Safety of *Mosaic* personnel

For the *Mosaic* trials personnel, both servicemen and scientists, the general levels of radiation exposure were low. About 5 per cent of them received a total of 0.5 mSv or more – one sixth of the normal *weekly* working rate of 3 mSv. The exposures of the cloud sampling crews were lower than expected, and those of the HMS *Diana* crew were below 0.2 mSv, which was the threshold of measurement. Only eight men received over 50 mSv. The two highest exposures during the whole operation were incurred by two of the senior scientists present, who volunteered to collect early samples from near to ground zero. They knew that such sorties would mean high exposures – but less than the special higher integrated dose – and they undertook them, with the scientific director's permission, after carefully weighing the value of the scientific information to be gained. The Royal Commission found little to criticize in the areas of personnel safety: it concluded that health precautions for servicemen were 'generally adequate' and that 'all efforts were taken' to limit the exposure of the crew of *Diana*.[52]

Safety of the Australian population

If *Mosaic* was acceptably safe for the participants, how safe was it for the Australian population? By far the greater part of the fallout was carried out to the open sea but, as we have seen, low levels of radioactivity reached the mainland. Adams reported to the *Mosaic* Executive that the highest level detected was a third of Level A, which gave a safety margin of three for Aboriginals and twelve for others. The Royal Commission noted that fallout had been deposited on the mainland, something acknowledged by the British Submission, but also noted that the fallout levels were less than the *Mosaic* Level A, and also less than the *Buffalo* Level A for Aboriginals.[53]

As at previous trials, there were radiological surveys by low-flying aircraft to detect ground surface activity (to be supplemented if necessary by ground survey teams), but for the first time there was also a static monitoring system. The Memorandum of Arrangements (Appendix A) had specified that 'in collaboration with the United Kingdom government the Australian government [would] set up a chain of fixed monitoring stations at agreed sites in Australia' (clause 9). At these stations fallout was collected on air filter papers and on strips of gummed film.[54] By the time of *Mosaic*, 29 stations were in action along the north-west coast and at strategic points throughout the continent. Sampling began before G1 and continued daily until the end of July, and then every four days for some time thereafter. In addition, water and mud samples from 14 reservoirs all over Australia and Tasmania were taken from March to August. There was also (as we shall see – Chapter 9), an extensive study of uptake of radioactivity in the thyroids of sheep and cattle.

Altogether, there was a wealth of information about fallout from *Mosaic*. The samples from reservoirs showed no radioactivity above normal background levels, and the fixed monitoring stations showed no airborne radioactivity in any of the large population centres – Adelaide, Brisbane, Melbourne, Perth and Sydney. From the fallout readings at the 29 stations it was possible to derive an upper limit for the integrated (total) dose of gamma radiation that people at each place would receive. However, from these same fallout readings different ranges of dose might be derived, according to the assumptions made. Three sets of calculations have been done. The first by the AWTSC shortly after *Mosaic*, is extremely conservative and based on pessimistic assumptions, which do not suggest that the Committee was indulgent to the trials or complacent about safety.[55]

At Port Hedland, where the highest activity was found, the AWTSC calculated the individual radiation exposure, from G1 and G2 together, as 58 millirems (580 microsieverts) over 50 years. This dose, however, depended on four unlikely assumptions: that the recipient remained at Port Hedland for 50 years; that he was out of doors all the time; that he wore no clothing; and that the contamination was reduced only by radioactive decay, with no weathering. As a suggestion had been made that the gummed film might be only 62 per cent efficient, the figure of 58 millirems might have to be multiplied by 1.6, giving 93 millirems.[56] (This was one-third of the normal weekly working limit of 0.3 rem for test personnel or for radiation workers). Of the radiation doses which the AWTSC calculated on these assumptions, only six were over 25 millirems and twenty were 6 millirems or below.

In 1983 the Australian Ionizing Radiation Advisory Council (AIRAC) reviewed the AVITSC figures, using the original data from the 29 monitoring stations.[57] It was unrealistically conservative, AIRAC thought, to assume that weathering would not reduce contamination, or that people would remain in one place for 50 years, with no clothing or shelter. As most of the calculated 50-year exposure would be received in the first six months, AIRAC integrated the dose over six months only and ignored weathering, as little would occur in such a short time. It then produced revised figures based on alternative assumptions: (i) that people were out of doors all the time, and (ii) that they spent a normal amount of time indoors; the shelter factor used in the calculations was taken from the 1977 Report of UNSCEAR. The second set of figures would provide, it said, a reasonable upper limit of the possible radiation dose for most of the population.

Table 7.1 shows the comparative figures for the six places in Australia with the highest fallout reading after *Mosaic* (AIRAC gives the

Table 7.1   The six places in Australia with the highest fallout reading after *Mosaic*

	AWTSC	AWTSC (with 1.6 factor)	AIRAC (i)	AIRAC (ii)
Broome	42	67	12.5	5.0
Fitzroy Crossing	25	40	7.7	3.1
Liveringa	25	40	9.0	3.7
Noonkanbah	38	61	8.9	3.5
Onslow	34	56	8.2	3.3
Port Hedland	58	93	21.0	8.5

figures in microsieverts but they are shown here in millirem for easier comparison).

By any existing standards, the largest lifetime dose of gamma radiation due to *Mosaic* – even based on the more pessimistic AWTSC figures – was insignificant. The highest dose, at Port Hedland, was less than the amount of radiation the average Australian receives annually from natural sources. All the figures calculated for Port Hedand are only a small fraction of the annual limits, obtaining in 1956 or today, for radiation workers and for members of the public, as Table 7.2 shows. (These figures – except item 4 – are given in millirems for easy comparison. The figures for 1, 3, 8 and 9 are integrated doses, whereas those for 2 and 4 to 7 are annual.)

In 1985 Wise and Moroney – whose reassessments of *Hurricane* and *Totem* have already been referred to – also reassessed the public health impact of the three later series of trials, in 1956 and 1957. For these, especially for *Buffalo* and *Antler*, they had much better data, from the static monitoring stations. They used these fallout records – correcting for proven inefficiencies of the monitoring techniques used – and other contemporary data, including radiological surveys and records of cloud trajectories, and they brought to bear on them the most up to date knowledge on radiation pathways.

Their calculations, covering all twelve nuclear explosions from 1952 to 1957, yield a population dose about 30 times higher overall than that of AIRAC, largely because the contribution of ingested radioactivity was dominant in their analysis.[58] However they warn that their population-weighted averaged doses may be too low by a factor of 2, or too high by a factor of 10. No comparison of their Mosaic figures with those of AWTSC and AIRAC is made here, as they are not on a directly comparable

Table 7.2   Doses of gamma radiation exposure at Port Hedland and ICRP annual and lifetime limits

Doses	Millirems
1 Integrated dose at Port Hedland: calculated from fallout measurement by:	
(a) AWTSC	58
(b) AWTSC (increased by factor of 1.6 to compensate for suggested inefficiency of monitoring 'sticky film')	93
(c) AIRAC	
(i) without shelter factor	21
(ii) with shelter factor	8.5
2 Annual exposure of average Briton or Australian to background radiations (including radon, thoron and their daughter products)	200 approx.
3 Exposure of average Briton or Australian to background radiations over 70 years	14,000 approx.
Limits	
4 UCRP-based annual limit for radiation workers (1956)	15,000 milliroentgens
5 ICRP-based annual limit for radiation workers (1959(77)	12,000 millirems in one year and 5,000 per year on average since age of 18 – dose equivalent
6 ICRP annual limit for radiation workers (post-1977) for 50 years of occupational exposure	5000 millirems effective dose equivalent
7 ICRP limit in any one year for individual members of the public (post-1958)	500 millirems – dose equivalent
8 Lifetime limit for radiation workers proposed by Medical Research Council (1956)	200,000 millirems dose eqivalent
9 ICRP lifetime (70 years) limit for individual members of the public (1985)	7,000 millirems effective dose equivalent

basis. The conclusions that they draw from them, and from their studies of all other tests, about the public health impact on the Australian population are discussed in Chapter 12.

What of Aboriginal safety? At the Royal Commission hearings, Martell was questioned about this, and acknowledged that Aboriginal safety had not been an issue, for two reasons: the Monte Bello Islands themselves were uninhabited, and although this was not the case with the mainland, the G1 and G2 clouds had not been expected to cross the coast.[59]

Penney pointed out that 'we would have looked to the Australians for advice' on Aborigines living on the mainland, and although the Commission was critical of the British for failing to properly consider the possibility of Aborigines, it also noted that this was 'unquestionably the responsibility of the AWTSC'.

8
Buffalo – 1956[1]

The first Maralinga trial

Operation Buffalo, in September–October 1956, broke new ground; the first major trial at Maralinga, its planning was from the outset bound up with the planning and preparation of the new permanent range, and the Australians were more closely involved, especially through the Maralinga committee and the AWTSC (see Chapter 6). *Buffalo*, with four shots, was more extensive than the three previous trials and included the first airdrop from a bomber aircraft with an operational weapon. Associated with the weapon tests was a substantial programme of biological studies and target response experiments. A novel feature was the so-called 'indoctrination' exercise, designed to give some 200–300 officers a practical understanding of atomic weapons and their effects and of the nature of atomic warfare. Altogether it was a big and complex operation.

Besides the scientific and technical preparation for *Buffalo*, the British and their Australian colleagues had four serious concerns. How could the Australian public be informed and reassured? What should be the radiological safety standards for the Australian population? How could meteorological forecasting and the prediction of safe firing conditions be improved? Most immediately, would the range be ready in time?

The rationale for testing

In contrast to the hurried timetable for *Totem* and *Hurricane*, *Buffalo* allowed much more time for the planners. Work began in mid-1954, with the operation (then known as *Theta*) originally scheduled for April–May 1956. Planning considerations put the date back to September–October, however. Suitable meteorological conditions were more likely at that time of year, and it will be noted that all mainland tests took place during that period.

Despite the long lead-time, everybody was affected by the speed at which new ideas appeared. The orderly sequence of development was interrupted by the *Mosaic* trial. It will be recalled that a contingency plan was made in case the required amounts of lithium deuteride were not available for *Mosaic*, in which G2 would have been fired at *Buffalo*. Details were not worked out, but action was taken to procure and build a 300 ft tower at Maralinga. The contingency plan was cancelled when it became clear that *Mosaic* would proceed as planned.

The 1954 plan for *Theta* envisaged four shots: a 10-kiloton test of the *Red Beard* experimental warhead; two 1–5-kiloton ground and/or tower bursts; and an air drop of a Service weapon.[2] This is reasonably close to the pattern of the actual operation two years later, for which a number of rationales can be identified.

The first was the test of Aldermaston's new warhead, *Red Beard*. Britain's first operational weapon, *Blue Danube*, was a very large bomb indeed: at 24 feet long, 5 feet in diameter and weighing 10,000 lb, even the RAF's largest bombers could only just carry it. In November 1953 the Air and Naval staffs issued an Operational Requirement for a smaller weapon (that is, smaller in size, not necessarily in yield) that could be carried by tactical aircraft rather than the large bombers needed for *Blue Danube*.[3]

The new warhead was codenamed *Red Beard*, and while the basic design was very similar to that of *Blue Danube*, some innovations in implosion technique (specifically the 'air lens') had allowed for a reduction in size. These reductions were quite dramatic: *Red Beard* was only half the size of *Blue Danube* and weighed only a fifth as much. Testing this new warhead represented the first purpose for the *Buffalo* trials.

A second, closely related reason for developing smaller atomic warheads was related to the H-bomb decision of 1954. Thermonuclear weapons require fission or atomic explosions as a 'trigger'. Therefore H-bombs encompass a small-scale atomic warhead known as a primary, and this necessarily places a premium on keeping this relatively small. The *Red Beard* implosion assembly, codenamed *Tortoise*, offered clear possibilities in this respect, since its key advantage lay in allowing significant reduction in size.

By early 1956, *Red Beard* had been included in British designs for the *Green Granite* thermonuclear warhead,[4] and with the *Grapple* trials only a year away, testing of the primary was very important. In fact, knowledge of thermonuclear triggers was accorded sufficiently high priority for

Pilgrim to suggest running further tests, to run concurrently with *Buffalo*, at Monte Bello.[5] He considered this 'quite feasible', provided the meteorological conditions would be acceptable (which they probably would) and that the Admiralty would be able to provide the required support (which it certainly would not). The idea was not taken up.

A third reason was boosting of fission warheads. The *Mosaic* trials, as Penney pointed out, had demonstrated that 'we have not made a fundamental mistake', but work on boosted bombs continued. The Service request in OR 1127, which produced *Red Beard*, had also stipulated variable yields (later versions went up as high as 50–100 kilotons[6]) and the growing need for bombs of higher yield, reduced size and the enhanced yield-to-weight ratio kept the boosting concept alive.

Pilgrim had mentioned the possibility of a ground burst in his 1954 note, and this formed a fourth purpose of *Buffalo*. The case in favour of such a test was set out in November 1954 by E. P. Hicks, an expert in fallout prediction.[7] Ground bursts create much more fallout than air bursts, because exploding the warhead in contact with the ground creates far more dust particles which are irradiated by the explosion, but Hicks noted that 'we know very little indeed' about ground bursts beyond this fact. The same was true for the Americans, who had freely admitted as much to their British counterparts, and Hicks pointed out that a British ground burst might therefore provide 'useful bargaining counters'. Information on the cratering and ground-shock effects was also thin. Moreover, the fallout data from an atomic ground burst could be used to estimate contamination levels from hydrogen bombs: data provided by the Americans had suggested that this was a relatively simple calculation, according to Hicks. His conclusion was that 'the ground burst [is] the only effects trial worth pursuing', an opinion clearly shared at Aldermaston.

A fifth rationale was a first for the British: a service operational test of a *Blue Danube* bomb. It was felt necessary to experiment with an RAF drop of the *Blue Danube*, since at the time none of the British nuclear weapons had been tested like this. The physics package itself had already been tested, of course, but not the weapon in its full operational form.

Thus the four *Buffalo* shots were driven by weapons development objectives (*Red Beard*, boosted weapons, thermonuclear primaries, the service drop) and weapons effects (the ground burst). They also provided opportunities for target response and, in a new development, indoctrinees.

The target response and biology programme

Maralinga afforded greater opportunities than Monte Bello or Emu Field for target response experiments, and this advantage had been one of the arguments for the permanent range. Nevertheless, in its unfinished state and with scanty water supplies, the range could accommodate only limited extra numbers at *Buffalo*, and proposed experiments had to be rigorously scrutinized. At an early stage in planning, the *Buffalo* Executive (Buffalex) asked government departments to submit bids, and it set up a target response sub-committee to coordinate them. With its assistance, J. T. Tomblin, Pilgrim's deputy, and later the target response coordinator, E. R. Drake Seager, produced order out of the chaos of proposals.

The Services put forward an extensive programme, to which the Australian Services also contributed. It included the exposure of six Swift aircraft; three Centurion tanks; guns of various types; ammunition and explosives; structures (including bridges, runways and sheds); equipment (Service clothing, respirators, radio sets, telephones and instruments of various kinds); medical supplies; and materials (plastics, paints, packaging, etc.). Not all these items were the 'real thing': with the main future threat believed to be H-bombs, many of the structures used were models scaled down so that the atomic explosion would have a similar effect to a thermonuclear explosion on a full-scale structure.[8]

The Services also had a strong interest in some of the work of the Biological Group, which had an extensive and – by British standards – ambitious programme. When Buffalex invited bids, the Medical and Agricultural Research Councils (MRC and ARC) replied promptly that they wanted to take the opportunity of validating certain laboratory conclusions in the field, as well as carrying out biological experiments that were possible only with an actual weapon detonation.

They proposed two different ingestion studies and some blast-effect experiments. For the first, they wanted to pasture some grazing animals on an acre of grassland sown and maintained in the fallout area within a few miles of the explosion. These animals would be slaughtered at the site after a few days, and autopsied to investigate the uptake of radioactive fallout. For the second, they wanted to determine the effect of fallout on sheep downwind of the test area; samples of tissues and organs would be required for analysis, and in this biological monitoring programme they needed the cooperation of the Australian agricultural scientists. For both types of investigation, the MRC recommended joint Anglo-Australian teams, especially as these studies were of particular interest to the Australian authorities. The blast experiments were expected to use mice and a few large animals, say ten sheep, in shelters. Penney commented on the proposals:

I have to admit that the suggestion rather frightens me, because I know from experience what tremendous complications arise at trials when animals are included, especially large animals like cows and sheep. The building of shelters and the introduction of test animals is another matter of great complexity ... very difficult to get useful results.

Plans for the experiments were discussed in May 1955 by the Research Councils and Aldermaston, and then by a biology subcommittee of Buffalex chaired by Dr J. F. Loutit of the MRC. It was agreed that the ingestion experiments could not be simulated by sprinkling radioactive material on grass, and that the grass must be exposed to real contamination downwind of the explosion. As the direction of the fallout could not be determined until a few hours before firing, it would not be practicable to sow a sufficiently large sector of pastureland; about 100 trays of grasses, 18 inches square and 9 inches deep, would have to be strategically placed shortly before firing. This would limit the number of sheep that could be grazed, but six would be the minimum. They would not be taken into the area of the explosion or exposed to an injurious level of external radiation.[9]

The blast experiments were to be done for Dr (later Lord) Zuckerman, who was investigating for the War Office the effect of hydrostatic pressure in a blast wave on living creatures. Much of his programme was carried out in the laboratory, using small animals and a simulated blast wave in a shock tube; to extrapolate with confidence from small animals to man, he needed experiments with intermediate-sized animals, such as goats. The experiments would be concerned only with the blast wave and not with radiation or heat, or with secondary effects of blast, and the caged animals were to be placed in hollow pits or shelters to reduce secondary or thermal injuries. The numbers proposed were 200 mice, 140 rabbits and 20 goats. All this would mean a few extra trials staff and some additional facilities.[10]

These plans were approved in August 1955 for submission to British ministers; the use of live animals was clearly a politically sensitive topic in Britain. On 29 August Eden sought Australian agreement. In a message to Menzies he wrote:

> We are naturally anxious to make the fullest use of the opportunity afforded by these trials to carry out experiments to cover not only matters of purely military interest but also those affecting the assessment of the effects of atomic warfare on both public health and agriculture. ... The authorities responsible for research into medical and agricultural aspects of atomic explosions are pressing for the

inclusion in the trials of a number of experiments which involve the use of live animals. This is always a contentious subject and we have therefore ... reduced the programme to what we regard as a minimum. ... It covers experiments for which an actual weapon explosion alone can give the necessary conditions. ... I should be grateful for your sympathetic consideration.

There is another associated matter. We are anxious to study the effects of distant fallout from atomic explosions on the bone tissue of animals. A conventional way of doing this would be to arrange for the collection of bone samples from sheep or rabbits from a number of widely separated places in Australia. This could, I believe, readily be done by your agricultural services and I should be grateful for your agreement in principle so that our experts may make an approach to yours.[11]

With this message went a description of the proposed experiments. Menzies agreed but, as the use of live animals could arouse considerable public interest, he wanted Australian scientists to be given full information about the experiments so that the Australian government could deal effectively with any critical comments. Eden thanked Menzies warmly. Indeed, without the active participation of Australian scientists at Maralinga and in the universities of Sydney and Adelaide, the experiments would have been quite impracticable. The following month Dr Scott Russell, of the ARC and the Department of Agriculture, Oxford University, went to Australia to meet Professor J. Wood, of Adelaide University, who was to be the Australian adviser on the programme, and his team of animal and plant experts.

Besides the animal experiments on blast effects and the two ingestion studies, there were several other biological studies. One involved the weekly collection of sheep thyroids from three sheep stations 150–200 miles from Maralinga, to be assayed for radioactive iodine. Another was a survey of local flora and fauna after Rounds 1 and 2. A third was the exposure to radiation of cereals ripe for harvest. Other activities included the collection of fission product samples and contaminated soil to be flown back to the United Kingdom for experimental use by the MRC and ARC.[12]

The Biology Group planned two other sets of investigations not involving animals, which were important for both civil defence and the protection of troops. The first, conducted by Dr W. J. H. (later Sir John) Butterfield, of the MRC, was into the hazards of broken glass, since it was known that flying glass from broken windows had been a serious source of injury in Japan. In one of these experiments, glass samples were place in steel fragmentation boxes at various distances up to 10 miles from ground zero. In another, glass fitted in steel window frames was mounted in four 8 ft wooden packing cases. In both experiments telephone directories fixed inside the box or packing case were used to catch the glass projectiles, and to enable calculations to be made of the depth of penetration.

The second set of investigations was to be carried out using human dummies. A total of 78 dummies, designed to resemble humans in height, weight, centre of gravity and ballistically (that is, in how they would fall through the air) were used in these experiments.[13] Despite recurrent stories, it is not true that live soldiers were used (see below). Thirty of the dummies, dressed in Army uniform, were to be positioned at various distances from ground zero, some standing, some crouching and some prone. Some had accelerometers in the chest cavity. Forty-eight other dummies were to be placed in tanks, scout cars and various other vehicles; in groups with field guns or anti-aircraft guns; in large steel shelters; and in medium machinegun pits. The experiment was concerned with blast rather than radiation or thermal effects; the object was to see how soldiers could best be protected, or could protect themselves, from injury by blast from an atomic weapon.

In the *Buffalo* Summary Plan of April 1956 one section was devoted to the Biology Group, which numbered 16 in all. The group leader was Dr Scott Russell, and his deputy was Dr Butterfield. There were six Australian members (from the Commonwealth Scientific and Industrial Research Organization – CSIRO), and one Canadian scientist. The group was to be assisted by Professor H. R. Marston of Adelaide University, chief of the CSIRO Division of Biochemical and General Nutrition, and three of his staff. Professor P. L. Krohn and Dr J. McGregor, of Birmingham University, were also members, and there were others from the MRC, the RAMC (Royal Army Medical Corps) and Harwell.

The Indoctrinee Force

The proposal that servicemen should attend the trials was first made, and agreed by the British Chiefs of Staff, early in 1955. The War Office considered this to be 'of the greatest importance' in view of the fact that virtually no service personnel had witnessed an atomic explosion or had any realization of its effects.[14] *Buffalo*, it was thought, would be an opportunity 'to spread the confidence which comes from personal experience and dispel fear of the unknown'. The Americans had already made use of atomic tests to indoctrinate whole formations of troops, on a scale that the British could not begin to emulate.

The Australian government agreed in principle in June 1955. At first 400 'indoctrinees' were envisaged, but this number was too ambitious and plans were worked out for 250. Places were allocated to the British and Australian forces, predominantly to the two armies. The RAF's *Buffalo* commitments were already so heavy that the Air Ministry did not want any places on the Indoctrinee Force (IF). The Chiefs of Staff approved plans in December 1955, and nominations were called for – all officers, most of them captains, majors or lieutenant-colonels. After many changes, due largely to the Suez Crisis which began to loom in July 1956, there were eventually 178 British officers and civilians, about 70 Australian officers and five from New Zealand.

The stated purpose was to enable these selected officers:

(a) to experience the effects of a nuclear explosion;
(b) to examine the effects of such explosion on the ground and on weapons and equipment;
(c) to pass on their experience to other members of the Armed Forces at the conclusion of the trial.

The programme for the IF was to consist of lectures and general instruction very much on Staff College lines, including syndicate work and the writing of original appreciations of military aspects of the new weapon. Before round 1, there would be a tour of the range, particularly to see the target response material: the nuclear explosion would be observed from a stand at a distance of about $4\frac{1}{2}$ miles; and there would be a post-firing conducted tour to see the effects of the explosion. The timetable of instruction for the first week was intensive, with highly expert lecturers, including Penney, and lecture topics ranging over 'blast, genetics, nuclear physics, nutrition, meteorology, heat effects, ionization and decontamination'. The Army officers were to be much impressed by the importance of meteorology – and by their 'abysmal ignorance' of it.

Preparing the range

The original *Buffalo* plan set 1 August 1956 as the arrival date of the main scientific party at the range, and 29 August as the first possible firing date for Round 1,[15] but by the beginning of 1956 the prospect of completing the Maralinga range in time for a major trial in

September/October looked uncertain. Progress made on the site by the Kwinana Construction Group was unsatisfactory, but in the forward area, for security reasons, work was to be done by servicemen, not the civilian labour force. The Australian task force – including an augmented Army field engineer troop and RAN and RAAF personnel – was due to arrive soon.

The task force moved into 43 Mile Camp (see Map 5) in February as planned. Their morale, it was reported, was high, despite a shortage of water for washing, and temperatures up to 105° F in the shade and a ferocious 132 °F on the ground.

Clearly, to meet the deadlines, a lower standard of construction would have to be accepted and even some of the major work, as well as minor jobs, would have to be deferred until after *Buffalo*. Serious delays were caused by an Australian dock strike and the continuing shortage of water; however, by late June it appeared that the basic essentials would be ready by 31 July. The advance scientific party arrived on 20 June, but the village was not yet habitable; buildings were unfinished, the power station was not yet functioning, water was scarce and hygiene was appalling.[16] The scientists had to join the task force at 43 Mile Camp for two or three weeks. The water supply, from four bore holes, was still disturbingly inadequate. Then, ironically, the range was deluged with continuous heavy rain for three weeks, which further delayed progress, especially on road and runway construction.[17]

The main body of the scientific staff reached Adelaide in July. Then, instead of coming by special train to Watson as originally planned, they were flown to Maralinga by the RAF in parties of 50; the last – which included Roy Pilgrim, the deputy director of the trial – arrived on 17 August.[18]

Very soon, between 19 and 23 August, the IF of some 250 men would be arriving also. The Australian Army had set up a separate camp for them, 11 miles from the railhead at Watson and 12 miles from Maralinga village; officially named Gundulph, it was usually called Eleven Mile Camp, or Seaview Holiday Camp.[19]

Weeks before, on 1 August, Reginald Maudling, the British Minister of Supply, had written to Beale, his opposite number in Australia, to express satisfaction at the completion of the range and gratitude for Australian cooperation. At the same time he wrote to the consulting engineers, Sir Alexander Gibb and Partners, to thank them, and in particular to commend the indefatigable resident engineer.[20] But considering the immensely difficult conditions and the impossibility of working during the hottest weeks of the summer, there had been too little time, and much work was still unfinished when the Kwinana

Photograph 1   Cable-laying in the Monte Bellos. For *Hurricane* some 150 miles of cable had to be laid between the islands.

Photograph 2   Before *Hurricane* – Dr W. G. Penney confers with the Scientific Superintendent, Dr L. C. Tyte.

Photograph 3 On board HMS *Campania* at Monte Bello. Right to left: L. C. Tyte, W. A. S. Butement (Chief Scientist, Commonwealth Department of Supply and Development), Captain A. B. Cole RN, Rear Admiral A. D. Torlesse, W. G. Penney, L. H. Martin (Melbourne University) O. M. Solandt (Chairman, Canadian Defence Research Board).

Photograph 4 A re-entry party at *Hurricane*, wearing protective clothing. Light-coloured clothing was used for later trials to minimize heat stress.

Photograph 5 At Emu Field – Sir William Penney with C. A. Adams (left) and E. Titterton (right).

Photograph 6   The terrain at Emu Field.

Photograph 7   Operation Hotbox – the aircrew and their Canberra at *Totem*. Right to left: Group Captain D. A. Wilson (observer), Wing Commander G. Dhenin (pilot) and Wing Commander E. W. Anderson (navigator).

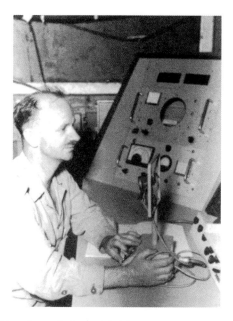

Photograph 8   Firing Control – Ieuan Maddock at *Mosaic*.

Photograph 9 Maralinga – Eleven Mile Camp, the home of the *Buffalo* Indoctrinee Force.

Photograph 10 The warhead for the 'Marcoo' test at the *Buffalo* series being lowered into its pit. Uniquely at Maralinga, the test was conducted at ground level to provide information about cratering effects.

Photograph 11

Photograph 12

Photograph 13

Photographs 11–13 This dramatic 'before, during and after' sequence shows the effects of an atomic explosion on a Land Rover placed 600 yards from ground zero at the *Buffalo* trials. Photograph 11 was taken shortly before detonation; Photograph 12 by remote camera as the blast wave engulfs the vehicle; Photograph 13 shows the same jeep after the explosion. The experiment was part of the Target Response programme to assess the effects of nuclear explosions on military equipment.

Photograph 14 Dummies were used to study the effects of atomic explosion on servicemen and to determine the best methods of protection. The dummies used at *Buffalo* were well made and very life-like.

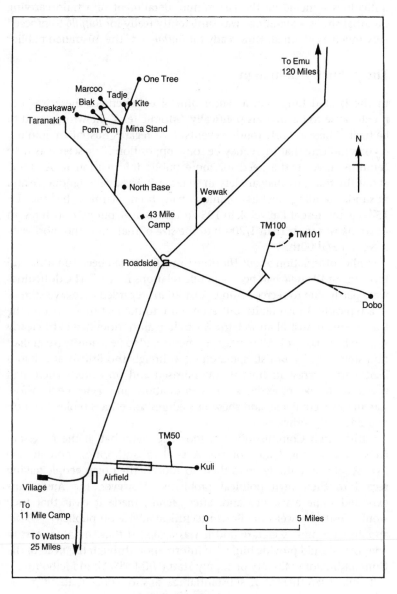

Map 5 The Maralinga range

Construction Group handed over. However, after all the delays and difficulties – including the last-minute derailment of a train carrying essential stores – Maralinga was sufficiently ready for *Buffalo* to proceed very much as planned. How ready for *Buffalo* was the Australian public?

The publicity campaign

In the United Kingdom, a senior official commented, there was not much cause to be anxious politically. 'Atomic tests', he wrote, 'tend to be treated here as fairly routine events ... As regards Australian opinion, reports indicate that there may be some opposition'. The scientists were certainly alive to the need for more public information in Australia about the trials, to allay anxiety in so far as it was due to ignorance and misunderstanding. Public opinion had been alarmed by the US 15-megaton test at Eniwetok in 1954 (*Castle Bravo*), but no British test in Australia was more than 1/200th of the size of that shot, and most were less than 1/1000th.[21]

Public information about *Hurricane* and *Totem* had been too little and too late, and *Mosaic* had been a public relations fiasco.[22] The difficulties were partly due to secrecy (some Australians regarded excessive secrecy as a typically British fault), but even more to the fact that, because the trials were on Australian soil, the Australian authorities had to be clearly seen to be in control. All public statements had to be made by Australian ministers, not by British spokesmen, although the British also had a legitimate interest in how it was released and presented. There had therefore to be procedures for consultation and agreement before statements were made, and these procedures sometimes broke down on one side or the other.

British High Commission staff took the view that, if the necessary facts were in the hands of the Australian authorities, notably the AWTSC, it was 'entirely up to them to educate their own people having regard to their own political problems'. However, the Australians expected some assistance and, after *Mosaic*, made it clear that they would positively welcome British technical advice on publicity.[23] Beale appointed a press secretary and it was arranged that the Aldermaston scientists should provide him with information through the head of the United Kingdom Ministry of Supply Staff (UKMOSS(A)) in Melbourne.[24]

By mid-1956 there were substantial reasons for concern about public relations. Up to this time, there had been little opposition in Australia to the trials, but worldwide hostility to all nuclear tests was growing (see Chapter 5) and in Australia it naturally focused on the British tests.

Hurricane and *Totem* had been tolerated as 'one-off' operations, but the establishment of Maralinga as a permanent range implied a continuing programme of tests. By June 1956, 60 per cent of the Australian public was against the tests, according to an opinion poll, and the Opposition Party in Parliament had taken up the issue.[25]

Moreover since Maralinga was in the centre of the continent, assurances could not be given that the fallout would be blown out to sea, as at Monte Bello. The British scientists therefore had to be able to convince the Australian scientists, and through them the politicians and public, that the tests would not deposit harmful radioactive fallout on the mainland (at least, beyond the test area). It was always obvious that at Maralinga radioactive clouds would traverse much of the continent before reaching the coast. But after the G2 scare at Monte Bello, Beale had decided that the best line to take was to emphasize, as a guarantee of safety, that the cloud had gone out to sea. This, as we have seen, had not been a success and, as Adams ruefully pointed out, by focusing attention on whether or not the cloud had crossed the coast, Beale's statements had fostered two erroneous beliefs, both prejudicial to Maralinga.[26] The first fallacy that had to be belatedly explained away after Mosaic was that as long as the cloud did not cross the coast there would be no radioactive fallout on the mainland. The second was that no place under the trajectory of a radioactive cloud was safe. But the truth was that the deposition of fallout, not the cloud trajectory, was the crucial factor, and the trajectory was important only for prediction and cloud-tracking purposes. The real facts would have to be effectively presented to the Australian public before Buffalo if panic headlines were to be avoided.[27]

By mid-1956 there were serious problems, and in June, Penney was sufficiently concerned to raise the issue with Brundrett. He proposed three steps: to hold a press conference attended by himself and Beale; to give the AWTSC more detailed information about the *Blue Danube* and *Red Beard* warheads to be tested at *Buffalo* (including the amount of fissile material in each); and to give 'somewhat better treatment than I had originally proposed' to a party of Australian MPs who would be viewing one of the *Buffalo* shots.[28] The visit by the MPs had been agreed in response to a request from Menzies for a party of a dozen parliamentarians to watch some of the *Buffalo* shots. Penney had initially opposed their viewing more than one shot, but was now waiving that objection, and also offered to give the MPs a short talk.

Brundrett concurred on the political difficulties: 'The Australian situation is getting distinctly messy', he wrote to Richard Powell. 'I am sure

Penney is right in thinking we should be wise to take out an insurance policy'.[29] Penney's first suggestion of a press conference was eminent common sense, and the conference was held on 14 August, the day after his arrival in Australia. Penney, Beale wrote, was masterly. He was also invited to make a guest of honour broadcast, and gave some effective press conferences and radio and television interviews.

The second suggestion, about informing members of the AWTSC about warhead design, was more contentious. This was regarded as a radical departure from present British policy and also, more seriously, 'flatly contrary to our post-war understanding with the Americans'.[30] He conceded, however, that it might be done if strictly necessary, and the consensus appears to be that it *was* necessary. Brundrett discussed the idea with Penney, and they agreed that there would be no significant security risk in sharing the information with the restricted group of the AWTSC.

Moreover, Menzies had given the Committee strict instructions not to agree to the tests unless they were satisfied about safety, and the weapons details were the minimum that would allow them to make calculations on yield. Penney regarded the AWTSC as 'solidly with us, but conservative and apprehensive'. He and Brundrett both believed that permission to fire would be refused unless they shared the information. The Chiefs of Staff concurred and Brundrett obtained ministerial approval for the step in July.[31]

Pennney's third recommendation was also accepted, and the Australian parliamentarians were present for the first two shots at *Buffalo*. The pre-trial publicity campaign, strongly advocated by Penney, was launched in the summer of 1956. British ministers had wanted to keep publicity about *Mosaic* to a minimum (because it was mainly of a scientific character and was in aid of *Grapple*), but they agreed that *Buffalo* was quite another matter. Facilities should be offered to the press, and 15 Australian and British press representatives invited to witness the first shot.

The publicity plan included feature articles on Maralinga prepared by the Ministry of the Interior, articles by Howard Beale, and papers on scientific aspects of the trials written by British experts for use by the Australian authorities. A long article by Beale, dealing comprehensively with the trials, appeared in all the main daily newspapers on 6 August 1956. Australia, he wrote, had both the wide empty spaces and the facilities needed for atomic weapon tests which, he argued, were essential to the defence of the Commonwealth and also provided invaluable information on civil defence, crucial to the protection of the population in the case of an atomic war. He went on to describe the nature of fallout and to outline the findings of the recently published Himsworth and Bronk reports. Australia, he said, was firmly in control of the tests and, through the AWTSC, of the safety standards applied. As for the demand that tests should be stopped, he would strongly support an end to testing by all the nuclear powers – as proposed by the British Prime Minister – but not by Britain unilaterally.

The most telling contribution was probably the visit by Australian parliamentarians to Maralinga during *Buffalo*. It has been suggested that the publicity campaign was a brainwashing operation intended to ensure the continuation of the tests. It could also be considered simply as a way of providing the Australian public with sufficient information to understand the tests being carried out in their country, to give them the facts and to dispel some erroneous notions. Beale's articles, for example, were certainly informative, as well as enthusiastic and persuasive in tone.

Safety of the population

Once again, the safety of the Australian population depended on its exclusion from the danger area, on the setting of adequate safety standards and safe firing criteria, on accurate meteorological forecasting and fallout prediction, and on post-firing checks – by cloud-tracking aircraft, aerial and ground radiological surveys and monitoring. The network of fixed monitoring stations had been extended from 29 to over 80.

Exclusion from the danger area

In the area that would be affected by short-range fallout there were no stations, homesteads or missions, and the only danger would be to intruders or to Aboriginal nomads who might be moving across the range. As we have seen, Butement had assured Penney – who had no reason to doubt him – that no Aborigines lived on the range, few ever traversed it and none needed to. Butement clearly regarded the area as a vast, empty, arid and uninhabitable space.

The rocket range established in 1949 had already created a large prohibited area stretching across the continent from Woomera,[32] and a native patrol officer, W. B. MacDougall, had been appointed to cover the South Australia section; later his responsibilities were extended to Western Australia. There was at that time no coordinated Australian Commonwealth approach to Aboriginal welfare or to such major issues as reserves, segregation, protection of nomadic lifestyles, or assimilation, and the policies of the Western Australia and South Australia governments in those areas were different. MacDougall thought that the reserves should be gradually eliminated and that the Aboriginals should be assimilated and given opportunities in Australian society ('we have taken away their beliefs and customs and trespassed on their lands, and we have a moral obligation to give them something in return'), but meanwhile their interests must be protected.[33] One of his responsibilities was to identify ceremonial grounds or sacred localities and to advise the authorities on how to avoid giving unnecessary offence to the Aboriginals.

At first he had no staff and few resources for patrolling his enormous parish, in which he estimated that about 1,000 Aboriginals were living, though he had not been able to carry out the thorough population surveys he wished to do. In 1955 a young assistant native patrol officer, R. A. Macaulay, was appointed to work at Giles, where the new meteorological station was being built, in an area where Aboriginals had been living in virtual isolation from white men. MacDougall and Macaulay were responsible for assessing the Aboriginal situation at the time of tests at Maralinga, getting information from their own patrol activities, from local homesteads and missions, and from police and security officers. On the basis of this information and of air surveys (the value of which has been much debated) before each trial, the scientific director was advised, before he took a decision to fire, that there were no people in the danger area on the Range.

Shortly before *Buffalo* an Aboriginal gathering (or *corroboree*) took place near Mount Penrhyn and MacDougall was concerned that after the trial some of them might cross the fallout area on their way home. Arrangements were made for security and police officers, and the 20 members of the Australian Radiation Detection Unit (ARDU) engaged in fallout surveys, to keep watch for any parties, to tell them which way was safe and to move them out of danger if necessary.

Safety outside the danger area

Safety outside the danger area was, as before, a problem of intermediate range fallout. The primary requirement for safe firing was that such fallout should not cause anyone to receive a dose of radiation above the acceptable dose for members of the public; however, at the time of *Buffalo*, ICRP was still concerned with the protection of people occupationally exposed to radiation and had made no recommendations about limits for exposures of the public.

The secondary standard, derived from the radiation dose limit, was the level of radioactive material on the ground that it was calculated would give rise to that dose. It was defined in micro-curies per square metre. It may be noted that the micro-curies per square metre could not be measured directly but had to be derived from readings given by monitoring instruments which measured radiation dose rates either in counts per second or per minute (cps or cpm) or in millirads per hour.

The main business of the theoretical predictions staff was to plot the theoretical fallout contours, showing – for a warhead of a given yield and in various specific conditions – how far from ground zero the unacceptable levels of fallout would extend. It was the responsibility of the meteorological staff to provide forecasts so that the fallout contours could be predicted and advice given when it would be safe to fire.[34]

For *Buffalo*, the safety document (report 041/55) relating to fallout levels was one that Aldermaston scientists had produced in 1955 in succession to A32. It replaced the 'zero risk' level with level A, and the 'slight risk' level with level B (corresponding to 3 r and 25 r respectively). For *Mosaic* and *Buffalo*, levels of surface activity were calculated that – taking into account all kinds of radiation and all modes of exposure (external and internal) – would result in theoretical exposures at level A (3 r) or half of level B (12.5 r). These values were used for plotting fallout contours before a decision to fire was taken.[35]

It had been during *Mosaic* that Adams had suggested to the AWTSC that, as an additional safety factor, 1/2B should be adopted instead of B. The AWTSC had been concerned that the limits calculated by Aldermaston applied to people wearing clothes and living in houses, and had therefore asked the Aldermaston scientists to think about special limits to safeguard Aboriginals living in a tribal state, unprotected by buildings or clothing or footwear. The result was an appendix to report 0.41/55, produced in April 1956, which defined reduced levels A and B (later designated A^1 and B^1); these levels were lower by a factor of 5, a reduction that would entail a considerable extension of the fallout contours beyond the original A and B lines and would therefore impose more restrictive firing conditions.[36]

The AWTSC also decided that more information was needed about the number and distribution of Aboriginals in the areas outside the prohibited area which might nevertheless he affected by early, or intermediate, fallout. It is surprising that such an enquiry, which MacDougall had wanted, was not put in hand before the original decision to conduct trials at Maralinga was made, but it was at least made before major trials began there. A survey by MacDougall and Macaulay estimated the population in question at about 1,600, and the limit of their migrations at about 150 miles from the trials area.

A report by the AWTSC to the Prime Minister, via the Minister for Supply, set out the position and gave examples of fallout patterns from a nominal (i.e. 20-kiloton) detonation at Maralinga, using the most recent data from the two *Totem* shots, which had been fired in such contrasting meteorological conditions – T1 with practically no wind shear and T2 with a high degree of wind shear. In their report the committee recommended that level A should be used as the criterion for trials at Maralinga. It was lower than the level thought acceptable for a white population; at 3 r, it was only a quarter of half level B (used for *Mosaic*) and one eighth of level B which was understood to be the American standard for the Nevada test site. The whole matter was submitted to the Australian Cabinet which, in September 1956, approved the adoption of level A. But as Maralinga, unlike Monte Bello and Emu Field, was to be a permanent range, they made it a condition that fallout contours should not overlap so as to expose the same areas repeatedly.

It would be confusing to attempt to compare the various levels of surface activity, in terms of radioactivity per unit area, tabulated in the various scientific reports. What is important is the radiation exposure to which the levels correspond; the relationship between them is not a simple arithmetical one. The radiation dose limit for *Buffalo* was fixed with particular regard to the vulnerability of any Aboriginals who might be in a fallout region. Between *Hurricane* and *Buffalo* the dose limit, for external gamma radiation, had come down from 25 r ('slight risk' or level B) to 12.5 r (half level B, for *Mosaic*) to 3 r (level A). It should be remembered that these were the radiation standards used for planning; they were not actual radiation exposures.

It may well be argued that both the British and Australian the authorities had been slow to take account of Aboriginals in their fallout calculations. It may also be thought that the various arrangements made to keep Aboriginals away from danger were insufficient. However the AWTSC, once set up, took the safety of the Aboriginals seriously, and the British scientists – with limited knowledge of the problem, and necessarily relying on Australian information, advice and action – had always been concerned about it. The wider question of Aboriginal interests, the restrictions on their movements and the denial of access to territory is a separate one (see Chapter 13).

Planning the operation

It was always apparent that *Buffalo* would not be an easy operation. Maddock, in a prescient note in 1954, said that this first trial 'with a fair number of bangs', given the 'somewhat depressing meteorological probabilities', would mean a long time at the site unless plans were made to minimize delays in every way. The whole duration of one operation, and the sequence of preparation, should be limited, he said, to about six hours so that opportunities could be quickly seized. The trials staff were very likely, he thought, to strike a similar period to that before *Totem* 1, with consistently unfavourable meteorological conditions; staff morale was vital in such a situation. The airdrop would present novel problems; though the weapon was intended to fire high above the ground, the worst must be assumed – that is, that the radar fuses would fail to function. If the weapon detonated on impact with the ground, contamination would be severe and the ground shock considerable. Before the live drop, both the RAF and the telemetry group would therefore need practice drops, including drops with small H E bombs.[37]

The interdepartmental executive committee that functioned as Mosex or Buffalex, according to the matter in hand, held its first meeting on 11 November 1954. Penney was appointed as scientific director of *Buffalo*, and Pilgrim was his deputy and chief planning officer. Later, Air Commodore C. T. Weir RAF was appointed as Task Force Commander. Planning, and visits to and from Australia, proceeded throughout 1955 and early 1956, and the problems of Maralinga and *Buffalo* were inextricably intertwined. The main preoccupations of Buffalex were the readiness of the range, the target response programme, the biological experiments and the Indoctrinee Force (see below).[38]

By March 1956 an outline timetable had been drawn up, and a summary plan was ready in June. This plan set out the organization of the trials staff. The scientific groups came under the headings of HQ, Safety, Weapon, Measurement and Target Response; those concerned with safety were the meteorology, theoretical predictions, health physics and decontamination groups. Australians were to staff the seismological, meteorological and radio-flash measurement groups, and were to make a big contribution to the health physics and target response work. Twenty-five Canadians were to take part as a radiation detection unit (RDU).

As before, there were to be considerable RAF and RAAF contingents, responsible for air patrols, surveys, cloud sampling and tracking and so on, but on this occasion the RAF was to have the new and demanding task of assembling and dropping the test bomb. A provisional timetable gave 1 August 1956 as the date of arrival of the main scientific party, 22 August for the scientific rehearsal of Round 1, 26 August for the operational rehearsal and 28 August as the beginning of standby. The order of firing was expected to be tower burst, ground burst, second tower burst, air burst. Practice flights for the live airdrop were planned to begin on 12 September.

Except for the airdrop, firing was expected to be early in the morning, at 07:00 hrs (local time). The timetable required that on each day of standby, meteorological forecasts were to be made at 07:00 hrs, 14:00 hrs and 19:00 hrs. If the last was favourable D-1 would be declared and the firing phase would begin; forecasts would follow at midnight, 02:00 hrs and 06:00 hrs, with wind balloon ascents at 05:00 hrs and 06:15 hrs; at 06:55 hrs, the scientific director would give instructions to start the master clock, and firing would take place. After firing, movement control would be established at Roadside and a mobile health unit (the health physics 'circus' of caravans) would be set up.

The plan envisaged a total of 1,350 men at Maralinga. There would be 200 scientists from Aldermaston and Harwell, 70 from other departments, 30 Australians and 50 Canadians. The Indoctrinee Force was expected to number about 250. There would be 500 RAF and RAAF personnel, and about 250 Australian servicemen responsible for keeping the range and the camps running. There would besides be various short-term visitors – the Australian parliamentarians, six high-ranking US observers, and journalists. The numbers were much larger than had been envisaged when Maralinga was planned, and the village and the camps would certainly be overcrowded at times.[39]

The four shots are fired

One Tree – Round 1

The first round, One Tree, was to be a tower-mounted test of the new plutonium warhead, *Red Beard*. Though its expected yield was about 16 kilotons, it was much smaller in dimensions than the Mk I bomb, *Blue Danube*. Round 1 was also the main target response round, and the one to which the Australian parliamentarians and the press were invited.[40]

Standby was declared on 11 September, with Martin, Titterton, Butement and Dwyer, of the Australian Weapon Tests Safety Committee, all present. The party of Australian parliamentarians, led by Beale, had left Canberra by air for Maralinga on 10 September, and it was hoped that Round 1 would be fired soon after they arrived. Meteorological conditions had been favourable for two or three days before standby, but then the weather changed; firing was cancelled on 12 September, and the parliamentarians had to return disappointed.

Conditions continued unfavourable from 13 to 18 September. A revised schedule of forecasts was then introduced, allowing for either morning or evening firing (at 07:00 or 17:00 hrs), and the timetable was compressed into 12 hours or less, instead of 24. Maddock had been right two years earlier! On the statistical evidence available, not more than one satisfactory occasion in a month was likely to occur; however, experience at the site showed that other opportunities occurred but remained favourable only for a few hours. The change of plan imposed a heavy load on the meteorological group, and Penney cabled home urgently for an additional meteorologist to reinforce the team; he arrived on 1 October. A Canadian scientist and another Australian were also added.

Firing on 20 September was again cancelled, but preparations for firing on the 21st continued through the night. The parliamentarians from Canberra arrived once more, but were again disappointed. 'We have had a tough night', Penney signalled Aldermaston:

> Met forecasts, originally rosy, got progressively worse, until we ended with forecast and observed winds over wide area showing less than degree variation ground to 35,000 ft pointing precisely at Oodnadatta. [See Map 3.] With several homesteads nearer could not prejudice future of Range, and therefore cancelled without last-minute fight with Safety Committee undoubtedly ending with their veto. Showed Press and Parliamentarians non-secret apparatus, and hope we made deep impression on care which we exercise and quality of our work. Three of most important Labour leaders appeared to become friendly and sympathetic. Press had discovered reason for postponement so saw them and told them what they knew already. I believe that this abortive night may have valuable long-term effects ... I have done my best to win confidence of Australians and keep long-term use Maralinga ... Everyone here behaved magnificently and took the disappointment like men. Parliamentarians will not return for first shot, but some may come to second shot, which is much easier.

Another alert was declared for 23 September, but by the evening of the 22nd rapid changes in low-level winds caused yet another cancellation. The weather remained unsuitable until the 25th, when forecasts for the morning of the 26th were promising. Penney signalled:

> Tried again last night and cancelled in last few minutes. Winds at cloud height were rapidly turning towards south. Firing opportunity was real but lasted six hours and we missed. Main worry Safety Committee thunderstorms Adelaide to Melbourne. This was political

and not safety. Last minute telephone consultation Martin to Beale resulted in advice to postpone. I should probably have delayed one hour at last minute because of danger to Maralinga and small settlements on railway and would then have postponed.

Speaking for people at site we are going to try to catch every firing opportunity that is safe. Am asking Safety Committee to get Beale and Menzies approached to accept political disturbance due to counts in rainwater magnified by the trouble makers.

Real culprit is completely exceptional weather. Conditions vary widely every few hours and Australian meteorological grid cannot cope with fine structure.

Am studying arrangements firings but not easy. Have Olympic Games dates in mind but still believe weather will not continue bad. [The Olympic Games were to be held in Melbourne in November 1956.]

Grateful advise if my No. 1 priority not to prejudice future of Maralinga is correct. Difficult for me here because I cannot fully assess strength of trouble makers raising scares by rainwater counts. We can never guarantee that activity will not be found in rain 500 or more miles away.[41]

At Aldermaston, Cook swiftly drafted a firm response: 'You should exert all possible pressure to be allowed to fire when conditions are safe. You should not be deterred from exerting pressure by political troublemakers raising scares. Number one priority in your present circumstances is to fire the rounds under safe conditions. The future of Maralinga takes second place'.[42]

Cook sent this draft to Jackson at the Ministry of Supply, who discussed the matter with Brundrett and How, and produced a very different re-draft: 'it is important to retain the confidence of the Australian government and to reassure Australian opinion so that we can carry on at Maralinga in future years. While therefore you should not be deterred from exerting pressure to fire under safe conditions by chance of troublemakers raising scares, you must take note of political objections represented to you by official sources and which are real to the Australian government'.[43]

Jackson stressed to Cook that 'We cannot, particularly in the early days of the range, afford to ride roughshod over Australian political opinion'. This discussion was about crossing a bridge when one comes to it, but Cook and Jackson clearly differed over *which* bridge. The unspoken word here is, of course, *Grapple*. Failure to complete *Buffalo* would have serious knock-on effects for the 1957 trials, and Cook at

Aldermaston clearly regarded that outcome as more serious than the possible loss of Maralinga. At the Ministry, Jackson, Brundrett and How were keenly aware of the political implications of the range, and they were prepared to accept an Australian veto of the tests (including one they regarded as unjustified) if that was the price to be paid for keeping it. If necessary, *Grapple* would simply have to be rescheduled. The Ministry's view prevailed, and it was Jackson's draft that was sent to Penney.

Apparently the Australian journalists were sharply critical of the cancellation, alleging that Beale had prevented the firing on political grounds. What happened was that the Safety Committee had informed him that the winds would carry the clouds over Adelaide and perhaps Melbourne; possible thunderstorms there would result in high Geiger counter readings. Though not necessarily dangerous, they would cause anxiety. Beale confirmed their advice not to fire, but as we have seen Penney decided against firing without waiting for the AWTSC to say no. Press signals also suggested that Maralinga was an unsuitable site for atomic weapon trials and that there was dissension among the scientists there.[44] There must certainly have been much frustration, but it had been known from the beginning that favourable opportunities would be elusive.

Then at last, at 06:00 hrs on 27 September, the forecast was good and, thanks to the new compressed timetable, Round 1 was successfully detonated at 17:00 hrs, in conditions that were considered completely satisfactory but short-lived, during a minor interruption in the prevailing westerly air stream. Penney described the test in a cable to Cook at Aldermaston:

Cloud top 38 compared calculated 29 ... Think yield was as expected and cloud height theory is in error and unreliable. Cloud top went right into tropopause.[45] High level cloud moved just north of east at 70 knots and should pass coast line north Brisbane during morning. Low level secondary cloud 15(?) moved ENE. Aircraft tracked both clouds during the night. Magnificent work. Congratulate Air Ministry. Panic here all night because winds began to stack at all local stations. Ground surveys at nearest inhabited places show nothing more than total dose infinity one tenth roentgen or one-fifth level A. All safety worries gone. Think we have excellent complete records. Will [send] second report late tonight. Everyone cheerful.

After the explosion the main cloud, and a secondary cloud that formed between 16,500 and 23,000 ft, moved almost due east. Its height was some 12,000 ft in excess of the estimation, and this failure in their calculations worried the theoretical predictions group. The upper-level winds were from 254°, with little angular wind shear, but changes in the lower-level winds caused the slow-settling fine material in the atmosphere to diffuse to the north and west. The nearest inhabited area in the fallout path was at Coober Pedy, 197 miles from ground zero. The main cloud crossed the east coast about 18 hours after firing, and the secondary cloud some 12–18 hours after that. No rain was observed in the area over which the main cloud moved, but on the afternoon of 29 September rain brought down some radioactive material in the Brisbane-Lismore area. Fallout from Round 1 is discussed on pp. 166–70, together with that from the other *Buffalo* shots.

When the scientists had had a few days to assess Round 1, Penney sent a further report to Aldermaston:

> Lovely blast records. Blast yield 17 kilotons ... Complicated fallout pattern but most complete survey we have ever had ... Target response and medical side had high percentage excellent results ... Still puzzled by height of cloud ... Hope to shoot ground burst this Thursday but rain threatens. We shall be ready ...

The story of the first round at *Buffalo* exemplifies the problems the scientists had to face. The problems for the biology group of having repeatedly to deploy and then remove their animals, grass trays and so on, were especially trying, to scientists and animals alike. It also shows how determined Penney and the AWTSC were to wait for the right conditions, even if the Australian parliamentarians had to make two abortive flights to Maralinga. From their point of view, the repeated cancellations must have been reassuring, even if frustrating.

Marcoo – Round 2

Round 2 was the ground burst, using a *Blue Danube* device with a low yield Mark I uranium core.[46] It will be recalled that firing on the ground would give information about fallout, cratering and ground-shock effects, on which the British scientists had little information. Nor had the Americans, and it was hoped that sharing the results might encourage their fuller cooperation. This possibility had been discussed at the British Joint Services Mission in Washington DC, and the Americans had been sufficiently interested to offer the use of their instruments, and even to attend Marcoo to take measurements of their own.[47]

Brundrett, however, firmly resisted the latter idea. 'The Americans', he wrote to Penney,

are trying very hard to find out the exact state of progress in the UK atomic weapon projects without so far being willing to commit themselves in advance to full mutual exchanges. While in the past we may have gained from our very free attitude to UK releases to the US, I think you agree that we are now reaching the stage where the advantages of such an attitude are more questionable and may in fact do more harm than good.

Penney fully concurred and added, 'They would find out far too much about the weapons themselves'. Thus the offer of instruments was accepted, in so far as they were required, but no more.[48]

The low yield of the test warhead meant a predicted low cloud height, and therefore if lower level winds were suitable it would be safe to fire even when a strong westerly air stream persisted at altitudes above 10,000 ft. The Australian parliamentarians returned once again to Maralinga, and this time there was no long wait.

The warhead was lowered into a concrete pit, and Round 2 was fired on the afternoon of 4 October, at 16:30.hrs (local time). Of the AWTSC, Titterton, Dwyer and Stevens were present. Penney reported:

Second shot appears to be exactly as predicted. Worried at last minute by approaching rain. Fallout 100–200 miles very slight. Shear exceeded right angle. Main cloud very dispersed. Expect very low level counts if there is rain at E coast. Best estimate yield just under 2 kilotons. Have had solid rain for last 8 hours. Parliamentary party delighted with their visit – and very friendly.

There were good fallout data up to 30 miles, and no contamination could be found further away, though the cloud was somewhat higher than predicted and just penetrated the region of the westerly air stream. Moving almost due east the cloud crossed the coast 25–30 hours after firing; a secondary cloud at about 5,500 ft drifted away very slowly over the desert to the north-west and was soon too diffused to be tracked by aircraft. The lower-level winds were from the south, and the high-level winds were westerly, with a large angular wind shear. Fallout was thinly spread over a wide sector; deposition in inhabited areas was negligible, and the ARDU ground survey reported zero readings.

The bomb made a crater 160 ft across, perhaps 40 ft deep, with steep sides and surrounded by a lip 4–10 ft high. After Round 2 came heavy continuous rain 'More gales', Penney signalled, 'thunder and heavy rain, see Ecclesiastes chapter 1 verse 6'.[49] His message, decoded with the help of a Bible, read: 'The wind goeth toward the south and turneth about unto the north; it whirleth about continually and the wind returneth again according to his circuits'.

Kite – Round 3

Penney decided to change the original order of the shots, making the airdrop Round 3 instead of Round 4. It was to be a Service operational test of a *Blue Danube* bomb, and originally the expected yield had been some 40 kilotons, which would have produced little fallout from firing at an altitude of about 1,200 ft. But there was a remote possibility that the fusing system might fail and that the bomb would hit the ground before exploding. A ground burst of 40 kilotons would be quite unacceptable, and various safety devices were considered that would prevent detonation on impact. Maddock had suggested at a very early stage that the special characteristics of a ground burst meant that planning would have to proceed on worst-case scenarios: that is, that the bomb would detonate on impact and that all safety devices would fail.[50] This meant scaling down the yield by a great deal, and, after correspondence with the AWTSC in the person of Professor Martin, it was decided – because of the risk, however slight, of a ground burst – not to use a standard production *Blue Danube* bomb. A low-yield version with a reduced fissile component was used instead, to be dropped from a Valiant bomber and fused to detonate at 500 ft.[51] The expected yield was 3 kilotons.[52]

Titterton and Dwyer, of the AWTSC, were present for the shot. It was successfully carried out on 11 October, at 15:30. hrs. Later, Penney reported back to Aldermaston:

> RAF did a lovely job. Brilliant flash and fireball. Some trees set on fire and many scorched. Terrific dust cloud and stem. Impressive scar on desert, surface torn and rocks scattered in central area. Atmosphere very dry and stable with big inversion at 14 000 ft where cloud stopped as predicted. Blast and heat indicate 3 to 4 kilotons, nearer 3 ... We shall be ready for the last shot early afternoon Thursday ...

There was a small amount of low-level fallout on Maralinga village some hours later – not dangerous but a slight nuisance because it affected instruments there. Otherwise fallout from Round 3 was minimal.

Breakaway – Round 4

Martin, Butement and Dwyer were present at the site for Round 4. The device was essentially a variant of the *Red Beard* warhead with a small quantity of the light elements inserted to supplement data obtained from *Mosaic*. The device was to be exploded on a 100 ft tower. A somewhat larger yield that from Round 1 was thought to be possible, so this shot, Penney said, would need excellent weather. If they were unlucky, there might be a wait of two weeks, but he thought this most unlikely. Two favourable firing occasions were just missed on 18 October, because rain had flooded the instrumentation sites. Standby was then declared, but on 19 October the meteorologists predicted a light northerly component in low-level winds; this might cause contamination of Maralinga village. Conditions were good on the 21st but it was a Sunday, and Sunday firing was not permissible. Shortly after midnight – on the 22nd – the round was successfully fired, with an estimated yield of rather less than 16 kilotons. 'Beautiful clear night with full moon until 10 minutes before shot, then suddenly thick cloud 2,000 [ft] above ground', Penney cabled. 'Rather spoilt night vision test and ruined cloud photography ... Safety aspects extremely satisfactory ...'

The cloud rose some 35,000 ft and reached the coast just south of Darwin within 24 hours; no rain fell in the areas over which the cloud passed. There was no secondary cloud. Because of extensive wind shear, the radioactive material became widely diffused and was deposited very thinly over an arc from Darwin to Newcastle. The highest reading by the ARDU ground survey was obtained at Ingomar, 190 miles from ground zero.

Target response and the Indoctrinee Force

The IF, due to arrive at Maralinga at the end of August, was expected to stay 10–14 days; it turned out to be 41 days, and longer for some men. The Australian Army prepared a camp with great efficiency, 12 miles from Maralinga Village and 11 miles from the railhead at Watson. Conditions at Eleven Mile Camp were spartan, and high winds, rain and the all-pervading red dust made the tents uncomfortable, although the food was reported to be excellent. The first party arrived at Maralinga on 20 August and most of the British group was there by 29 August. This was the date for which the first shot had been planned, but as we shall see it had to be repeatedly postponed. The IF was kept busy meanwhile, and not only with academic work. Even before the first group arrived, working parties were organized for various tasks on the range, where preparation was behindhand because of bad weather, and the indoctrinees were set to work building a biological laboratory, erecting aerials, digging weapon pits, laying cables and preparing target response materials. The brigadier commanding the IF found it 'a pleasure to watch highly responsible senior officers manipulating power drills, filling sandbags and cleaning up 25-pounders with complete abandon and a certain lack of skill', and they all took their turn at washing up and other camp tasks.

During the long wait, the GOC, Central Command, Australian Army, lived at Eleven Mile Camp with the IF and remained until after Round 1. The delay and the working party schemes benefited the indoctrinees, who – even though they were not living in the village – were able to get to know the scientists and to learn a great deal more about atomic weapons and atomic tests. The formal training programme too was extended, thought it was somewhat erratic at times because of repeated standbys and 1.30 am reveilles in order to arrive in good time at the spectator stand.

Round 1 was eventually fired on 27 September, and on D + 1 and D + 2 all the indoctrinees, wearing protective clothing and respirators, entered the target response area in small parties, each led by a conducting officer and with one IF member briefed to monitor radioactivity. They were taken on two-hour tours to inspect the area and the target response items, and afterwards each man passed first through an experimental Army decontamination centre, designed for use by a unit in the field, before going through the civilian Health Control. After showering, no one was found to be contaminated, and no one received as high a dose as the permissible 3 r.

Most of the IF left on 30 September, but at Penney's suggestion the military authorities agreed that 65 officers should remain for Round 2. Their time was fully occupied between rounds, with more training, discussing tactical problems relating to the low-yield warhead, and digging shelters with overhead cover. Twenty-four of the indoctrinees were in these shelters to experience the ground shock produced by the Round 2 explosion, and four others were in a Centurion tank in the same area.

Contaminated clothing trials were also carried out by 24 volunteers, wearing three different types of clothing. The officers moved in groups through a fallout area three days after the detonation; some were in a vehicle, some marched along a track, and some crawled 30 yards 'in the accepted military manner' and then marched through the bush. Health escorts accompanied each group. The object was thoroughly practical – to discover what types of clothing would give soldiers the best protection against radioactive contamination in conditions of warfare. Exposures were satisfactorily low (see pp. 170–1).

The indoctrinees were 'shaken by the devastating effects on weapons and equipment' of this very small bomb; they realized 'the devastating effect on the morale of troops not expecting one, and/or not knowing what to expect'. One hardy soul, however, would have liked to be 'much closer, in a properly constructed infantry position'. The lectures had been well worthwhile, but films, demonstrations and lectures were no substitute for the real thing. Discussion of the effects with fellow officers and scientists had been very valuable. The experience would be a stimulus to further study. They would be able to lecture and carry out their training duties with greater conviction and authority. As field commanders they would have more confidence. As their comments showed, most of them found the whole experience professionally rewarding.

In spite of delays and discomfort, the atmosphere of Eleven Mile Camp was cheerful. In their spare time, which must have been scanty, there were cricket, chess, darts and volley ball, as well as botanical walks, fossil hunting and conversation. One officer wrote later, 'All British indoctrinees will always remember the friendliness of the Australian and New Zealand officers ... and the sharing of good times and bad, hardship and alcohol'. 'Throughout the whole of the six weeks', wrote another – it sounds almost too good to be true – 'in conditions that were sometimes frustrating, I never heard of one cross word being spoken, nor was there even a jarring note'.

A story about troops being used as human guinea pigs in the *Buffalo* operation had appeared in the London *Daily Mail* on 2 February 1956 and was picked up by the Australian press the next day. About 200 troops, it said, all volunteers, were to be disposed in danger areas in a new type of dugout, which scientists would share with them. The troops would be told that there was 'some margin of danger'. Pressed strongly by the Australian newspapers for comment, Beale told them that servicemen would be present as observers but certainly not as guinea pigs.

A similar story that gained currency in 1984 was that soldiers were placed close to ground zero to demonstrate the effects of an atomic explosion on human beings. This story arose from a Chiefs of Staff paper, by that time in the Public Record Office, that outlined plans for atomic weapon trials and for associated investigations of 'the detailed effects of various types of explosion on equipment, stores and men with and without various types of protection'. One reader assumed wrongly that this meant using troops for the purpose. What the plans really involved was the placing of dummies in various positions and at various distances from ground zero, as described earlier. The dummies used at *Buffalo* were well-made and were dressed in Army uniform; photographs show them to be extremely lifelike.[53]

Thirty of the dummies had been left exposed in the open, in standing, crouching and prone positions, and a further 48 exposed in vehicles and shelters. The results showed that, contrary to what might be expected, those in vehicles and even in earthworks could suffer much greater injury than those exposed in the open.[54] These injuries were principally caused by displacement, or being thrown about by the force of the explosion. The target response team took some rather disturbing photographs of the dummies before and after detonation.

Buffalo in retrospect

Operation Buffalo was completed in an overall time of 26 days in spite of persistently bad weather. The long period of planning had paid dividends, and so had experience gained in previous trials.[55] The AWTSC reported to the Australian Prime Minister that stringent safety conditions had been imposed for all firings; detonation had occurred only when Safety Committee members were present and their British colleagues had arrived at the considered opinion that no dangerous effects would arise. Subsequent analysis of the data, they said, showed that the safety measures were successful; there had been no risk to any human beings, livestock or property at any time during the series.

Meteorology and fallout

Meteorology, as always, was a major preoccupation. For this first Maralinga trial, past meteorological data that would have made it possible to estimate the frequency of good firing conditions were almost nonexistent. The desired conditions that had been originally defined were found to occur only once a month or less; there were only two such periods during the whole operation – once just before Round 1 and once just before Round 4 – and neither could be used. The wind structure at Maralinga turned out to be so complex, and so difficult to forecast in detail, that little confidence could be placed in the predicted fallout pattern. The most important consideration was that the fallout should be along a safe line; provided the fallout direction was acceptable, the contamination would remain within permissible distances in most wind conditions.

The extra meteorological facilities in use for *Buffalo* – including the new station at Giles (the mobile station between Maralinga and Broome) and improved communications with the Central Weather Bureau in Melbourne – had been invaluable, but still better meteorological provision was required; meteorologists never had enough information, Penney thought. At Maralinga, firings had to be carried out in essentially transient conditions markedly different from those expected, and, to catch these fleeting opportunities, procedures at future trials would have to be so streamlined that all groups would require only 9–12 hours' notice and could maintain a state of readiness for a further 12–18 hours. Experience at *Buffalo* showed the need for still more detailed meteorological information, especially better upper air observations, for predicting suitable weather conditions and rain and for tracking radioactive clouds. Penney commented:

By a combination of good judgment and good luck, the offsite fallout from *Buffalo* was minute. Every university, and numerous cranks, were waiting with Geiger counters to detect radioactivity. They got either zero results or such minute traces that many of them were convinced that the margin of safety was even greater than we claimed. Sooner or later, however, there is going to be rainfall with 20,000 cpm and then the political scare will start again. This amount of radioactivity is quite safe but a carefully reasoned case will have to be presented.[56]

Aerial and ground surveys were, as previously, carried out after each round. From the two tower bursts – Rounds 1 and 4 – fallout was detectable at about 200 miles downwind; after the ground burst (Round 2) at about 60 miles. (Fallout from a ground burst is unlike that from a tower burst because a large proportion of the radioactivity is left behind when the cloud rises.) From the airdrop (over Kite – Round 3) the fallout was purely local and very small in quantity.

Adelaide University, which ran a regular monitoring programme to measure the radon and thoron content of air due to emanations from rocks and soil, found a marked increase in radioactivity for 12–14 October. It fell away rapidly and would not have been shown by rainwater monitoring as these were rainless days. H. R. Marston, the head of the laboratory concerned, concluded that after the *Kite* shot the plume had passed close to Adelaide and had contaminated the city and surrounding countryside. (See Chapter 9 for a further account of Marston's report.)

The AWTSC report makes clear that the plume did not pass within 160 miles of Adelaide. The primary cloud moved east and crossed the coast in the Newcastle area. However a slight temperature inversion just below 6,000 ft trapped a small quantity of radioactive material, and the veering of light low-level winds after the explosion caused a southerly diffusion of slowly settling material of low activity, which was detected in South Australia, Victoria and New South Wales between 12 and 16 October.

As in the case of *Mosaic*, fallout was measured at fixed monitoring stations all over Australia, which were in operation from 27 September to 5 November. Water and sludge samples were also taken from 16 reservoirs, and rainwater was collected at 13 meteorological stations. Detectable rises in radioactivity were found in samples from these reservoirs, but were too small to have any health significance for human beings or livestock. Of the rainwater samples, most of the activities measured were very small; the highest were at Oodnadatta and Brisbane. Even if the water had been collected as run-off water from roofs and used for drinking, the AWTSC calculated that the maximum dose to the whole body would have been 0.2 r, which would have been of no consequence, but in a normal household water tank a large dilution factor would have reduced the dose correspondingly.[57]

As after *Mosaic*, readings from the monitoring stations were again used by the AWTSC to calculate the maximum integrated gamma doses. From Round 1, 11 out of 86 stations gave results of 1 millirem or above. Only four were 3 millirems or above; the highest was 22 millirems, at Lismore where rain had occurred shortly after the shot. From Rounds 2 and 3, there were no doses above 1 millirem; most were zero. Round 4 gave many zero results, but eight were of 5 millirems or over; the highest was at Birdsville, Queensland (11 millirems).

The combined *Buffalo* results showed that radiation doses in six of the main population centres – Canberra, Adelaide, Melbourne, Perth, Darwin and Sydney – were 1 millirem or less; the figure for Brisbane was 2 millirems. Elsewhere the highest figures were 24 millirems at Lismore, 15 at Marree and 12 at Birdsville. The places which had received most fallout from *Mosaic*, such as Port Hedland, were untouched by *Buffalo*.

The AWTSC doses for *Buffalo*, as for *Mosaic* (see p. 135), were recalculated by the AIRAC and comparative figures are shown in Table 8.1 for the three highest instances.[58]

The AWTSC figures are for doses integrated over 50 years, with no allowance for weathering or shelter. The AIRAC figures (as explained on p. 134) are integrated over six months; they do allow for weathering and shelter, and to calculate the corresponding dose for a person without clothing or shelter, the figures have to be multiplied by 2.5.

The figures may be compared with ICRP limits, and with the figures for annual exposure given at the end of Chapter 7. *Buffalo* exposures are far below the A level – or 'zero risk' level of 3 r (3,000 millirems) recommended by the AWTSC and approved by the Australian government.

The network of monitoring stations was planned to provide an extensive coverage of the Australian mainland, but it would be assumed that some higher doses might have occurred elsewhere or as a result of 'hot spots'. Wise and Moroney, in their 1985 study, estimated higher external radiation doses from *Buffalo* for two other places, Coober Pedy and Ingomar, where fallout contours for Rounds 1 and 4 overlapped (as they were not supposed to do), as shown in Table 8.2.[59] Their figures for total population doses are much higher than the highest AIRAC and AWTSC figures, largely because of a much greater contribution calculated for internal radiation. It should be remembered that Wise and Moroney state that their figures may be ten times too high, or too low by a factor of 2. Their assessment of the total dose to the whole Australian population (over all time) from fallout from the four *Buffalo* shots is 250 man-sieverts

Table 8.1 The AWTSC radiation doses and comparative AIRAC doses for *Buffalo*

Location	AWTWC (millirems)	AIRAC (millirems)
Lismore	24	3.5
Marree	15	2.7
Birdsville	12	1.5

Table 8.2 External radiation doses from *Buffalo* for Coober Pedy and Ingomar

	Effective dose equivalent (millirems)	
	External dose	Total
Round 1		
Coober Pedy	20–68	120–400
Ingomar	17–30	100–180
Round 2		
Coober Pedy	4.5	2.6
Ingomar	12	72

(25,000 man-rems), or about one-third of that from all 12 nuclear explosions from 1952 to 1957. The possible public health impact is discussed in Chapter 13.

The Royal Commission took a more critical approach. It found fault with all four decisions to fire, which it concluded had violated pre-trial criteria. The One Tree shot was found to have been fired when fallout was predicted to exceed the agreed limits.[60] The British government accepted this, but argued that the agreed safety contours were 'appreciably overestimated' and that this wide margin of safety ensured safe firing.[61] On Marcoo, the Commission accepted that all Level A fallout lay in uninhabited areas, but also pointed out that rain had fallen only 250 miles from the firing site, well inside the 500 miles agreed as the accepted limit.[62] That was tacitly accepted in the British Submission, which similarly pointed out that there was no fallout recorded in inhabited areas and only very small readings elsewhere.

The fallout on Maralinga village at the Kite shot, caused by adverse winds, was noted by the Commission, which argued that the test ought to have been postponed. The British Submission acknowledged that Kite was fired in 'a decaying weather situation', but it should be noted that fallout was slight.

Human safety

The Commission reserved its strongest criticism for the attention, or more accurately lack of it, given to Aboriginal safety. It is noted above that exposure limits for people living in a traditional lifestyle had now been included in the safety criteria, correcting the fault in the A32 criteria used at *Totem*. However, the principal deficiency was found to lie in the arrangemeand willy-willies coming from the Timor Snts for ensuring that no Aborigines would roam through the range. Contrary to the advice given by the AWTSC, which claimed that there would be no Aborigines within 170 miles of the firing sites, the Commission found that parts of the range were in use and that arrangements for ensuring Aboriginal safety demonstrated 'ignorance, incompetence and cynicism'.[63] The 'Pom Pom incident', in which an Aboriginal family were found to have camped in the vicinity of the Marcoo crater, was cited as a case in point, and while the British Submission pointed out that the family had been checked for contamination and found to be clear, the Commission's judgement was that 'if Aborigines were not injured or killed as a result of the explosions, this was a matter of luck'.

Regarding servicemen's safety, of the 1,250 test personnel for whom there are radiation exposure data, 24 received more than 3 r (19 of them in the Services, none of them Australians). In three cases, 5 r was exceeded, but there were none over 10 r for the whole operation. The Royal Commission found safety arrangements for test personnel to have been 'well-planned and sound', and rejected the allegations that any men had been used as 'guinea pigs'.

Bombs on a shoe-string

Previous trials had been planned with little time for preparation and with barely adequate resources. *Buffalo*, the biggest and most elaborate, had the advantage of a longer planning period – though none too long for the work involved – and had the largest scientific staff. It was still a rush, because of the delays at the range and the uncertainties about its completion (or rather its partial completion, as a good deal of work was still left to be done after *Buffalo*). Resources, of both men and material, were barely sufficient. The most serious handicap, one senior member of the trials staff wrote later, was lack of adequate transport and mechanical handling plant. The planners had had to cut requirements below the essential minimum to keep down high transport costs; and insufficient allowance was made for servicing or contingencies, or for additions to the scientific programme.

The Australians had made an invaluable contribution, besides providing the range. The Range Commandant and the Services task force had done 'a magnificent job' (Penney's words) 'in the forward area and in providing domestic support'. In all, well over 400 Australians, about 100 of them civilians, took part in *Buffalo* – in the task force, in the Indoctrinee Force, in the target response programme, as meteorologists, as security officers, as members of the health physics and biological teams, in ARDU and as observers in a seismic survey designed to investigate the ground shock effects of atomic explosions.

Rumours that Maralinga was unsuitable as a permanent testing ground for atomic weapons were dismissed; nothing better, it was said, could be found anywhere in the British Commonwealth. In all the circumstances this was no doubt true, but from a meteorological point of view Maralinga – like Monte Bello – had been far from ideal, and had never looked very promising.

9

'There Must be Further Trials to Come': Weapons Planning, 1956–57

The years 1956 and 1957 were climacteric in the British nuclear weapons programme. The technology of nuclear explosives by 1956 was being rapidly developed against a political backdrop that nuclear weapons tests might soon be banned by international agreement. Aldermaston, encouraged by ministers, the Foreign Office and the military, sought to consolidate into established technology the maximum amount of knowledge and hardware. In the situation, the quickest and cheapest was not necessarily what would have been the best if the development time had been longer.

The test programme had to be flexible. From month to month, the priority of terms in the programme changed. In total, many more shots were considered and partly planned than could possibly be managed. The results of one shot often caused an immediate modification or even the cancellation of a shot that was in the course of preparation.

Mosaic and *Buffalo* took place in 1956, but plans were already going forward in early 1956 for a series of high-yield tests, to be held at various times in 1957 and collectively called *Grapple*. A completely new test range with different characteristics was to be established on two remote islands in the Pacific: Christmas Island and Maiden Island. In spite of all this activity, Aldermaston scientists decided it might be possible also to manage another series of tests in 1957 at Maralinga. The precise make-up of this series was changed several times and several codenames were used, but in the event the series was held in September/October 1957 with the code name *Antler*.

The pressure of work on Aldermaston's staff was severe. In January 1956 there were only about 225 scientists (some 700 scientific and technical staff altogether) of whom 100 or more were abroad at any one time for long periods, and many others were engaged at Aldermaston in trial planning, preparation of trial weapons and devices, and support for the teams overseas. (There had been about 150 scientists – and fewer than 400 scientific and technical staff – soon after *Totem* in 1953.) Moreover, trials were only part of Aldermaston's work; other tasks ranged from theoretical research to production of parts of the Service weapons for the defence stockpile. It is commendable that the trials staff managed to write up the trials data as comprehensively and in such detail as they did; it is hardly surprising that there appear to be some gaps in the reports literature.

Shifting plans

As we saw earlier, British weapons testing after the 1954 H-bomb decision had entered a new phase. The trials in Australia became concerned with developing more efficient fission weapons for operational use, and also smaller fission primaries to enable thermonuclear primaries to be built for delivery on ballistic missiles. In 1958, John Corner at Aldermaston noted that the trials in Australia had, among other things, achieved their objective of confirming that 'a fundamental mistake' had not been made in attempts to develop the megaton weapon requested by the Chiefs of Staff. This applied particularly to *Mosaic*, and following those trials it was concluded that there were only two practical routes to megaton weapons. These were large-yield fission bomb, known as Type A and a thermonuclear warhead using a technique known as the double bomb, or Type B.[1]

The task of perfecting the latter was given a strong sense of urgency by the gathering pace of moves towards a partial or complete international ban of nuclear testing. It was recognized in Aldermaston and Whitehall that Britain might not be able to withhold international pressure for long enough to allow development to be completed. That eventuality would potentially curtail the two main goals of British nuclear policy: it could halt the development of British-designed megaton weapons and, as a direct consequence, end the possibility of renewed Anglo-American collaboration, since the British had always recognized that such collaboration would almost certainly depend on Britain producing its own design for a thermonuclear weapon. The events of 1957–58, therefore, represent a defining moment for British policy, since those two goals were both reached during that period. At the series of Christmas Island H-bombs tests codenamed *Grapple*, Britain successfully tested its first

H-bomb. The following year, the 'great prize' of British nuclear policy, the re-establishment of Anglo-American collaboration, was achieved. These events are the subject of this and the next chapter. In this chapter, we look at the intertwined planning for the first two trials series of 1957 – *Grapple* at Christmas Island and *Antler* at Maralinga. It is impossible to understand the latter properly without the former, as the planning for *Antler* was, as we shall see, heavily contingent on the results achieved at *Grapple*.

In Chapter 10, we examine the *Antler* trials themselves, followed by the next series of Christmas Island trials and then the re-establishment of collaboration with the United States.

The origins of *Antler*

The codename *Sapphire* was given in early 1956 to a second series of tests that the Aldermaston scientists contemplated holding at Maralinga in 1957, if possible. It was clearly understood that the details of the shots could not be defined at that time, but provisions had to be made in forward plans.

In July 1956, Cook had drawn up a list of objectives to be covered by atomic tests. Some would have to wait, and it would be some time before it was clear which shots would be ready by September 1957. Soon afterwards, he and Penney discussed the two main *Sapphire* objectives. The first, said Penney, was to investigate lightweight weapons of low yield using plutonium; the second, to study new weapon principles opening the way to cheaper, lightweight, high-yield warheads for a ballistic missile. At this time the world's first long-range rocket able to deliver a nuclear warhead had not yet been made, but it was known that the USSR had been engaged since 1953 in a major effort to develop one; their first test ICBM (intercontinental ballistic missile) was launched in August 1957. The Americans had six crash programmes during the 1950s, and their first test ICBM was launched in December 1958.[2]

The urgency of the *Sapphire* tests was less to meet production dates for weapons than to beat the ban on tests, which might be stopped internationally – or in Australia for local reasons – before the weapon scientists had gathered essential information. If major trials were to be mounted at Maralinga in the latter part of 1957, the Australian government would have to be approached soon, even though it was too early to put forward firm proposals. In September 1956 advance information about the trials for which agreement might later be sought was despatched to the Australian government. This information had to cover all the possibilities. There might be up to five tower tests; the scientific party would be smaller than for *Buffalo*; there would be no target response programme. The AWTSC must in due course be satisfied on the safety aspects. The range staff required would be a basic 228, increasing to 354 during the preparatory phase, and 400 during the operational phase. If it was difficult for the Australian government to provide the whole force, the British government would have to consider supplementing whatever numbers Australia could provide.[3]

It was still not possible to state with clarity what would be tested at *Sapphire*; the results of *Buffalo* had not yet been fully evaluated, and results of the *Grapple* tests in mid-1957 would also impact on the planned Maralinga tests. It was none the less recognized that planning considerations meant that some outline plan had to be prepared. In November 1956, Penney and Jackson drew up a list of five possible objectives for the Defence Research Policy Sub-Committee on Atomic Energy.[4] The first was to check weapon yield against compression, partly in aid of developing low-yield warheads. Second was to continue the investigations into core boosting tested at *Mosaic* and *Buffalo*, but this time using tritium. Third was the possible development of an atomic gun shell for the Army (these plans subsequently produced the *Yellow Anvil* design, but were never tested). Fourth was continued work on *Red Beard*, this time using a small loading tube. And fifth, perhaps most important, were 'investigations in aid of development of thermonuclear warheads'. Penney did not specify the last of these any further, but was referring to the development of atomic primaries for thermonuclear weapons.

By early December, the Sub-Committee had officially sanctioned the request for a set of trials at Maralinga, and the priorities were summarized for the Chiefs of Staff by Brundrett: 'the development of warheads for sur-face-to-air guided weapons, of small megaton weapons, and of versions of *Red Beard*'.[5] The second of these should *not* be taken to imply that small megaton weapons would be tested in Australia. Rather, as Mancroft noted for the Prime Minister in January, the tests were to 'increase our scientific knowledge so as to enable us to produce smaller initiators for megaton weapons'.[6]

Meanwhile, the Air Force had objected to the codename *Sapphire*, which they pointed out was already the name of an aero-engine.[7] The operation was renamed *Volcano* by someone with no public relations sense, and then to *Antler* after the Australians had – not surprisingly – complained.[8]

In January 1957, a more detailed outline plan for *Sapphire* was produced. There would be up to five shots, two of which were to be on 300 ft towers and three suspended from balloons. There were six possible tests to be conducted, and thus one would have to be deleted later. Cook's list was as follows:

(a) a 5-kiloton warhead to be used for a surface-to-air guided weapon;
(b) a test 'at the edge of theory' for an even smaller warhead;
(c) a Service test of a *Red Beard* with a new safety loading device;
(d) a core boosted *Red Beard*;
(e) tests on techniques relating to the *Short Granite* thermonuclear device to be tested at *Grapple*;
(f) tests of different techniques with the same object which could be worked into the rounds at (a) and (b) above.

The balloon project, begun in late October 1956, was novel, though it was known that the Americans had used balloons at the Nevada test site. The advantage was that the test weapon could be suspended very high in the air, so that the explosion would not suck up contaminated material from the ground (including tons of metal from the tower itself) and the amount of fallout would be greatly reduced; at such altitudes the fine radioactive particles would return to earth very slowly, allowing more time for dispersal and radioactive decay. Britain had considerable experience of balloon operations, though not of course for this use, but if the technique could not be developed successfully, all the detonations would have to be on towers and the programme would have to be recast.

The plan was to lift two of the test weapons by a double or triple balloon system using 110,000 cubic ft balloons, and the third by a double or triple system using smaller balloons (70,000 cubic ft). By the end of the 1956 contracts had already been placed for the development and production of balloons and handling gear and for hydrogen sufficient for three shots. A final decision on the use of balloons would have to be made by the end of January 1957.[9]

The estimated total of scientific staff was 200, with the addition, it was hoped, of some Canadian scientists to help with radiological surveys and health physics. The Services would again be asked to help, especially with health physics and control. The air support required would be similar to that for *Buffalo*, but with the balloon operating personnel and without the airdrop. Meteorology would be an Australian responsibility as at *Buffalo*, but four or five British staff might be needed as reinforcements. No target response programme was envisaged, but the plan was later changed to provide for a modest programme; no IF was included. The preparatory phase of the operation would be from 1 March to mid-August, and the operational phase from mid-August to 28 days after the last firing. Once again the timetable would be very tight. It would require all stores to be packed and shipped at the beginning of April; all stores to be delivered and all site engineering work to be finished by 1 August; all scientific staff to be on the range by the end of August. The first possible firing day would be at the end of September and the operation should be completed by mid-November.

The Defence and Service Ministers strongly agreed that *Antler* was essential and urgent, and the Foreign Secretary concurred. However, the Prime Minister, asked to give his approval for both *Grapple* and *Antler*, endorsed the former but asked, 'Are the other trials really necessary?'[10] A minute prepared for those briefing the Prime Minister set out the rationale for *Antler*:

> If *Grapple* is successful we shall have tested a rather primitive and a rather more advanced kiloton weapon and have exploded one or more fairly crude megaton weapons. Further trials would be necessary to improve these weapons and also to carry out tests in connection with a range of smaller warheads for Surface-to-Air Guided Weapons, shells and the like. Unless, therefore, we are on the one hand to content ourselves with fairly primitive weapons and on the other hand to forgo the development of small warheads, it is clear that there must be further trials to come.[11]

The primary aims, the Prime Minister was told, were to develop nuclear warheads, small in physical size and yield, for defensive use in surface-to-air guided weapons; to develop more efficient (Service) versions of the tactical aircraft bomb, *Red Beard*; and to increase scientific knowledge in order to produce smaller fission bombs as triggers for megaton weapons.

An approach to the Australian government, with detailed proposals, was becoming urgent if the trials were to be in 1957.[12] Recent US disarmament proposals made it particularly important to go ahead with essential nuclear testing without delay. The Foreign Secretary added that, apart from these proposals, growing public opposition to tests might make it more difficult to carry out tests in 1958; so too might future reports of the recently set-up UN Scientific Committee on Effects of Atomic Radiation (UNSCEAR). However *Buffalo* had not aroused much foreign comment in 1956, and tests at Maralinga in 1957 might attract little attention, especially as they would be overshadowed by the *Grapple* tests in the Pacific.[13] The Prime Minister agreed that plans should proceed as rapidly and quietly as possible, even though they might be affected by whatever emerged from the current discussions on disarmament.[14]

The proposed plan was forwarded to the Australian government on 12 February 1957. They accepted it, but soon their decision seemed likely to be reconsidered.[15] Penney wrote giving further details to Martin, as chairman of the AWTSC, but the AWTSC felt unable to recommend final approval by the Australian government without further investigation. The Committee's doubts, Martin wrote to Penney, arose from the magnitude of some of the proposed yields and from lack of knowledge about the use of balloons. Martin had advised the Minister for Supply that Titterton, shortly to become chairman of a reconstituted AWTSC, should visit the United Kingdom immediately to discuss *Antler* plans. If possible he should return via Nevada to get the general feel of American balloon experiments. Butement would be visiting England at the same time.[16]

Penney, previously informed of this suggestion, had already approached Admiral Strauss, chairman of the US Atomic Energy Commission, to explain the position and to ask if Titterton might visit the Nevada test site. Two of the Aldermaston staff, Tomblin and Saxby, with an RAF balloon unit officer and an RAE official, had already been invited there to see the American balloon work, which differed considerably from the techniques the British were developing. Penney wrote to Strauss:

> There is, of course, an agreement between the Australian and British governments about tests at Maralinga. The Prime Minister of Australia has a Safety Committee and ... one member is Professor Titterton who you will recall made distinguished contributions at Los Alamos in the early days. The Australian government have asked me if I would be willing to request that Professor Titterton be allowed to visit Los Alamos and possibly Nevada to see how the fallout problems at the Nevada site are handled. He would be particularly interested in the fallout computer ... and also any work you have done on balloons. There is understandable anxiety in Australia about the dangers of fallout from atomic tests but the successful operation of Operation *Buffalo* last year did a great deal to allay fears. However the continuous agitation against tests will undoubtedly regenerate some public nervousness about fallout in Australia. The Australian government wishes to prepare accurate and convincing publicity to counteract this nervousness, and it would be a valuable point for them if they could claim that a member of the Prime Minister's Safety Committee had visited Nevada. Your excellent publicity showing how you have

run so many tests in Nevada without mishap or hazards has had a great effect in Australia.

This useful visit duly took place.

Grapple in context

By 1956, Penney was confident that a fission bomb could be built with a megaton range (that is, over 400 kilotons), but it would consume large amounts of scarce and expensive highly enriched uranium. In those circumstances, accumulating the desired stockpile of bombs would be a slow process. By contrast, the double bomb design (later known as a two-stage or staged design) would be more economic in its use of fissile material, but its size and efficiency would be heavily dependent on the development of fission weapons of reduced size.

British double bomb design at this time comprised a number of variations on the same basic theme, under the family codename *Granite*. These used a small fission device (generically known by Aldermaston as a 'Tom' and later described as a primary or trigger) in order to initiate the thermonuclear reaction in a secondary device (generically known as 'Dick' and later as a secondary).[17] The concept was speculative, but by 1956 enough was known for Corner to note that 'the task was to find the points at which the double bomb might fail and to correct them'.[18] That is to say, there was sufficient confidence in the design to obviate the need to find another technique altogether. Some of the work required to find these critical points took place at Maralinga: the *Antler* series of 1957, for example, involved testing atomic primaries for use in thermonuclear weapons.

The accelerating pace of nuclear weapon development in the US and the Soviet Union gave a sense of urgency to their British counterpart, if the UK was to maintain some technological parity with its closest ally and its defining adversary. An added urgency, perhaps a greater one, was the looming possibility of a test ban. As Ian Clarke has noted, one consequence of this was that the British position on a test ban was ambivalent, to say the least.[19] This ambiguity was the product of conflicting priorities.

On the one hand, a test ban would freeze British progress short of its goal of thermonuclear weapons, and consequently cut off the prospects of both a nuclear weapons stockpile and renewed collaboration with the US. The possibility that Washington might throw its weight behind a complete ban appeared to be very real. A Cabinet paper of October 1956 stated this clearly: 'it is possible that at any moment the United States might decide that they now know so much about nuclear weapons that they could dispense with any further tests. In this event it is possible that they would, with no adequate warning to us, change suddenly their present position and announce their willingness to abolish tests, without taking into account whatever might then be the state of the British nuclear weapon programme'.[20] The paper highlights not only the British sense of vulnerability to the test ban negotiations, but also their unease over the US. Clearly, the Cabinet did not trust Washington to consult London, or take its concerns into account, when deciding whether to force the pace of the negotiations. The Prime Minister himself noted later that several Cabinet members suspected that the US harboured secret plans to 'sell us down before we have a stockpile sufficient for our needs'.[21] There is also a tacit admission that Britain might find it difficult to stand alone as the only nuclear testing state when the other two nuclear powers had agreed to implement a ban.

On the other hand, there were some incentives for Britain to support a test ban. The possibility of nuclear proliferation beyond the three existing nuclear powers, for example, would be strongly curtailed. The US was known to favour a ban in principle, and British support might enhance the prospects of renewed collaboration: the price to be extracted, bearing in mind the sacrifices this would entail for the British nuclear development programme, could be access to technical assistance. Moreover, the growing domestic opposition to nuclear testing was making itself strongly felt.

Consequently, Britain was in a tricky position in the test ban negotiations. A breakthrough in its nuclear development via the *Grapple* and *Antler* trials would not only help to beat the ban, but would also give much needed elbow room for the British negotiating position in Geneva over a test moratorium by reducing the need to head off any imminent ban. Such was the international context for the three nuclear test series of 1957: *Grapple, Antler* and *Grapple X*.

The *Grapple* tests

A great deal about the first round of tests, the *Grapple* series of May–June 1957, has been, in the public realm at least, obscure and misunderstood: fission weapons have been erroneously described as fusion weapons, and H-bombs as mere disguised atom bombs.[22] The tests are, in fact, better described collectively as megaton-range trials (400+ kilotons) rather than thermonuclear ones. Britain tested two designs for a two-stage thermonuclear warhead (codenamed *Short Granite* and *Purple Granite*) and one boosted fission warhead codenamed *Orange Herald*. This reflected the dual drivers of British nuclear weapons testing: the technological imperative to perfect the H-bomb design, and the strategic imperative to produce a megaton weapon that could be fitted onto a delivery system such as a ballistic missile or aircraft. The delivery date to the RAF of the latter, codenamed *Yellow Sun*, was March 1958.

The early planning for *Grapple* involved a concept known as *Green Granite*, which Aldermaston described as 'an experimental assembly involving the only economical way of achieving multi-megaton warheads'.[23] The trick of H-bomb design was to use the radiation produced by the atomic 'Tom', or primary, to produce the ferociously high compression required to implode the second-stage, 'Dick', and thus start a thermonuclear reaction. This technique, known as radiation implosion, was a central feature of the *Grapple* planning from early 1956.

The *Red Beard* design was important in this regard. Originally developed in response to an Operational Requirement submitted by the Army and Navy, the warhead also had applications as an H-bomb primary. The *Red Beard* design, it will be recalled, had been successfully tested at the *Buffalo* trials, and another version was tested again at *Antler* in 1957.

The forced pace generated by the test ban threat, and the uncertain status of development, are both illustrated in the firing programme for *Grapple* and also the *Antler* tests, both of which went through several significant changes prior to the actual trials. This is true for most of the nuclear test programme, of course, but the *Grapple* and *Antler* programmes contained a number of changes that hinged on the results of actual firing *during* the series, rather than on research conducted at Aldermaston.

One such option was *Green Bamboo*. This was a megaton bomb of the concept known as Type A, and used thermonuclear reactions to boost a large fission warhead. *Green Bamboo* suffered from recurrent assembly problems that were never satisfactorily resolved, and by Spring 1957 it had been removed from the firing programme. None the less, a *Green Bamboo did* go to Christmas Island for the *Grapple* trials, to be used only if the now-favoured design (the two-stage thermonuclear warhead originally referred to as Type B and now known as the *Granite* family of designs) did not work.

A second optional warhead was *Orange Herald Large*, a boosted fission 'political bomb' only to be used as a last resort if all other rounds failed to produce a megaton-range explosion. Unlike *Green Bamboo*, *Orange Herald Large* was not taken to Christmas Island. A third contingency warhead, less politically driven than *Orange Herald Large*, was *Green Granite*. This was a version of the *Short Granite* design, to be tested only if the latter failed to produce results. The key difference was the distance between the primary and secondary: *Short Granite*, as its name implies, placed the two closer together, producing a smaller and hence more manageable warhead.

Three rounds were fired at the first *Grapple* trials, and the result was summed up by William Cook: 'We haven't got it quite right, and we shall have to do it all again.'[24] This should not, however, be taken to imply an unsuccessful trial. In the cases of the experimental designs used in the first and third rounds, success should be judged more by technique than by yield. The yields were undeniably disappointing, but the demonstration of 'proof of principle' was a significant success. Production of a megaton explosion was more a political imperative than a technological one at *Grapple*, and Penney had been aware from early 1957 that the experimental assemblies might not produce yields greater than 200–300 kilotons.

The first round, *Short Granite*, was fired on 15 May and produced a yield of 300 kilotons; an order of magnitude greater than anything Britain had exploded before, but certainly well short of a megaton or even megaton range. However, some important confirmations of correct technique were obtained, chiefly radiation implosion. As Penney put it, *Short Granite* showed that 'our principles were right'. The low yield was due to problems with the secondary, but attempts to correct this in the *Purple Granite* round of 19 June were unsuccessful and in fact counter-productive: *Purple Granite* produced a lower yield of 200 kilotons. Further testing was therefore required, but, as Cook noted later, *Short Granite* 'did work correctly as a double bomb and all stages did operate'. Consequently, the plans to fire *Green Granite* were abandoned.

The performance of *Short Granite* also meant the cancellation of two rounds planned for the *Antler* trials. These rounds, known as R1 and R2, and also as 'Tom' and the 'radiation round', were to investigate problems in the *Granite* design, should it have failed at *Grapple*. Particular problems were Rayleigh-Taylor instability and radiation implosion, both of which could be investigated at Maralinga. The success of the *Granite* design at Christmas Island obviated the need for these two rounds.

The other round at *Grapple* was *Orange Herald Small*, fired on 31 May with a yield of 700–800 kilotons. Although this round was not the 'political bomb' of *Orange Herald Large*, it achieved the political purpose of providing a megaton-range explosion. The round has sometimes been referred to as simply a very big atomic weapon; Corner, for example, described it as 'a simple megaton fission bomb'. None the less, the round was reported in the press as an H-bomb test; *The Times*, for example, reported enthusiastically, but entirely erroneously, that 'a great multi-coloured fireball above the central Pacific today heralded Britain's second hydrogen bomb test'.[25]

The yield of *Orange Herald Small* appeared to be the largest that could be obtained from such a design, which, as Cook explained to the Defence Minister, Duncan Sandys, left the two-stage *Granite* design as the only realistic route to the megaton warheads that were the aim of British strategy, and this in turn demanded further tests. Sandys concurred and gave the go-ahead for more trials at Christmas Island, but placed a heavy emphasis on maintaining strict secrecy ('more than Top Secret', as he put it) on the disappointing yields at *Grapple* and the need for further tests. The reasons for this are not hard to find.

Cook himself had noted after *Grapple* that 'we shall have to do it all again, provided we can do so before the ban comes into force'. His choice of words in the latter half of that sentence makes it plain that a test ban was now regarded as a certainty, and in fact the Foreign Office had already warned that this could be mere months away. It would be politically indelicate, to say the least, if Britain were to be negotiating an imminent test ban while simultaneously planning a series of thermonu-clear tests at Christmas Island. The plans should therefore be kept secret for as long as possible; hence also the secrecy on the *Grapple* yields, which would have made it very clear to negotiators on the test ban that further testing was a necessity.

Planning the *Antler* shots

The results of the first *Grapple* series in May and June made it possible to omit some of the originally planned *Antler* rounds, but since the over-heads of the operation were high, it would be uneconomical to reduce the programme too drastically. Moreover, the prospect of a ban on tests made it desirable to gain as much knowledge as possible without delay. However, fissile material was costly and government pressure to make economies in research and development meant that a sound justifica-tion was needed for each shot. Further – apart from the cost – supplies of fissile material, as Penney warned urgently, were small and must be con-served; tests must not use up an undue proportion of the military stock. This meant that tests of a final design might have to be foregone for weapon designs that were well understood.

In mid-June, up to seven possible shots were still under active consid-eration. The first two were different versions of a small warhead codenamed *Blue Fox*. This was a prototype warhead for a surface-to-air guided missile (SAGW), and, referred to as simply 'test in principle leading to 5 kt warhead for Stage $1\frac{1}{2}$ SAGW', had been on the draft firing list drawn up by Cook the preceding January (see above). *Blue Fox* was an all-plutonium warhead with yield range of 5–15 kilotons (although 6 kilotons was expected), intended for anti-aircraft missiles but with possible applications in the *Bloodhound* anti-missile system, and also as a thermonuclear primary.[26]

Also on the June list was an even smaller warhead than *Blue Fox*, codenamed *Pixie*. In contrast to *Blue Fox*, which appears to have been a comparatively uncontroversial choice, the test of *Pixie* was contested at several points.

The list also included up to three versions of *Red Beard*. These were a 'pure' *Red Beard* (that is, with an unmixed core) intended for Service use, a mixed plutonium/uranium *Red Beard* also intended for Service use, and another mixed version for use as a primary at the forthcoming *Grapple* X trial. The seventh possible test was known as a 'radiation round', intended to investigate the principles of radiation implosion if the *Grapple* trials of May 1957 were unsuccessful in this regard.

Blue Fox and Pixie

It was planned to test *Blue Fox* in boosted and unboosted form, but only the latter was eventually used at *Antler*. Although the boosted *Blue Fox* had an anticipated yield of up to 30 kilotons, Cook noted that the *Orange Herald* test at *Grapple* in May, which showed little or no advantage in core boosting, suggested that 15 kilotons was more likely.[27] This implied that the probable yield of a boosted *Blue Fox* would in fact be very close to the maximum yield of the unboosted version, and this seems to have obviated the need for testing.

The plans for testing *Pixie* had a much more difficult trajectory. It will be recalled that the January firing programme, when *Antler* was still known as *Volcano*, had included a test 'at the edge of theory' for a very small warhead: this became *Pixie*. It was a very lightweight weapon, weighing only 250 lb, with a plutonium core and an experimental, small-diameter implosion system. It had an expected yield of about 1 kiloton, and had potential applications in SAGWs such as the Navy's *Seaslug* missile.[28] It also had possible uses as an anti-ballistic missile weapon, especially if its high plutonium content could disable enemy nuclear weapons through the 'R1 effect'. R1 was the name given to 'the specific effect of "neutron poisoning" or "delayed neutron production" in the core of an incoming warhead'. This could 'greatly reduce, for a short time, the potential yield of a fission warhead or H-bomb primary'.[29] This caused great concern for the British offensive weapon designers, who by 1957 were working on modifications to the *Green Granite* thermonuclear design to counteract the effect and create what was described as 'immunity' to it.[30] However, the discovery of the effect also served to 'encourage the idea of nuclear warheads for SAGW' in the UK throughout 1957.[31]

Pixie therefore had some potentially important applications if the workings 'at the edge of theory' could be fully explored. However, it was a very new and untried design, also used large amounts of plutonium relative to its yield of only 1 kiloton or so. This was potentially an advantage in the production of neutrons for disabling enemy nuclear warheads, but the fact remained that plutonium was scarce and very expensive; Penney pointed out that a single *Pixie* contained nearly enough plutonium to produce two *Red Beards*.[32]

The cost-effectiveness of testing *Pixie* was exacerbated by the need to make economies prior to *Grapple*. In April, finances were tight enough to make it necessary to slice £1 million from the trials budget, and it was decided to defer a decision on testing *Pixie* until after the *Grapple* trials were completed. The deletion of the *Green Bamboo* weapon from the thermonuclear trials saved enough money to pay for *Pixie*, but the question of whether the trial was technologically necessary remained.[33] The design's experimental nature, its extravagance with scarce financial and material resources, and the fact that more progress had been made with another small warhead in *Blue Fox*, meant that the case in its favour was not decisive.

Cook and Cockburn both felt that the need for very small, lightweight warheads militated in favour of testing Pixie, especially given that the test ban possibility meant that *Antler* could be the only opportunity to do so.[34] Cook pointed out that theories of warhead design did not yet extend to devices of Pixie's weight and size, and therefore testing would be required.[35]

Penney therefore appears to have been in something of a minority, because he argued several times that the rationale for testing *Pixie* was thin. His concerns failed to win over the rest of the Committee, however, usually because of growing concerns about a test ban. In the run-up to *Antler*, he was sufficiently concerned to write to the Deputy Chiefs of Staff in August expressing his reservations, which were convincing enough for a meeting to be hastily convened on 26 August.

Here, Penney explained that *Pixie* was 'entirely an experimental assembly; it was not a weapon or the prototype of a weapon', and described it in illuminating terms: '*Pixie* was originally a model scale HE implosion assembly produced as a quicker method of testing implosion theory than a large assembly like *Blue Danube*. These experiments involved no fissile material and were purely part of the experimentation required to design implosive systems. It had later been suggested that it might be useful to try the effect of including a plutonium ball; but it would be far better, if circumstances allowed, to agree upon a specific Service requirement and to develop a round for test in 1959'.[36]

Penney's concerns failed to produce a decision to abandon the test of *Pixie*. The clinching argument at the August meeting was (again) the test ban: if *Pixie* was not tested at *Antler*, it might be impossible to test *any* similar design in future. Hull appears to have spoken for most at the meeting when he argued that the question was not whether *Pixie* itself would be a warhead design in its own right (Penney had convinced them that it would not be), but rather whether it would be 'a useful contribution to progress in that direction and would have a reasonable chance of making such a development possible'.

The decisive factor therefore was less the intrinsic merit of the design than the looming probability of a moratorium or ban on testing. The choice was, therefore, one of testing now or possibly not at all.[37]

'Tom', *Red Beard* and the 'radiation rounds'

Helping the case for running *Pixie* was the less crowded schedule for *Antler*. By this *Blue Fox* boosted had been abandoned, as had three other planned shots, referred to as the Service *Red Beard*, mixed *Red Beard* and the 'radiation rounds'.

The radiation rounds at *Antler* had a number of different variations, principally designed to investigate radiation implosion in thermonuclear weapons, and had a very large yield indeed for a mainland test: a note by Corner estimated around 80 kilotons.[38] Quite what the Australians would have made of a test of such size is uncertain, but the round does not feature in firing programmes after late June, and the cable of 16 July stated that 'results of Operation *Grapple* have caused us to reconsider the nature and number of rounds for *Antler*'.

After the *Short Granite* shot at *Grapple*, Penney noted to Brundrett that 'our principles were right' and the test had achieved 'radiative implosion'. This success at Christmas Island obviated the need to run a 'radiation round' at *Antler*, and the test was abandoned.

Economics had also ended plans to test the Service *Red Beard*. Planning from December 1956 onwards had referred to versions (note the plural) of the *Red Beard* warhead, including the pure plutonium version tested at

Buffalo, but including a safety device known as a loading tube. A new 'mixed' version of *Red Beard* with a plutonium core in a highly enriched uranium shell, also including the loading tube, was also planned. Unlike the pure *Red Beard*, this version had yet to be tested.

At the end of July, both versions were scheduled for testing, but at a meeting on the 30th, Brundrett canvassed opinion on whether either was necessary. Fissile material was extremely scarce, and it was here that Penney noted that *Pixie* contained almost enough plutonium for two *Red Beards*. Given the majority in favour of testing *Pixie*, Richard Hull of the War Office came up with a solution: *Pixie* and mixed *Red Beard*, neither of which had yet been tested, would be fired at *Antler*, and the pure *Red Beard* could go into production without further testing.[39]

Three rounds were therefore selected. The first, to be fired at Tadje, was to be *Pixie*. The second, to be fired on a tower at Biak, was *Blue Fox*, now renamed *Indigo Hammer*. The third device, to be fired from a balloon assembly at Taranaki, was the mixed *Red Beard*.

One final change was made at very late notice. At the meeting precipitated by Penney's last-minute letter to the Deputy Chiefs about *Pixie*, the mixed *Red Beard* was removed from the firing programme and replaced by a test referred to as 'Tom'. This was, confusingly, *also* a mixed *Red Beard*, but one configured solely as a primary for the forthcoming *Grapple* X trials rather than as a weapon in its own right.

This was due to the decision not to use the *Short Granite* design as the 'interim weapon', the megaton bomb the British would deploy until they had a fully functional thermonuclear weapon. The *Granite* design required a loading tube as a safety device, and thus the primary to be tested at *Antler* needed to have this feature. However, shortly before the August meeting, it was decided that the 'interim weapon' would be *Violet Club* (also known as *Knobkerry*), a fission weapon derived in part from *Orange Herald*. This did not require a loading tube, and in consequence the mixed *Red Beard* that *did* possess such a device was less of a priority at *Antler*. Although this version had applications as a primary and as a weapon in its own right, in the final round at the trials, it was the function as primary that was uppermost: hence the decision to switch to the version without a loading tube once the 'interim weapon' decision had been made.

Summary

By the time of the actual trials, *Antler* had gone through more changes in plans than any of the other tests at Maralinga. The fact that the last change to the programme was made with barely days to go before the trials began is evidence of how fast and fluid was the pace of technological research at Aldermaston. As a result of the tests before *Antler*, the British scientists had acquired the knowledge to produce three types of weapon:

1. a fairly efficient tactical bomb of nominal yield, which could be carried in a Canberra as well as a V-bomber;
2. an extremely expensive high-yield warhead for a ballistic missile; and
3. a medium-to-large-yield free-falling bomb, or a warhead for a propelled bomb, which was heavy and which could only be carried in a V-bomber.

They did not as yet have the knowledge necessary to produce small kiloton warheads for defensive missiles or small tactical weapons, to make (comparatively) inexpensive megaton weapons, and to maximize a weapons stockpile from a given cost in nuclear materials.

Antler would lead to significant progress. It would become possible to produce a much cheaper and operationally safer tactical bomb; preliminary ideas on the design of small tactical and defensive weapons would have been tested; and the way to major design changes in thermonuclear bombs might be opened. But if no more tests were possible after 1957, the British would still be unable to make efficient use of nuclear materials, in comparison with either the Russians or the Americans, who could produce larger stockpiles of weapons from similar quantities of nuclear materials. There was a pressing need to continue kiloton and megaton tests after 1957 for these reasons. Moreover the Services, following the lessons of military history, began to enquire if nuclear weapons could be made more resistant to attack in combat situations, thereby raising a new range of problems in component development and design.

10
Antler and After[1]

In mid-April 1957 Penney put forward a detailed programme for *Antler*, on the assumption that it would be modified by the results of the first *Grapple*. The *Antler* programme consisted of a maximum of six rounds, including two of 80 kilotons as free air bursts, each suspended from a balloon assembly. Safety and fallout precautions, he said, would be based on the maximum expected yields, and the fallout on the range and at distances up to 200–300 miles would in no case exceed the *Buffalo* tower shots. The balloon shots would give very high clouds and the debris would be in very fine particles. The main meteorological conditions required would be fast upper winds, with no expectation of rain below the cloud tracks; the cloud would then quickly clear the mainland, and the fallout on Eastern Australia would be similar to that of *Buffalo*. Trials with balloons had been very successful. All the safety precautions would be discussed with the AWTSC.

There would be a small target response programme after all; Penney was sceptical about target response but the Service departments in particular had insisted that no opportunity should be missed and that these expensive experiments must be utilized to the full.

The Trial Director was to be the very experienced C. A. Adams, with Dr J. A. T. Dawson GM as his deputy and J. T. Tomblin as Trial Superintendent. The Services Commander was Air Commodore W. P. Sutcliffe, and the RAF task group was commanded by Group Captain H. A. S. Disney. There would be 22 scientific groups, totalling 170 men, and a target response team of 25. There would also be 28 Australians forming the Australian Radiation Detection Unit (ARDU), 11 Australians in the meteorological unit and 17 Canadians. The whole scientific and technical staff would number about 320. The Australian Range Commandant's staff of 450 would support the entire operation.

The biggest single contribution, as at *Buffalo*, was to be made by the RAF. The RAF air task force, with 31 aircraft and about 700 men, would cover all the flying activities that are now familiar – transport services, meteorological flights, photography, safety and security searches, cloud sampling, cloud tracking, and so on – as well as aircraft decontamination, and would also provide the 70-strong balloon unit. Twenty-five RAF regiment personnel would be attached to various groups, in particular to the health physics group. The task force's main base was to be at RAAF Edinburgh Field, 15 miles from Adelaide, whereas most of the operational flying would be from Maralinga. The Shackletons were to be based 1,400 miles to the west, at RAAF Pearce, near Perth. This situation, Group Captain Disney commented, was like having a headquarters in London, a forward airfield near Berlin and meteorological aircraft east of Leningrad. The vast distances involved – the great distances within Australia as well as the distance from the United Kingdom – are easily forgotten.

A new timescale for the standby and firing phases, even more stream-lined than that developed for *Buffalo*, was to be used, in order to take immediate opportunity of transient weather conditions. All the activities that had to be carried out immediately before firing were to be completed in six hours for tower rounds or eight hours for balloon rounds. Members of each group had to know precisely how the timing of their activities fitted into the overall pattern so that Control could make appropriate arrangements for moving and accounting for each man present in the Maralinga area.

The special advantages of the balloons were not confined to reducing fallout. Their use had three operational advantages: it did away with the civil engineering effort required for erecting towers; weapons of larger yield could be detonated without infringing the safety criteria; and the absence of contamination at ground zero meant that, instead of using a new firing site for each round, a permanent firing site could be set up, with a permanent cable system for instrumentation. The disadvantage was that the weapon could not be positioned so precisely. There were other problems too, as will be seen later.

The balloons to be used were developed from the designs of those used during the Second World War to discourage low-level air attacks, and were procured in cooperation with industry and the RAE establishment at Cardington, former home of the great airships of the 1920s and 1930s. If successful, the technique was likely to be used in future trials, as indeed it was for the first and fourth shots in the *Grapple Z* series at Christmas Island in August–September 1958.

The *Antler* programme was again modified in July 1957 as a result of information obtained from *Grapple*, and the Australian government was informed that it would be possible to reduce the number of rounds and the maximum yield. Instead of five or six shots, there would be only three, two on 100 ft towers and one on a balloon assembly; the maximum yield of the last would be 25–30 kilotons and of the tower rounds less. Penney would send full particulars to the Safety Committee.

This reduction must have been a great relief to the Australian authorities. For the British it meant welcome economies in a programme the costs of which were anxiously counted – by the leading scientists as well as by the Treasury – and a simplification of the timetable; six shots, with all the rehearsals between, might have proved difficult or impossible to squeeze into the time available if weather conditions turned out as unfavourable as they had been in 1956.

Safety arrangements

Reorganization in Australia

Rules for the safety of test personnel were, as before, governed by the Maralinga Radiological Safety Regulations (see pp. 103–4). For the Australian population, radiation safety standards were to be the responsibility of a new body, the National Radiation Advisory Committee (NRAC), set up as the result of an Australian reorganization after *Buffalo*.

Martin had proposed in December 1956 that the AWTSC should be reconstituted as a three-man committee – with Titterton as chairman, L. Dwyer, head of the Commonwealth Meteorological Bureau, and D. Stevens, head of the Commonwealth X-ray and Radium Laboratory (CXRL) – to be responsible for all public safety aspects of the atomic weapon tests. He suggested that another committee be set up with more general functions, as the national authority on all radiological hazards. It should advise the government, through the Prime Minister, and should include medical scientists, nuclear physicists and experts in human, animal and plant biology. Its scope would be similar to that of the UK's Medical Research Council's Committee on Hazards to Man of Nuclear and Allied Radiations the Himsworth Committee (see p. 80), but unlike the latter it was to be a permanent body.

Martin's recommendations, with suggested names, were submitted to the Ministers for Supply and Defence, and the formation of NRAC was agreed in May 1957, under the chairmanship of Sir Macfarlane Burnet, a medical scientist of the greatest eminence. This was a wise, indeed overdue, change; the NRAC not only met wider needs outside the scope of the AWTSC, but it was also more fully representative in having biological scientists in its membership.

The new AWTSC forwarded a report to the NRAC on 30 July 1957 on safety levels for radioactivity in fallout from atomic weapon trials, and it was considered at an NRAC meeting on 26 August. In this report, the AWTSC explained the basis of the standards it had approved for the general population. The external gamma dose recommended by ICRP was 0.3 r a week for a working life-time, and for beta radiation 1.5 rep a week. ICRP considered a level permissible if ten times the weekly dose was not exceeded in a period of ten weeks; thus for a single trial period – approximately 13 weeks – the external dose should not exceed 3 r (gamma) and 15 rep (beta). Though ICRP recommendations already embodied large safety factors, the AWTSC had decided to recommend a further safety factor, setting the external radiation limit for the public at 0.5 r (gamma) and 2.5 r (beta). For internal radiation, the AWTSC recommended as a limit an integrated dose of 0.5 r from all sources. AWTSC concluded by noting that the highest integrated dose so far recorded in any inhabited area was a factor of 10 below these limits, and the doses generally recorded were many orders of magnitude lower.[2]

Safety limits for *Antler*

For Round 1 of *Antler*, firing criteria were based not on 0.5 r but on the requirement that predicted fallout contours were such that half level A (equivalent to an exposure of 1.5 r gamma and 7.5 rep beta) would not be exceeded in any populated spot. Level A, it may be remembered, was defined in the Aldermaston report 0–41/55 as that level of surface radioactivity that would not give rise to any observable effect on people living under 'civilized' conditions – i.e. wearing footwear and some clothing.

For Rounds 2 and 3 the criteria were changed, following the NRAC's acceptance of the AWTSC report. The predicted fallout contours should have been based on a surface radioactivity equivalent to an external gamma exposure of 500 milliroentgens (0.5 r) and 2.5 rep of beta. This would have been a more restrictive limit than that for Round 1. However, by some failure of communication, the limit actually applied was simply 0.5 r (gamma). This was a reduction compared with 1.5 r, but because of the varying beta component, exposure of surface tissues could be up to 40 times that from the gamma. The 0.5 r limit, with no corresponding beta limit, was actually a slight relaxation, though not one intended by the AWTSC.

These changing limits are complicated and are difficult to compare, as they are defined in so many ways – in terms of radiation dose; as units of activity per square metre; as levels A, B, zero risk, slight risk, and so on. The important point is the limit on the radiation exposure of members of the public that is implied. This had been reduced from 12.5 r (gamma) and 25 rep (beta) at *Mosaic*, to 3 r and 15 rep at *Buffalo*, and then to 1.5 r and 7.5 rep for *Antler* (Round 1). These are limits and do not imply anything about actual activity levels or actual exposures.

The efforts made to ensure that no Aboriginals strayed into potential hazard areas before or during *Antler* appear to have been more thorough and systematic than for previous trials. The air task group reported as follows:

The Aboriginal tribes have complete freedom in South Australia but tend to stay within their own reserves where there are mission posts from which they obtain medical services etc. The Native Affairs Officers exert a great influence over the tribes by whom they appear to be highly regarded, so there is no great difficulty in preventing a large-scale influx into the Range area. Nevertheless there is always the possibility that individuals or isolated groups of Aboriginals or other people might enter the area by accident or with malicious intent. Searches of the Range area were therefore flown by day and night [by Varsity aircraft] during the last 48 hours before each shot. Detailed briefing for all searches was prepared in collaboration with the Range security staff, a member of which normally flew on each search.

The Varsity crews flew low, searching for Aboriginal campfires but none was found and there were no incidents.

Meteorology

The meteorological provisions made for *Buffalo* were enhanced for *Antler*. Besides the meteorological stations at Maralinga itself and at Giles, a mobile unit operated from Giles. The Maralinga meteorological office received surface three-hourly synoptic charts from the Commonwealth Bureau at Melbourne, as well as daily prognostic and upper air charts and extended period forecasts. Perth provided daily prognostic statements, giving valuable information about weather approaching from the west. Precipitation forecasts came in from all over Australia. The Southern Ocean analysis was received every 24 hours. Daily wind observations, by radiosonde or radar, were sent in from 18 stations; a new radar station was set up at Woomera and two new radar sets were installed by the British authorities at Albany and

Carnavon. Additional upper wind soundings were requested from at least seven other stations after each firing, to assist with cloud tracking. RAF Shackletons based at RAAF Pearce made routine meteorological flights over the ocean south of Australia, and special sorties were flown by RAF Canberra and Varsity aircraft.

The Maralinga village meteorological office was well equipped – though it wanted rather more space, some fluorescent strip lighting and a wire screen so that the door could be left open in hot weather. With excellent communications – telephone, telex and Mufax – it had a wealth of information pouring in. The importance of meteorology in the trials was very fully appreciated. Dwyer was a member of the AWTSC, was present at the weapon trials and was involved in the firing decisions. There were some meteorological deficiencies at the early trials, but by the time of *Antler* everything that could possibly be done to ensure safe firing conditions was done.

Public relations and privileged observers

By May, the UK High Commissioner in Canberra, Lord Carrington, was anxious about Australian public opinion. 'I have just returned from Maralinga', he wrote on 29 May. 'There has been a good deal of comment ... for some weeks past about nuclear tests. This has naturally been brought to a head by the explosion at Christmas Island' (actually off Malden Island, some 450 miles south of Christmas Island). Public opinion, he thought, would find it hard to understand why atomic tests of this kind need continue after a high-yield bomb had been successfully exploded. There would be much opposition from Dr Evatt and the Labour Party – Evatt had recently challenged the government to conduct a referendum on the continuation of tests – and sensational and alarmist articles in the newspapers about radioactivity and strontium-90 were to be expected. It was difficult to see what could he done, and he had only one remedy to prescribe:

> Sir William Penney has established in Australia a reputation which is quite unique ... His appearance, his obvious sincerity and honesty, and the general impression he gives that he would much rather be digging his garden – and would be, but for the essential nature of his work – have made him a public figure of some magnitude in Australian eyes. If he can be persuaded to come out before the tests start, if only for a few days, to give one or two interviews and then hand over to his subordinates ... a great deal of unpleasantness might well be saved.

This letter was passed on to the Minister of Defence, Duncan Sandys, but the suggestion was not adopted, partly because Menzies was confident that *Antler* would not give rise to any particular trouble but also because he was anxious not to focus a spotlight on the trials. The policy was one of minimum publicity and a low profile.

The British government was considering issuing a statement about *Antler* when it was overtaken by events early in June. Reports appeared in the Australian press that because of adverse Australian public opinion all the atomic testing facilities might be moved to Christmas Island. Beale, the Minister for Supply, denied these rumours and said that British scientists would shortly be arriving to prepare for a new series of tests at Maralinga later in the year. The explosions, he said, would be small compared with those taking place in the South Pacific and no hydrogen bomb would be tested.

The British decided that since Beale's statement had aroused no interest or comment, an announcement in the United Kingdom was unnecessary, but a draft statement was agreed with the Australian, for use if questions had to be answered, especially about the balloons. The obvious question was, what would happen if the balloon system escaped its anchorages while carrying an atomic device? The answer was that the system included exhaustively tested safety devices that would eliminate the possibility; and they would if necessary bring the balloons and the atomic weapon safely to the ground, in the highly unlikely event of a breakaway. Nevertheless as an extreme back-up measure an armed aircraft would stand by to shoot down the balloons before they could drift far.

The Australian authorities agreed with the draft announcement, except on one point. Titterton was anxious to avoid any reference to the use of aircraft to shoot down the system, even if a direct question were asked. He believed public fears would be enhanced rather than allayed by an admission that there was any possibility at all that the balloons might break loose and might then have to be shot down. If a question was asked, the possibility should be denied categorically, and if there was a leak about the armed aircraft on standby, the answer should be simply that this was a duplicate safety measure. Beale agreed with Titterton, who produced an alternative draft that the British accepted. The statement never had to be used, no doubt to the relief of everyone concerned.

Press comments in Britain and Australia mounted during August. Penney, it was said, would be at Maralinga, but might not be director of the trials; four or five rounds would be fired, two of a type not previously tried; one of the rounds would be a 'simple triggering device for a pocket

H-bomb'. The *Adelaide Observer* carried a lengthy and accurate article on the use of balloons. In response to press enquiries, Beale released part of the agreed statement about safety of balloons, but it attracted no publicity; the Prime Minister's Department apologized for not telling the British beforehand. A press announcement was released on 29 August:[3]

> The forthcoming tests of atomic weapons in the kiloton range which, with the cooperation of the Australian government, are being held at the Maralinga proving ground in South Australia, will begin in September. They will be directed by Mr C. A. Adams, chief of research at the Atomic Weapons Research Establishment. In agreement with the Australian government, facilities are being provided for the attendance of observers from Commonwealth and allied countries.
>
> Meteorological information to ensure safe conditions for the tests will be provided by the Australian meteorological service. Individual firings will take place only when the Safety Committee of the Australian scientists appointed by the Australian government have agreed that conditions are such as to ensure no risk to the people and stock of Australia.[4]

With Australian agreement the British extended an unprecedentedly wide invitation to observers. NATO countries were invited to Round 3; Commonwealth countries that had defence relations with Britain – Canada, New Zealand, Pakistan, South Africa – to Round 2. As on earlier tests, six US observers were asked as a reciprocal courtesy, and 24 Australian observers, besides 20 Australian parliamentarians. A press party of, say, 20 was to be accommodated. Although the Prime Minister, Harold Macmillan, thought the invitations 'an extraordinary proposal', the Defence Committee approved them.[5] Fourteen countries (not including Australia) accepted, but Belgium, Canada, Greece, India and South Africa refused. The logistics for these observers were not easy; most of them had to be accommodated in Adelaide and flown to the range just before the round was fired, and any postponed firings meant flights back and forth and much time spent waiting. Some of the observers found their visit well worthwhile, but others were disappointed or critical.

The balloon project

There had been mysterious indications from the United States during 1956 that ways had been found of firing test weapons so that fallout was much reduced. One way, it appeared, was to use balloons, which made it possible to detonate the weapons at a much higher altitude than if they were placed on a tower. Balloons for *Antler* were discussed in October 1956. Twelve hydrogen-filled balloons would be needed, able to lift loads of up to 9000 lb and to operate in wind gusts of up to 30 knots. RAE was to supervise procurement, while Aldermaston was to deal with development, and field trials were to be held at Cardington, Bedfordshire, in February 1957. A great deal of ancillary equipment – cargo cradles, pulleys, shackles, winches, etc. – was needed. An RAF balloon unit would have to be trained for the job (which it was agreed would be carried out under the direction of the AWRE Range Facilities Section). Millions of cubic feet of gas would have to be procured from Australian industry and stored on the site.[6]

A contract had been signed for 110,000 cubic foot balloons; but by July 1957 it was clear that the firm could not produce them in time, so that balloons of 70,000 cubic foot capacity – modified versions of an existing type used in a project called *Blue Joker* – had to be ordered. An attempt was made to modify the smaller balloons and upgrade them to 110,000 cubic feet, but they proved aerodynamically unsatisfactory.

Twelve 70,000 cubic foot balloons were shipped to Maralinga, for use in firing the third round of *Antler* and for preliminary practice. But even before standby for Round 1 there was trouble. The balloons when inflated were not kept in hangars, as at Cardington, but were moored in the open air. On 4 September there was a meteorological warning of lightning, and winds gusting up to 40 knots. The three inflated balloons were winched down to 100–150 ft; then an occluded front passed through the site and there was a violent increase in wind speed and turbulence. The balloon crews could hardly see the balloons through the swirling sand. One balloon burst into flames; a second, diving and turning in the wind, was too dangerous to approach, and then it, too, ignited. A third balloon was also destroyed. A fourth, much smaller balloon was lost later; this balloon was used for exercise purposes and was not fitted with the anti-escape devices used for the main balloons. An inquiry was held and a report made to the Air Task Group Commander that same day.[7]

Further bad weather losses might well occur and Adams asked urgently for a spare balloon and rigging to be flown out from Britain. On 2 October, in good flying conditions, another balloon suffered an over-pressurization split during a practice hoist because its vent valve failed in a closed position; this fault was corrected.[8]

However great their advantages over towers in reducing fallout, balloons were not an easy option in adverse weather conditions, but they were used successfully for *Antler* and later at Christmas Island.

Standby

The first standby for Round 1 was declared on Thursday, 12 September, soon after midnight, and the complex routine of calculations, briefings and conferences began. Cloud heights were calculated and fallout patterns predicted on the basis of the latest wind forecasts for the envisaged time of firing; they were presented at a pre-firing conference attended by the Trial Director, his Deputy, the Trial Superintendent, the members of the AWTSC, meteorological and theoretical predictions staff, the Services Commander and the Air Task Group Commander. Regular meetings were then planned for 07:00 and 19:00hrs, when the meteorological outlook for the coming 24 hours would be studied; the earliest possible firing times would be, respectively, at 14:00hrs or 07:00hrs next morning.

If conditions remained promising, further meetings were arranged. At the first, more refined calculations of cloud height were presented, with predicted fallout safety contours. If the meteorological outlook was satisfactory, a second conference was held in two hours or so to study recalculated cloud heights and fallout contours and to decide whether or not to declare Z hour – i.e. to begin the firing phase. If Z hour was declared, a third conference was arranged for 2–3 hours before the intended firing time (F hour). This conference – beginning at Maralinga village and then moving to Forward Control at Roadside – would go on intermittently until half an hour before F hour, with updated predictions if any changing meteorological data were available, and with special attention to the forecasts of rain in regions over which the cloud would pass. So much meteorological material was flowing in, and so much effort was applied to analysing all the relevant data throughout the pre-firing period, that those responsible for firing were well supplied with information on which to make their decisions. The duties were shared between British and Australians, and the order to fire was not given unless and until all present – and in particular the AWTSC members – were satisfied.

Round 1 – Tadje

The first standby for Round 1, on 12 September, was soon postponed; a second standby on 13 September was also cancelled for some reason – not apparently because of the predicted fallout contours. A conference at 23:00hrs that day predicted favourable conditions on 14 September, with upper winds improving during the afternoon. Z hour was declared at 06:00hrs on the 14th, a further conference an hour later confirmed the firing time of 14:30hrs, and the final conference began at 11:30hrs and continued until the weapon was fired at 14:35hrs (local time).

Conditions were almost ideal, with an intense anti-cyclone over the Great Australian Bight, and the cloud track did not enter the rain areas predicted in the east and south east of the Continent. The cloud height, predicted first as 10,000 ft and then as 8,300 ft, was actually 9,500 ft; however, the local fallout pattern was not exactly as predicted because of variations in the wind field. The theoretical predictions staff concluded that an error of about 15 per cent must be expected and that it was unlikely to be improved significantly by using more extensive forecasts.

A feature of this test that was later to cause concern and misunderstanding was the novel use of cobalt metal for so-called radiochemical 'diagnostic' purposes – i.e. as an aid to measuring the nuclear efficiency of the explosion. It was not a good idea and was not repeated. When the Australian range staff later found small pellets of radioactive cobalt scattered around the Tadje firing site, they were very puzzled. Besides causing an unforeseen type of surface activity, the pellets gave rise to a later, totally unfounded, suspicion that the British scientists had been working on a new type of nuclear weapon incorporating cobalt-60; this was not the case, but the suspicion persisted.

More seriously, as the Royal Commission pointed out, the Australian Health Physics Representative (AHPR) had not been informed that cobalt would be used at the Tadje test. Consequently, the AHPR (Mr Turner) made the discovery himself by accident, during routine surveys for radioactivity. The British Submission protested that the AWTSC had been informed, but it became clear during the hearings that the only member of the AWTSC thus apprised was Titterton. For reasons that, to say the very least, are not obvious, Titterton appears to have kept this information to himself, and decided not to inform either the rest of the AWTSC or Turner before the test.

Giving evidence to the Commission, Titterton claimed that he wished to give the AHPR 'a bit of a test'.[9] This was rejected in the Commission's report, which concluded that the British ought to have informed the AHPR themselves about the cobalt (this was not disputed in the British Submission), and also that Titterton had 'contributed to an unnecessary radiation hazard' in his apparently unilateral decision to keep the Committee and Turner in the dark.

Round 2 – Biak

The first day of standby for Round 2 was a week later, on 21 September. Firing phases were cancelled on 21 September and again on 24 September because of likely rain areas. On the evening of 24 September it seemed that a brief opportunity would occur on the morning of 25 September, but fog was forecast for the early morning, and at about midnight hope of firing at 07:00hrs was abandoned. Another conference half an hour later was held to consider firing later in the morning; maps were prepared showing the fallout contours for a detonation of between 6 and 10 kilotons. There seemed a good chance of firing at 10:00 hrs and Z hour was declared at 03:30hrs. The final meeting began at 07:00hrs in Maralinga village, moved to Forward Control at Roadside, and continued until 08:30hrs. Wind forecasts then showed that the Taranaki site would probably have low levels of radioactivity deposited on it, but the decision was taken to fire at 10:00hrs (local time) as planned and to accept the difficulties that might arise.

The yield was about the expected 6 kilotons, but the cloud was much higher than predicted – up to 24,000 ft instead of 14,600 ft – and so some change in the direction of maximum fallout was likely. A secondary cloud was apparently formed at about 15,000 ft. No rain had been forecast for any area within 300 miles of the cloud track, and the cloud did not pass through any rain area. The weather conditions were generally very good, except that winds at the lowest level were rather light and not very favourable in direction, and as expected they deposited low levels of radioactivity on the Taranaki site.

Round 3 – Taranaki

The first day of standby for Round 3 – the balloon round – was 7 October, but no attempt to fire was made for two days. From 6 October onwards the upper level winds were favourable but winds up to 1,000 ft had too great a northerly component. By the early hours of 9 October, the upper wind structure was deteriorating. There was now a difficult problem of timing. The adverse low-level winds seemed likely to improve soon, but if firing was delayed too long the favourable upper winds would be lost, perhaps for several days.

A meeting at 06:00hrs on 9 October studied maps showing fallout contours assuming the maximum yield of 50 kilotons – a large safety margin as the probable yield would be up to 30 kilotons. The main cloud height was predicted as 28,300 ft (for 30 kilotons) or 37,000 ft (for 50 kilotons), with a secondary cloud at 13,000 ft or 19,000 ft. The upper winds that were forecast would not carry radioactive material into any of the expected rain areas in the south cast of the continent. Z hour was declared and the firing phase began, with an expected firing time of 16:00hrs. A second meeting confirmed the decision and the final meeting began at 13:00 hrs in Maralinga village and then moved to Roadside. By F hour the lower wind directions were much improved, and when the weapon was fired at 16:15 hrs (local time) the local contamination that had seemed possible did not occur. The near-calm conditions prevailing during the firing phase were not ideal from the point of view of fallout, but they greatly eased the difficulties of handling the balloons and hoisting the weapon, and the operation went very smoothly.

The yield was about 25 kilotons and the height of the cloud – 23,000 ft, with a secondary of cloud at 10,000 ft – was rather less than expected. Cloud tracking showed that the main cloud moved rapidly away to the east; though at higher levels its course was less to the north than had expected, it was over rain-free areas.

Reporting on *Antler*

Operation *Antler* had gone very smoothly apart from the early troubles, and the balloons had performed well on the day. The briefing routines and pre-firing meetings were efficient and streamlined. All the meteorological arrangements had worked well although, surprisingly, the forecasting errors were greater than for *Buffalo* – perhaps because of the general atmospheric conditions in 1957 compared with those in 1956. Altogether 452 forecasts had been made. The RAF meteorological flights had been invaluable; some took place in appalling weather and heavy demands were made on the aircrew, but they always completed their observations and the meteorologists had great confidence in them.

The RAF's low-level radiological surveys by Varsity aircraft and helicopters had been improved as a result of more reliable equipment. After *Buffalo*, better navigational equipment and a more accurate altimeter had been asked for, since the accuracy of aerial radiological surveys depended on the aircrew knowing precisely their position and altitude. The Decca navigator, introduced before *Antler*, proved excellent, though more accurate altimeters were still needed. Improved navigational equipment and more effective calibration techniques had enhanced the reliability of these surveys, and correlation with the results of ground monitoring by mobile units was good. However the relationship between air readings and the radiation dose rate on the ground was complex and some uncertainties still existed.

Fallout

For Round 1, the varied direction of the upper winds had spread the radioactive material widely and thinly over the continent to the north of Maralinga, and the fallout had not coincided with the rain areas in the south east coastal regions. For Round 2, again, wind shear had dispersed the main cloud very widely to the north-east and east of Maralinga. For Round 3, the main cloud moved east and then north-east towards the Queensland coast, missing the rain areas in New South Wales and Victoria as predicted.[10]

The network of fallout monitoring stations was in operation from 10 September to 24 October, and 12 stations – including Adelaide, Melbourne, Sydney, Brisbane and Darwin – collected rain samples, but no radioactivity above background level was detected. As a further check on fallout, measurements were made at intervals after each round on the thyroid gland of sheep grazing in various places up to 250 miles from the test site. Three radionuclides were found – iodine-133 and xenon-131 (detectable only in a few cases), and iodine-131, a radioisotope of iodine with a half-life of eight days which, if ingested, concentrates in the thyroid. The highest concentration of iodine-131 found in the thyroids was negligible compared with the level considered by American and British agricultural scientists to be harmless to grazing sheep. (For H. R. Marston's report on radioiodine in the thyroid of sheep and cattle, see below.)

The Commission concluded that although the permitted contamination levels were higher than those agreed for *Buffalo*, Rounds 1 and 2 at *Antler* had fallen within limits, while the third round had slightly exceeded Level A for 'people living in primitive conditions' in some regions.

Health and safety

Safety of test participants

At *Antler* 1,500 test personnel were recorded as having been exposed to radiation; only 424 had exposures above the threshold level of detection, and 17 received over 3 r. No civilians and no Australian citizens received more than 5 r during the trial: five members of the Defence Services did; two exceeded 12 r and one received 15 r, but all were within the special limit of 25 r. The two highest were the pilot and safety observer of the Canberra aircraft engaged on primary air sampling after Round 3. It was believed that for yields of less than 60 kilotons an aircraft could collect samples 30 minutes after the explosion without exposing the crew to more than about 3 r; this figure was slightly exceeded for Rounds 1 and 2, but for Round 3 an exposure of 10 r accumulated unexpectedly quickly and the pilot had to fly out of the cloud before completing a single pass. The observer described vividly the appearance of the fireball and the formation of the cloud as seen from the Canberra orbiting at 30,000 ft. Flying into the cloud, he wrote, was like 'entering a reddish brown cloud of smoke which was at first very thick but rapidly thinned to a paler colour. During the first few seconds ... the instruments indicated high activity, and almost before we had realized what had happened the "Charlie" meter was registering 10 r. We immediately took action ... but it was more than 20 seconds before we got clear. However the time taken to clear the cloud added very little to the dose recorded ...'

The health physicists had difficulty in obtaining the previous radiation histories of the crews, and some officers had apparently been employed as sampling crews on several trials: experience must have been invaluable in these specialized operations. Though they were apparently still within the limits set for the trials and within the lifetime limits shortly to be recommended by the ICRP, they were for the time being undoubtedly incurring a greater annual radiation exposure than most workers in the nuclear industry received in a year: however, it should be remembered that many radiation workers would continue to be exposed throughout their working lives.

Safety of the population

The theoretical radiation doses received by the population were again calculated by AWTSC using the fallout data from the monitoring stations. The highest cumulative dose of gamma radiation was 4 millirems, integrated over 50 years, as in previous calculations for *Mosaic* and *Buffalo*, and as before making no allowance for shelter or weathering. The four highest values, and the revised figures calculated by the Australian Ionizing Radiation Advisory Council in 1983 (AIRAC No. 9) are shown in Table 9.1. The AIRAC figures for *Antler*, as for *Buffalo* and

Table 9.1 Four highest radiation values, and the revised figures calculated by the Australian Ionizing Radiation Advisory Council in 1983, for *Antler*

	AWTSC (millirems)	AIRAC (millirems)
Bourke	4	0.8
Mackey	4	0.1
Thargomindah	3	0.5
Townsville	3	0.2

Mosaic, are much lower than the AWTSC for the reasons previously explained (Chapter 7, pp. 133–4). The *Antler* doses – even the higher values calculated by the AWTSC – are clearly far below the 'half level A' (equivalent to 1.5 r or 1,500 millirems) that the AWTSC had stipulated before Round 1, and less than 1/1000 of the average Australian's exposure to natural radiation in 50 years. However, higher exposures might well have occurred in places where there was no fixed monitoring station, so AIRAC calculated the radiation doses along the central fallout line from each of the *Antler* explosions. From Round 1 the fallout track, as determined by aerial survey, did not pass over any inhabited area, and the fallout would therefore have caused no radiation exposure.

After Round 2, the ARDU survey showed that the highest level at any inhabited place was at Coober Pedy, 146 miles north-east of Maralinga. There the dose, integrated over six months, was 15 millirems (or 6 millirems allowing for shelter).

For Round 3 – the balloon round – the close-in fallout, on the range and nearby, was very low; further out from ground zero it was more than expected, though not high. The ARDU survey found the highest level of fallout at any inhabited place at Mulgathing, 144 miles east of Maralinga. There the radiation dose, integrated over six months, was calculated at 13 millirems (or 5 millirems if an allowance was made for shelter). Wise and Moroney assessed the population dose from *Antler* as 149 man-sieverts (14 900 man-rems), or about one-fifth of the total from all the tests in Australia.[11] Most of the *Antler* dose was contributed by Round 3.

The Royal Commission's findings on Antler reserved strong criticism for the treatment of the Aboriginal population, and Beale was a focus of condemnation for 'dogmatic replies based on false assumptions and inaccurate information'. The Commission concluded that, as with the other tests, 'inadequate attention was paid to Aboriginal safety', and that the patrols designed to ensure that the range was clear were 'neither well planned nor well executed'. Responsibility was laid at the feet of C. A. Adams, on the British side and the AWTSC on the Australian side.

Antler Postscript

A postscript to the major trials appeared as a paper by an Australian scientist, H. R. Marston, published in August 1958 under the sober title 'The accumulation of radioactive iodine in the thyroids of grazing animals subsequent to atomic weapon test'.[12] It contained valuable new scientific information on iodine-131 – an important constituent of fallout – and a great amount of meticulously researched data. It did not indicate high levels of iodine-131 contamination. Nevertheless the paper was very controversial at the time and later. Before it was published, it was described as 'dynamite to the uninformed'. Why was this? And why were attempts made – it was alleged – to suppress its publication?

It was controversial for two reasons: first, because of comments that Marston made, and did not make, on his data; second, because of the paragraphs he included on other fission products, especially strontium-90, in which he drew erroneous inferences from his iodine-131 results with no supporting experimental data. These comments and inferences sounded alarming. He wrote, for example, of 'heavily contaminated areas', 'repeated dressings' of radioactivity, and precipitations in 'areas more or less thickly populated'. Writing of strontium-90 he said that the contamination of any part of the earth's surface by fallout from the stratosphere was quite small when compared with the contamination of parts of Australia with fallout from the troposphere after recent weapon tests.

To understand the story of the Marston report it is necessary to go back to its origins, and also to look at the research on strontium-90 being done at the time.

Iodine-131

Iodine-131 is one of the most abundant fission products of an atomic explosion and though short-lived – with a half-life of eight days – it is radiologically important. The thyroid gland of animals and human beings is avid for iodine and will absorb iodine-131 if it is present, with a consequent risk of thyroid cancer. Animal thyroid measurements by an American scientist, published in 1954, had indicated that, at existing levels, iodine-131 from weapon tests in the United States was no hazard to animals or human beings.[13] The AWTSC, with the new permanent range being set up on the Australian mainland, wanted to be able to assess the Australian situation. They accordingly asked Marston to undertake a survey, starting well before trials began at Maralinga, in order to establish a baseline. He was to obtain thyroid samples from sheep and cattle and make iodine-131 measurements using scientific equipment supplied by Aldermaston.

Marston, of Adelaide University, was head of the Division of Biology and General Nutrition of the Commonwealth Scientific and Industrial Organization (CSIRO); as we have seen, he and his laboratory assisted in some of the biological experiments at *Buffalo*. A distinguished scientist in the field of animal health and nutrition, he was also by temperament controversial.

He began his survey at the end of April 1956, and by mid-December had measured more than 230 thyroid samples from 26 areas in northern and north-eastern Australia that were likely to be traversed by plumes from explosions at Maralinga. When he began sampling he expected nil results until after the first *Buffalo* firing in September. At first, the iodine-131 content of all his samples was below the level detectable with his apparatus. But a few days after the first *Mosaic* firing (G1) on 16 May he found iodine-131 in many samples from across the country, and after G2 on 19 June the concentrations increased by a factor of 100 or more. Marston did not consider these levels dangerous, but he was surprised and angry because they showed that *Mosaic* had deposited radioactivity quite extensively on the mainland, despite assurances that this would not happen and that the fallout would be blown out to sea.

After *Buffalo*, his iodine-131 measurements rose, predictably but less than he had expected. Meanwhile, his laboratory in Adelaide, which had a long-standing interest in radioactivity in air caused by emanations of radon and thoron from rocks and soil, continued its periodic air sampling; this was unrelated to weapon tests and had never shown any response to them. However, after the third *Buffalo* shot on 11 October an increase in radioactivity in the air suggested to Marston that the plume had passed close to Adelaide – a conclusion that authoritative evidence does not support (see Chapter 8). But even if it gave a correct picture of fallout over Adelaide, it was still irrelevant to a report on iodine-131 in animal thyroids.

The figures in Marston's 26 tables of thyroid measurements showed that the iodine-131 levels in inhabited and stock rearing areas were all well below safety limits; the highest figure he recorded was about on per cent of the so-called 'Scott Russell' safety limit, which was based on the maximum iodine-131 concentration in milk for infants, the critical group. Yet Marston's paper did not say this, or compare his measurements with this or any safety standard.

Strontium-90

Another fission product abundantly produced in atomic explosions is strontium-90. It has a half-life of 28 years and (like calcium) is deposited in bone if taken into the body through the food chain; then, by irradiating neighbouring bone marrow, it can cause leukaemia or aplastic anaemia, or may in the long term give rise to bone tumours. Strontium-90 was causing increasing concern to American, Canadian and British scientists, and its significance was underlined in June 1956 by both the Bronk and the Himsworth reports on nuclear hazards (see pp. 80–1).

The US research programme on strontium-90 was known as *Sunshine*.[14] In October 1956, American, British and Canadian scientists met in Washington to arrange to collaborate on *Sunshine*, by comparing strontium-90 levels in samples of soil, food, milk and animal and human bones in the three countries. Penney quickly suggested to Martin, as chairman of the AWTSC, that Australian samples should also be collected from locations 150–200 miles from Maralinga, at regular intervals before and after weapon trials. Plans were worked out over the next few months; the collecting methods were specified by Scott Russell and the samples were to be despatched to AERE, Harwell, which had the necessary facilities and expertise for strontium-90 analysis, and where the techniques used had been standardized with those of American and Canadian scientists. The results would be evaluated at Harwell by a group of biologists expert in internal radiation. Detailed arrangements were agreed at a meeting at Harwell at which Titterton was present for the AWTSC.

Meanwhile Marston, who was not involved in the strontium-90 work, used his iodine-131 results to make calculations about strontium-90 and included these vague, but somewhat alarmist, conclusions in his report on the iodine-131 survey. They were, however, not only unsupported by any experimental data but were based on faulty assumptions about the behaviour of strontium-90. A valid assessment of the strontium hazard could not be made in this way, but only on the basis of experimental data obtained from the assay of representative bone samples. Such an assessment was later published in Nature, in 1961 (see p. 208).

Open publication

Marston presented his paper to the AWTSC early in 1957, when a copy was sent to Aldermaston and was discussed with Harwell scientists, with Scott Russell, and with Loutit of the Medical Research Council.

Penney's chief comment, which he sent to Titterton as AWTSC chairman, was that the paper contained a small amount of technical matter, in two graphs, that could reveal weapon design information. If this was included, the whole document would have to have a high security classification; however, these graphs were not essential to the text and if they, plus two sentences, were omitted, open publication would be possible. This condition was purely a matter of the security of weapon information, and had nothing to do with any debate on radiological safety. As for the paragraphs about strontium-90, etc., Penney said that if they were published they could be answered by scientific argument.

The AWTSC reconsidered the draft in August 1957 and referred it for an independent opinion to Sir Macfarlane Burnet, chairman of the new National Radiation Advisory Council (NRAC).[15] An Aldermaston scientist visiting Melbourne in November saw the final version and confirmed that the security objections had been met. He said that 'unscientific assumptions' remained about strontium-90 in relation to iodine-131 measurements, but they were 'patently conjectural'; publication was not opposed.

The *Australian Journal of Biological Sciences*, after consulting independent referees, finally published the paper in August 1958. It still included four paragraphs on strontium-90, and argued that the ingestion of bone-seeking isotopes by grazing animals might be inferred directly from measurements of iodine-131 in the thyroid. These speculations were valueless compared with the mass of scientific data becoming available from the analysis of bone and other samples, and published in the first report of UNSCEAR, which also appeared in August 1958. A 1961 report on strontium-90 in Australia recorded an increase in late 1958 and early 1959, but noted that levels in bone were still one-third to one-half of levels in the United States and Britain.[16]

The controversy generated much heat, and publication was delayed by 18 months. Marston felt aggrieved and thought he was being muzzled. We have not seen the Australian documents, but know of no attempt in Britain to suppress his research results. It was unfortunate that he was determined to include in his valuable report on iodine-131 extraneous passages about strontium-90 on which he had no experimental data and which was being extensively researched by many other scientists.

Grapple X, Y and *Z*

The first *Grapple* trials, wrote Corner, 'demonstrated that we did not understand the working of the final thermonuclear stage in Dick'. In the case of *Short Granite*, the necessary calculations were hampered by a lack of computing power; the readjustments for *Purple Granite* had therefore been 'a last-minute attempt to improve it by eye', as he put it. Research at Aldermaston was therefore greatly facilitated by the arrival of a new computer which accelerated the calculations necessary for the design of the thermonuclear stage. In fact, it has been argued that, by enabling the calculations for the *Grapple X* trial, the new computer was indirectly responsible for the successful revival of Anglo-American collaboration in 1958.[17]

The primary for the *Grapple X* test required some modifications. It would need to be lighter than the primary used for *Short Granite* in order to achieve the aim of a megaton yield from a 1 ton device. Several ideas were discussed, and the primary eventually used, a mixed *Red Beard*, was the one tested as 'Tom' suspended under the balloon assembly at Taranaki as the final shot in the *Antler* series.

Grapple X performed comfortably above expectations: the first round produced a yield of 1.8 megaton.[18] This was enough to obviate the need to run the diagnostic round and also the test of the improved design that had also been scheduled. *Grapple X* was, then, a one-round trial. The impact of this on the Anglo-American talks is discussed below.

With the political and strategic goal of megaton weapons achieved, the aim of testing became predominantly one of technique. The two-stage *Granite* design used at *Grapple X* was once again employed at *Grapple Y*, but the secondary now incorporated considerably more lithium, and the uranium content was sharply reduced. This, together with the calculations facilitated by the new computers, would mean much more of the yield would come from thermonuclear reactions. The eventual yield of the *Grapple Y* round, fired on 28 April 1958, was 3 megatons. The technological significance of this was matched or perhaps exceeded by the political benefits of demonstrating to the US that British technique had reached the stage of being able to exploit fully the destructive potentiality of thermonuclear explosions.

The *Grapple* series reached its final stage with the *Grapple Z* trials over August–September 1958, shortly before the restoration of Anglo-American collaboration. The *Grapple Z* trials had been planned from well before *Grapple X*, partly driven by the ultimate aim of a 1 ton megaton warhead, but also driven by the concerns over the R1 effect and the concerns to make UK warheads invulnerable to it (see above pp. 184–5). It was thought that the R1 effect might be lessened, or perhaps negated altogether, if the amount of vulnerable fissile material in atomic weapons and fissile thermonuclear primaries could be reduced. One way to achieve this was through boosting fissile reactions with thermonuclear material, something the British had already investigated but with little success. Boosting had initially been pursued as a means to economize on scarce fissile material, and also to make weapons lighter and thus easier to deliver via missile, but the uncertain potential of R1 gave it a new urgency. The plan for *Grapple X* was therefore to continue development of the double-bomb *Granite* design and to investigate boosting in primaries: the aim was thermonuclear weapons that were lighter and immune to R1. The tests were held between 22 August and 23 September

1958, and involved two boosted primaries (*Pennant* and *Burgee*) and two H-bomb designs (*Flagpole* and *Halliard*).

The events of 1957–58, therefore, represent a defining moment for British nuclear policy. At the series of Christmas Island H-bombs tests codenamed *Grapple*, Britain successfully tested its first H-bomb. The following year, the 'great prize' of British nuclear policy, the re-establishment of Anglo-American collaboration, was achieved. At the same time, this led directly to a reduced need to use Australian territory for further nuclear trials, and by 1963 to the abandonment by the UK of the Maralinga testing range, into the construction of which so much effort and so many resources, both British and Australian, had been poured in the period 1955–57.

'The relationship is wonderful now': restored collaboration[19]

Ian Clarke has noted that although the Anglo-American 'special relationship' – if there is such a thing – is usually associated with the provision of the *Trident* missile and its antecedents, the exchange of nuclear weapons information is probably far more significant.[20] The efforts to re-establish the wartime nuclear collaboration between Britain and the US had been central to British policy from the instant the McMahon Act became law in 1946, but by the mid-1950s two factors had become closely bound to these efforts. The first, of course, was the constant knowledge that the best way, and probably the *only* way, for this to be achieved was for Britain to demonstrate something approaching technological parity with the US. That is to say, the US would almost certainly not show Britain the nuclear technique, but might be prepared to help Britain improve on it.

The second, as mentioned above, was the possibility of a test ban. We have seen that Britain was uniquely vulnerably to a ban, and that it did not entirely trust the US to take that into account when making policy. The nagging suspicion that Washington might decide to throw its weight behind an all-out ban was to some extent soothed by a secret agreement put together at the March 1957 summit in Bermuda, by which the two sides agreed that they would not submit any proposals to the test ban negotiations without first consulting each other. Although this did not allay the fear that the US might change its position, it did at least remove the prospect of this coming out of the blue.

None the less, the British policy at the test ban negotiations was aimed at protraction and delay of an agreement, something the British were not shy of using to their advantage with the Americans, whom they regarded as growing increasingly sympathetic to a ban. Macmillan noted to Eisenhower in January 1958 that, 'We could not accept the abolition or suspension of tests in the present state of our knowledge. But if you were prepared, after an amendment of the Atomic Energy Act, to make your knowledge available to us, our position would be different'.[21] Eisenhower was sympathetic, and indeed was regarded by the British as generally in favour of an amendment to the McMahon Act.

Although the President's sympathy was an asset, it was one that could not be realized as long as the general opposition elsewhere in Washington prevailed. Amending the Act required an Act of Congress, where the environment was rather less congenial than in the White House. A change in that position would require something to alter the international context from the point of view of legislators in Washington. As if to prove Macmillan's own saw that it is 'events, dear boy, events' that produce changes in policy, an event of far-reaching implications arrived in late 1957 to produce exactly the shift in context that the British needed. This was, of course, the launch of the Soviet satellite Sputnik on 4 October, four days before the final test in the *Antler* series and a month before the *Grapple X* shot in the Pacific.

The implications of Sputnik were twofold: first it shook America's confidence in its technological lead over the USSR; and second it raised the imminent prospect of an intercontinental-range missile that could target the US itself. This sudden extension and dramatization of the Soviet nuclear capability produced an opportunity that the British Ambassador in Washington, Harold Caccia, spotted instantly: 'with luck and judgement, we should be able to turn this in some way to our special advantage'.[22]

For Eisenhower, Sputnik also presented an opportunity. He wrote later: 'Our defenses were cooperative – why could not our research be cooperative also? ... Our atomic energy laws had been written when we thought we had a monopoly on this branch of science. Now, when many of our former secrets were known to our enemies, it made no sense to keep them from our friends. I wanted the law changed'.[23]

Macmillan, who saw his chance as clearly as Caccia, moved quickly and set up a meeting with Eisenhower, held in Washington less than three weeks after the launch of Sputnik. This meeting was the breakthrough. The developments of the following year proceeded on the foundation laid at Washington in October 1957, at which the principles of technological collaboration and information exchange were agreed. The Declaration of Common Purpose, issued after the meeting, stated: 'The President of the

United States will request the Congress to amend the Atomic Energy Act as may be necessary and desirable to permit of close and fruitful collaboration of scientists and engineers of Great Britain, the United States, and other friendly countries'.

Implementation of this principle was to be discussed by two study groups, one on nuclear cooperation led by Sir Edwin Plowden and Lewis Strauss of the US AEC; the other on wider defence cooperation led by Sir Richard Powell and Donald Quarles. These groups had a number of technical sub-groups working for them, including a nuclear sub-group that involved Penney, Brundrett and Cockburn on the British side, and whose report laid the foundations for amending the McMahon Act.

The amended Act went before Congress on 10 June 1958, and passed into law on the 30th. Wording the amendment had not been entirely straightforward. Alliance politics in NATO dictated that the US ought not to name Britain in legislation on atomic sharing (hence the phrase 'and other friendly countries' in the Declaration), but the Joint Committee on Atomic Energy was also unhappy with the prospect that, by applying in principle to *any* other 'friendly' state, the Act might be a blank cheque for nuclear proliferation. In short, information should be exchanged with the British alone, but without explicitly saying so. The circle was squared by stating that only countries that 'have developed capacity in the weapons field *when the Act goes into force*' (emphasis added) would be eligible. Since the only states other than the US that had 'developed capacity' in nuclear weapons were Britain and the Soviet Union, the door was effectively shut to others.

With the Act suitably amended, negotiations on the information to be exchanged could proceed. A meeting was arranged for Washington in August 1958 but much remained to be decided. The likely price for American nuclear weapons information was British agreement to a test moratorium. Macmillan had told Eisenhower that he was prepared to do this, but only if assurances were forthcoming that Britain would obtain the information it required to perfect its weapons programme, particularly immunity to R1 and weight reduction of warheads.

Eisenhower was sympathetic, but the AEC was far more cautious: exchange of information was not to be an unrestricted flow across the Atlantic. The Committee drew up a list of what could be discussed at the forthcoming bilateral, which did not include immunity and weight reduction. Quarles informed Eisenhower that the list would not meet the needs stipulated by the British, and the President overruled his Committee in firm terms. With this agreed, both governments agreed that a test ban could be in place after 31 October.

None the less, opening exchanges at the first bilateral on 27–28 August were rather cagey. Although aware of British requirements, the US contingent were not fully informed of exactly how advanced the British programme was. The amendment only stipulated a 'demonstrated capacity', and the Americans therefore required some demonstration of the technological status of the British programme, while the British themselves naturally wanted to play their hand to its fullest advantage.

Eisenhower's instructions to the AEC did not extend to provision of *anything* the British requested, and the US delegation was still strictly limited in the designs it was allowed to show. These amounted to information on 3-megaton and 4-kiloton warheads, with any further disclosures requiring AEC and Presidential authorization. These designs were similar to those to be tested at *Grapple Z*, and hence were of limited use. The British responded with details of *Green Grass*; the two- and three-stage *Halliard* designs planned for *Grapple Z*; the nuclear artillery shell design *Yellow Anvil*; and a design for a small boosted warhead.[24] They also explained, in some detail, the recent history of their weapons development programme, and their current requirements.[25]

These exchanges helped clarify technical status and outstanding requirements, and the Americans were sufficiently struck with British weapon design to request a change in the firing schedule for *Grapple Z*. It is also worth noting that, despite the initial caution in the opening exchanges, information on the American warhead design subsequently anglicized by British scientists, the Mk 28, was given at this session.

The following month, the exchange was finalized at the Sandia bilateral. Here, the US provided information on a number of designs, including a three-stage H-bomb similar to the *Halliard* design; a lightweight missile-borne warhead, the Mk 47; and a boosted tactical warhead, the Mk.45.[26] The British expressed an interest in producing an anglicized version of the Mk.28 and Mk.47 designs at the Sandia bilateral; the Mk.28 was subsequently converted into the UK *Red Snow* warhead and used in the *Yellow Sun Mk II* gravity bomb, the *Blue Steel* guided bomb, and planned for use in the subsequently cancelled *Blue Streak* missile. The month after Sandia, the British further decided to pursue an anglicized version of the Mk.44 warhead in preference for *Blue Fox/Indigo Hammer* and also *Pixie*.

Even by the standards of the British nuclear programme, the events of 1957–58 represent startling progress at dizzying speed. Within the space of 16 months, breakthroughs in thermonuclear development, megaton warheads and Anglo-American collaboration had permanently changed the technological and political face of British nuclear weapons development.

The establishment of the test moratorium on 31 October 1958, which subsequently became an all-out ban on above-ground nuclear testing in 1963, effectively meant that there was now no going back. Atmospheric testing at Maralinga and Christmas Island came to an end. In Australia, however, work on the so-called minor trials continued until 1962. This work, which would leave behind considerably more problems than the major tests, is the subject of Chapter 11.

11
Kittens, Rats and *Vixens*[1]

The story of the atomic trials in Australia would be incomplete without an account of the supporting experimental work that began at Emu Field in 1953 and continued at Maralinga from 1958 until 1963, six years after the major trials ended. Five different kinds of experiment, involving some 550 events, were carried out during those years. They were not nuclear explosions, but they were an important element in the weapon programme. What was their nature and purpose? When and how were they conducted? What were their political and safety implications?

What the minor trials were for

The various minor trials were codenamed *Kittens*, *Rats*, *Tims* (which were similar to *Rats*) and *Vixens*. The first three were purely weapon development experiments, and tests of components and materials; the two types of *Vixen* trials, A and B, were concerned with safety.

Kittens, the first experiments, were to develop and improve initiators. In an atomic bomb, an implosion system using conventional explosive is used to compress the fissile material in the core – plutonium or highly enriched uranium – very rapidly, and at the instant of firing a device called an initiator produces a supply of neutrons to initiate a chain reaction in the fissile material. The efficient functioning of the weapon depends on the timing, intensity and rate of neutron output from the initiator. In the *Kittens* experiments, small quantities of radioactive and other materials were mounted in an assembly of conventional (i.e. chemical) explosive. Various configurations and combinations of materials were tried – for example, radioactive polonium and non-radioactive beryllium. The effect of the chemical explosion was to mix the polonium with the beryllium, thus allowing alpha particles to bombard the beryllium and so release neutrons. The output of neutrons after the explosion was measured by sensitive detectors coupled to oscillographic recorders. *Kittens* trials took place in 1953 at Emu Field, and in 1955, 1956, 1957, 1959, 1960 and 1961 at Naya, an area on the east of the Maralinga site.

Tims and *Rats* began later, in 1955 and 1956 respectively. They were experiments in which a conventional explosive was fired in a simulated weapon assembly; the resulting movement of the materials, and the passage of shockwaves through the assembly, were precisely measured and recorded. Natural uranium, which is non-fissile and only slightly radioactive, was used in the mock weapon to simulate the fissile material used in a real weapon. Though similar in purpose, *Tims* and *Rats* used different techniques of measurement. For *Tims*, the methods – telemetry probes, high-speed photography and radiography – were external. For *Rats*, an intense, short-lived gamma-ray source, the size of a pea, was placed inside the non-explosive assembly; using gamma-ray detectors a picture of the event was obtained from the inside – Pilgrim said it was like taking an inside-out X-ray – and flux-time records were made at a nearby recording station.

Tims and *Rats* dispersed natural uranium locally, but the radioactivity was too low to be hazardous. These experiments took place in the Australian desert rather than in Britain, where they could have been conducted safely if necessary, because of a ministerial undertaking made in 1954 that no experiments using fission products or any other hazardous material would be carried out at Aldermaston's range at Foulness.[2] Though this statement referred specifically to Foulness, it was held to apply generally, and was reaffirmed in 1956.

Tims experiments took place on the Maralinga Range in 1955, 1956–61 and 1963 in an area called Kuli, and *Rats* each year from 1956 to 1960 at Naya and Dobo.

Vixens were safety experiments, which began in 1959. The first series was concerned with the consequences of accidents, especially fires, involving nuclear weapons, radioactive materials or reactors. It was important to know what would happen to the radioactive and toxic materials if a large fire broke out. Would they burn, and how widely would they be dispersed? Would they be carried downwind in the smoke, or would they remain in the debris of the fire? The burning experiments in this series were later called *Vixen A*, to distinguish them from the B series which began in 1960.

Vixen B was a study of the inherent safety characteristics of nuclear warheads. Safety in the *Blue Danube* and *Red Beard* designs had principally been assured by keeping their fissile cores and non-nuclear assemblies physically separate from each other until they were to be used. The designs which followed, however, were intended to be stored and moved with the cores in place. The effects of detonating the explosive accidentally during manufacture, storage or transport, therefore, had to be investigated, however unlikely such accidents were. These *Vixen B* experiments were of serious practical importance, for both the armed services and the public; they were also the most likely to cause significant contamination, especially by dispersing plutonium. *Vixen B* experiments differed from all the other minor trials since they used fissile material in a simulated weapon. The quantity was reduced and the experiment was arranged so as to limit the chain reaction to an amount of fission energy that was quite insignificant in comparison with the chemical explosive used. Nevertheless there was a fission reaction, and some fission products resulted; moreover, plutonium debris was dispersed. These experiments had both political and safety implications, far more than any of the others.

There were *Vixen A* experiments in 1959, 1960 and 1961 at Wewak, and *Vixen B* in 1960, 1961 and 1963 at Taranaki, near the firing site of the third *Antler* round.

Kittens

The initiator experiments started very modestly with five shots at Emu Field in 1953 in an area ('K site') about 8 miles from the *Totem* firing site and 5 miles from Emu Village. They began before the main *Totem* trial and were carried out on 26 and 30 September and 6, 14 and 17 October. Ground contamination was very light outside a 40 ft radius, though some radioactive debris was thrown up to 400 yards, but the maximum extent of the danger area, some 20 miles downwind, was well within the main *Totem* danger area.[3]

The scientific results led to an improved design for a simpler and considerably smaller initiator. The scientists wanted to follow up with ten more shots in September 1954, perhaps in Australia again.[4] However a site in the United Kingdom would doubtless save time and expense, and a third possibility was in Alberta, as suggested by Dr Solandt of the Canadian Defence Research Board. The best site found in the United Kingdom was in an area beyond Wick, in the far north of Scotland, where the bulk of contamination would be carried out to sea. One crofter would have to bought out if this site was to be used. Penney did not like the idea at all.[5] The weather at Wick was unreliable; it rained constantly; the high humidity would be bad for electronic instruments. Contaminated debris would be a problem, and though the hazards of downwind contamination were probably acceptable, he could not give the local authorities an honest assurance that they were zero. Besides, it would be difficult to get the site ready in time. Australian weather, by contrast, would be ideal. *Kitten* firings in the desert, far from the nearest people and stock, would be 'safe for certain'. A permanent range in Australia was intended in any case and, for the range staff, occasional minor trials would usefully fill in the gaps between major trials. There might not even be much difference in cost between Australia and the United Kingdom.

Proposals for *Kittens* in South Australia in September–October 1954 were approved, and Penney was instructed to discuss the technical aspects with Butement, the chief scientist of the Australian Department of Supply. But before the Australian government had been formally approached, Penney visited the United States and there acquired fresh information that made initiator tests unnecessary in 1954. They might be wanted in 1955, but even this was uncertain pending the results of new research work at Aldermaston.[6] It was not until August 1954 that Penney confirmed the need for initiator tests the following May.[7]

Meanwhile, the Australian government seemed favourably disposed, but wanted safety data on the tests. Martin, the Australian defence scientific adviser, visiting London in the summer of 1954, had discussions with Penney which satisfied him on safety. Plans for the permanent proving ground, as we saw in Chapter 6, were worked out between the Australian authorities and the Wilson mission from the United Kingdom during November and December 1954; these plans included arrangements for *Kittens* early in 1955, either at Emu Field or in a section of the Maralinga Range where they would not interfere with the main construction work. In December the Australian government confirmed its agreement to the tests, subject to detailed examination of the safety data, and promised the help of 20 Australian personnel for three months. Aldermaston produced a safety document, *The Scope and Hazards of Kittens 1955*, in February, which the Australian government referred to Martin.[8] He considered the hazards slight, but recommended that a standing committee should be set up to advise. This was the origin of the Australian Weapons Tests Safety Committee (AWTSC); though it was to be mainly concerned with the major programme of nuclear tests – *Mosaic, Buffalo* and *Antler* – it was first set up in connection with the small programme of much less hazardous minor trials, which were not nuclear tests.

The AWTSC recommended acceptance of the 1955 *Kittens*, and work began on the *Kittens* site at Naya to the east of what was to be the main range. A team of a dozen scientists arrived from Aldermaston in April. With Australian agreement, on the advice of the new safety committee, the plan was extended to include some timing experiments of the type later called *Tims*, and the whole programme was completed successfully between May and July 1955.

The British asked for further *Kitten* tests in early 1956 and six were carried out uneventfully in March. After 1956 the *Kittens* experiments became only a small part of annual programmes of minor trials; *Kittens* featured in 1957, 1959, 1960 and 1961, and they ceased after 1961 when they were no longer considered necessary because other methods of neutron initiation had been developed.

Tims

Penney explained the need for experiments of the *Tim* type to the Atomic Energy Authority board in April 1956. The success and efficiency of nuclear weapons depended largely on the degree of compression of fissile material, and the synchronization of the operation of the neutron initiator with the instant of maximum compression. These depended on several variables. As a guide to design, mathematically ideal circumstances could be calculated, but unless the theory was checked by controlled experiment, the calculations could not be confidently applied to practical designs. To obtain the design data needed for their weapons programme, the scientists required about 100 non-fissile firing trials.

The obvious site was Maralinga, but to save staff and time and to avoid delays in interpreting results, an alternative and nearer site was desirable. Aldermaston's range at Foulness (used for explosive firings) was out of the question. A suitable alternative would be the range belonging to the Chemical Defence Experimental Establishment (CDEE) at Porton, less than an hour by road from Aldermaston. Here localized hazards could be confined well within the range, which was fenced and controlled. Some radioactivity would, however, inevitably be carried beyond the boundaries, and ministers would have to be consulted. One argument advanced in favour of Porton was the financial saving.[9] Another was that as the British tests in Australia gave rise to radioactivity there, it would be embarrassing to prohibit tests in the United Kingdom on the grounds that the British public could not accept 'the possibility of extremely small and quite safe exposures to occasional radioactive conditions of this kind'. A hazard assessment was made jointly by the Harwell health physicists and the MRC's laboratory (the Radiobiological Research Unit, located alongside the Atomic Energy Research Establishment) at Harwell. After consulting the Oxford agricultural scientist Scott Russell, they concluded that the experiments could be safely undertaken at Porton, provided that there was detailed monitoring after each shot and that overlapping of contamination from various shots was avoided. However, ministers were adamant that the experiments could not take place in the United Kingdom; any publicity might have repercussions on the Atomic Energy Authority's other activities (the first civil nuclear power programme had been announced in February 1955). *Tims* experiments had to be held in Australia. They duly took place at Maralinga, with AWTSC approval, during September and October 1956, in the intervals between the *Buffalo* shots.

Minor trials in 1957 and 1958

By 1957, minor trials had diversified and grown in scale since the 1953 *Kittens*, and some people thought that additions were made too readily and uncritically.[10] The programme for 1957, approved by the Australian government in December 1956, included *Kittens*, *Tims* and *Rats*, up to 88 firings in all. It was carried out from March to November – 21 *Kittens*, 44 *Tims* and 23 *Rats*. In 1958 there were 27 *Rats* and 71 *Tims* firings between April and November.

As the programmes became larger and more complex, there was increasing discussion and argument between the British and Australian authorities, largely for political reasons. The minor trials never attracted press or public attention in Australia, but international developments were taking place that were soon to put a temporary stop to major trials and to set a question mark against at least some minor trials.

Maralinga and the moratorium

In April 1958 President Eisenhower had responded to a Soviet declaration – immediately after a series of H-bomb explosions in Siberia – that the Soviet Union was unilaterally suspending nuclear weapon tests. Eisenhower, moving away from his previous insistence that nuclear weapons could be discussed only in the context of general disarmament, offered separate talks on the idea of a test ban, and suggested a technical conference on inspection and detection of tests. More US H-bomb tests – the *Hardtack* I series – began at once in the Pacific and lasted from the end of April to mid-August; Phase II continued from mid-September to the end of October. Meanwhile, during July and August, a Conference of Experts to Study the Possibility of Detecting Violations of a Possible Agreement on Suspension of Nuclear Tests met in Geneva. It included American, Russian, British, Canadian and French representatives. Four methods of detecting and identifying nuclear explosions were considered: recording acoustic waves, locating and examining radioactive debris, recording seismic signals and recording radio signals. By the end of August it reached the conclusion that it was technically feasible to set up a workable and effective control system for the detection of violations of an agreement to cease nuclear testing.[11]

Early in August UNSCEAR had presented its first report. This report, compiled by scientists from 15 nations, came to similar conclusions to those of the Bronk and Himsworth reports of June 1956. It found that the radiation received from fallout so far was slight – only 5 per cent of that from natural sources – but warned that even a small rise in environmental radioactivity in the world might eventually cause appreciable damage to large populations. It estimated the additional deaths from leukaemia due to fallout as between 400 and 2,000 a year worldwide, but pointed out that even the higher figure was only a small fraction of the annual total of 150,000. The committee had voted down, by 9 votes to 5 a Soviet proposal to recommend suspension of all nuclear tests; the report did, however, urge member states to take steps to minimize the irradiation of human populations by nuclear weapon explosions as well as by medical and dental X-rays (the major source of man-made radiation exposures) and by atomic wastes.

Eisenhower proposed that test ban negotiations should begin on 31 October and pledged a one-year moratorium as soon as the talks began; the Russians agreed. The following month, September 1958, both sides mounted new tests, another H-bomb series in Siberia and *Hardtack* II in Nevada, which ended on 30 October. On 31 October a Conference on the Discontinuance of Nuclear Weapon Tests opened in Geneva. After the last Soviet firing was detected on 3 November, there begun a moratorium on nuclear weapon testing; it lasted for nearly three years, until September 1961.

The latest British test series at Christmas Island, *Grapple Z*, had been completed in September 1958, and *Lighthouse*, a projected kiloton trial at Maralinga in 1959, had been cancelled. Britain was most anxious, however, to continue with minor trials, some of them essential to the next of the *Grapple* series. It could not then be foreseen that further

Grapple trials would never take place and that *Grapple Z* in 1958 would be the last.

The minor trials were not nuclear explosions – they did not involve either significant fission or fusion – and they were considered by the British to be unaffected by the moratorium or by the Geneva negotiations. The Americans took the same view of their comparable experiments. However, in the circumstances it was feared that the use of the term 'minor trials' might be misleading, and Penney decided that they must in future be called 'assessment tests'.[12] 'We are changing the name', he told the Foreign Office, 'in order to prevent the possible interpretation that they are very small nuclear explosions'.[13] At the same time, in order not to prejudice negotiations in Geneva, instructions were sent to Maralinga that all firings involving radioactive materials must cease by midnight on 31 October.[14]

The new title was not at first introduced into correspondence with the Australians. Soon, however, it would be time to approach them about assessment tests in 1959. As a preliminary move, the British view of the tests and their exemption from the moratorium was disclosed to the Australian representative in Geneva. He seemed unsurprised.[15]

The term 'assessment tests' lasted only a year, and by late 1959 another title, avoiding the word 'test', became politically desirable. For the future, the work was to be known as 'the Maralinga Experimental Programme', or MEP, and the plan for each year was to be designated MEP 1960 (or MEP 60), MEP 61, and so on.[16] The new title encapsulated a decision that the experimental work was to continue at Maralinga, but even this had come into question in 1958 during appraisals, at Aldermaston and in Whitehall, of future test policy. One possibility discussed was transferring the assessment tests to Christmas Island.[17] Another was the use of the Nevada test site, which had been informally suggested by American scientists to a visitor from Aldermaston. (The bilateral agreement providing for technical cooperation in the uses of atomic energy for mutual defence purposes had been concluded in July 1958.) The Nevada idea had its attractions – an appreciable saving in staff, possibly some financial savings and intangible gains in closer cooperation with the Americans. Practically, the chief disadvantage would be loss of independence and flexibility. Politically and strategically, Aldermaston felt that it might be inexpedient to withdraw all work from Maralinga.[18]

To establish that these weapon experiments – and the safety experiments already contemplated – would be permissible under a test ban treaty, Aldermaston scientists were seeking a definition of a nuclear explosion which would permit them while preventing even small-scale major trials. It proved extraordinarily difficult, scientifically and legally. Penney at first suggested that the term nuclear explosion should be held to mean 'explosions which are a consequence of the deliberate release of nuclear fission, or nuclear fusion, or both'.[19] British and American scientists continued to seek a definition which could be included in a comprehensive test ban treaty, but the complex arguments about reaction times (10^{-6} seconds? 10^{-8} seconds?) and energy yields (10 ton TNT? 10 lb TNT?) need not concern us here, as a Comprehensive Test Ban Treaty was not achieved until 1996. A definition was irrelevant to the Partial Test Ban Treaty (PTBT) eventually agreed in 1963.

New departures in the 1959 programme

The 1959 assessment tests were planned to take place from early March to November.[20] Such programmes, lasting for nine or ten months of the year, meant that – even without major trials – the range was almost continuously operational. Three teams a year of Aldermaston staff, each of some 20–25 men, were engaged in them at Maralinga each year, as well as the numerous Australian and British staff permanently on duty there.

For 1959, there were to be 21 *Kittens* firings at Naya in March and May; 22 *Rats* firings at Dobo, a new site in the Naya area, from May to June; and about 64 *Tims* firings between May and December in the *Tims* areas TM100 and TM101 (see Map 5, p. 147). The approval of the Australian government was requested in January 1959 and a safety statement followed; approval was given six weeks later.[21] Subsequently, as we shall see, experiments of a new type – the *Vixen* safety experiments – were added to the programme. The arrangements in the safety statement were based on the latest (1958) ICRP recommendations: outside the safety boundaries for each firing site the radiation levels were not to exceed those for members of the general public, i.e. one-tenth of those recommended by ICRP for the protection of radiation workers in atomic energy establishments, universities and hospitals. The airfield and Maralinga village were both well outside the safety radii. All the tests would create a local inhalation hazard around the point of burst and would leave areas of radioactive contamination out to about 60 yards. The scientists would take action to remove the worst contamination and would survey, mark and map the remaining contaminated areas. Each team leader, before leaving Maralinga, would take all reasonable steps to make the areas and buildings safe and would give the scientific superintendent in overall charge of operations a map showing radioactive areas. He in turn would satisfy himself that everything required had been done, and finally would hand over to the Range Commandant (an Australian Army Officer) a composite map showing radioactive areas and buildings, with a signed statement detailing the residual radioactivity and specifying the precautions to be taken. Then, for the inter-trial period, these areas would become the responsibility of the Range Commandant, along with the remainder of the range. He was assisted by the Australian health physics representative (AHPR) who would make regular surveys and some special measurements. The AHPR was accountable to the Commandant, but also was to make technical reports to Aldermaston and to the AWTSC.

The first *Vixens*

Hazards from accidents to nuclear weapons in transport or storage were much discussed during 1957/58. In March, Penney called together scientists from Harwell, Risley and Aldermaston to consider them. In April, two Aldermaston scientists attended a conference in Washington and brought back information about American experiments that had been going on since 1955, and about accidents involving nuclear weapons that had already occurred. American data were still far from complete, especially on the dispersion of plutonium in a fire.

Experimental work at Maralinga seemed essential. However, burning trials using plutonium and beryllium were unprecedented and could be open to political misrepresentation: 'a careful approach to Australia' would be needed. Three possibilities were suggested. First, Titterton might be told the reason for the tests, given estimates of the contamination, and then asked how best to obtain political clearance.[22] Second, the Australian government might be approached directly through the normal channels, that is, through the Commonwealth Relations Office and the High Commission in Canberra. Third, the new tests might be assumed to be covered by the approval already received for the 1959 programme, and particulars might simply be forwarded to the AWTSC as an amendment – an unworthy suggestion. The first course was adopted, and Titterton was asked for his advice on the best way of getting the Australian government's agreement to the *Vixen* shots. The object of the proposed *Vixen* experiments – 'to study the dispersion of plutonium, uranium and beryllium when released in particulate form by explosions or fire, and to obtain information which will permit estimates of hazards downwind in case of accidental release' – was explained to him. Two trials were proposed, each using 200 g of plutonium metal, to be burnt in a controlled petrol fire. There would be no breathing hazard beyond 3,600 yards and no deposition hazard beyond 2,500 yards.

Within a month, Titterton replied that the AWTSC recommended acceptance of the extended programme, and a formal request from London to Canberra was sent a few days later.[23]

These *Vixen* experiments – later called *Vixen A* to distinguish them from the B type introduced in 1960[24] – had a special feature. They were the only experiments to use balloons – not to be confused with the balloon systems used for major trials. They were flown to carry meteorological instruments, especially anemometers, and radiological instruments for measuring radioactivities at high altitudes. These were needed in order to correlate the measurements of airborne and deposited radioactivity resulting from the fire with micro-meteorological conditions. Estimates of radioactive dispersal under various meteorological conditions, in case of a real accident or fire, could then be made.

Unfortunately, the unpredictable weather of Maralinga was bad for balloons, and in a violent storm during the *Vixen* series in 1959 two balloons tore their mooring cables apart and broke free. This was the first of three such occurrences.

MEP 60 – the 1960 Maralinga experimental programme

General proposals for a 1960 programme, to include *Tims*, *Rats* and *Vixens*, were sent to Australia in October 1959, with the hope they would receive no publicity.[25] Although the experiments were not nuclear tests, it would be embarrassing if they were talked about while test ban discussions were going on in Geneva.

During December 1959 plans for new safety experiments were being evolved at Aldermaston and discussed by officials and ministers. The object was not, as in the 1959 *Vixens*, to investigate the hazards arising after an accident, but to study how the weapons themselves could be made accident-proof. A question of particular interest was 'one point safety'. For a nuclear weapon to operate properly, an accurately formed implosion was necessary, but an accidental initiation of the conventional high explosive at a single point would produce a very distorted implosion which would not create a full nuclear explosion but might trigger a limited, and small, fission reaction. The new *Vixen B* experiments were planned to produce design information to give assurance that this would not happen. Actual warheads were not to be used in the experiments and the amount of fission would be minimal, equivalent to grams, or at most a few pounds, rather than to tonnes of TNT.

American scientists were planning similar experiments for 1960, but, it was argued, it would be wrong to rely entirely on American data.

Nuclear weapons now being made in Britain to American designs – as a consequence of the 1958 bilateral agreement on collaboration in atomic energy for defence purposes – incorporated substitute materials of British origin, and some design modifications. Independent tests were therefore essential for assessing their safety during manufacture, transport and storage of the weapons. It was doubtful that such tests could be concealed.

Ministers considered the case for the new experiments and their implications for the Geneva Conference. They decided that the experiments would be necessary as long as Britain continued to manufacture, transport and store nuclear weapons, and Britain must try to make sure that they were not prohibited by any agreement to suspend tests. The US authorities should be consulted about tabling a draft article defining nuclear explosions that would not preclude these safety experiments, and British representatives should be prepared to put the case frankly to the Soviet delegation at Geneva.

As for the Australian government, ministers said that Titterton should be asked informally for his advice on the best approach, though the Commonwealth Relations Office would have preferred direct communication through the normal channels. Two senior Aldermaston scientists, Newley and Pilgrim, left for Australia a few days later. They reported on their return that Titterton saw no objection in principle to the *Vixen B* proposals and would advise the Australian government accordingly if asked. He regarded the new experiments as a logical extension of *Vixen A*; the approval already given by the government for the 1960 programme would, he believed, adequately cover them, provided a satisfactory safety statement was submitted. He thought a formal approach undesirable, as it would force the government to consider the specific nature of the experiments, and how they varied from those already approved. Then Newley asked him about the long-term radioactivity that the experiments would create on the Range. In Titterton's view it was acceptable, provided it did not extend beyond the range boundaries; in any case, Maralinga was being considered as a disposal ground for Australian radioactive waste.

Titterton's advice was well received in Britain and his help was much appreciated. The chairman of the Atomic Energy Authority, Sir Roger Makins, agreed that it was wise to avoid formal communications on 'these contentious experiments' and to proceed without going through formal channels. This, Makins conceded, involved a slight risk that the Australians might raise some objections later on. It had been suggested, he said, that instead of the usual channels the matter might be take up at the highest level, with Menzies, but this might lead to 'some danger of confusion and possibly irritation at the Australian end'.

Aldermaston despatched a safety statement for MEP 60 to Canberra, and Titterton replied in April that the AWTSC had accepted it, but would require advance notice of each *Vixen B* firing, and wanted more information about the contamination of the range. This was sent in May. A formal approach was made to Canberra in June, but the Australian government was slow in replying. Normally, Makins had commented, it did not enquire into details of British experiments, and approval was always given subject to AWTSC acceptance of a detailed safety statement.

If this had hitherto been the case, it was no longer so; the Australian authorities, especially the Department of Defence, were not happy. In August, Titterton was astonished to learn that permission for *Vixen B* had not yet been sent. The situation – a silly one, he said – had developed without his knowledge, or he would have intervened earlier.[26] The Department of Defence was demanding information to allow it to decide on the 'political safety' of the experiments, as distinct from the environmental safety which was the business of the AWTSC.[27] Martin (Defence scientific adviser and former AWTSC chairman) 'spent a lot of time complaining that too little was put on paper between the UK and Australia'. If it was to be agreed between the two governments that information about present and future trials was to be given to the Department of Defence, as well as the AWTSC, Martin would insist on less discussion and more paperwork. He would want to know, for example, the total amounts of high explosive, fissionable and radioactive materials used in each round, the expected height of the cloud, and the fallout patterns.

At last, in September, news came from Canberra that the extended MEP 60 was approved and the four *Vixen B* firings could proceed at once.

More trouble with balloons

MEP 60 had more problems before it was completed in October. There was another loss of balloons. After the previous breakaway, the design of the balloons had been modified, but in a thunderstorm on 23 September seven balloons broke loose simultaneously. Five were recovered on the range, but two were lost.

Titterton wrote Aldermaston a critical letter about this and other matters. The balloons did not concern the AWTSC, he said, except when they passed over the boundaries of the range. It was to be hoped this would never happen again, but some level must be set for the permissible level of radioactivity on any balloon that was to be flown. Apart from safety, if anyone were to identify a lost balloon, or if a small child were to pick up a piece of balloon fabric, the Australian government could be politically embarrassed.

The AWTSC asks more questions

Titterton's letter continued with a list of questions. In the *Vixen B* experiments, had there been an approach to criticality in any round? What information about the results could be given to the AWTSC? What did the residual radioactivity consist of? The committee felt strongly that the materials ought to be named; vague descriptions like 'fissile material of long life' and 'toxic material' were unsatisfactory. The committee had complete confidence in the safety assessments, but it wanted to be able to reject criticisms from elsewhere about insufficient information, and to regularize the difficult position in which it found itself after the 'recent fuss', especially about balloons. Could general descriptions be given of the various types of experiment – *Tims*, *Kittens* and *Vixens* – and the radioactive clouds associated with them? Until it had received Aldermaston's views on these matters, the committee felt that it should not make a recommendation to the Australian government about the next programme.

Pilgrim replied fully on each point, giving a summary of the purpose and method of each of the five types of experiment. He enclosed a detailed technical note on the meteorological conditions required for firing, and on how the safe distances were calculated using the latest ICRP recommendations. He promised reports on the 1959 *Vixen A* burnings very soon, and on the 1960 *Vixen B* firings in a few months. The latter had gone very much as predicted; the small, controlled amount of fission which occurred was adequate for experimental purposes but radiologically insignificant. It was agreed that in order to provide the fuller information which the AWTSC was now asking for, safety statements would be more detailed and explicit, and therefore highly classified. The safety statement for the 1961 programme, already sent, was being revised accordingly.

MEP 61

Plans for MEP 61 were in hand well before MEP 60 finished. MEP 61 was expected to be similar but on a rather smaller scale. It was to run from March to November or December. Some Aldermaston scientists would arrive in February, and the number on site would rise to about 100 during

April, when *Kittens* and *Vixen A* and *B* firings would be in progress. About 250 range staff would also be needed, with a contingent of Royal Engineers who had taken part in the 1960 *Vixen* series, and a few RAF personnel for decontamination duties. The numbers engaged in these programmes, though nothing like those at major trials, were considerable, and *Vixen* firings were said to have something of the appearance and atmosphere of a small major trial.

A request for approval was sent to Canberra in late September. The safety statement followed and, under a new arrangement agreed between ministers in the summer, a copy was sent to the Department of Defence, as well as to Titterton for the AWTSC. But when scientists began arriving at Maralinga in February to start firings in March, MEP 61 had not yet been approved. The Australian Department of Defence, inspired by Martin, wanted further information, and more was sent, but it did not satisfy the minister, Athol Townley. He had specific instructions from the Prime Minister to satisfy himself about the Maralinga experiments from the political as well as the safety point of view. Especially since the balloon incident of 23 September, the Australians had become extremely sensitive about Maralinga. They felt that they really did not know what was going on there and now they were determined to do so. If it was believed that nuclear weapons were being tested there during the moratorium, public opinion in Australia would be united against the government and it would be accused of opposition to disarmament – and this in a general election year.

At the beginning of March, the Prime Minister's Department (said to be 'plainly embarrassed' by it) despatched a strongly worded letter, in terms personally approved by Townley, protesting about inadequate information. He was anxious not to delay the programme but could not agree to it on the strength of the two documents received from the United Kingdom. A senior British officer familiar with the trial programme should visit Australia at once to brief him and his departmental advisers, and should be authorized to disclose any information – other than on weapon design – needed to enable the minister to fulfil his responsibilities to his government.

Peter Thorneycroft, the British Minister of Aviation, replied affably, and Dickins, the Director General of Atomic Weapons, accompanied by Pilgrim from Aldermaston, departed promptly for Australia. Their visit produced instantaneous results. They had long meetings with Martin and Defence Department officials – during which Martin disconcerted them by asking why implosion experiments could not be done in Britain if they were so safe – and two meetings with Townley. He quickly agreed to advise approval of MEP 61, subject to satisfactory precautions for balloons and to the omission from the *Vixen A* series (the burning experiments) of a device that looked like a real bomb; he was understandably afraid its appearance might lead to false rumours. (Devices externally resembling bombs had been used in the 1959 *Vixen* series.)

All difficulties appeared to be resolved. Townley and Thorneycroft exchanged friendly, and grateful, messages. But within a few days, on 22 March, a thunderstorm struck Maralinga. Ten balloons, all inflated, were bedded down. Fortunately, all were clean of surface radioactivity. Four broke loose in the fierce gusts of winds: on three the safety devices worked, but the fourth escaped, leaving a broken ripcord and trailing 600 ft of flying cable. A search for it began in the darkness. A report of the incident reached ministerial level within hours and Townley was furious. A board of enquiry was set up at once, and balloon flying and *Vixen A* firings were suspended. It seemed that balloons might be banned for the future, but the embargo was lifted three weeks later and the *Vixen A* series was completed. There were no more after 1961.

Another, much less serious problem arose over *Vixen B*. Titterton, as AWTSC chairman, complained that the 1961 *Vixen B* firings had violated the western boundary of the permitted firing sector in a minor way and had spread radioactivity outside the area agreed with the AWTSC. There was a good deal of internal argument at Aldermaston as to whether the alleged violation had actually occurred, but all the senior Aldermaston scientists, including the Director, found even the possibility of a minor violation disturbing and insisted that every effort must be made to avoid the slightest infringement of agreements between Aldermaston and the AWTSC.

MEP 61 ended in December, and the same month an Australian general election returned Menzies and his government to office with the slenderest of majorities. A different result would probably have meant very different official attitudes towards further experiments at Maralinga.

MEP 62

In August 1961, while MEP 61 was still in progress, British intentions for 1962 were conveyed to Canberra. Beginning in March, up to ten *Vixen B* shots, 30 *Kittens* and 80 *Tims* were planned. The full costs of the experiments and any subsequent safety arrangements would be borne by the United Kingdom. As usual, publicity should be avoided. There would be the usual health physics precautions, and a safety statement was coming.

One novel safety feature of MEP 62, codenamed *Waterlily*, was a large steel vessel, like a small gasholder, that was to be used to contain *Vixen B* explosions.

The AWTSC accepted MEP 62 with slight reservations; firing arcs must be strictly observed and more restrictive conditions should be applied to firings at Taranaki. Formal approval was given by Australia in November.

By January the programme had to be reviewed. Circumstances had changed radically since it was planned. The Geneva negotiations had broken down and the moratorium had ended. The Soviet Union had resumed nuclear testing in the atmosphere in September 1961, and had detonated a 58-megaton device in October. The United States had also resumed underground testing later in September. Atmospheric tests in the Pacific came later, in April 1962. In March a joint Anglo-American test (*Pampas*) was to be carried out underground in Nevada, and the British were also to participate later in the year in the American *Dominic* series, for which the United States would use Christmas Island as one of their bases. The original MEP 62 was obsolete, and furthermore British resources would be heavily engaged in *Pampas* and in Operation *Dominic* (in which the UK support task was codenamed *Brigadoon*).

A modified programme (incidentally dropping the *Waterlily* idea) was sent to Canberra. The *Vixen B* series would now be only three or four shots, and not before October; a reduced *Tim* series would begin in September; *Kittens* would take place concurrently. After all the build-up for a programme starting in March or April, the British authorities were very apologetic about the last-minute change, but Maralinga could expect a full workload in 1963. No one, however, could clearly foresee the course of nuclear weapon development or nuclear testing and the future of the range was undeniably in question. British officials found the situation *vis-à-vis* Australia uncomfortable, and the High Commission staff in Canberra tried hard to find some way of presenting the Australians with less embarrassingly laconic statements.

By the time *Pampas* had taken place, the technical position had changed again. The analysis of results would take time, and firm decisions about MEP 62 could not be made before the end of May, if then. Probably MEP 62 would not be required at all; it was an embarrassing position. The Australians were told without delay and were very understanding, albeit concerned about the 80 or so range staff they maintained. It was agreed that Australian and British manpower at Maralinga would have to be run down, and the range put on a care and maintenance basis, but more work was likely in 1963 and subsequent years, and no satisfactory alternative site existed.

The Australians asked for definite information about 1962, 1963 and the long-term prospects, and an appreciation was given to them in June. There would now be no MEP in 1962, but as long as nuclear weapons were in service, experiments at Maralingà would be necessary. Planning for 1963 would begin shortly, but MEP 1963 would contain no new types of experiment.

The Maralinga staff position was inevitably fluid. It was difficult for the Range Commandant to maintain morale throughout 1962, but the time was profitably used for a much needed tidying up exercise, which greatly improved the appearance of the place.

MEP 63

Originally, plans for 1963 included only *Tims* – about 12 shots, beginning in October – and up to six *Vixen B* shots, beginning in March. No *Vixen A* experiments were intended, and so no balloons (other than small meteorological balloons) would be used. Proposals were sent to Canberra in September 1962, but were soon modified to include extra *Tims*. The actual programme – 16 *Tim* shots and five *Vixen B*s – was all in March and April.

When Pilgrim, together with a new DGAW, L. T. D. Williams, visited Australia in December they found the Australians anxious on two counts. First, they clearly wanted tighter Australian control in the future. Martin emphasized that though he was recommending approval of MEP 63, he would not agree to a programme in 1964 without more information about what was being done. He seemed uncertain about what further information he would be seeking, but his attitude was one of suspicion. The Minister for Defence, Athol Townley, could not resist the opportunity of referring again to the balloon incidents of 1960 and 1961, which had not been serious in themselves, but which had eroded confidence. However, he was not so much worried about safety at Maralinga – he was content to leave the details to the AWTSC – as about political embarrassment. The government was constantly aware of its narrow majority, and was sensitive to the slightest possibility of trouble at the range. An untoward incident there might create a public impression that the government had little control over events on Australian territory.

The second anxiety of the Australian authorities was about the future of the range. They felt that Australia got nothing for her contribution and indeed that neither side was getting value for money; the cancellation of MEP 62, and the very few firings proposed for 1963, prompted doubts as to whether the continued existence of the range was justified. Williams apologized again for MEP 62 and explained the reasons for cancellation, unforeseen when MEP 62 was planned. But he assured the Australians that Britain would need a facility like Maralinga as long as she had a nuclear deterrent.

The Australians reassured Williams and Pilgrim that approval for MEP 63 would be forthcoming. Discussions then touched on what might happen to Australian nuclear policy if Menzies were to retire soon, as seemed likely. (He did not, and continued as Prime Minister until 1966.) A Labour government might even want to make Australia a nuclear-free zone.

The visitors also had talks with Titterton who suggested that the political worries of the Defence Department should not be taken too seriously. But the general view in Australia was he had overplayed his hand and that he had by this time little influence except on matters of safety.

The 1963 experiments took place uneventfully. There were 16 *Tim* firings, all in April, and five *Vixen B* shots were fired in March and April, with such success that Aldermaston notified the Australians in June that no more would be needed that year. Nor would a second series of *Tims* in the last quarter of the year. MEP 63 was over by the end of May and – though it was not realized at the time – it was the last ever at Maralinga.

The minor trials in retrospect

The minor trials did not deploy ships, aircraft and large numbers of men as did the twelve nuclear tests. But they were a continuing and very considerable commitment for Aldermaston for ten years, and were an important and integral part of the weapons research and development process (especially the *Kittens*, *Tims* and *Rats*). Minor trials, especially the *Vixens*, were the justification after 1957 for the continued use of the Maralinga range, which had after all only accommodated two major trials.

There had been a certain amount of publicity for the nuclear tests and a great deal of press and public interest in them in Australia. It was not so with the minor trials (under their various titles). Outside official circles, very few people apparently realized that Maralinga was being used for these experimental programmes, and that it continued to be used after *Antler*. The two *Vixen* series – which were on a much larger scale and involved more people, including Australians – were more likely to attract notice. But the British authorities were particularly anxious to avoid any publicity about the *Vixen B* series during the Geneva negotiations, since there was no agreed definition of nuclear explosions which would specifically exclude *Vixen B*.

Rules for the radiological protection of the minor trials participants were the same as those for major trials ('The Maralinga Radiological Safety Regulations'). Exposures were kept very low. In 550 events, 1,120 men were exposed to radiation: no one received more than 5 r, and only five of them exceeded 3 r; for nearly 800, exposures were at or below the threshold of detection. The public health hazards of the minor trials were nonexistent at the time. Unlike the nuclear tests, they produced no fallout beyond the range boundaries. However they caused greater residual surface radioactivity, some of it extremely long-lived owing to dispersed plutonium around, and downwind of, *Vixen A* firing sites at Wewak and *Vixen B* sites at Taranaki. Thus it was the minor trials, not the nuclear tests, which had the more significant long-term effects – though limited to range areas – on the Australian environment.

12
The Maralinga Range after 1963

In the period since 1987, two issues have dominated public concerns over the Maralinga range and the tests that took place on its territory. The first was the clean-up of the range after it had become clear that the original exercise in *Operation Brumby* had been inefficient and, in places, ineffective. The second was the emotionally charged issue of compensation for ex-servicemen for illnesses that were attributed to their presence at nuclear testing. This is dealt with in Chapter 13.

Closing down the Maralinga range

The Maralinga range, created at a cost of some £10 million, covered 20,000 square miles which included a test area of some 100 square miles. Maralinga village, built on high ground in thickly wooded country, consisted by 1959 of aluminium huts providing accommodation for some 750 men, and with kitchens catering for up to 1,600. There were well-equipped laboratories and workshops. There were also a church with resident chaplain, a power-station, a small, well-equipped hospital, a well-stocked and comfortable mess, library, bank, post office, shop, cinema, swimming pool and facilities for tennis, cricket, football and golf. The staff of the range, the Maralinga Range Support Unit (MARSU), were drawn from six armed services, 70 per cent from the United Kingdom and 30 per cent from Australia; it totalled about 120 between trials and 450 during a major trial, and was under a commandant from the Australian army.

Maralinga was a large commitment for the Australians. For the British it was a considerable investment and an essential facility for the nuclear weapons programme. In 1956, the Ministry of Supply expected no major trials there in 1957, but looked forward to regular, perhaps annual, trials from 1958 onwards. However, a major trial, *Antler*, did take place at Maralinga in 1957, but no more after that, for within two years of its completion three important factors altered the position of Maralinga.

The first factor was an Anglo-Australian one. Australian public opinion was increasingly restive; the Menzies government, anxious as it was to be fully cooperative, could not ignore the domestic political implications. A Gallup Poll in 1952 had shown a majority in favour of the tests (58 per cent, with 29 per cent opposed). However, opinion moved steadily against them, until in 1957 the poll showed a majority of 49 per cent against the tests and 37 per cent in favour. The British were well aware of what the Australian public opinion could mean for Maralinga, especially if there were to be a change of government: there were general elections in 1954, 1955, 1958 and 1961. However, after Maralinga was established, the new test range at Christmas Island had been acquired. Though set up expressly for high-yield trials, which were impossible at Maralinga, its use if necessary for kiloton and minor trials as well was an option that was seriously considered. Christmas Island had some disadvantages, but the decided advantage that its geographical position and the prevailing north-easterly winds meant that fallout would not be a problem.

The second factor bearing on the future of Maralinga was an Anglo-American one. The bilateral agreement of July 1958 created a fundamentally new relationship between the United States and Britain in the nuclear weapons field. It made possible the sharing of weapons data and designs, and radically changed the British weapons programme. By 1962 it led to joint weapon tests, underground, at the Nevada test site and to cooperation in atmospheric testing in the Pacific.

The third factor was an international one. In 1957, the future of all atmospheric nuclear weapon testing had become uncertain, with international discussions of a possible scheme to limit nuclear tests. The object of this scheme was to reduce global fallout in view of increasingly powerful public opinion against atmospheric testing all over the world. The British government's position was clear; it was prepared to discuss limitation of tests, but not suspension – a quite separate issue that it would only consider as part of a comprehensive disarmament agreement. At the Anglo-American Bermuda conference in March 1957, Eisenhower was concerned about public anxiety over nuclear tests, but believed it essential that the tests should continue. The British Prime Minister was no less concerned about public opinion. A public statement was made from Bermuda that the US and British governments would conduct their tests in a manner that would limit the radiation they produced to well below dangerous levels. It proved impossible to agree on an international scheme for limitation, but then events took a new turn and the test ban question was disengaged from that of comprehensive disarmament. Negotiations began in Geneva that resulted in the nuclear test moratorium that lasted from November 1958 to September 1961.

Besides planning for the assessment tests (or minor trials) which they intended to continue during the moratorium, the British made provisional plans for major trials, since no one knew how long the moratorium would last or what would be the results of the Geneva Conference on the Discontinuance of Nuclear Weapons Tests which opened on 31 October 1958. During 1958 some thought was given to the possibility of underground testing at Maralinga if atmospheric tests only were banned. (The United States had carried out two underground tests in Nevada in March 1955, three in 1957 and eleven in 1958.) But the idea did not seem promising; the only suitable site was 250 miles from Maralinga, and in an Aboriginal reserve.

The British thoroughly reviewed their test policy in December 1958 and Duncan Sandys, the Minister of Defence, advised the Prime Minister in January 1959 that no further high-yield tests were needed until the spring and no kiloton tests until the autumn of 1960, depending on the outcome of the Geneva Conference. It was decided for planning purposes to assume the indefinite suspension of all British nuclear tests – atmospheric, underwater or underground. This decision would be reconsidered if the Geneva Conference failed to reach a comprehensive agreement for the cessation of all nuclear tests. Neither the Australian nor the US government was to be informed until ministers had been able to consider the results of the Geneva negotiations.

Apart from its use for assessment trials, Maralinga was still important to the British authorities. If the Geneva Conference failed, they wanted the option to resume major trials there. The Director of Aldermaston argued that the cessation of major trials enhanced the importance of the minor experiments to support weapon development and safety research being conducted at Maralinga. Meanwhile, it was staffed and run at a reduced level, to support the assessment tests and MEPs, but requiring long notice for preparation of any possible major trials in future.

In September 1961 the moratorium ended and, as we have seen, the USSR resumed atmospheric tests at once. The United States, too, began testing, but underground in Nevada; then from April to November 1962 they carried out an extensive programme of atmospheric testing – the *Dominic* series – in the Pacific. No American detonation was as large as the 15-megaton *Castle Bravo* shot of 28 February 1954, but the USSR detonated a 58-megaton device in 1961 and two 30-megaton devices in 1962; 1962 was the year of the largest total yield – 108 megatons. More global fallout was created between September 1961 and October 1963, when the Partial Test Ban Treaty came into force, than in all the previous years of atmospheric testing. However British atmospheric testing was not resumed, either at Maralinga or Christmas Island, after the moratorium ended.

The situation changed again in 1962 when the British had the opportunity of a joint major trial (*Pampas*) underground, at the Nevada test site. This, and the Anglo-American cooperation in *Dominic*, made the function of Maralinga more uncertain. But the range was still needed for minor trials, and as an insurance against the possibility that the Nevada test site might not be open to the British for major trials if they were required later: the 1962 arrangement had been ad hoc, with no guarantee for the future.

The following year, 1963, the PTBT was signed in August, and came into force in October. It prohibited atmospheric but not underground tests so, although it ended the worst fears of fallout, it did not halt nuclear weapons development. The British authorities again reviewed the future of Maralinga during the summer, in the light of the PTBT, which Australia as well as the United Kingdom had signed. It was agreed that Maralinga was the best site for the experiments involving nuclear materials that would still be needed, and that the Australian government should be asked that the range should be kept on a care and maintenance basis, ready to come into operation at six to nine months' notice.

Discussions went on in 1964 between Britain and Australia, and in the Maralinga Board of Management, and there was some suggestion of a further programme in 1966 (MEP 66), but the Memorandum of Arrangements was due to expire in March that year unless extended by mutual agreement (see Appendix A). Meanwhile, clean-up operations continued. Where possible radioactive debris was collected and buried in pits in special disposal areas; chain mesh fences with posts set in concrete were erected; and all the fences carried durable warning signs. The clean-up culminated in an operation, codenamed *Hercules V*, by an Aldermaston team. After its completion, the range was considered safe on a care and maintenance basis, with reduced staffing and no health physicists present.

In 1965 the feasibility of using Maralinga for underground testing, if the Nevada test site was not available, was again considered. It would have been very expensive to develop an underground test facility there however, and the political as well as the geological and engineering problems were formidable. There seemed no further justification for maintaining the range, even at the minimum level, just to accommodate an occasional *Vixen B* experiment, and the British government finally informed the Australian government that the range would no longer be required after the expiry of the Memorandum of Arrangements.

The AWTSC was asked to advise on any additional measures that ought to be taken before the range was closed down. The detailed requirements that they laid down were carried out in 1967 at Maralinga and Emu Field by an Aldermaston team, in Operation *Brumby*. Debris and pieces of glazing from sites of the major trials were collected and buried; where the soil surface was contaminated with plutonium that could not be removed it was ploughed into the earth; and in some cases clean soil was spread over as a top cover. The AWTSC reported that their requirements had been fulfilled. At the ground zeros of the major trials, radioactivity was low enough to meet ICRP standards for continuous exposure of members of the public (0. 5 r a year), but at two areas used for minor trials there were still appreciable levels of plutonium contamination in the soil. The AWTSC considered that unrestricted access could be allowed to all but a few small areas, and they could be occupied on a short-term basis without risk. However, patrols at regular intervals would be advisable, for general surveillance and to dissuade any visitor from staying too long in areas unsuitable for permanent occupation.

The British authorities formally withdrew from the range, and a Memorandum on the Termination of the Memorandum of Arrangements (see Appendix B) was signed on 23 September 1967. As from 21 December the United Kingdom was released from all liabilities and responsibilities except for certain claims covered by clause 11 of the original Memorandum. This was confirmed in January 1979 after the British had agreed to an Australian request for the 'repatriation' of 0.5 kg of recoverable plutonium buried at Maralinga.

There were to be two further investigations, in 1977 and 1985. The first arose out of a proposal in 1972 that the Australian government should relinquish control of Maralinga. The Australian Ionizing Radiation Advisory Council (AIRAC) was asked for its views on what restrictions, if any, were still necessary. The Council saw no reason why the greater part of the range should not be relinquished at once, but recommended a field study of the whole range. This study was eventually carried out in 1977 by Australian scientists and published by AIRAC in January 1979 as AIRAC 4. It recommended that an area sufficient to include the sites of major and minor trials, and the burial ground and airfield 'cemetery' where radioactive material was buried should remain under government administration; the remainder of the range could be released. A further survey should be carried out not later than 1987.

This survey was done in 1985. The major trial sites were re-examined, all the experimental sites were re-surveyed, and the sites at which plutonium had been used were studied in much greater detail. The results showed that at the sites of the major trials (including the *Totem* sites at Emu Field) radioactivity would have decayed in the next 40 years sufficiently to allow continuous occupation. The main hazard remaining on the range was from the plutonium and associated americium (a daughter product of one of the plutonium isotopes) dispersed over comparatively large areas by the minor trials; if the plutonium-239 in the most contaminated area at Taranaki were air-borne in 'dust-raising activities', long-term occupation would entail radiological risks from inhaling or ingesting the dust. This survey, using more sophisticated portable instruments than those available earlier, drew attention to the widely scattered plutonium-contaminated fragments, distinguishable from the finely divided material and present in varied concentrations – from a few to less than one per square metre. These could be dangerous if found and picked up by, for example, souvenir hunters. The amount of plutonium buried in shallow pits and spread around an area of approximately 1 square mile at Taranaki-and smaller areas at Wewak, TM 100 and TM 101 – was substantial. 'Disposal of radioactive waste of this nature in this manner', the report concluded, 'cannot be considered acceptable current practice'.

The minor trials had left more trouble behind them than the big explosions.

The Royal Commission and the Maralinga clean-up

When the range was established at Maralinga, its long-term future was hardly considered. The Memorandum of Arrangements made no stipulations about the condition of the area when no longer required, beyond saying that the UK government 'accepted liability for such corrective measures as may be practicable in the event of radioactive contamination resulting from tests on the site' (see Appendix B). When the range was closed down the United Kingdom, as we have seen, undertook various cleaning operations, culminating in *Operation Brumby* in 1967. Long-term or permanent habitation of contaminated areas was considered unlikely by the AWTSC, though they thought that short-term occupancy by itinerants passing through was possible and ought to be taken into account. These assumptions formed the basis for the clean-up operations.

When the range was relinquished by the United Kingdom in December 1967, it became the responsibility of the Australian Federal government. It remained to be decided how long they would have to retain control of it; how long it would have to be fenced, guarded and supervised; and when it could be released for possible other uses. Maralinga was surveyed in 1974 and again (together with Emu Field) in 1985. In 1984 a Land Rights Act passed by the Australian Parliament gave Maralinga to the Tjarutja tribe; but what use would they be able to make of it? By early 1985, residual fission product radioactivity at six of the seven major trials sites (Tadje was the exception) was low and, by 1977 ICRP standards, would decay sufficiently in 50 years to permit 'continuous occupancy' – an interesting term that no one would have applied to these regions 30 or 40 years earlier, and one that some old Maralinga hands would find it difficult to view as realistic today. One consequence was the setting-up of a Royal Commission by the government of Australia to enquire into the British tests in Australia and their consequences, including the impact of the remaining contamination upon the rights given to the tribe.

The British government's submission to the Royal Commission had, in fact, attempted to prevent any serious consideration of the clean-up issue. The submission noted that there had been four clean-up operations prior to *Operation Brumby*,[1] but went on to qualify the 1985 study's conclusion about acceptable current practice by pointing out that 'not only was there no established current practice at the time of *Operation Brumby* about the disposal of plutonium waste, but there is still no internationally established practice'.[2] Moreover, the submission pointed out that the British government had explicitly drawn the Australian government's attention to the existence of surface level plutonium contamination at the Taranaki site during *Operation Brumby*, and that this had not prevented the signing of 1967 Memorandum pronouncing the Australian government satisfied with the decontamination, and releasing the UK from further obligations.

The conclusions of the British submission that relate to Maralinga were as follows:

- Whether there should be further decontamination work at Maralinga depends upon a number of factors, one of which is the future use of the area by Aborigines. There is no evidence of the numbers or pattern of movement of Aborigines in the now unrestricted areas around

Maralinga. Unless and until it is known whether there is a real likelihood of the small area around Taranaki being used to any significant extent, the Commission cannot begin to make a reasoned judgement on what further decontamination or protective work there is necessary.

- In addition, there is not sufficient evidence in various disciplines to enable the Commission to determine what, if anything, needs to be done and how, [and] what it would cost ...
- Only at 4 of the ground zeros at the nuclear test sites are the external doses above those equivalent to the ICRP limits for members of the public. They present little hazard to the casual visitor. Within about 50 years the radioactivity will have decayed so as to enable permanent habitation at these grounds in the unlikely event of it ever being sought.[3]

This case cut very little ice with the Royal Commission, which was heavily critical of virtually all concerned with the clean-up. In the first place, the AWTSC assumption, which also figured in the British submission, that long-term habitation of Maralinga was unlikely was rejected by the Royal Commission, which also concluded that the *Vixen* trials should never have been held at Maralinga at all in light of the long half-life of the plutonium used there. The Royal Commission went on to state that neither AWE nor AWTSC was aware of the plutonium-contaminated fragments at Taranaki, TM101 and Wewak, and that their subsequent discovery effectively changed the equation on the adequacy of the clean-up. In essence then, all bets were now off.

The AIRAC reports also came under fire. The AIRAC 4 report of 1979 was described as 'useful but limited', while the AIRAC 9 report of 1983 was written off as 'not an adequate scientific account of the testing programme'. In particular, AIRAC 9 was accused of introducing a bias by only interviewing those who had an interest in arguing that safety procedures were satisfactory, and failing to seek out evidence and witnesses that would testify to the contrary.

The Commission's conclusions on Maralinga ran like this:

1. The Maralinga range is not acceptable in its present condition and it must be cleaned up.
2. The aim of the clean-up should be to allow Aborigines access to the test sites without restriction ...
3. The following hazards must be dealt with before the Maralinga range can be considered suitable for unrestricted access by Aborigines:
   (i) plutonium contamination at Taranaki, TM100, TM101 and Wewak;

(ii) pits at Taranaki and TM101 containing plutonium-contaminated debris; and

(iii) uranium and beryllium contamination at Kuli ...

4. A Maralinga Commission should be established to determine clean-up criteria, oversee the clean-up and coordinate all future Range management ...

5. The cost of clean-up of the Maralinga range should be borne by the UK government because the previous clean-up in 1968 was clearly inadequate and based on insufficient information.[4]

The Australian government pondered these recommendations, and announced its decision in September 1986. The first three of the above recommendations were accepted, the fourth rejected, and the fifth only partially accepted: rather than an independent Maralinga Commission, the government felt that a Department of State body would be more appropriate, the Maralinga Rehabilitation Technical Advisory Committee (MARTAC).

The recommendation that the entire cost be borne by the UK government was rejected, but the likely costs had not yet been determined. A Technical Assessment Group (TAG), comprising five scientists (two Australian, two British and one American), was established in February 1986 to investigate clean-up criteria and associated costs. The basis for the clean-up criteria was that the land was to be returned to its traditional owners, Maralinga Tjarutja, who would use it to support an outstation lifestyle. On that basis, it was decided that for those living on the land in such a fashion, the annual risk of fatal cancer following inhalation of contaminated soil should be less than 1 in 10,000 by the age of 50.[5]

MARTAC and the TAG

Having set the criteria the clean-up would need to meet, the TAG reported back to MARTAC with a range of options in November 1990. The Australian government's preference, upon which it would negotiate a UK contribution, was for a plan referred to as Option 6(c), which had four major components. The first was the removal and reburial of the soil that had been ploughed during *Operation Brumby*, which was still heavily contaminated with thousands of plutonium fragments, some of them large enough to attract attention as souvenirs.[6] The second component was for the pits in which contaminated MEP equipment had been buried (known as 'formal debris pits') to be stabilized using a new technique called 'in situ vitrification' (ISV; see below); the third was for the 'informal debris pits', which had been used for more general rubbish disposal, to be sifted for any contaminated debris and the contents reburied at the same site; and the fourth was for the plumes from the *Vixen B* trials at Taranaki to be delineated and marked at the 5 mSv/yr mark. The total contaminated area here was 120 square km (46 square miles), and complete clean-up was financially prohibitive.[7]

The Australian government decided that the rehabilitation work would not commence until the UK had agreed to make a significant contribution to the clean-up and pay the entire for compensation to Maralinga Tjarutja. The latter had been set at $A45 million. The UK response, which came in late 1991, refused to pay for Aboriginal compensation but agreed to make a contribution to the clean-up. In June 1993, it was agreed that the British contribution to the clean-up would be $A45 million, about 42 per cent of the total operational budget of $A104 million. With the UK still refusing to offer any contribution to Aboriginal compensation, the Australian government finalized a sum of $A13.5 million with Maralinga Tjarutja, considerably short of their original claim. With this final agreement in place in December 1994, the clean-up could begin in earnest. The Australian Parliament gave the go-ahead on 27 June 1995, and the installation of facilities and equipment commenced on 15 September.

The task

Despite the Royal Commission's heavy criticism of *Operation Brumby*, the original clean-up had in many cases been very effective, and in others the remaining contaminants were of sufficiently short half-life to no longer be a significant problem.[8] However, plutonium contamination still represented a radiological danger at five sites: Taranaki, TM100, TM101, Wewak and the airfield cemetery. Contamination with uranium, which is not radiotoxic but is chemically toxic if ingested, was found at Kuli.

(i) Taranaki

The Taranaki site had been the location for a 27-kiloton major test during *Antler* (a balloon-borne shot that left little long-term contamination behind), some of the *Vixen A* trials that investigated the effects of burning and explosives, and all of the *Vixen B* trials in which the effects of explosive detonations were assessed. The contamination at Taranaki, which was the heaviest at the five sites, took two forms, the first being the contamination from the explosive detonations of plutonium. A total of about 22 kg (48.5 lb) of plutonium had been dispersed in this fashion, and the TAG airborne radiological survey had identified four major plumes at Taranaki, the longest of them 28 km (17 miles) long. The plumes consisted of finely divided dust and many thousands of plutonium fragments. The survey had checked for americium (Am[241]), an isotope produced by the radioactive decay of plutonium, and it transpired after the 1985 survey that the British estimates of plutonium contamination here had been in error by a factor of ten or more.[9]

The second form of contamination was the formal debris pits. The *Vixen* B trials, which had produced the heaviest contamination, had detonated the explosives in large, heavy steel structures called featherbeds. After the trials, the featherbeds, together with their concrete mounting slabs and soil from around the firing point, were buried in these pits which were then capped with concrete.[10] A total of 21 pits were recorded. In contrast to the plumes, assessment of the level of plutonium contamination in the pits proved to be problematic, with estimates varying from 20 kg to well under 1 kg of plutonium (44 lb and 2 lb).[11] The TAG hedged its bets and estimated 2–20 kg, while the UK Ministry of Defence suggested 2.2 kg. It later emerged that both these figures were substantial overestimates: the final amount found was 650 g.[12]

However, the real problems with the Taranaki pits lay were with the total volume of material buried in them, and with the concrete caps that were supposed to protect the contents. As work began, it became clear that the British had grossly underestimated the volume of buried material: it was eventually ascertained that 5,589 cubic metres (197,381 cubic feet) had been interred, against an official British figure of 1,388 cubic metres (49,018 cubic feet).[13] Equally seriously, it rapidly became clear that the concrete caps did not completely cover their pits, and in some cases did not cover them at all. Each cap was supposed to cover the pit by 0.9 m (3 ft) on all four sides, but several pits turned out to have misaligned caps, and in two cases (Pits 2 and 18) the cap was some distance from the pit: the cap for Pit 18 was 4 m (13 ft) away, and that for Pit 2 was fully 12 m (39 ft) away.[14] A total of six unrecorded pits were found with no cap at all, but contamination in these cases was very low.

(ii) TM100 and TM101

These two sites were the locations for the fissile material compression trials using natural or depleted uranium, and a similar run of trials in the *Rats* series using uranium and some very strong gamma sources. Regarding the latter, *Operation Ayres* in February/March 1960 had removed a heavily contaminated 'hot box' that had contained thorium isotopes used at the *Rats* trials, and decontaminating the building that had housed it. The building itself was dismantled in *Operation Ayres 2* in 1962. A total of 1.2 kg (2.6 lb) of plutonium was used in explosive dispersal, of which 500 g (1.1 lb) was returned to the UK in 1979. The TAG survey detected a high concentration of plutonium contaminated fragments, with a total activity of 9 GBq, over an area of 1.5 square km (0.57 square miles).[15] The TM100 site had a formal debris pit containing an estimated 70 g of plutonium along with assorted trial debris, including heavily contaminated drums of bitumen.

(iii) Wewak[16]

This had been the site of some of the *Vixen A* trials. The TAG survey detected 6GBq of Am^{241} activity over a contaminated area of 2.7 square km (1 square mile). The plutonium contamination was mostly from explosive dispersal using 0.57 kg (20 oz) of plutonium; burnings of 0.41 kg (14.8 oz) had concluded with nearly all being recovered at the time. Two concrete caps that were labelled as covering formal debris pits turned out to be firing pads.

(iv) Airfield cemetery

Despite the funereal name, this had been a storage site for radioactive waste, and no bodies were interred in the cemetery. No trials had taken place there, but it was the location of 18 formal debris pits containing some short-lived but highly radioactive waste. The pits were categorized according to radioactivity: the 11 pits in Category 1 were high-level activity (mostly thorium 232, but some plutonium and cobalt), the three pits in Category 2 were medium activity (less active thorium, plutonium and cobalt), and the remaining four pits in Category 3 were low-level.[17] In 1979 500g (1.1 lb) of plutonium had been removed from the cemetery and returned to the UK.

(v) Kuli

This had been the site of some of the *Tims* trials on compression of fissile material. About 7,000 kg (15,432 lb) of uranium had been explosively dispersed, contaminating the area with fine dust and fragments. This did not present a radiological hazard, but the substance is toxic if ingested, and it was also feared that the bright yellow colour of the fragments might attract crawling babies.[18] The TAG had estimated that there were also three formal debris pits on the site, but two of these turned out to be concrete firing pads. The third was left in situ.

The clean-up

The task thus involved principally the clean-up of the contaminated surface soil, and the formal debris pits. The first of these was relatively straightforward, the second less so.

(i) Clean-up of contaminated surface soil

The contaminated soil at Taranaki, Wewak and the TMs was cleared under three criteria set by MARTAC. They were:

1. The average level of surface contamination should not exceed a stated level of Am^{241}, which varied from site to site (see below).
2. No fragments with a radioactivity level above 100kBq of Am^{241} should remain.
3. Any fragments with activity of more than 20kBq should not be scattered at more than 0.1 per square metre of ground.[19]

This meant removal and disposal of large amounts of contaminated soil, to a depth of about 150 mm (6 in). In practice, soil removal boundaries were always set by the fragment and particle criteria, since surface-level contamination was usually too low to be meaningful, other than at Taranaki.[20]

Although the material to be cleared had a significant portion of relatively large fragments, a great deal consisted of sub-millimetre particles and fine dust. This raised the problem of how to ensure that no contaminated soil was lost or displaced during removal. Removing dry soil presented risks of recontamination of surrounding areas, risk to workers from dust, and possible contamination of filters and machinery. Conventional soil removal usually involves applying water to prevent dust formation, but this has disadvantages of its own, including the problem of contaminated mud sticking to machinery. After some debate, it was decided that the balance of disadvantage favoured using the dry method with some advance spraying of soil surfaces.[21]

At Taranaki, the site of the *Vixen B* plumes that left the heaviest contamination, it was decided that the stated level of surface contamination should not exceed 40 kBq/m^2 of Am^{241}. This was considerably over the 3 kBq/m^2 that was the benchmark for unrestricted occupancy of land, but a complete treatment of the plume area was deemed too costly in environmental and financial terms.[22] Thus it was decided that the land would be marked as unfit for permanent habitation of camping, although there was deemed no risk to those passing across the area. An area of 1.5 square km (371 acres) of land, and 262,840 cubic metres (9,253 cubic feet) of soil, was cleared at Taranaki. The contaminated soil was then reburied in a specially dug trench.

All of the soil burial trenches at Maralinga had to meet the same basic criteria: all contaminated soil was to be buried under at least 5 m (16 ft) of clean fill, and a minimum of 3 m (9.8 ft) of the clean fill was to be below ground level. The clean fill was to be sloped to prevent water leaking into the contaminated soil, and the soils and rocks used for the clean fill was to be sequenced in such a way as to also minimize water ingress.[23] The soil burial trench at Taranaki was 206 m long, 141 m wide and 15 m deep (676, 463 and 49 ft respectively). Taranaki was also the site of a debris burial trench, containing the ISV melts and other contaminated debris from the formal debris pits, and an ISV burial trench containing other ISV debris, the concrete caps, 1,200 cubic metres (42,379 cubic feet) of laboratory waste from the airfield cemetery, and assorted other waste.[24] Like all disposal pits at Maralinga, the Taranaki pits were marked with a concrete plinth and metal signposts warning of buried radioactive material.

A perimeter boundary was also marked at Taranaki, delineating the area where full-time human occupancy would lead to potential dosage of above the general policy limit of 5 mSv/yr. Later measurements suggested that the figure at Taranaki was in fact less than 1 mSv/yr, but it was none the less felt that this still represented an unacceptable hazard for infants. Consequently a 412 square km (159 square miles) area is still marked as unfit for habitation or camping, although hunting and passage through the area present no hazard. The actual area of the plumes is only 108 square km (42 square miles), and much of the enclosed land is in fact uncontaminated.[25] The boundary is marked by posts carrying warning signs every 50 m (164 ft).

For the TMs, the 'stated level' criteria were set at 1.8 kBq/m^2 at TM100 and 4 kBq/m^2 at TM101. The fragment criteria were the same as for other sites, but at the TMs the fragments were more easily collectable, and so all fragments above 30 kBq/m^2 were collected.[26] In total, 68,365 cubic metres (2,414,378 cubic feet) were removed to trenches, together with 24,100 cubic metres (851,116 cubic feet) from the formal debris pits and another at the nearby Tietkens Plain cemetery pit, and 550 cubic metres (17,658 cubic feet) from the informal debris pits.[27] This was buried in a soil burial trench marked with the usual concrete plinth and metal signposts.

At Wewak, the 'stated level' was set at 1.8 kBq/m^2 for the plumes area and 0.7 kBq/m^2 for the plutonium burning site. A total of 45,070 cubic metres (1,591,692 cubic feet) of soil was removed. Together with the concrete firing pads once thought to be pit caps, it was buried in a trench, covered with clean fill and marked with plinth and signposts. At the airfield cemetery, three of the debris pits were judged to present no hazard and were left undisturbed. All Category 1 and 2 pits, plus one of the Category 3 pits, were exhumed and the debris buried in the ISV burial trench at Taranaki.[28] The cemetery now has only background levels of radiation. The uranium fragments scattered at the Kuli site were scavenged by hand, but it was decided the site should remain one of restricted occupancy. After clearance, boundary markers were put in place marking out the area of more than 5 kBq/m^2 of uranium activity.[29]

(ii) The formal debris pits

These presented some difficult problems. The TAG had recommended the use of the ISV technique to stabilize the pit contents. This innovative technique was still in its infancy, but had been pioneered by the US Department of Energy. ISV works by sinking electrodes into the ground and then using electricity (up to 4 Mw) to heat the soil to 1,400–2,000° C. This melts the soil, which subsequently cools into a vitreous/ceramic mass that is highly durable and weather-resistant: it is 2–5 times stronger in compressive strength, and 5–10 times stronger in tensile strength, than unreinforced concrete. The process is expensive, but is a highly effective means of dealing with radiotoxic waste. The TAG had originally regarded ISV as the 'default option' for all pits containing radioactive debris, but the escalating cost of the process led to it being applied only at Taranaki, where the large amounts of plutonium thought to lie in the pits (20 kg, or 44 lb) made ISV the safest option.[30]

A total of eleven pits at Taranaki were treated using the ISV technique, before an explosion during the 'melt' at the eleventh pit on 21 March 1999. No one was injured, but the ISV plant itself was badly damaged by the explosion and by molten debris.[31] The ISV programme was curtailed while an investigation took place. Initial conclusions by the contractor were that drums of 'an explosive material such as ammonium nitrate fuel oil' had been buried in the pit by the British and had exploded under the high temperatures of the melt. However, an independent report commissioned by MARTAC decided that this was 'most unlikely', and MARTAC itself eventually rejected active explosive material as the cause. The causal factor was never identified and, as a result, as the ISV contractor informed the Australian government the week after the explosion, 'because we cannot be sure of the pit contents, we cannot guarantee a similar event will not occur'.[32]

This double uncertainty was compounded by other problems that were emerging. MARTAC had ordered the excavation and inspection of four of the pits treated with the ISV process, as part of a quality assurance practice, and problems became apparent. One was that the steel from which the featherbeds were constructed had a melting point above that of the surrounding soil, and as a consequence large quantities of contaminated steel remained unmelted and sank to the bottom of the melt. This was judged by MARTAC to present an unacceptable hazard.[33] Nearly all the Taranaki formal debris pits had this problem. A second issue was that the pit debris contained large amounts of lead originally used for radioactive shielding, which unlike the steel had a melting point well *below* that of the surrounding soil. The result was that the lead melted much more quickly, leaked into the soil, and failed to be incorporated into the vitreous/ceramic mass. It was estimated that about 9 tonnes of lead had leaked out into unmelted soil in this way, and that it could be a transport medium for plutonium.[34] A third problem was cost. The original estimate for the ISV process had been $A25 million, a figure which later turned out to exclude all but the ongoing operating costs and thus was optimistic, to say the least.[35]

The three problems had all emerged before the pit explosion, and in fact MARTAC had been discussing a 'hybrid option' involving carrying out the ISV process inside a special pod.[36] After the explosion, however, MARTAC recommended abandoning all ISV, and the programme was never started again. There was some controversy later about the exact reason for the curtailment of the process, which is discussed below. The eleven melts at Taranaki had their contents excavated and reburied in the ISV and debris burial trenches. The excavated pits were then surveyed for any residual contamination and refilled with clean soil.

The rationale for using the ISV process as Taranaki was that the large expected amounts of plutonium presented radiological hazards if the waste was exhumed from the pits without being stabilized first. It will be recalled that the actual amount of plutonium at Taranaki turned out to be considerably lower than the expected amount, but this uncertainty did not exist in the other formal debris pits, which all had much lower concentrations of contaminated material (none had more than 70 g, or 2.5 oz, of plutonium). This, plus the escalating cost of ISV, combined to compel MARTAC to conclude that ISV for the other formal debris pits was neither suitable nor financially viable.[37] Consequently, these pits were excavated and the contents reburied under the requisite 5 m of clean fill.

(iii) Informal debris pits

As well as the formal debris pits, a number of informal pits were discovered.[38] These were essentially rubbish tips, and the British kept no records of their number, location or contents. The Maralinga process uncovered a total of 74 pits, and categorized them according to radiological hazard. Category 1 pits, of which there were 13, were judged to present no radiological hazard and were left untreated. A further 60 pits were designated Category 2, meaning that they presented no hazard but required removal and reburial of some material that was protruding above ground. Only one pit was designated Category 3, requiring the exhumation and reburial of the contents: some bitumen contaminated with 60 micrograms of plutonium was found in this pit. Other assorted debris removed from the pits and individually reburied included a vacuum cleaner contaminated with 7 micrograms of plutonium, a steel plate contaminated with 0.2 micrograms and a trailer contaminated with 1 microgram. These were buried in the trenches dug for the TM and Wewak soil.

Criticisms

The MARTAC Report was published in 2003. Criticism of its activities had in fact featured recurrently during the run-up to publication, particularly after the cancellation of the ISV programme. Some of the criticism came from a former MARTAC member, Mr Alan Parkinson, and had two basic elements. The first was that the ISV process should not have been cancelled. It will be recalled that a number of factors had featured in the decision to abandon ISV, in particular the lower than expected levels of plutonium, the escalating costs and the explosion in Pit 17. The reasons for the explosion were never satisfactorily identified: MARTAC concluded that there was no decisive evidence on the cause, and this uncertainty appears to have strongly influenced the decision not to continue.

Mr Parkinson's argument was that it was, in fact, the cost put on the ISV process by Gutteridge, Haskins & Davey, who had been awarded the contract without tender, had been what put an end to the ISV process. This does not, however, explain the uncertainties created by the explosion: the fault there was not with the ISV process itself, but with the unknown contents of the pits and the lack of clear evidence for what had caused the explosion.

The second key criticism was that the method of soil and debris disposal fell some distance short of good practice. The burial procedure adopted by MARTAC stated that at least 5 m of clean fill should cover the debris, but that only 3 m is required to be below ground level; in other words, it was permissible for up to 2 m (7 ft) of fill to be above ground level. This does not necessarily imply that the debris is only 3 m below ground level: the contaminated pit debris at Taranaki is 7.5 m (25 ft) below this level. However, the case put by Mr Parkinson was that the practice of exhuming contaminated soil and debris and then reburying it elsewhere was an unsatisfactory method of disposal that compared unfavourably with practices elsewhere, such as the US. He argued that, at the very least, the disposal trenches ought to have been lined with concrete, and it emerged from some leaked official notes from a MARTAC meeting that at least one other member of MARTAC had concurred. The notes recorded that Dr Mike Costello of MARTAC had stated, 'I don't believe that shallow burial is (1) within the spirit of the UK NRPB code ... or (2) that it's accepted current practice. However I'm outvoted by my colleagues. I have experience with plutonium at Sellafield in the UK, there are much smaller quantities of plutonium there. The amounts varied yet, while miniscule, it had to be enclosed in concrete. I don't believe this shallow burial is the best that we can do, as it could be encapsulated in concrete'.[39]

MARTAC's recommendations

At the end of the clean-up, the Environmental Monitor undertook a survey of Maralinga to make a revised assessment of the likely doses via inhalation (the most likely form of dosage) of those living on the land. All were comfortably under the safety line.[40] The Taranaki plumes remained the most contaminated area, with an estimated dose of 3.6 mSv/yr for a child of ten.

A further assessment was made of the safety of the burial trenches in terms of the risk of 'inadvertent human intrusion'.[41] Deliberate human intrusion was not considered, as it was assumed that a deliberate intruder would be aware of the hazards. The inadvertent intrusion scenarios ranges from archaeological surveys (plutonium has a half-life of thousands of years) to consumption of roots that had drawn water from contaminated ground. Only the possibility of an archaeological dig was found to present a risk significantly above 1 mSv/yr.

MARTAC then put forward five recommendations for the future management of the Maralinga range:

1. To perform a risk assessment of the final condition of the site, based upon an agreement between the Commonwealth, the State of South Australia, and Maralinga Tjarutja.

2. To identify from the risk assessment the risks that require long-term management ...
3. To prepare an agreed 'roles and responsibilities agreement' for the execution of the management plan.
4. To create an oversight group that would track the execution of the management plan ...
5. To ensure that there is a mechanism to allow the Department to request additional funds for unforeseen problems arising at the site.[42]

That the MARTAC clean-up was necessary at all tells its own story: the range at Maralinga was not left in a fit state when it was dismantled, and neither Britain nor Australia ought to have signed the agreement that stated it was. It is true that standards shifted in the intervening period, and that, as with so much of the Anglo-Australian nuclear relationship, what was acceptable in the 1950s and 1960s was inconceivable a couple of decades later. In that respect, retrospective condemnation of those responsible for making decisions should be treated with great caution. None the less, the fragments of plutonium scattered on the ground, the unaccounted-for material in the debris pits, and the slipshod placing of the concrete caps, are evidence of work that was unacceptable by past or current standards. Cleanup, then, was an irrefutable necessity. The controversy that attended the MARTAC operation has yet to abate, and it is not the function of this book to take sides on issue.

13
Health and Safety and the National Radiological Protection Board Studies

How were radiological safety standards for test personnel set?

It is sometimes suggested that the tests were conducted without proper care for radiological health and safety, or that the weapon scientists worked to their own rules. This is untrue, as the standards were set for the UK by the Medical Research Council (MRC) and were based on the recommendations of the international committee of scientists of the highest standing, the International Commission on Radiological Protection (ICRP). The ICRP standards were applied to the employment of radiation workers who might be occupationally exposed to radiation for up to 40 years. The dose limits were determined by the ICRP with the object of ensuring that these workers' health risks were 'small compared to the other hazards of life'.[1]

Thus radiation workers were under an occupational risk on a very different scale from, for example, contemporary miners, construction workers or deep-sea fishermen. For the latter, the risks were short-term and immediate, rather than to their long-term health. Test participants had equivalent dose limits to those for full-time radiation workers, but were much more protected and were not expected to work for long periods of time. These ICRP standards were used as the basis for the whole system of radiological protection at the tests. This system involved, for example, the establishment of safe distances from ground zero, the definition of various danger zones and the strict control of access; the use of protective clothing where necessary; personnel monitoring of all those potentially exposed to radiation, mainly by use of film badges; decontamination; environmental and monitoring, chiefly of air, soil and water. The British had the advantage of acquaintance with a Los Alamos publication of 1950, 'The Effect of Atomic Weapons', which contained a wealth of scientific and technical information and experience (it was useful too to the Soviet bomb tests).

The long-term effects of test participation

Did radiation exposures at the trials nevertheless cause illness many years later? Most of the men at the trials were young, and indeed many of them were doing their two years' National Service. The scientists were mostly young too, and since the conditions were physically tough they had to be fit. In all, there were about 25,000 servicemen from Britain, plus civilian scientists, 8,000–10,000 Australians, and a small number of Canadians, making a total of about 35,000 participants. These young men are now middle-aged or elderly. Some have died. Cases of illness, especially cancer, have been reported, and radiation exposure at the atomic weapon trials has been blamed.

It is generally accepted that levels of radiation exposure too low to have any immediate effect may lead to long-term damage to health, notably cancer; the latent period may be only a few years for leukaemia, or up to 30 years for solid tumours. These long-term effects are 'stochastic'; that is, the amount of the radiation dose does not affect the severity, only the probability, of the damage. For radiological protection planning purposes the ICRP assumes that risks can be extrapolated to lower doses in direct proportion to the dose, and that the risk is linearly related to exposure. However, radiation is by no means the only cause of cancer, and, generally speaking, radiation-induced cancers cannot be distinguished from others. In the Western world more than 20 per cent of all deaths are due to cancer. There are, in all, rather more than 130,000 cancer deaths a year in the United Kingdom of which, it has been estimated, 5,000 may be due to natural sources of radiation. Many of the British test veterans would by now be suffering from cancer or would have died if they had never been at the trials. But it is inevitable that some, knowing that radiation can cause cancer, should associate their illness with the trials.

The total radiation – i.e. the 'total collective dose equivalent' – received by the 25,000 or so UK test participants is about 176 man-sieverts (Sv). On the basis of ICRP and UNSCEAR figures for dose-risk relationships, the number of extra cancer deaths that might be expected is about one; the estimate is considered unlikely to be too low by more than a factor of three or four.

Problems of causality

Very high exposures to radiation (say more than 3 or 4 Sv) will, in the absence of medical treatment, result in immediate injury, severe radiation sickness and death before long. In such cases the cause of the injury is immediately and appallingly apparent. At the time of the British weapon tests only two such cases were on record, both in the United States (Los Alamos). Ordinarily, however, a causal link between a case of cancer and a previous radiation exposure is virtually impossible to establish, for three reasons.

First, the 'lag-time' between low-level radiation exposure and the appearance of cancer may be very long, sometimes up to 40 years. Second, there is no specific and recognizable radiogenic cancer. This is in contrast to such occupational diseases as pneumoconiosis in miners and mesothelioma in asbestos workers, where the disease can be conclusively traced to a single cause. Third, cancer is very common in the UK and one in three men will suffer from it during their lifetime. Therefore, as test participants or radiation workers age, a large and increasing number of cancer cases is to be expected. The only means of ascertaining what proportion of such cases may be due specifically to past radiation exposure is therefore statistical, a question to be answered by the epidemiologists. Epidemiological studies by their nature cannot determine the cause in individual cases.

The National Radiological Protection Board (NRPB), now the Radiation Protection Division of the Health Protection Agency, together with scientists from the Imperial Cancer Research Fund, has conducted a large epidemiological study of test participants in the UK for many years. This study has compared cancer mortality and morbidity (i.e. registrations of these diseases) in British test veterans with that in a control group of men not involved in the trials but otherwise closely matched (e.g. as to date of birth, Service, rank, and tour of duty in the tropics.) The NRPB study was carried out to see whether there are differences between the two groups, in cause of death, and age at death or of developing cancer. The whole investigation was conducted as a soundly based epidemiological study to answer the concerns raised by allegations that the health of participants has been affected. Three reports have been published, and as we shall see, they now cover 40–45 years' experience in over 20,000 test participants. The next section describes these three reports.

The Australian Commonwealth Department of Health also undertook a survey in 1982–83 of the health of Australians who had participated in the tests. It was done under considerable pressure and was something of a rush job. From Maralinga security records and Department of Defence data, nearly 15,000 men who might have been involved were identified, including many construction workers who left the sites before any trials began. A further 472 were 'self-identified'. Over 8,000 were traced and questionnaires were sent to them; 2,536 replies were received and analysed. Every effort was made in the time available to collect and examine radiation records, but it could not be claimed that complete lists or exact individual exposures were obtained. In particular, there were some gaps in the information on RAAF air and ground crews. Nor was the control group well defined. The report concluded, after comparing test participants and controls, that the study did not support the view that there was evidence of increased mortality that might be attributable to radiation. A very much more thorough study of Australian test participants is presently being carried out.[2]

The NRPB studies

In 2003, NRPB published its third report into cancer and leukaemia rates among British servicemen present at the UK's atmospheric nuclear tests.[3] Before examining the conclusions of the study, it is useful to describe its background and origins.

Background to the study

In 1982, the thirtieth anniversary of the first British atomic weapon test, the BBC news and current affairs programme *Nationwide* invited veterans of the tests at Christmas Island to contact the programme with memories and experiences. A total of 330 people responded, and the programme enlisted the help of the University of Birmingham in making a statistical analysis of the data received.

The first results of this analysis were published in 1983. The Birmingham researchers found 'evidence of an abnormally high incidence of leukaemia and other reticuloendothelial system (RES) neoplasms'.[4] This conclusion was made on the basis that the *Nationwide* respondents reported a total of 27 deaths from leukaemia among test veterans. Working on an estimate provided by the Ministry of Defence (MoD) that about 8,000 servicemen had been at the Pacific tests, the researchers estimated that the expected rate of leukaemia should have been 17.2. In short, the test veterans appeared to be more susceptible to the disease by about half as much again, and the researchers recommended further study. An eminent group of scientists, including the Nobel Laureate Josef Rotblat, responded to the Birmingham finding by recommending 'an independent body ... to conduct a full investigation into the morbidity, mortality and perhaps genetic effects on these men'.[5]

However, in a follow-up letter published later the same year, the Birmingham researchers withdrew some of their conclusions. It appeared that the MoD had underestimated the total number of servicemen present at the tests, which was now thought to be 12,000 rather than 8,000. This substantially raised the expected rate of leukaemia, and the 27 known deaths from the disease were now set against an expected number of 29.9. In other words, while an incidence of 27 deaths from a group of 8,000 was anomalously high, 27 deaths from a group of 12,000 was about the national average. However, their studies had also detected an apparent excess of leukaemia cases in those veterans aged under 30 (42 cases reported against an expected 30.4), which contrasted oddly with a noticeable *deficit* of cases in those aged over 30 (seven cases against an expected 14.2).[6] The waters were sufficiently muddy for the team to recommend 'a comprehensive follow-up of all men involved in nuclear weapon tests', and this was the rationale for the NRPB study.

The first two NRPB studies

It is important to stress that the NPRB's three studies were *epidemiological* exercises. That is to say, they were designed to investigate the incidence and distribution of a disease, rather than its cause. To put it another way, the aim was to ascertain whether test veterans *as a group* were more prone to cancers, and not whether individual cases of the disease could be put down to presence at a nuclear explosion. Epidemiology is therefore about associations (in this case the association between test participation and cancer/leukaemia), and statistical strength is the key.

Three studies, published in 1988, 1993 and 2003, had at least three significant advantages over the original Birmingham study. First, the NRPB had a much clearer picture of how many men were involved in the tests. Although no comprehensive list of participants was ever compiled, by the time of the 2003 report a list had been compiled of 21,357 men who had been involved in a total of 27,505 appearances at tests (some had been to a single test whilst others had been at several). The Birmingham researchers had been compelled to rely on rough estimates by the MoD about the true figure, and the uncertainty had caused such differing results in their two reports.

Second, the Birmingham study had been able to work with only the 330 self-selected respondents to the *Nationwide* appeal, whereas the NRPB's group was an estimated 83 per cent of the total. And third, the NRPB's study involved a carefully designed control group against which to assess cancer and leukaemia rates among test participants. The control group was drawn up on the basis of comparable age, type of armed service, rank and period in the tropics. In short, it was designed so that, as far as possible, the study was comparing like with like: the only significant difference between the groups was that one contained men who had participated in the tests and the other did not.

The first NRPB study, released in 1988, identified a total of 22,347 participants, an estimated 83 per cent of the total. It reported that the relative risk was greater only in the cases of leukaemia and multiple myeloma (MM), a form of bone cancer.[7] There had been six deaths from MM against none in the control group, and 22 from leukaemia against six in the control group. However, interpretation was difficult because levels of leukaemia and MM in test veterans were similar to those in the UK population as a whole, while levels in controls were much lower.

The study went on to note that the evidence 'was confusing, and on balance we conclude that there may well have been small hazards of both diseases associated with participants in the programme but that this has not been proved'. For this reason, a follow-on study was recommended, and specifically two topics required further investigation: the apparently increased risk of leukaemia and MM, and the risk of other forms of cancer.

The follow-on study was released in 1993, and the interpretations of its predecessor on leukaemia were reviewed in the light of the new evidence.[8] The second study found that rates of leukaemia and MM in the additional seven years of follow-up were slightly lower in test participants than in controls and the controls had rates similar to those of the general population. This made it more plausible that the low rates of these diseases in controls seen in the first analysis were due to chance. The overall conclusion was that 'participation in nuclear weapon tests has not had a noticeable effect on particpants' expectation of life or on their risk of developing cancer or other fatal diseases'. However, it was noted that 'the possibility that participation in the tests may have caused a small risk of leukaemia in the early years afterwards cannot be ruled out'.

This difficulty was partly due to the fact that the leukaemia cases were not concentrated in participants known to be exposed to radiation, involved in a particular operation, or employed in a specific job. Thus it was difficult to trace the disease to any specific cause.

The run-up to the third NRPB study

The 1993 report, despite hedging on the leukaemia risk, was very conclusive in its general deduction: that test participation produced no appreciable rise in cancers or decrease in general life expectancy. During the next few years, however, a growth in public pressure from test veterans combined with the emergence of potential new evidence to eventually prompt a third NRPB study.

The year the second study was published, two test veterans took a case before the European Court of Human Rights in Strasbourg. They were Ken McGinley, who was present at five of the *Grapple* series of tests in 1958, and Edward Egan, who was present at *Grapple Y*. Both were prominent members of the British Nuclear Test Veterans Association (BNTVA), a group established by McGinley in 1983. Both had claimed a war pension on the grounds that their participation had subsequently caused severe illness. The UK authorities had rejected the claims, and the two men had then gone to the Court of Human Rights, claiming that the MoD had withheld documents that might have proved a link between the tests and their illness. In 1998, the Court rejected the claim, albeit by a narrow margin of 5 to 4, and a subsequent appeal by the two was also rejected in January 2000.

Throughout the 1990s, stories continued to surface of the use of servicemen as 'human guinea pigs'. This vivid and highly charged phrase, containing undertones of callousness in authority and lack of knowledge, consent or protection in participants, was recurrently used. The Royal Commission had investigated the 'guinea pigs'' claim in 1985, and concluded that there was no proof that any such work had taken place. At the heart of the controversy was exactly what counted as 'guinea pig'-type experiments. The phrase suggests that individuals were irradiated without their knowledge or consent in order to see what would happen to them.

There is no reliable evidence that the former ever happened, but it has always been known that protective clothing was tested by monitoring how effectively it worked when in use. The object was to assess how well protective clothing worked, *not* to see what happened when an individual was irradiated. In fairness to the BNTVA, their claim is not based on the argument that participants were the victims of experimentation, so much as that they were either inadequately protected or that their subsequent illness is wrongly unrecognized as being related to test participation. In response, the British government's case has been that only a small contingent of test participants (the 1,716 recorded as having a non-zero dose) had actually been exposed to measurable amounts of ionizing radiation at all. This claim rested on the assumptions that witnessing a nuclear explosion did not automatically mean exposure to harmful levels of ionizing radiation, and that those who *were* at risk were given protection as and when necessary and tested for radiation exposure.

These assumptions, when taken in conjunction with the NRPB's conclusion that test veterans were no more susceptible to cancers or early death than comparable individuals, formed the basis of the British government's claim that cancers, leukaemias and MM among test veterans could not reasonably be attributed to participation at a nuclear test.

Sue Rabbitt Roff of Dundee University initiated a further development in a *New Scientist* article published in 1999.[9] In it, she argued that 'a significant number' of test participants had contracted or died from MM, in greater numbers than could be explained by chance fluctuations in the annual rate. Specifically, her study reported more than double the total number of cases of MM reported by the NRPB, and two-thirds of that number had appeared *after* the NRPB studies had ended. This appeared to suggest that the rate of MM was increasing with time, and in fact the Defence Minister, John Spellar, accepted that this was the case in a letter to Roff in 1998, although he also restated that it was not yet demonstrated that radiation from nuclear tests was the cause.

The apparently accelerating rate of MM suggested that the NRPB's conclusions might have been drawn prematurely. On 25 February 1999 it was announced that the NRPB would conduct an investigation of the incidence of MM among test participants, funded by the MoD. An Oversight Committee of independent experts was set up to review the study, and at its first meeting in November the Committee recommended that the study should cover other causes of death and other forms of cancer than solely MM.

The third study

The third NRPB study took place in an atmosphere of some public controversy. The 'guinea pig' accusations had resurfaced in May 2001, when documents from the Australian official archives were published, describing how a group of twelve servicemen were asked to walk across contaminated ground in order to test the effectiveness of their protective suits (these documents were published in the UK in 1984 during the Royal Commission hearings). Some of the controversy surrounded the subgroup of test participants referred to in the NRPB study as *Group A* and *Group B*. The former comprised members of the Indoctrinee Force and the Target Response Force from *Buffalo*, the RAF ground and air personnel involved with flights through mushroom clouds, and members of the crew of HMS *Diana* which had sailed through the *Mosaic* fallout cloud. A total of 759 men were in this group. Group B comprised AWE employees and those directly involved in the MEP.

The NRPB published its third report in February 2003. The study was an extended follow-up of the group studied in the previous reports. The study is publicly available, and for the purposes of this narrative it is appropriate to focus on the three aspects that were the cause of most controversy. These were the claims that participants had not received adequate protection from radiation exposure; that the general mortality rate was substantially higher than it ought to have been; and that the incidence of leukaemia and MM had been underestimated in previous studies.

(i) Dosage and radiation exposure

Formal records of exposure are only available for those participants who were issued with dosemeters (film badges). In total, only 21 per cent of participants were given badges, and thus these are the only men for whom files are kept in the AWE Health Physics (HP) records. This does mean that four-fifths of participants had no means of checking exposure, but the UK government's case has always been that participation does not automatically mean exposure took place, and that all those who were at risk were issued with dosemeters.

It should also be noted that the figure of 21 per cent is potentially misleading. This is the number issued with badges as a percentage of the entire group of participants in the whole test programme. In practice, the proportion of men issued with badges varied between individual tests. The highest proportion was at *Hurricane*, where 96 per cent were issued with dosemeters, and the MEP, which included Group B and where 92 per cent had badges. *Totem* had 74 per cent, and *Buffalo*, which included the Indoctrinee Force and the Target Response Group, had 61 per cent. Numbers dropped off very sharply for the *Grapple* tests: only *Grapple Z* had a proportion in double figures, with 14 per cent. The reason for this was that, by the time of the *Grapple* trials, scientists were more able to identify who would be at risk and to issue them with dosimeters. In the earlier tests, this was more uncertain and therefore caution dictated that all or most staff be issued.

Of the 21,357 test participants, a total of 1,716 are recorded as having had a non-zero dose; that is to say, a dose that was large enough to register on a dosimeter. Figure 13.1 shows the distribution of dosage as a percentage of that total. An important Rubicon, so to speak, is the usual annual dose limit, 50 mSv, and the table shows that only 5 per cent received a dose in that category. Of the tests prior to *Grapple*, for which

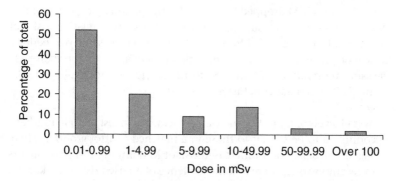

Figure 13.1 The distribution of radiation dosage as a percentage of total doses among test participants

larger numbers were issued with badges, only *Totem* showed greater than half as recording a non-zero dose (75 per cent). *Buffalo* had 49 per cent, *Antler* 43 per cent, MEP 38 per cent and *Mosaic* 32 per cent. The *Grapple* tests had a high proportion of non-zero doses (up to 95 per cent), but very small numbers were issued with film badges there.

(ii) Mortality rates and incidence of illness

The general mortality rate among test veterans differed sharply from the Dundee study. Of 21,357 participants, 4,902 or 22 per cent had died by 1 January 1999, which compared well with the control group number of 5,217 (23.4 per cent). The SMR (standard mortality rate) for leukaemia was 106, and 40 test participants had died of the disease (excluding chronic lymphatic leukaemia) by 1999, nearly twice the 23 in the control group. This produced a relative risk of 1.83. For MM, 21 had died of the disease, against 18 in the control group, giving a relative risk not significantly different from 1. In terms of incidence, the relative risk of leukaemia was 1.41, although the relative risk was higher the first 2–25 years after test participation. During that period, 29 veterans developed leukaemia against ten in the control group. The same pattern was also seen for mortality, where the rate of death was three times higher for veterans than for the control group in that period. For incidence of MM, the relative risk was not significantly different from one.

The NRPB report also investigated the comparative rates of mortality and incidence since the publication of its second report in 1992. The Dundee study's conclusion had suggested that incidence increased sharply after the cut-off date for the second NRPB study, but the third NRPB report indicated that this was not the case. The relative risk for mortality from MM dropped from 1.90 for the period up to 31 December 1990 to 1.21 for the subsequent eight years. The relative risk for incidence of the disease fell from 2.05 to 0.79 over the same two periods. Leukaemia, excluding chronic lymphatic leukaemia, stayed approximately the same: mortality went from 1.84 to 1.81, incidence from 1.46 to 1.39.

The NRPB's general conclusion was that

> overall levels of mortality and cancer incidence in test participants have continued to be similar to those in a matched control group ... There was no evidence of an increased risk of MM among test participants in recent years ... there is some evidence of a raised risk of leukaemia among test participants relative to controls, particularly when focusing on chronic lymphatic leukaemia, although the relative difference in rates between the two groups appears to have narrowed with increasing follow-up ... Taken overall, the possibility that test participation caused a small absolute risk of leukaemia other than CLL [chronic lymphocytic leukaemia] cannot be ruled out.

(iii) Entitlement to compensation

At this point in the narrative, it is worth briefly examining the responses of other governments to the question of test veteran's entitlements.

The United States takes the presumptive approach to the question of entitlement. That is to say, in order to be eligible for all necessary health care (the US has no NHS) and also compensation, an individual need only prove that he was present at a test and has one of a schedule of diseases listed as linked to radiation exposure. The list includes leukaemia (other than chronic lymphatic leukaemia, which is not thought to be linked to radiation exposure), 15 forms of cancer and MM.[10] There is no requirement for proof of exposure to ionizing radiation beyond evidence of presence at a particular location during a test: it is presumed that a test veteran was exposed to radiation, and that this exposure is as likely a cause as any of their illness. Moreover, a test veteran who has an unlisted disease does not necessarily lose the entitlement to compensation. Provided that medical opinion can demonstrate that the disease may be linked to radiation exposure, entitlement to health care and compensation can still be granted. This system may be termed 'double presumptive': there is a presumption of exposure to ionizing radiation *and* a link to later disease among test participants. This has been US law since the 1988 Radiation-Exposed Veterans Compensation Act (R-EVCA).

In Australia, a review of all perceived anomalies in veteran's entitlements was published in January 2003. This included a comprehensive review of the entitlements of Australian participants in the British atomic tests. These participants did not qualify for benefits under the current Australian law regarding veterans, the 1986 Veterans Entitlement Act (VEA), since that did not cover peacetime service before December 1972. They did however qualify under the 1988 Safety, Rehabilitation and Compensation Act (SRCA).

The salient part of the SRCA is Section 7:1, which relates to disease or death related to exposure to ionizing radiation. Like the US R-EVCA, Australian entitlements here presume that a person subjected to ionizing radiation who subsequently develops a disease associated with such exposure is entitled to compensation; it is presumed that exposure has materially contributed to the disease and it is for the government to prove otherwise. However, there is an extra burden of proof, which is incumbent upon the claimant rather than the government. Like their US counterparts, Australian claimants must demonstrate that they were present at a test and have a disease associated with exposure to ionizing radiation, but unlike the US claimants, Australians must further demonstrate that they *were* exposed. Like the UK and unlike the US, the Australian government does not regard presence at a test by itself as reasonable proof of exposure. Consequently, as the *Australian Review* noted, 'only a small percentage of claims made under the SRCA by participants in the tests have been successful'.

Proving exposure retrospectively is difficult if not impossible, and consequently Australian test veterans also claimed that they ought to be entitled to compensation under the VEA. As mentioned above, they did not qualify under the defence service entitlements of the VEA, but the Act also gave provision for hazardous service compensation regardless of when it was carried out. Here, therefore, the participants needed to demonstrate that their presence at a test represented 'hazardous non-warlike service'. It was this that led to the review of entitlement.

After looking at 160 submissions and also the recommendations of the 1988 Royal Commission, the Review Committee concluded that 'by common sense and by any reasonable measure, service in the test operations must be regarded as involving hazards beyond those of normal peacetime', and consequently recommended that test veterans should be entitled to health care benefits under the VEA. Moreover, the Committee further concluded that VEA compensation coverage ought to be extended to those participants 'placed in danger from ionizing radiation'. However, it stopped short of fully endorsing the 'double presumptive' model of the US. Despite finding that existing records of radiation exposure were 'problematic', the Committee could not recommend that exposure should be presumed to have taken place by virtue of participation. Instead, it noted that the Australian equivalent of the NRPB study was also investigating the possibility of estimating dosage for each test participant, and it urged that the study (scheduled to be published in late 2005) be finalized as quickly as possible.

Thus the Australian system appeared to be moving towards a halfway house between the British and US systems. Participation in a test was recognized as hazardous and worthy of health care benefits, but not yet of compensation. For the latter to be provided, clear evidence of exposure to ionizing radiation would have to be provided, and would not be assumed. By the end of 2002, only ten participants had succeeded in securing compensation.

New Zealand followed a similar system. Studies of mortality and cancer incidence among New Zealand test participants came to similar conclusions to the NRPB report. It found that there was 'little evidence of an increased risk for non-haematological cancers' (that is, leukaemias) and that for leukaemia a similar excess risk existed to that found by the NRPB study.[11] In 1999, the New Zealand government extended full war disablement pensions to participants in the *Grapple* tests, but none the less held to the position that there was no evidence that New Zealand participants had been exposed to ionizing radiation.[12] However, in 2001 the government awarded the New Zealand Nuclear Test Veterans Association (NZNTVA) a grant of NZ$200,000 for an investigation of the possibility of a test for exposure to ionizing radiation. The investigation was to be carried out by the Institute of Molecular Biosciences at Massey University in New Zealand, and began with a pilot study of DNA samples of 50 test veterans to look for genetic damage that could be linked to radiation exposure.

Conclusions

From an epidemiological perspective, the NRPB appears to provide much the strongest evidence on possible risks to participants in the UK nuclear weapons tests. Three studies involving the great majority of participants have produced almost identical broad conclusions – overall death rates in test participants as a group are similar to those in a group of comparable individuals (or 'control group'), and participants are not significantly more prone to cancers, the most established radiation-related diseases. This does back up the UK government's stance that participation should not be taken to *automatically* mean exposure to ionizing radiation: if it were otherwise, then signs ought to show up in an epidemiological survey, which they have signally failed to do.

Therefore, it is highly unlikely that a fourth NRPB study, should one take place, will produce a change in current British government policy, barring the emergence of some startling new evidence. It is far more likely that any change in policy on this issue will come as a result of non-epidemiological evidence, such as that which may emerge from the Massey University study.

From a policy perspective, the choice is quite stark: either to follow the US example of presumptive compensation, or else to continue to require proof of exposure. Apart from those in Groups A and B, who are known to have been exposed and for whom records of the size of exposure are available, there is not yet a formula for such proof. If the New Zealand study comes up with a test, it changes things. If such a test does turn out to be feasible and reliable, then it will have the greatest relevance for participants in the *Grapple* tests, where only a small percentage of participants were issued with film badges.

14
In Retrospect

In retrospect, the 1950s saw nuclear weapons developments that could lead to the destruction of civilization, or even the extinction of the human race and many other forms of life. The technology of thermonuclear explosives was being developed by the United States and the Soviet Union, who were about level in advancement. The United Kingdom was four or five years behind, but had a more limited programme.

While the weaponeers were developing thermonuclear technology, great changes were taking place in other areas of military engineering. Rocketry was making sensational advances, pointing towards missiles with ranges varying from a few hundred miles to many thousands of miles. Electronics, computers and instrumental advances generally indicated that it would be possible to deliver a missile accurately within a distance less than the radius of destruction of a nuclear explosion. The combination of thermonuclear warheads with precise rocketry, countermeasures notwithstanding, had by 1970 produced the military situation where East and West could destroy each other, whichever fired first.

All of these developments were foreseen in the 1950s by some politicians, military men and scientists, but only dimly. The continuing policy of the West was to be one of deterrence, and within that policy the United Kingdom insisted on having an independent component judged by the government of the day to be sufficient 'to deter'. France took an even stronger line in regard to nuclear weapons, and acquired a nuclear arsenal and delivery system at least as powerful as those of the United Kingdom.

The international and political aspects of the military balance of power in the world are outside the scope of this book, but it must be noted that it was the British perception of the great political significance of military nuclear power that led to the British nuclear weapon programme, with its constant updating. However, by 1960 the United Kingdom had given up the attempt to develop its own strategic delivery systems. But it did share in the advances in electronics and computers that are an essential part of nuclear weapons systems.

The main task seen by the British governments in the 1950s was, first, to build an atomic bomb and then to develop the technology of thermonuclear explosives in sufficient detail to make possible the manufacture of nuclear warheads. The means of delivery were to be the V-bombers, and later the Polaris missile, bought from the United States and carried in British nuclear-powered submarines.

The need for tests was implicit in the political decision after 1945 to produce nuclear weapons. Looking back at the test programme from the vantage point of 2006, our perspective must be different from what it would have been at the time of the tests. Were the trials worthwhile? What did they achieve? And at what cost? Were they conducted with due care for the safety of the men taking part and of Australian and world populations? And if so, were they really safe or did they cause illness and death?

The nuclear task

Hurricane in 1952 – three years after the first Russian atomic explosion – was a successful test of a plutonium device, but it was not a weapon and needed further work to develop it into an atomic bomb for the RAF. If some of the British scientists had thought of this bomb as 'the deterrent' and their definitive goal, they soon found new objectives before them. For some, there was the challenge inherent in the very nature of nuclear energy. For all, there were new requirements from the Services to be met – for smaller and lighter bombs, for bombs of high, low and intermediate yields, and for varied designs for different purposes. But, above all, within a few weeks of *Hurricane* came the world's first thermonuclear explosion – an American test of a 10-megaton device – and a Russian thermonuclear weapons test followed a few months later.[1] Just as Britain was acquiring an atomic bomb capability, the Americans and Russians were acquiring infinitely more powerful hydrogen weapons, and the whole strategic scene changed. In the summer of 1954, the British government decided that British scientists too should develop and hydrogen bombs. It was a race of Lewis Carroll's Red Queen variety, in which 'it takes all the running you can do, to keep in the same place. If you want to get somewhere else, you must run at least twice as fast as that'.[2]

The programme of research and development of a thermonuclear weapon (as well as the production of a stockpile of A-bombs) was daunting, though it started with one immense technological advantage – knowing that it could be done. But Penney's scientific staff, by American standards, was very small indeed, and he was persistently worried about staff shortages in some skills and disciplines. Some of the scientists he most wanted were impossible to recruit; even within the atomic project, the work lacked the appeal of Harwell, partly because the weapon scientists – instead of attending conferences, publishing reports and building up scientific reputations and career prospects – had to hide their lights under a bushel of super-secrecy.

Penney had other difficulties to face. The intrinsic scientific research problems were formidable. His computing facilities were inadequate, hardly one-tenth of those Los Alamos commanded. Supplies of fissile material were also a cause for anxiety, since the growing demands for it on Hinton's industrial group could scarcely be met, and material used on tests was at the expense of the stockpile. Thinking had to take the place of experiment as far as practicable. Other supplies besides fissile material were sometimes scarce or late in delivery, because of production problems. This was especially true of the special materials needed for the hydrogen bomb, for which novel production processes had to be designed and new plant built at great speed. A trial planned many months ahead might depend crucially on whether a small quantity of some essential material was delivered on time.

The achievement

The weapon tests were an essential part of the postwar defence policy of both Labour and Conservative governments. Without them there could have been no acquisition of a British nuclear deterrent, and as such they were highly successful. The first British test had been seven years after the first American and three years after the first Russian atomic test. But within five years of *Hurricane* the British had progressed from a clumsy atomic device to a megaton hydrogen bomb, and had developed a range of atomic weapons that Britain thought would meet her needs. The timescale, as has recently been emphasized,[3] was short compared with that of the American and Soviet hydrogen bomb programmes. From the Defence White Paper in February 1955 to the first megaton-range airdrop at Christmas Island in May 1957 was only 27 months; even from the Cabinet decision of mid-1954 it was only 34 months. By either figure, it compares with 76 months for the United States and 60 months for the Soviet Union. Britain's entire programme of major trials was compressed into less than six years compared with 17 (postwar) years for the United States and 14 years for the Soviet Union,[4] up to the Partial Test Ban Treaty of 1963. Of course, the United States and the Soviet Union developed a much wider range of nuclear warheads and delivery systems than did the United Kingdom. Then too the British had brought back from Los Alamos the earliest American ideas about the 'super' – the H-bomb.

These few years of intense and unremitting effort produced much more than a small stockpile of British-made military hardware. Ever since 1946, when the United States had so abruptly ended the wartime atomic partnership and agreements, Britain had striven to renew them and had made some promising but unsuccessful attempts. During the years of nuclear independence, restoration of nuclear interdependence with the United States had been a primary aim of Labour and Conservative governments; it had taken priority over relationships with European and Commonwealth friends and allies. The weapons trials, leading up to the trials at Christmas Island, demonstrated both Britain's nuclear competence and her value to the United States as a partner. They showed that cooperation with the British would no longer be – as an American senator had once said – like trading a horse for a rabbit.[5]

American perception of the advantages of partnership was enhanced by the launching of Sputnik I in October 1957, which aroused American fears that the Soviet Union was overtaking the United States in technological achievement. President Eisenhower invited Prime Minister Macmillan to Washington for talks about cooperation on the military applications of nuclear energy, and at their conclusion a Declaration of Common Purpose was issued, in which the President committed himself to seek the amendment of the Atomic Energy (McMahon) Act so as to 'permit close and fruitful collaboration of scientists and engineers of Great Britain, the United States, and other friendly countries'.[6] The McMahon Act, which had prevented collaboration on nuclear weapons for twelve years, was amended on 2 July 1958, and the very next day a comprehensive bilateral defence agreement was signed.[7] In May 1959, a further agreement placed Britain in a highly favoured relationship by enabling her to buy component parts of nuclear weapons and weapons systems (but not nuclear warheads) from the United States.[8]

These agreements effectively pooled the two countries' scientific expertise in nuclear weapons where both had a requirement, adding Aldermaston's knowledge and skills to those of Los Alamos and Livermore. What the Americans wanted was not actual British designs but another source of ideas, access to the brains of Penney and his scientists, and the capacity of another weapons laboratory that could make independent and original contributions.

They got a better bargain than they expected when to their surprise it became clear that, during the years of separate development, the two countries had reached very much the same understanding of the physics involved (though the Americans were clearly ahead, especially in engineering design). Moreover, they soon realized that the British scientists had developed some techniques that they did not possess and were anxious to share.[9] They were 'amazed to learn how much we already know', the Prime Minister wrote, and 'this was a major factor in convincing them that we could be trusted with more information than they probably intended originally to give us'.[10]

Circumstances were favourable for a bilateral agreement in 1958, but negotiations – even with Sputnik assistance – could not have succeeded without Britain's proven achievements in nuclear energy and especially in nuclear weapons. Penney and his men provided Macmillan with a powerful case, and he gave credit to them for a 'tremendous achievement', of which they had 'every right to be proud', enabling Britain 'to keep virtually abreast of the United States in this complex and intricate business of nuclear weapons development'.[11] To this 'tremendous achievement', and all that it implied, Australia had made a most generous – and indispensable – contribution.

Besides their primary purpose, the weapon trials had served as convincing demonstrations to the United States of Britain's scientific and technological status, and the resulting agreements of 1958 and 1959 created a unique relationship of nuclear interdependence, which – with periodic renewals – has powerfully shaped postwar British history. For the British, the new relationship gave access not only to American data and experience, but also to materials such as uranium-235 which could be supplied by the United States much more cheaply than they could be produced in British plants. It increased the potential of both countries and optimized the use of resources. The aims of postwar British nuclear policy had been triumphantly achieved, but the achievement of interdependence meant that the independent deterrent was no longer totally independent.

Costs

Though small by American and Soviet standards, the major British trials were large and costly operations. Six of the nine series involved long-distance naval expeditions; all nine involved, in total, hundreds of aircraft and thousands of civilian and Service personnel; massive amounts of money were spent on engineering and construction work in remote and inhospitable areas, to be written off in a few years at most.

No estimate of the total expenditure on weapon tests is attempted here. The costs were small in relation to the results achieved with so few trials and so few shots – only 21 – and Macmillan, Chancellor of the Exchequer before he was Prime Minister, certainly considered them very cheap. Financial statements showing total expenditure on trials are unlikely to be found, since the costs were shared among various Service and civilian departments and the Atomic Energy Authority, and were subdivided among general departmental expenditure on salaries, Service pay, travel, civil engineering and supplies. Moreover, figures for the cost to the British Treasury would still give an incomplete picture, since they would not include that borne by Australian government departments.

Estimates made in February 1957 for the Lord President of the Council give a round figure of £39 million for four trials (presumably *Hurricane*, *Totem*, *Mosaic* and *Buffalo*), but it is not clear exactly how that total is made up. Including fissile materials, the cost is put at £15 million a year, declining after 1957–58 to £10 million a year or less. These annual costs were less than 10 per cent of the £150–160 million a year estimated for development and production of nuclear weapons and delivery systems, and that figure was itself only 10 per cent of the defence budget.

Whitehall officials noted approvingly how cost-conscious the scientists were. Even so, as we have seen, the scientists were always under pressure to reduce expenditure and pare down their requirements. At all the trials, resources were barely adequate, and insufficient allowance was made for contingencies or for equipment breakdown. It was a strangely parsimonious attitude on the part of a government that attached overwhelming importance to an independent nuclear deterrent.

In relation to the magnitude and the momentous consequences of the trial programme, it was undeniably cheap. Its objectives were quickly fulfilled, with only 21 shots fired. The tenth, at Christmas Island in May 1957, was a thermonuclear bomb dropped from a V-bomber. In comparison, the Americans' first airdrop (at Bikini in 1956), was their 67th.

The tasks assigned to the scientists had been carried out rapidly, effectively and with a minimum of testing. The small number of shots meant huge savings. Costs were low not only in terms of logistics, but also in scarce and costly fissile material. Britain had ordered a nuclear arsenal with the approval of the majority of the public, for even after 1958, when CND was most active, opinion polls showed consistent support for the nuclear deterrent. Britain's scientists and engineers had delivered it promptly, and at a bargain price.

The safety of the Australian population

Trials personnel were a small and special population – male, mostly young and passed medically fit for service in arduous conditions. All were under health physics and medical supervision. Protection for members of the public was quite another matter. Any risks they ran were involuntary; they included vulnerable groups, such as children and pregnant women, and they could not be individually monitored. They had to be protected from radiation hazards in the first place by keeping them out of the danger areas, and then by seeing that fallout did not harm them outside those areas.

No entry

The regions of the tests – the Monte Bello Islands, Emu Field and Maralinga – were so barren that they were uninhabited and the only problem in excluding people from them was the reputedly small number of Aboriginals travelling across the Maralinga range. Penney had enquired particularly about the Aboriginals when Maralinga was first considered and had been reassured. The Australian security authorities were given the task of controlling access to the range and warning the nearest Aboriginal communities. Patrolling the range was undertaken by Aboriginal Welfare Officers and Commonwealth 'peace officers', with the help of land patrols and low-flying RAF air searches before firings.

There have been various stories of Aboriginals on the range. One well-documented instance was in May 1957 (between *Buffalo* and *Antler*) when an Aboriginal family named Milpuddie – husband, wife, little boy and baby girl – walked across the range and were discovered at a place called Pom Pom near the health physics control unit. They were monitored and the boy was found to be very slightly contaminated, so they were all showered. The radiation dose they had received during the walk and while camping at Pom Pom was estimated at 6–7 millirems (60–70 microsieverts) or about 1/70th of the present ICRP short-term non-occupational limit of 0.5 rem in a single year. It is impossible to prove conclusively that the Pom Pom incident is the only one, despite the efforts made to ensure that no one strayed into the prohibited area. The AWTSC believed at the time, and reported to the Australian Prime Minister, that these efforts were effective, and that no Aboriginals were nearer than

170 miles. AIRAC later came to a similar conclusion. Many people present at the time, and working in areas where intrusions were likely to have been observed, still maintain that there were no other events, though there have been various stories of Aboriginals wandering or camping on the range.

Fallout

Protection of the public against fallout beyond the danger area depended on firing criteria and meteorology, as we have seen repeatedly. Weather data had to be combined with theoretical calculations of bomb yield, cloud height and particle distribution, and confidence established that favourable conditions would persist for long enough to permit preparation, firing and subsequent safe dispersal of radioactive debris – ideally giving 24 hours of stable conditions after firing to allow the cloud to disperse. At any point in this process there was room for uncertainties and for the unforeseen. Meteorology was as much an art as a science, and still is an inexact science. Before the trials, not much was known about the weather patterns of either the Monte Bello islands or the Central Australian Desert. Much was learnt in the course of the trials, but, in the earlier ones especially, there were some meteorological problems, partly due to having too few weather stations. Cloud heights were sometimes predicted incorrectly, winds changed direction unexpectedly, or the expected shear pattern failed to materialize. Even so, no catastrophes such as the 180-degree change of wind direction at Bikini in March 1954 occurred (see Chapter 5). Meteorological facilities and methods improved during the decade, and by the time of *Mosaic* the network of weather ships, weather stations and long-range reconnaissance flights extended from the Cocos Islands in the west to Christmas Island in the east and from the equator to Antarctica. No evidence exists of pressure being exerted on the trials staff to fire in meteorologically unsafe conditions, for political or any other reasons. Errors occurred, as at *Totem*, but there is no indication in the records of any of the trials that the trial director ordered a firing in conditions that he believed to be unsatisfactory, against his better judgement and that of his colleagues (including Australian and British meteorologists and members of the AWTSC).

Before *Mosaic*, as we have seen, fallout monitoring stations were set up and were soon increased to provide an extensive monitoring network across the Australian continent. Evidence from these stations was that radiation exposure of the population due to fallout from the 1956 and 1957 trials was slight. As we saw in previous chapters, from the readings at these stations the AWTSC calculated the lifetime radiation doses to people in these locations from each of the *Mosaic, Buffalo* and *Antler* shots, and in 1983 AIRAC revised the calculations on what it considered a more realistic basis. (All the figures were, of course, theoretical doses, not measured doses to actual persons.) A possible weakness of both assessments was that they used readings from the monitoring stations only. These were widely distributed, and were planned to give representative coverage, but fallout can be patchy and some higher readings might have been found at other places.

Then, in 1985, a new appraisal of the fallout and its public health impact was made by two scientists of the Australian Radiation Laboratory, Wise and Moroney, whose work has been mentioned earlier in connection with the individual trials. Wise and Moroney took into account not only the data from the monitoring stations and the AWTSC and AIRAC work, but all the other information available on yields, radiological air and ground surveys, cloud trajectories and meteorological conditions. For *Hurricane* and *Totem*, before the monitoring stations were set up, they made conservative calculations based on all the available information and extrapolation from later trials. They applied more recent worst-case assumptions about the pathways by which radioactivity can reach man, and because of the consequent large additional contribution from internal radiation their figures were generally a good deal higher, and thus more pessimistic, than AIRAC'S. They stressed that the emphasis on external radiation at the time of the tests was consistent with the best contemporary practice and reflected the limitations of the knowledge available then of the environmental transport of radionuclides.

Wise and Moroney – who warned that their figures could be ten times too high, or too low by a factor of 2 – calculate the population dose from all twelve shots in the major trials as 700 man-sieverts (70,000 man-rems) or about 1/60th the natural background dose over the same period of time. This extra dose averages 70 microsieverts (0.7 millirem) per person. The statistical result of applying the ICRP's risk coefficient to the population dose of 700 man-sieverts may be a total of seven fatal cancers and seven serious hereditary effects expressed in the first two generations – probably fewer. For individual people the numerical risk of serious detriment to health was higher in those population centres which received greater fallout than elsewhere, but within such a small overall figure was obviously still very low. Even if the Wise and Moroney figures, and the ICRP estimates of risk, are too low by factors of 2, the effect of the atomic weapon tests on the health of the Australian population appears to have been very minimal. The estimate of perhaps seven (or probably fewer) cancer deaths may be compared with over 500,000 cancer deaths in Australia since the early 1950s, of which total, background radiation and medical uses may account for 5,000.[12]

The Aboriginals and the land

Months before *Hurricane*, the British Prime Minister was asked in the House of Commons what steps were being taken to protect from harm the Australian Aboriginals likely to be in the neighbourhood of the impending atomic bomb test. He replied that there was no danger whatsoever to the health or safety of the people of Australia.[13] The planners did not know of the whereabouts of any Aboriginals in the north-west of Australia, within 200 miles or so of the Monte Bello Islands, but in any case it was intended to fire only in conditions that would prevent fallout reaching the mainland.

Penney was anxious about the safety and welfare of Aboriginals around Maralinga and, as we saw in Chapter 6, he was given assurances by Butement. Measures were taken to warn homesteads and Aboriginal communities and to patrol the range – particularly in areas in the direction in which the fallout was destined to occur – before firings. But the two Native Welfare Officers had an impossible task; their function was to do everything practicable to persuade natives to keep out of the way of operations, but they had no vehicles of their own, no radio communications and a vast area to cover.

The health effects, if any, of the tests on the Aboriginals are difficult to establish because of the lack of health and other records, and because of the general background of ill-health; the condition of the Aboriginals in the 1950s was very poor, suffering as they did from malnutrition and recurrent severe epidemics, especially of measles and influenza. If Wise and Moroney's estimates, of perhaps seven fatal cancers and seven serious hereditary effects in a population of ten million are accepted, the incidence in the Aboriginal population – even if disproportionately high – must have been very small. In the group that probably incurred the highest exposure, at Wallatinna, the estimated dose indicated a probability of much less than one fatal cancer.[14]

However, the test programme undoubtedly had an adverse effect on the Aboriginals' lives. Howard Beale, the Australian Minister for Supply, asserted that the natives were not deprived of their tribal grounds. The area over which watch was kept for native movements during test periods was, he said, very arid and was uninhabited, no natives had been found there and so none had been interfered with. It is true that there was no forced removal of communities, as occurred at Bikini and Eniwetok. A decision had been taken some time earlier to move the tribes associated with the Ooldea Mission, before a permanent proving ground was in question. Having already removed the Aboriginals, the Australian government was not averse to using the deserted region, and acceded to the British request. Some care was taken not to encroach on reserves or tribal hunting grounds. But to the contemporary Australian authorities the deserts were simply vast, empty, useless spaces. They did not appreciate the Aboriginals' attitude to the land, and had little understanding of their social organization or of their journeys to visit relatives and sacred sites and to attend ceremonial gatherings. The decisions were taken by people with little or no knowledge of the Aboriginals. They wanted to ensure that the Aboriginals did not come to harm by wandering into danger areas, but there was to be no question of 'placing the affairs of a handful of natives above those of the British Commonwealth of Nations'.[15]

This is hardly surprising. At that time Aboriginals had no rights as citizens; they did not, for example, get the right to vote until 1967. The Constitution expressly stated that 'in reckoning the numbers of the people of the Commonwealth ... Aboriginal natives shall not be counted'.[16] For years it had been expected that they would solve the dilemma of a property-owning advanced society confronting nomadic people without a sense of individual property by dying out or being assimilated; in the 1920s and 1930s there were said to be only a few thousand left who preserved some semblance of their tribal culture.[17] When in 1972 a committee of enquiry recommended land grants for Aboriginals forced off their customary hunting grounds by pastoralists in the Northern Territories, there was still opposition.[18] The Whitlam government proposed extensive welfare measures and the suspension of grants of mining leases on Aboriginal reserves, but these policies were reversed by the Fraser administration which followed.

In four other areas – Taranaki, Wewak, TM100 and TM101 – there were still significant surface densities of plutonium, resulting from the minor trials and especially from the *Vixen* safety experiments (see Chapter 10). Taranaki was the largest and most heavily contaminated, and there were also various sites where radioactive materials are buried in shallow pits, a manner of disposal that some experts do not regard as acceptable current practice in an area where access and habitation are unrestricted. The clean-up of these facilities, as we saw in Chapter 12, was controversial and fraught with difficulties.

The people most affected by the atomic weapon tests programme of the 1950s were the Aboriginals, because of damage to their way of life rather than directly to their health. They had no rights and their interest in the land was not realized or respected; but this was, and had been, their general situation and was neither new nor peculiar to the weapons trials.

Health and safety of test personnel

It has frequently been suggested, and accusations continue, that the weapon trials were conducted without regard for health and safety. The evidence is anecdotal and it is impossible to discuss numerous individual stories, but criticism follows several general lines. It includes allegations that international radiation protection standards were flouted and that the trials staff drew up their own more accommodating rules; that safety rules and procedures were inadequate or were not enforced, and test personnel were not warned of radiation hazards; that film badges were not issued or were not collected, and exposures were not recorded; that protective clothing and respirators were not provided when they were necessary. Stories have been told of men being used as guinea pigs and deliberately exposed to danger to study the effects of radiation. It has been suggested that the Australian population was put at serious risk from fallout and that some people were harmed as a result; that shots were fired in unsafe weather conditions, either through error, or deliberately because time was too pressing to wait for safe opportunities; that insufficient care was taken to protect people, especially Aboriginals, from wandering into danger areas; that when things went wrong, the facts were suppressed and the public was deceived.

If all these accusations were true, the scientists must have been guilty of ignorance, incompetence or a cynical disregard for safety, or all three, and there must have been a gigantic conspiracy among many scores of them. We have tried to consider without prejudice as much of the evidence as we could and before coming to any conclusions, to weigh up its credibility bearing in mind the state of knowledge at that time.[19]

Radiation standards

The radiation protection standards used at the trials were based on the ICRP recommendations. As Penney said: 'ICRP was our bible'. However in 1950, the postwar ICRP was just resuming its interrupted work, with a brief set of Recommendations on the protection of workers routinely exposed to radiation for a working lifetime. It did not deal – as it was to do later – with 'one-off' special emergency exposures or with compensatory lay-off periods after a higher dose, nor did it differentiate between occupational and non-occupational standards, either for individuals or populations.

The ICRP maximum permissible dose (MPD) of 0.5 roentgen (r) a week, equivalent to 25 r in a year, was exactly reflected in the normal working rate of 0.5 r a week applied to trials personnel and, like ICRP, the trial orders emphasized also that radiation exposure should be kept as low as possible. The integrated doses approved for use at the trials in certain circumstances were not set by the weapon scientists themselves, but by an independent Medical Research Council panel; the panel included members of ICRP, and was *au fait* with research and clinical data, with ICRP thinking and with current American standards and experience. Integrated doses did not at this time appear in ICRP Recommendations but were to do so well before the end of the decade. It may be worth noting here that ICRP Recommendations embodied an extremely wide international consensus of scientific opinion, and were not handed down from the mountain engraved on tablets of stone. Ideas were discussed for months or years before they appeared in a formal report, and the initial input into ICRP was from United States, British and Canadian scientists and scientific committees and from tripartite conferences on radiological protection. There is therefore nothing surprising or suspect in the adoption by the United States or Britain of radiological protection rules in advance of publication by ICRP.

ICRP occupational standards developed during the decade; by 1958–59 there was no weekly MPD, but instead limits of 3 rems a quarter or 12 rems a year (subject to a limit on accumulated dose which was related to age and which averaged 5 rems a year).[20] The considerable changes since the early 1950s in ICRP Recommendations on occupational exposure, reflecting increased knowledge of radiation effects, have not invalidated the basic standards of that time. Judged by those standards, the documentary evidence shows that the rules adopted for trials personnel were completely acceptable. The record of radiation exposures indicates that the standards were met; most test personnel received much less radiation than the normal working rate, and only a small number (six) received the higher exposures that were authorized to facilitate certain tasks such as ground surveys, collection of crater samples, and special flights.

To say this is not to prove that the trials were necessarily safe. It may be argued that the standards, the ICRP's Recommendations, were inadequate. There is a body of scientific opinion today that believes that existing ICRP standards are insufficiently rigorous and should be tightened up, perhaps by a factor of 10; however, most scientists believe equally strongly that ICRP standards are sound and are not in error by so much as a factor of two. This debate is undecided and will remain so until further and conclusive evidence is available. Meanwhile, what ICRP may or may not decide in the future is irrelevant in judging how the weapon trials were conducted.

Safety in practice

Standards are necessary but not sufficient to give assurance of safe operation, since they have to be embodied in rules, procedures, organization and discipline, and put into effect by staff with adequate resources. Information and instructions have to reach all parts of the organization; all concerned need to know and understand the rules and comply with them. Standards, plans, rules and procedures for the trials are all well documented, but in the nature of things there is more uncertainty about application and compliance – how it all worked out in real life. It would be miraculous if everything had gone perfectly according to plan; some things certainly went wrong and are so recorded.

In addition to the records, there are numerous anecdotes. Although it would be wrong to ignore or dismiss them without investigation, accounts of events 30 years ago, told in good faith, may be unreliable. (This is especially so if they are second-hand accounts, or related by people only slightly involved who may not have understood the events well at the time.) This is not the place to discuss individual stories, but rather to try to form a general picture from the available information, in particular from contemporary records. The mass of the evidence shows that the health and safety of the trials participants were regarded very seriously and that a great deal of trouble was taken over radiological protection. Film badges were duly issued and collected and doses recorded; movements were effectively controlled and men did not wander at random within danger areas; monitoring and decontamination of personnel was careful and systematic; protective clothing and respirators were available and were issued for work in contaminated areas. Undoubtedly, some film badges were lost, as happens even in routine factory operations, but it is believed that losses were few in the case of people entering contaminated areas. It is possible, but unlikely, that some film badges supplied for Service officers to issue to their men may not all have been handed out and returned. A few people may have broken rules, ignored instructions or cut a corner. Some men, especially perhaps young servicemen, may have had a cavalier attitude to safety, either out of ignorance or bravado. The scientists' familiarity with radiation sometimes bred contempt and a few were scornful of the stringent precautions. Penney had a 'blacklist' of them, but most of them had too much respect for radiation hazards to be careless, and they included men with many years' experience in high explosives research, who were habitually cautious. The men who incurred the highest exposures were themselves highly qualified scientists and doctors; for example the *Hot Box* pilot and observer at *Totem*, and the various scientists who collected crater samples at *Totem* and *Mosaic*. They took small calculated risks themselves for scientific purposes, voluntarily and in full knowledge of the radiation hazards.

The few deficiencies that existed in the health and safety arrangements were mainly due to weaknesses in overall organization of the operations or to failures of communication between the main elements engaged. Especially in the earlier trials, the different elements were run almost independently, and Captain Cooper, Penney's technical aide, commented (as we have seen) on the need for stronger headquarters control. The most obvious example was the lack of radiological protection for the air and ground crews of the RAAF Lincolns used at *Hurricane* and *Totem* in Harwell's programme of long-distance air-sampling flights.

Radiation limits at the trials were adequate by the standards of the time and stand up well, even by today's standards. Whether these standards were maintained in the actual operations cannot be established with the same certainty, but the radiation records show exposures of test personnel that compare very favourably with those of radiation workers in the atomic laboratories and factories. No one received a recorded dose anything like large enough to cause immediate physical or health effects, such as radiation burns or radiation sickness, and these do not appear in any of the medical reports. As for the suggestion that men were used as guinea pigs, it is untrue (see Chapter 8).

For some reviewers, the use of epidemiological studies (as we have done in Chapter 13) marks the authors as establishment stooges who accept suspect 'official' information uncritically and ignore independent evidence. The NRPB studies provide the most complete and reliable picture of the health experience of British test participants as can be imagined. We have been able to give only a short outline, but anyone who reads the reports carefully, in full, cannot fail to be impressed by their comprehensive character, the enormous mass of data collected and the meticulous methods of analysis. However, anecdotes are quicker to read, easier to understand and more emotive. As a consequence, they tend to have much greater public and journalistic appeal, and an impression has become widespread that the atomic tests were carelessly and irresponsibly conducted and that large numbers of participants have suffered grievously in consequence. These sufferings are matched in the 22,000 men in the NRPB control group, and in the general population, where cancers and leukaemias are widespread. Every case is tragic, and every one deserves our heartfelt sympathy. Cancer is a sad fact of our world. It is sometimes demanded that we should study 'independent sources', but there are no such sources known to us that offer a valid alternative. So we can only conclude that 'overall levels of mortality and cancer incidence in UK nuclear weapons test participants have continued to be similar to those in a matched control group'.

The atmosphere

Finally, what did Britain's tests in Australia add to the global fallout? Besides close-in and intermediate fallout in Australia, British weapon tests contributed to the global fallout that occasioned worldwide anxiety in the 1950s and early 1960s – between *Castle Bravo* in 1954 and the PTBT in 1963. Up to the time the treaty came into force, there were nearly 400 nuclear detonations in the atmosphere, 212 by the United States, 161 by Soviet Union, 21 by Britain (twelve in Australia and nine at Christmas Island) and four by France.[21] The total fission yield has been estimated at about 195 megatons (111 megatons from Russian, 72 from American, 11 from British and less than 0.2 from French tests).[22] Thus British tests contributed just over 5 per cent of the pre-1963 fallout; slightly over 4 per cent of that from all atmospheric tests up to 1980. The scale of the British programme kept environmental, as well as financial and resource, costs low.

The biggest detonations were by the Soviet Union – one of 58 megatons in 1961 and two of 30 megatons in 1962 – and the total fission yield for 1961–62 is estimated at about 85 megatons. The biggest American shot was the 15-megaton *Castle Bravo* in 1954; American shots were smaller but more numerous than the Russian, and after 1957 a high proportion were carried out underground (and a few at high altitudes) to minimize fallout.

Global, or long-range, fallout was deposited in a band of latitudes around the world, centred on the latitude where the explosion occurred. (The smaller the explosion, the narrower the band of latitudes containing the fallout.) It is true that high-yield explosions, made a mile or more above ground level, produced a cloud that rises well into the stratosphere; the radioactivity was contained in very fine particles that remain in the high atmosphere for a considerable time, and the radioactivity therefore had time to spread over the whole hemisphere. Some is taken into the other hemisphere by the slow exchange of air across the equator, but by the time some radioactivity had moved into the other hemisphere the activity had been greatly reduced by natural decay. It is therefore a good approximation to assume that the fallout from any explosion took place only in the hemisphere where the explosion occurred.

Fallout from the British tests in Australia therefore remained in the southern hemisphere, where there was a high probability of its being deposited in the oceans and harmlessly dispersed. It did not add to the heavy contamination of the densely populated countries of the northern hemisphere, where by 1958 the United States, Britain and Japan had three times the world average of accumulated fallout.[23] By early 1959 the level measured in Britain rose for the couple of months to almost one-third of the natural background.[24] In 1983 the figure for all cancers in the United Kingdom was 130,000 a year, of which perhaps 1,250 could be attributed to natural sources,[25] 330 to medical exposures, seven to fallout, six to occupational exposure, two to nuclear waste and five to miscellaneous sources; the actual numbers are probably smaller. Britain, as we have seen, has received decidedly more fallout than the world average, but even so the cancers due to fallout were about 1/50th or less of those due to medical exposures, and 1/80th of those due to natural sources of radiation. The risks associated with medical radiation were, and still are, much higher statistically than those of fallout; though they are not perceived as such, since medical radiation is largely non-controversial, and the patient receiving radiation does so voluntarily and stands to benefit personally.

Radiation doses from fallout have seldom exceeded a few millisieverts, but have been delivered to very large populations. Fallout from past atmospheric detonations will continue to irradiate the peoples of the world for very many generations, but at an extremely low rate. The total dose – past, present and future – is estimated to be about 4 millisieverts (400 millirems) for each member of the world's present population; this is equivalent to two years' exposure from natural sources. The present annual dose is about 0.01 millisieverts (1 millirem), compared with about 2 millisieverts (200 millirems) from natural sources. The best estimate is that fallout increases the risk of dying from cancer by, at worst, about one chance in 40,000. There is probably a real risk, although it is not exactly known and individual cases are not identifiable. Fallout is not a substantial hazard to human health. But it might have raised the levels of environmental radioactivity to a serious extent if testing had continued for some years at the 1961–62 rate. In Britain, for example, consideration was given on at least one occasion to stopping supplies of fresh milk for children because of increasing levels of radioiodine.[26]

The 1963 decision to end atmospheric tests, by the United States, the Soviet Union and Britain, was indeed highly desirable and was universally welcomed; it ended a period of intensive testing which produced 85 per cent of the world total of fallout.

Three thoughts on fallout

Paradoxically, the Australians received far less fallout from all atmospheric weapon tests, including the twelve British shots in Australia, than did the British themselves, with no weapon tests in their own islands. Up to 1963, when the PTBT ended Russian, American and British atmospheric tests, the population of the British Isles was exposed to levels of strontium-90 three times greater than was the Australian population. In the years following the Treaty, however, the ratio changed slightly because of French atmospheric tests in the southern hemisphere.

Australia willingly accepted the British weapon test programme and cooperated generously and effectively in it. But the Australian continent has been subject involuntarily to fallout from tests carried out by other countries as well, and it is ironic that the Australian population received seven times as much fallout from other nuclear tests as it did from the British tests on Australian territory.

As to the worldwide effects of fallout, it is impossible to estimate realistically what harm might result over thousands of years from that ten-year period of heavy testing by the United States, the Soviet Union and Britain. However, effects on the health of large populations can be very approximately assessed from the collective dose. For example, as we have seen, it has been estimated that, out of 130,000 cancer deaths a year in the United Kingdom, seven, or probably fewer, may be due to fallout. Worldwide, although individual instances cannot be identified, many cases of injury to health must have been caused by global fallout, and to these injuries the British tests must have made some contribution, although a very minor one since they created a small fraction of the total fallout, and moreover in the less populated hemisphere. 'Statistical deaths' may often be implicit even in the most humdrum and everyday of government decisions. But the British decision to possess, and therefore to test, nuclear weapons was not an everyday decision; it was a most momentous one. It was made, as Penney said, in the sober hope of bringing nearer the day when world war was universally seen to be unthinkable. Whether it justifies the possibility of additional cancer deaths or genetic defects – however unforeseen, unintended and few – must be a matter of opinion. Those who think the possibility was not justified should nevertheless look at the tests – and the defence decisions that led to them – in the light of the times and not only in today's light. Those who think it was justified must accept that some unknown, but relatively small, degree of harm was part of the cost of Britain's nuclear policy.

Appendix A
Memorandum of Arrangements between the United Kingdom and Australian Governments

Atomic weapons proving ground – Maralinga

Introduction

1　The Australian Government and the United Kingdom Government being agreed on the desirability of establishing a proving ground for atomic weapons and the Australian Government having offered to make a site available for this purpose in South Australia, this Memorandum sets out the principles which the two Governments agree shall govern the establishment of this site as a proving ground and its use for atomic weapon trials.

Conditions as to occupancy of site

2　The Australian Government will make the site at Maralinga in South Australia as defined in the annex to this Memorandum available to the United Kingdom Government as a proving ground for atomic weapons for a period of 10 years which may be extended by mutual agreement.

3　The use of this site by the United Kingdom Government in accordance with this agreement shall be free from all rent and similar charges.

4　During the currency of this agreement the Australian Government will take such steps as may be necessary in accordance with the laws and regulations in operation in Australia to proclaim the area defined in the annex as a prohibited area.

5　On the termination of this Agreement the United Kingdom Government shall have the right to remove and dispose of all movable facilities and equipment provided at the expense of the United Kingdom Government.

Nature of the tests to be carried out

6　No thermonuclear (hydrogen) weapon will be tested on the site.

7　An agreement of the Australian Government will be obtained before any atomic test is carried out on the site. For this purpose the United Kingdom Government will provide the Australian Government with sufficient information about the nature of any proposed test to enable the Australian Government to satisfy itself that the test can safely be carried out on the site. Such information shall be made available only to properly authorised persons in accordance with the security arrangements agreed between the two Governments.

Safety

8　The United Kingdom Government will be responsible for undertaking all practicable measures on the site to ensure that any tests carried out there do not cause injury or damage to persons or property.

9　In collaboration with the United Kingdom Government the Australian Government will set up and operate a chain of fixed monitoring stations at agreed sites in Australia and will make the information from these measurements available to the United Kingdom Government.

Claims for compensation

10　The Australian Government will take all reasonable steps to exclude unauthorised persons from the prohibited area.

11　The United Kingdom Government undertakes to indemnify the Australian Government in respect of all valid claims arising out of the death or injury of any person or any damage to property due to tests carried out on the site, except for claims made by any employee or servant of a Government other than the United Kingdom Government authorised to be within the prohibited area specifically in connection with tests on the site.

12　The United Kingdom Government accepts liability for such corrective measures as may be practicable in the event of radioactive contamination resulting from the tests on the site.

Australian access to the site

13　Subject to such safety and security arrangements as are agreed by the United Kingdom Government authorised officers of the Australian Government will be allowed access to the site.

14　By agreement with the United Kingdom Government the Australian Government will have the right to construct and/or install facilities and equipment for tests in the course of atomic weapon trials on the site and to send official observers to be present at any test on the site.

Information and effects

15　The United Kingdom Government will provide the Australian Government with all the data compiled as a result of the tests on the site about the effects of atomic weapons for both civil defence and military purposes. Such data shall however only be made available to properly authorised persons in accordance with the security arrangements agreed between the two Governments.

16　The Australian Government will similarly make available to the United Kingdom Government information about the results of tests of Australian facilities or equipment tested on the site.

Control of the project

17　A Joint Committee of Australian and United Kingdom representatives under the chairmanship of a representative of the Australian Department of Supply will be set up in Australia to consider all matters of joint concern in relation to the establishment and maintenance of the proving ground and to the arrangements for any trials thereon as may be approved from time to time and to advise the responsible departments through their respective representatives. The functions of the Committee will include the co-ordination of all activities within Australia of the United Kingdom and Australian Government Departments and Authorities, and their agents concerned with the project, and such executive action in matters of joint concern in Australia as may be agreed by the representatives of both parties.

Financial arrangements

18 A separate financial agreement will be negotiated between the Australian and the United Kingdom Governments in regard of costs of this project.
19 Nothing in this agreement shall be regarded as precluding the participation in atomic tests on the proving ground of other members of the British Commonwealth of Nations as may be mutually agreed by the Australian and United Kingdom Governments.
20 Unless provided to the contrary in any separate financial agreement which may be made between the two Governments, this agreement shall be deemed to be made on the understanding that all costs will be to the account of the United Kingdom Government.

Memorandum of Arrangements between Australian and United Kingdom Governments in regard to allocation of the costs of establishing and maintaining a proving ground for Atomic Weapons in South Australia, and for any tests carried out thereon.

1 This document is intended to be read in conjunction with the Memorandum of Arrangements between the Australian Government and the United Kingdom Government concerning the establishment in South Australia of a proving ground for atomic weapons.
2 Complementary to the arrangements outlined in that document regarding the terms and conditions on which the Australian Government agrees to make the site at Maralinga available to the United Kingdom Government for use as a proving ground for atomic weapons, this Memorandum sets out the financial obligations of the respective Governments in respect of the establishment and maintenance of the proving ground and of the arrangements for holding such tests thereon as may from time to time be approved.

Allocation of costs

3 It is agreed that subject to paragraphs 4 and 5 hereunder, the United Kingdom Government will bear all costs in connection with the establishment and maintenance of the proving ground and of any tests carried out thereon.

4   The Australian Government will bear –
  (a) the cost of any agreed target response or other tests carried out specifically at the request of any Australian Government Department or Authority;
  (b) the expenses of any Australian personnel authorised at the request of the Australian Government to attend any trials held on the proving ground; and
  (c) the costs of providing such Australian Services personnel as are agreed upon by the Australian Government from time to time for specific tasks at the Maralinga Proving Ground.

5   The Australian Government will, through appropriate Departments and organisations, provide such administrative assistance as is practicable in directions appropriate to their functions without cost to the United Kingdom Government. Where, however, such assistance cannot be rendered without additional cost to the normal functioning of such Departments, the additional cost concerned will be met by the United Kingdom Government.

6   The Australian Government agrees that any installation or facility provided at the expense of the United Kingdom Government in Australia will remain the property of the United Kingdom Government and, as provided for in Clause 5 of the Memorandum of Arrangements, be subject to removal or disposal on termination of the main agreement.

7   If it is mutually agreed between the Australian and United Kingdom Governments that another member of the British Commonwealth of Nations should participate in tests on the site, the allocation of any expenses of personnel authorised to be present at the request of the said member government and of any costs of agreed tests carried out specifically at the request of the said member government will be separately arranged between the United Kingdom and Australian Governments and the other Government concerned.

8   The cost of fares of United Kingdom personnel travelling to and from Australia and whilst in Australia, and the cost of Australian personnel travelling to and from the United Kingdom and whilst in the United Kingdom, will be borne respectively by the United Kingdom and Australian Governments.

9   The provisions of this Memorandum of Financial Arrangements may be altered by mutual consent between the Australian and United Kingdom Governments.

7 March 1956

Appendix B
Memorandum Respecting the Termination of the Memorandum of Arrangements between the United Kingdom and Australian Governments of 7 March 1956, concerning the Atomic Weapons Proving Ground-Maralinga

The Government of the United Kingdom of Great Britain and Northern Ireland and the Government of the Commonwealth of Australia, desiring to terminate the arrangements set out in the Memorandum of Arrangements of 7 March 1956 between them concerning the Atomic Weapons Proving Ground – Maralinga (the 'Memorandum of Arrangements') and the Memorandum in regard to allocation of costs of the same date, hereby record the following matters:

(a) The United Kingdom Government have completed decontamination and debris clearance at the Atomic Weapons Proving Ground Maralinga to the satisfaction of the Australian Government.

(b) On 21 December 1967, the United Kingdom Government relinquished to the Australian Government the site at Maralinga, as defined in the Annex to the Memorandum of Arrangements, and transferred without charge to the Australian Government certain installations and movable stores in accordance with detailed arrangements agreed between the British Defence Research Supply Staff and the Australian Department of Supply.

(c) With effect from 21 December 1967, the United Kingdom Government are released from all liabilities and responsibilities under the Memorandum of Arrangements save that the United Kingdom will continue to indemnify the Australian Government in accordance with Clause 11 of the Memorandum in respect of claims for which the cause for action occurred after 7 March 1956 and before 21 December 1967.

Signed at Canberra this twenty-third day of September 1967.

For the Government of the	For the
United Kingdom of	Government of the
Great Britain and Northern Ireland	Commonwealth of Australia

Notes

1 Atomic Policies and Policymakers

1. The substance of this section is taken from Margaret Gowing, 'Britain, America and the Bomb', in *Retreat from Power*, ed. David Dilkes, Vol. 2 (London: Macmillan, 1981). For a full and detailed account, see Margaret Gowing, *Independence and Deterrence*, Vol. 1 (London: Macmillan, 1974).
2. Otto Frisch was responsible for the name of the Maud Committee. When Denmark was overrun by German forces, Niels Bohr in Copenhagen had sent a telegram to Otto Frisch ending: 'Tell Cockcroft and Maud Ray Kent'. Maud Ray, who lived in Kent, had been the Bohr children's governess. Not knowing this, Frisch thought it was a cryptic message (perhaps an anagram of 'ray-dium taken' meaning that the Nazis had confiscated the Copenhagen stock of radium). The name came to his mind when a non-informative title was later needed for the secret committee. Subsequent ingenuity produced the mythical interpretation – Military Applications of Uranium Detonation. (Alwyn McKay, *The Making of the Atomic Age* (Oxford: Oxford University Press, 1984), p. 54, and Margaret Gowing, *Britain and Atomic Energy 1939–45* (London: Macmillan, 1964), p. 45.)
3. The text of the Quebec Agreement is published as Appendix 4 in Gowing, *Britain and Atomic Energy 1939–1945*.
4. See Gowing, *Britain and Atomic Energy 1939–1945*, Chapters 6 and 10.
5. Gowing, *Independence and Deterrence*, Vol. 2, p. 205.
6. Attlee said, 'We had worked from the start for international control of the bomb. We wanted it completely under the United Nations. That was the best way. But it was obviously going to take a long time. Meanwhile we had to face the world as it was. We had to look to our defence – and to our industrial future. We could not agree that only America should have atomic energy' (Francis Williams, *A Prime Minister Remembers* (London: Heinemann, 1961), p. 113, quoted by A. J. R. Groom, *British Thinking about Nuclear Weapons* (London: Frances Pinter, 1974).)
7. H C Deb, Vol. 450, col. 2117, 12 May 1948:

   Mr George Jeger asked the Minister of Defence whether he is satisfied that adequate progress is being made in the development of the most modern types of weapons.

   The Minister of Defence (Mr A. V. Alexander): Yes, Sir. As was made clear in the Statement Relating to Defence 1948 (Command 7327), research and development continue to receive the highest priority in the defence field, and all types of weapons, including atomic weapons, are being developed.
8. Gowing, *Independence and Deterrence*, Vol. 1, p. 407.
9. Gowing, *Independence and Deterrence*, Vol. 1, p. 229.
10. Gowing, *Britain and Atomic Energy 1939–1945*, Appendix 8.
11. Gowing, *Independence and Deterrence*, Vol. 1, Appendix 4 (p. 82).
12. Gowing, *Independence and Deterrence*, Vol. 1, Chapter 6 and Appendix 9 (p. 241).

13. Gowing, *Independence and Deterrence*, Vol. 2, Chapter 16.
14. Gowing, *Independence and Deterrence*, Vol. 1, p. 450.
15. Cmnd 537 (HMSO 1958).
16. Gowing, *Independence and Deterrence*, Vol. 1, Chapters 2 and 12.
17. Later Lord Hinton of Bankside; a great engineer, who has been called the Brunel of the twentieth century. Accounts of Cockcroft, Hinton and Penney are given in Gowing, *Independence and Deterrence*, Vol. 2, Chapter 13.
18. It was believed by senior people in the project that the Prime Minister had intended to appoint Sir William Morgan, who had impressed him as the Chiefs of Staff representative in Washington, but that he had confused the names and so the letter was sent to 'the wrong Morgan' (Gowing, *Independence and Deterrence*, Vol. 1, p. 46).
19. Gowing, *Independence and Deterrence*, Vol. 1, p. 428.
20. This is not true. Gowing, *Independence and Deterrence*, Vol. 1, p. 434.
21. CAE note November 1953 and MOS GN 176/56 20/11/1956, AVIA 65/879.
22. AE(O)(54)54, CAB 134/751, and AE (O)(54)111, CAB 134/752.
23. Lloyd/DGAW 28/4/1956 and DFGAW/US(SAW) 22/5/1956, AVIA 65/870.
24. *Outline of Future Policy* Cmnd 124 (HMSO, 1957).
25. Cmnd 124 (HMSO 1957), Cmnd 363 (HMSO, 1958) and Cmnd 662 (HMSO, 1959).
26. Gowing, *Independence and Deterrence*, Vol. 2, p. 18.
27. Gowing, *Independence and Deterrence*, Vol. 2, p. 30.
28. Gowing, *Independence and Deterrence*, Vol. 2, pp. 6–7.
29. C. Driver, *The Disarmers* (London: Hodder & Stoughton, 1964).

2   Why Australia?

1. Margaret Gowing, *Independence and Deterrence*, Vol. 1 (London: Macmillan, 1974), p. 307.
2. Gowing, *Independence and Deterrence*, Vol. 1, pp. 336–7.
3. Gowing, *Independence and Deterrence*, Vol. 2, p. 478.
4. Gowing, *Independence and Deterrence*, Vol. 2.
5. Gowing, *Independence and Deterrence*, Vol. 2, p. 479.
6. Cherwell/PM, 21/11/1956, PREM 11/292.
7. Gowing, *Independence and Deterrence*, Vol. 1, p. 337.
8. Gowing, *Independence and Deterrence*, Vol. 2, pp. 478–9.
9. Much of the material for this section is drawn from Russel Ward, *History of Australia in the Twentieth Century* (London: Heinemann Educational Books, 1978).
10. S. Cockburn and D. Ellyard, *Oliphant* (Adelaide, Brisbane, Perth, Darwin: Axion Books, 1981), p. 187.
11. However, when the United States demanded the withdrawal of Australian scientists working on guided weapons in Britain the British refused. In this field, unlike atomic energy, they valued Commonwealth cooperation more than American information. E. Barker, *The British between the Superpowers 1945–50* (London: Macmillan, 1983).
12. For an account of these issues, see Wayne Reynolds, *Australia's Bid for the Atomic Bomb* (Melbourne: Melbourne University Press, 2000), pp. 92–115.

13. R. Ward, *The History of Australia in the Twentieth Century* (London: Heinemann Educational Books, 1978), citing Kevin Perkins, *The Last of the Queen's Men*.
14. Ward, *The History of Australia*, p. 337.
15. Ward, *The History of Australia*, p. 363.
16. Ward, *The History of Australia*, p. 245.
17. Cockburn and Ellyard, *Oliphant*, Chapter 14.
18. Cockburn and Ellyard, *Oliphant*, p. 229.
19. Tel CRO/Canberra, ES 1/1091.
20. Cockburn and Ellyard, *Oliphant*, p. 192.
21. Cockburn and Ellyard, *Oliphant*, p. 193.
22. Gowing, *Independence and Deterrence*, Vol. 1, p. 113.

3 *Hurricane* – 1952

1. Much of the material for this chapter comes from Margaret Gowing, *Independence and Deterrence* (London: Macmillan, 1974), Vol. 2, Chapter 24.
2. HER – High Explosives Research – the codename for the atomic bomb project in the Ministry of Supply (see Chapter 1).
3. The three limits also dealt with beta radiation, but details are omitted here for the sake of simplicity, since gamma radiation was the significant hazard.
4. Sir John Butterfield, Regius Professor of Medicine in the University of Cambridge, was present as a Medical Research Council scientist at *Hurricane* and later at *Buffalo*. In his view, the HER (later AWRE) scientists were very impressive and the tests were excellently conducted, though he criticizes the protective clothing used at *Hurricane* as ill designed for hot conditions.
5. The LCMs were small, flat-bottomed landing craft designed originally to land infantry on beaches.
6. Keith N. Wise and John R. Moroney of the Australian Radiation Laboratory (ARL).
7. Gowing, *Independence and Deterrence*, Vol. 2, p. 473.
8. Gowing, *Independence and Deterrence*, Vol. 1, p. 54.

4 *Totem* – 1953

1. The following are selected from at least 55 scientific, technical and operational reports on *Operation Totem*:

   Report T3/53, Operation *Totem*: Canberra flight report, October 1953 – Operation *Hotbox* (Group Captain D. A. Wilson RAFMS). See file ES 5/5 in PRO.
   Report T5/54, Operation *Totem*: Fission product sampling (D. T. Lewis and Lt. Col. L. J. Howard RA). See file ES 5/7 in PRO.
   Report T6/54, Operation *Totem*: Radioactive air sampling and analysis (H. J. Gale). See file ES 5/8 in PRO.
   Report T7/54, Operation *Totem*: Radioactive samplingdeposited radioactivity (R. S. Cambray and W. C. T. Munnock). See file ES 5/9 in PRO.
   Report T8/54, Operation *Totem*: Operation report (P. F. Cooper). See ES 5/10 in PRO.
   Report T12/54, Operation *Totem*: Meteorological services (Cdr F. L. Westwater RN and M. H. Freeman). See file ES 5/14 in PRO.

Report T45/54, Operation *Totem*: Nuclear radiation measurements (Lt. Col. K. Stewart RE). See file ES 5/47 in PRO.

Report T54/54, Operation *Totem*: *Totem* administration (J. V. J. Richmond). See file ES 5/56 in PRO.

Report T104/54, Operation *Totem*: Prevention and removal of radioactive contamination (J. Austin and D. G. Stevenson). See file ES 5/104 in PRO.

Report T106/54, Operation *Totem*: Prevention and removal of radioactive contamination – decontamination of aircraft and health control at Woomera and Amberley (J. Austin). See file ES 5/106 in PRO.

Report T8/55, Operation *Totem*: Fallout particles from *Totem* 1 and *Totem* 2 (G. George). See file ES 5/123 in PRO.

Report TPN124/55, A re-analysis of fallout data for *Totem* (E. M. L. Beale). See file ES 10/174 in PRO.

2. AWRE Report T8/54, 'Operation *TOTEM*: Operational Report by P. F. Cooper', ES 5/10, PRO.
3. PIPPA: Pressinsed Piles Producing Power and Plutonium
4. AE(O)(53)6, 20 January 1953, CAB 134/748 PRO.
5. *Ibid.*
6. 20/1/1953, AE(O)(53)6 CAB 134/748; 26/1/1953, AE(O)(53) 2nd meeting, CAB 134/747; 10/12/1952, Cherwell/PM, PREM 11/562; Totex meeting 15/1/1953, AB 16/1744.
7. Totex 1 (a), (b), (c), 1/1 (e), AB 16/1904.
8. Tel Canberra/CRO 8/10/1953, AB 16/1904; AEA(5)68 d. 8/6/1955; Report T8/54; AE(O)(53)7, CAB 134/748; AE(O)(53) 2nd meeting 26/1/1953, CAB 134/748; 2/2/1953, Minute by Chairman of AE(O), AB 16/1904.
9. Report T8/54.
10. Totex 2nd meeting 16/2/1953, AB 16/1744. Also undated notes on Lucas mission (February 1953) in AB 16/1904.
11. AWRE Report T8/54, 'Operation *TOTEM*: Operational Report by P. F. Cooper', ES 5/10, PRO.
12. AWRE Report T8/54, 'Operation *TOTEM*: Operational Report by P. F. Cooper', ES 5/10, PRO.
13. Notes on Lucas mission (February 1953), AB 16/1904.
14. *Ibid.*
15. Adams and Tomblin report, March 1953, ES 1/825.
16. Report T8/54; Totex meeting 2/4/1953, AB 16/1744; Tel CRO/Canberra, 28/3/1953, AB 16/1904.
17. Tel. Canberra/London 30/4/1953 AB 16/1904; Note of (Australian) *Totem* Panel meeting 24/6/1953, ES 1/831.
18. Report T12/54, Meteorological services, 1954, ES 5/14; Report T8/54.
19. Telegram Defence Department to UK High Commissioner Canberra, 20 June 1953, AB 16/1904 PRO.
20. J. L. Symonds, *A History of British Atomic Tests in Australia* (Canberra: Australian Government Publishing Service, 1985), p. 131.
21. Lloyd to Morgan, 6/10/1953, AB 16/1904.
22. Tel. Penney to Elmhirst, 12/10/1953, AB 16/1904.
23. Cable Penney to Cherwell and Sandys, 26 October 1953, AB 16/1904 PRO.
24. Note of meeting 25/10/1953, ES 1/831.
25. Cable Penney to Cherwell and Sandys, 26 October 1953, AB 16/1904 PRO.

26. Report T7/54, Radioactive Sampling Deposited Activity, ES 5/9; Report T4/55, Survey of Residual Contamination from Operation *Totem*, ES 5/118.
27. Report T8/54
28. Note of meeting 25/10/1953, ES 1/831.
29. Tel Exad 151 Penney to Cherwell and Sandys (n. d.), ES 1/831.
30. Report T8/54.
31. Report T104/54, Prevention and removal of radioactive contamination, 1956, ES 5/104.
32. Report T104/54; report (n. d.) by D. T. Lewis on file 0261 IV; minute Dale/Cooper, 5/9/1954, ES 1/838.
33. AWRE Report T78/54, 'Operation *TOTEM*: The Effects of an Atomic Explosion on a Centurion Tank', ES 5/77 PRO.
34. Report T3/54, Canberra flight report October 1954, Operation Hot Box, 1954, ES 1/5.
35. Evidence by Air Commodore D. A. Wilson to Australian Royal Commission 11/2/1985.
36. 'Through the Boom at Woomera', *The Aeroplane*, 18 December 1953, pp. 815–16.
37. AWRE Report T78/54, 'Operation *TOTEM*: Canberra Flight Report (Operation HOT BOX)', ES 5/5 PRO.
38. Report T106/54, Prevention and removal of radioactive contamination, Part 6: decontamination of aircraft and health control at Woomera and Amberley, 1955, ES 5/106.
39. AWRE Report T8/54, 'Operation *TOTEM*: Operational Report by P. F. Cooper', ES 5/10, PRO.
40. Reports T7/54 and T4/55; Report TPN 124/55, *Totem* nuclear trials, Woomera, Australia: reanalysis of fall-out data, 1/1/1955–31/12/1955, ES 10/174.
41. Tel Canberra/CRO, 8/10/1953, AB 16/1904.
42. Report T104/54, Prevention and removal of radioactive contamination, 1956, ES 5/104.
43. Report T4/55.
44. UK–Australian *aide-mémoire*, cited in British Submission, p. 126.
45. Adrian Tame and R. F. P. J. Robotham, *Maralinga–British A-Bomb Australian Legacy* (Fontana/Collins (Australia), 1982), pp. 143–4.

5   A Pregnant Pause: 1953–56

1. *Bravo* in the *Castle* series, with a yield of approximately 15 megatons. The first US thermonuclear explosion (*Ivy-Mike*) with a yield of 10.4 megatons, had been at Eniwetok in October 1952; it was not a weapon, but a huge cumbersome device the size of a house, using liquid deuterium, which had to be kept refrigerated. The first United States airdrop of a thermonuclear weapon was at Bikini in May 1956, in between the first and second shots of the British *Mosaic* trial at Monte Bello.
2. John Baylis, *Ambiguity and Deterrence: British Nuclear Strategy 1945–64* (Oxford: Oxford University Press, 1995), p. 180.
3. Baylis, *Ambiguity and Deterrence*, p. 182
4. Baylis, *Ambiguity and Deterrence*, p. 187.

5. Lorna Arnold, *Britain and the H-Bomb* (Basingstoke: Palgrave, 2001), p. 37.
6. Arnold, *Britain and the H-Bomb*, p. 40.
7. Arnold, *Britain and the H-Bomb*, p. 50.
8. Cmd 9391, Feb 1955, HMSO.
9. See Andrew Pierre, *Nuclear Politics* (Oxford: Oxford University Press, 1972), pp. 92–4.
10. H C Deb, Col. 1899, 1 March 1955.
11. Richard Rhodes, *Dark Sun: The Making of the Hydrogen Bomb* (New York: Simon & Schuster, 1995), p. 541.
12. They received external radiation doses estimated at up to 2 sieverts (200 r). Seven of them eventually had to have surgery for thyroid cancer.
13. Accounts of the *Lucky Dragon* incident can be found in *Bulletin of Atomic Scientists*, Vol. X, Nos 5 and 9 (May and November 1954); in Ralph Lapp, *The Voyage of the 'Lucky Dragon'* (London: Penguin, 1958); and in Robert A. Divine, *Blowing on the Wind:The Nuclear Test Ban Debate 1954–1960* (New York: Oxford University Press, 1978).
14. *Bulletin of Atomic Scientists*, Vol. XI, No. 5 (May 1955).
15. Divine, *Blowing on the Wind*, p. 13.
16. Quoted in *The Times*, 26 March 1954, p. 7.
17. *Ibid.*
18. Quoted in Jeff Hughes, 'The Strath Report: Britain Confronts the H-Bomb 1954– 5', in *History and Technology*, Vol. 19 (3) (2003), p. 261. 'Nuclear Weapons Publicity', 5 May 1954.
19. *Bulletin of Atomic Scientists*, Vol. X, Nos 8 and 9 (October and November 1954).
20. *Bulletin of Atomic Scientists*, Vol. XI, No. 2 (February 1955).
21. Peter Hennessey, *The Secret State: Whitehall and the Cold War* (London: Penguin, 2002), p. 134.
22. Hughes, 'The Strath Report', p. 272.
23. Himsworth/Salisbury u/d letter, PREM 11/1676.
24. Salisbury/PM 26/5/1956 and Gen 529/18 meeting, PREM 11/1676.
25. Bentley Glass, 'The Hazards of Atomic Radiation to Man – British and American Reports', *Bulletin of Atomic Scientists*, Vol. XII, No. 8 (October 1956).
26. Cmd 9780, June 1956, HMSO.
27. H C Deb, Vol. 546, No. 65, Cols. 2319–22.
28. De Zulueta/Hanna 3/12/1955, PREM 11/1676; Document of 5/12/1955, PREM 11/1676.
29. Salisbury and Selwyn Lloyd to PM 13/12/1955, PREM 11/1676.
30. Tel FO/Washington 355 of 24/1/1956, PREM 11/1676.
31. Tel Washington/FO 27/1/1956, PREM 11/1676.
32. See *Effects of Atomic Weapons* (1950), p. 35.
33. Notes on White House meetings 1/2/1956, PREM 11/1676; also on file 11/1/1/13(3), AB 6/1817.

6   Maralinga – A Permanent Proving Ground

1. Elmhirst/Stevens 8/7/1953, AB 16/1904.
2. Elmhirst/Stevens 8/7/1953, AB 16/1904.
3. Stevens/Elmhirst 30/7/1953, AB 16/1904.

4. Report by Lloyd, February 1954, AVIA 65/869.
5. See S. Menaul, *Countdown: Britain's Strategic Nuclear Forces* (London: Robert Hale, 1980). p. 61.
6. A verbatim record is reproduced in J. L. Symonds, *A History of British Atomic Tests in Australia* (Canberra: Australian Government Publishing Service, 1985), Appendix 11.2.
7. AE(O)(53)17th meeting 22/12/1953, CAB 134/747.
8. Report by Lloyd, 8/2/54, AVIA 65/869.
9. Undated report RD/3, AVIA 65/869 and AVIA 65/804.
10. Report 8/2/1954, AVIA 65/869.
11. Brief (unsigned and undated – May 1954), AVIA 65/869.
12. AE(O)(54)4, 11/1/1954, CAB 134/750.
13. AE(O)(54)54 of 6/5/1954, and AE(O)(54)66 of 1/6/1954, both in CAB 134/751.
14. AE(O)(54)54 of 6/5/1954, CAB 134/751; AE(M)(54)3rd meeting 27/7/1954, CAB 134/745.
15. AE(O)(54)54 of 6/5/1954, CAB 134/751; AE(M)(54)3rd meeting 27/7/1954, CAB 134/745.
16. At the same time they asked the Lord President to examine the possibility of the South Polar regions for atomic tests; a thermonuclear explosion from an aeroplane near the South Pole was being considered.
17. AE(M)(53)3, CAB 134/748; AE(M)(54)2nd meeting 23/6/1954; AE(M)(54)3rd meeting 27/7/1954, CAB 134/745; AE(O)(54)139, CAB 134/752.
18. CRO/Canberra tels 633 and 634 of 29/7/1954 on file AB 16/2966.
19. Canberra/CRO tel 658 of 2/9/1954 on file AB 16/2966.
20. AE(O)(54)139 of 12/11/1954, CAB 134/752.
21. AE(O)(54)139 of 12/11/1954, CAB 134/752.
22. Jehu/Dep Sec (MOS) 24/11/1954, AVIA 65/869.
23. AE(O)(55)2, CAB 134/754; AE(O)(55)2nd meeting 19/1/1955, CAB 134/753.
24. Tel Canberra/CRO, 19/1/1955, AVIA 65/806.
25. Note of mtg Misc/M(55)19 on 10/2/1955, AVIA 65/869.
26. Tel CRO/Canberra, 30/3/1955, AVIA 65/869.
27. Tel Canberra/CRO, 6/5/1955; Minute of 11/5/1955; both on AVIA 65/806.
28. Elkington/Serpell, 14/7/1955, AVIA 65/806.
29. Charleton, UKMOSS(A)/Donaldson, MOS, 5/3/1957, AVIA 65/806.
30. The Department of Supply (which provided the chairman and executive secretary), the Department of Defence, the Service departments, the Treasury, the Department of Works, the Australian Atomic Energy Commision (AAEC) and the Australian Security Intelligence Organization (ASIO).
31. The first *Grapple* series in 1957 in which the Australians were to play some part.
32. Canberra/CRO tel 134 of 2/2/1956 on file AB 16/2966.
33. See Symonds, *A History of British Tests in Australia*, pp. 290–1.
34. See Symonds, *A History of British Tests in Australia*, p. 294.
35. Prime Minister/Ministry of Defence 16/5/1955, in Symonds *A History of British Tests in Australia*, p. 294.
36. AE(O)(52)12 of 9/3/1952, CAB 134/746.
37. Canberra/CRO tel 250 of 21/3/1955 on file AB 16/2966.
38. See Symonds, *A History of British Tests in Australia*, pp. 295–6.

39. The British government met the capital cost and Australia paid for operation and maintenance.
40. Matthewman/Adams 11/8/1955, ES 1/721; Tel Canberra/CRO 27/1/1956, ES 1/397.

7   *Mosaic* – 1956

1. Below is a selection from 13 reports issued on various aspects of Operation *Mosaic*. In addition there is in the Aldermaston archives an interesting over-all report (no serial number) by the Operational Commander, Commodore Hugh Martell RN – ADM 296/4.

    Report T21/57, Operation *Mosaic*: Radiological Group Report (J. A. Hole). See ES 5/158 in PRO.
    Report T24/57, Operation *Mosaic*: Theoretical predictions (A. G. Matthewman). See ES 5/161 in PRO.
    Report T30/57, Operations *Mosaic* and *Buffalo*: Air Sampling equipment and techniques (Wing Commander A. W. Eyre). See ES 5/167 in PRO.
    Report T33/57, Operation *Mosaic*: Aircraft decontamination (D G Stevenson). See ES 5/170 in PRO.
    Report T63/57, Operations *Mosaic* and *Buffalo*: The Handling, servicing and decontamination of radioactive aircraft (D. G. Stevenson). See ES 5/197 in PRO.
    Report AWEC/P(57)202, Operation *Mosaic*: The fallout analysed with reference to HMS *Diana* (E. M. L. Beale). See ES 1/1127, 1128.
    Report 0.41/55, Safety levels for contamination from fallout from atomic weapons trials (G C Dale, Oct 1955). See ES 4/130 in PRO.

2. 'The History of British R&D on Atomic Weapons', printed in Lorna Arnold, *Britain and the H-Bomb* (Basingstoke: Palgrave, 2001), p. 237.
3. The 'Type A' design was similar to the Soviet model referred to as 'layer cake'.
4. CAW to Defence Research Policy Committee Sub-committee on Atomic Energy, 6 December 1955, in DEFE 7/915. *Green Bamboo* was originally planned for testing at the *Grapple* trials of 1957.
5. John Simpson, *The Independent Nuclear State: The United States, Britain and the Military Atom*, 2nd edition (London: Macmillan, 1986), p. xxi.
6. CAW to Defence Research Policy Committee Sub-committee on Atomic Energy, 6 December 1955, in DEFE 7/915.
7. Note dated 15 February 1956, in ES1/470.
8. 'Report of a Committee Set up to Consider the Requirements of AWRE in Atomic Trials', 10 August 1954, ES1/465. Precursors form in low ground bursts over certain surfaces, including desert sand, coral, and dry soil with sparse vegetation. See Samuel Glasstone, *The Effects of Nuclear Weapons*, 3rd edition (London: Castle House, 1980), pp. 124–5.
9. Admiralty letter 27/3/1956, ES 1/491.
10. Message from Admiralty, 15 December 1955, ES1/470.
11. Undated MS memo in ES 1/92.
12. Memo by A S Brown 9/11/1954, ES 1/498.
13. 'Brief on thermonuclear trials', 3rd August 1955, DEFE7/915.
14. *The Times*, 19 February 1955, p. 5.

15. Tel Canberra/CRO 597 on file AB 16/2370.
16. The *Hurricane* yield was approximately 25 kilotons and the expected *Mosaic* yields would therefore be about (or less than) 60 kilotons. In the event the second shot (*Mosaic* G2) had a yield of approximately 60 kilotons, that is about 21/2 times that of the *Hurricane* device, and about four times larger than that (approximately 15 kilotons) of G1, the first *Mosaic* shot.
17. There had been no formal facilities at previous trials. With the Memorandum of Arrangements and the establishment of the AWTSC the Australians would have to be given much greater facilities.
18. Tel Canberra/CRO 780 on file AB 16/2370; Undated memo in ES 1/92.
19. Admiralty progress report 21/6/1955, Mosex (55)M1 6/7/1955 and Mosex (55)P2 21/7/1955; all on AVIA 65/820.
20. Mosex (55)P3 (undated), AVIA 65/820.
21. Mosex (55)P4 14/9/1955 and (55)P10 2/12/1955, on AVIA 65/820.
22. Black/Adams 16/8/1955, ES 1/490.
23. Tel Canberra/CRO 906 on file AB 16/2370.
24. This was not so in the event, as uranium was used.
25. Tels CRO/Canberra, 10/9/1955, ES 1/488; Tel Canberra/CRO 906 on file AB 16/2370.
26. Tel CRO/Canberra 16/12/1955, AVIA 65/821.
27. Mosex (55)P12 December 1955; all on AVIA 65/820.
28. Mosex (55)P12, AVIA 65/820; Tel Canberra/CRO, 3/1/1956, AB 16/2370; CRO/Canberra tel 1531 d. 16/12/1955 on file ES 1/488; mtg 16/2/1956 on file ES 1/479; Operational Instruction No 6/56 d. 27/4/1956 on file ES 1/480.
29. Mosex (55)M3 5/10/1955, AVIA 65/820; Adams/Black 8/9/1955, ES 1/476; Report 0.41/55, Safety levels for contamination from fallout from atomic weapons trials (G C Dale, Oct 1955). See ES 4/130 in PRO; Mosex (55)M3 5/10/1955, AVIA 65/820. It has been suggested that the scientists should have known whether the proportion of such hypersensitive people was more common in some races than others; in particular, whether the Aboriginals might be more sensitive to radiation. There is no available knowledge on this subject. Knowledge of the effects of radiation on human beings was and is mainly derived from studies of either Japanese bomb survivors, or of radio-therapy patients (in countries where medical radiation is extensively used).
30. Mosex (55)M3 5/10/1955, AVIA 65/820.
31. Letter, Adams to Dr DH Black at UK MOSS Australia, 29 September 1955, ES1/468.
32. Admiralty progress report 21/6/1955; Mosex (55)P12 and Mosex minutes passim, all on AVIA 65/820.
33. Announcement dated 16/2/1955, AVIA 65/821.
34. Maddock report, 20/6/1956, ES 1/491.
35. Pilgrim/AWRE 21/6/1956, ES 1/491.
36. Maddock 20/6/1956, ES 1/491.
37. Adams/Penney 17/5/1956, ES 1/491.
38. Penney/Brundrett 29/5/1956, ES 1/491.
39. Cook to Vice-Admiral Clifford, 12 June 1956, ES1/471.
40. Maddock 20/6/1956, ES 1/491.
41. Jackson 20/8/1956, Adams 23/8/1956, ES 1/491; Wheeler 30/7/1956, AVIA 65/821.

42. Penney/Adams 31/5/1956 and 4/6/1956 on file ES 1/486.
43. Mosex (56)M5, AVIA 65/820; Wheeler/Lloyd 21/6/1956; Rouse/Allen 26/6/1956; and Allen/Witheridge4/7/1956, on AVIA 65/821.
44. Canberra/CRO tel 747 d. 21/6/1956 and CRO/Canberra tel 139 SAVING 23/6/1956, on file AB 16/2370.
45. Mosex (56)M5 11/7/1956, AVIA 65/820; rouse/Allen 26/6/1956, AVIA 65/821.
46. Adams/Lloyd 19/3/1956, AVIA 65/821.
47. The arrangements for clearing public announcements were as follows:

    (a) All public announcements or publicity arrangements in Australia to be submitted to the Australian authorities for approval.
    (b) All press releases in Australia to be made by appropriate Ministers.
    (c) All press releases to be agreed between UK and Australia before release – also time and date.
    (d) Some discretion allowed if UK requests that announcement be made in Australia other than by a Minister.

48. Penney/Brundrett 29/5/1956 and Cook/Jackson 4/10/1956, ES 1/491.
49. *Report of the Royal Commission into British Nuclear Tests in Australia*, Volume 1 (Canberra: Australian Government Publishing Service, 1985) p. 234.
50. *Ibid.*
51. *The Submission of the Government of the United Kingdom to the Royal Commission into British Nuclear Tests in Australia*, p. 343.
52. *Report of the Royal Commission into British Nuclear Tests in Australia*, Volume 1, p. 272.
53. *Ibid*, pp. 258–9.
54. Mosex (56)M5, AVIA 65/820.
55. W. A. S. Butement, L. J. Dwyer, C. E. Eddy, L. H. Martin and E. W. Titterton, 'Radioactive Fallout in Australia from Operation Mosaic', *Australian Journal of Science*, Vol. 20, No. 5 (21 December 1957).
56. By the American scientists, Eisenbud and Harley. See D. W. Keam *et al.*, 'Experiments on the "Sticky Paper" Method of Radioactive Fallout Sampling', *Australian Journal of Science*, Vol. 21, No. 4 (November 1958).
57. AIRAC No 9: British Nuclear Tests in Australia – A Review of Operational Safety Measures and of Possible After-effects.
58. Wise and Moroney calculate the collective dose equivalent commitments for *Mosaic* as 10 man-Sv (1000 man-rems) for G1 and 52 man-Sv (5200 man-re rems) for G2
59. Royal Commission, p. 260.

8   *Buffalo – 1956*

1. The following are selected from well over 100 reports relating to *Operation Buffalo*, of which nearly half dealt with target response investigations of effects on e.g. aircraft, vehicles, instruments, various structures, ordnance, ammunition, medical supplies, food, and a variety of materials (as well as biological studies).

T1/57 Operation *Buffalo*: The construction and operation of a Field Decontamination Centre (Major D. B. B. Janisch *et al*). See file ES 5/137 in PRO.

T8/57 Operation *Buffalo*: Meteorological services (H. R. Phillpot). See file ES 5/144 (Volume 1) and ES 1/145 (Volume 2) in PRO.

T11/57 Operation *Buffalo*: The dose received at various parts of the body by a man walking over contaminated ground (C. F. Barnaby) An anthropometric model, made of wood, was used – the so-called 'mahogany man'. See file ES 5/148 in PRO.

T18/57 Operation *Buffalo*: Target response – Biology Group (R. Scott Russell). See file ES 5/155 in PRO.

T22/57 Operation *Buffalo*: Decontamination Group report (D. G. Stevenson). See file ES 5/159 in PRO.

T33/57 Operation *Buffalo*: Aircraft decontamination (D. G. Stevenson). See file ES 5/170 in PRO.

T40/57 Operation *Buffalo*: The measurement of radiation dose rates from fallout (J. H. Howse and D. H. Peirson). See file ES 5/177 in PRO.

T49/57 Operation *Buffalo*: The radiation survey of ground-deposited radioactivity (J. J. Rae). See file ES 5/185 in PRO.

T51/57 Operation *Buffalo*: The aerial survey of radioactivity deposited on the ground (Sqadron Leader P. Clay). See file ES 5/187 in PRO.

T52/57 Operation *Buffalo*: The measurement of airborne radioactivity and ground contamination at 15 and 200 miles from Ground Zero (P. A. Carter). See file ES 5/188 in PRO.

T54/57 Operation *Buffalo*: The hazards to aircrew flying through atomic cloud (R. E. Holmes). See file ES 5/190 in PRO.

T25/58 Operation *Buffalo*: Theoretical predictions of cloud height and fallout (E. P. Hicks and J. D. McDougall). See file ES 5/229 in PRO.

T57/58 Operation *Buffalo*: Target response tests – Biology Group – the entry of fission products into food chains (J. F. Loutit and R. Scott Russell). See file ES 5/262 in PRO. The Appendix to the report, containing details of the location of sites, is in ES 5/263.

T2/59 Operation *Buffalo*: Target response tests – Biology Group – the effects of blast on dummy men exposed in the open (W. J. H. Butterfield *et al.*). See file ES 5/265 in PRO.

T4/59 Operation *Buffalo*: Target response – Structures Group – the effect on field defences (Major A. Trimmer and Major F. G. B. Maskell). See file ES 5/267 in PRO.

2. Note by Pilgrim, 'Overseas Trials', 25 August 1954, in ES1/718.
3. See file AIR 2/13728.
4. Lorna Arnold, *Britain and the H-Bomb* (Basingstoke: Palgrave, 2001), p. 91.
5. Minute by Pilgrim, 31 January 1955, ES 1/1135.
6. See the various versions of OR 1127 in AIR 2/13728.
7. E. P. Hicks, 'The Case for a Ground Burst at *Buffalo*', TPN 36/54, in ES 1/718.
8. Buffalex(55)P7 of 15/7/1955 on file AVIA 65/813; Buffalex(55)M1 of 4/3/1955 on file AVIA 65/812; 'Proposed Test Structure for Future Atomic Trials', December 1954, ES 1/718.
9. Buffalex(55)P3 of 22/4/1955 and (55)P6 of 11/7/1955 on file AVIA 65/813.
10. Michaels/Walker 25/3/1955 on file AB 16/2370.

11. CRO/Canberra tels 1014 and 1015 of 29/8/1955, ES 1/488.
12. AE(O)(54)126 of 23/10/1954; Buffalex(55)P6 of 11/7/1955 on file AVIA 65/813; Buffalo summary plan on AVIA 65/813; CRO/Canberra tels 1014 and 1015 of 29/8/1955 on file AB 16/2370.
13. 'Target Response Biology: Interim Summary Report of Trials Results', October 1956, in DEFE 7/1519.
14. Memo, 'Outline Army Requirements for Operation *Buffalo*', War Office to Buffalex, 4 February 1955, DEFE 7/914.
15. *Buffalo* summary plan, AVIA 65/813.
16. Cook/Le Cren 8/2/1956; Pilgrim/Lloyd 9/3/1956, ES 1/723.
17. Buffalex minutes of 3rd, 4th, 5th, 8th and 10th meetings; Buffalex(56)M8 of 8/8/1956, AVIA 65/812.
18. Buffalex(55)M1 and (55)M2, AVIA 65/812; Serpell/Lloyd 5/4/1955, AVIA 65/812; EXMAR 330 of 3/2/1956, AVIA 65/812.
19. Buffalex(55)P13 of 1/10/1955 and (56)P2, AVIA 65/813; CRO/Canberra tel 421 of 18/4/1955, AVIA 65/869.
20. Maudling/Beale 1/8/1956, AVIA 65/811;57/Misc/8858 (MT3) (undated), ES 1/733.
21. Elkington/Jackson 17/7/1956, AVIA 65/870; Buffalex(56)M7 of 11/7/1956, AVIA 65/812; Canberra/CRO tels 140, 141 of 2/2/1956, Buffalex(56)M9 of 10/10/1956 on file AB 16/2370.
22. Adams/Penney 9/7/1956, ES 1/725.
23. Allen/Elkington 13/7/1956, AVIA 65/814.
24. Buffalex(56)M6 of 6/6/1956, AVIA 65/812.
25. AE(M)(54)2nd Meeting 23/6/1954, AVIA 65/869; Buffalex(56)M6 of 6/6/1956, AVIA 65/812.
26. Adams/Penney 9/7/1956, ES 1/725.
27. Buffalex(55)P11, AVIA 65/813; Penney/Brundrett 19/6/1956, ES 1/725; unnumbered paper 29/8/1956 on file 0434 Iib. General report (u/d) on *Buffalo*, ES 1/733.
28. Penney to Brundrett, 19 June 1956, DEFE 7/916.
29. Brundrett to Powell, 20 June 1956, DEFE 7/916.
30. CWW to Brundrett, 20 June 1956, DEFE 7/916.
31. Cable from Penney, 21 August 1956, AVIA 65/815; Brundrett to Minister, 25 July 1956, DEFE 7/916.
32. For a history of the range, see Peter Morton, *Fire across the Desert: Woomera and the Anglo-Australian Joint Project, 1946–1980* (Canberra: Australian Government Publishing Office, 1989).
33. Native Patrol Officer Report, August 1956, in J. L. Symonds, *A History of British Atomic Tests in Australia* (Canberra: Australian Government Publishing Service, 1985), p. 393.
34. T 25/58 (see Endnotes).
35. Paper d. 23/7/1956, ES 1/725. Pilgrim/Hicks 6/10/1955, ES 1/722. Adams/Penney 9/7/1956, ES1/725. Paper d. 23/7/1956, ES 1/727.
36. AWTSC 5th meeting 2/3/1956; Buffalex(54)P4 d. 2/11/1954, AVIA 65/813.
37. Maddock/Tomblin 4/8/1954 on file ES 1/718.
38. Buffalex minutes of 1st and 3rd to 10th meetings are on file AVIA 65/812. Buffalex papers are on ES 1/733.
39. Signal EXMAR 330 of 3/2/1956 on file AVIA 65/814.

40. Penney/Brundrett 29/5/1956 on file LO 426; Buffalex(56)M6 of 6/6/1956 on file AB 16/2370; Undated brief on paper AE(O)(54)54 on file AVIA 65/869.
41. Signal HQ 77 Penney/Cook 26/9/1956 on file ES 1/741; Cook/Jackson 26/9/1956 on file AVIA 65/8128
42. Draft by Cook, undated, DEFE 7/1519.
43. Jackson to Cook, undated [?], AVIA 65/815.
44. Signal SM 1321 (u/d) Wheeler/Jehu on file ES 1/741.
45. Tropopause – the plane of discontinuity between the troposphere (the lowest layer of the atmosphere) and the stratosphere. The thickness of the troposphere varies from 20 000 ft at the North and South Poles to 60,000 ft at the equator.
46. The yield of a test warhead or device bore no necessary relation to that of a production bomb, since the yield of a given weapon could be varied at will.
47. Letter, Major-General Luedecke to Colonel Stewart, 16 March 1956; Stewart to Brundrett, 3 April 1956; both in DEFE 7/916.
48. Brundrett to Penny, 13 April 1956; Penney's response 18 April 1956; both in DEFE 7/916.
49. Signal Penney/Cook 9/10/1956, ES 1/741.
50. Maddock to Tomblin, 4 August 1955, DEFE 16/236.
51. Brundrett noted the smaller fissile component used at Kite, and could not help mentioning that because this was not standard issue in *Blue Danube*, the weapon dropped had to be regarded as 'a purely experimental drop'. Note by Sir Frederick Brundrett to Chair CoS, 17 December 1956, DEFE 7/896.
52. Penney/Brundrett 25/6/1956 on file ES 1/724. Pilgrim/ACAS(Ops) 9/3/1955 on file ES 1/47. Martin/Adams EXBUF20 of 29/11/1955 on file ES 1/722. Pilgrim's diary on file ES 1/728.
53. Buffalex target programme requirements on file AVIA 65/813. COS(53)239 d. 20/5/1953 (cited in *New* Scientist, 9 February 1984).
54. 'Target Response Biology: Interim Summary Report of Trials Results', October 1956, DEFE 7/1519.
55. Undated report ('*Buffalo* got off to a shaky start ...') on file ES 1/733; Buffalex(56)M10 of 12/12/1956 on file AVIA 65/812.
56. Penney/Musgrave 5/3/1957 on ES 1/755.
57. *Australian Journal of Science*, October 1958 (Butement, Dwyer, Martin, Stevens and Titterton).
58. AIRAC 9.
59. Keith N. Wise and John R. Moroney, *Public Health Impact of Fallout from British Nuclear Tests in Australia 1952–1957* (July 1985).
60. *Report of the Royal Commission into British Nuclear Tests in Australia*, pp. 285–6, 299.
61. *Submission of the Government of the United Kingdom to the Royal Commission into British Nuclear Tests in Australia*, p. 421.
62. *Report of the Royal Commission*.
63. *Report of the Royal Commission*, p. 323.

9 'There Must be Further Trials to Come': Weapons Planning, 1956–57

1. Lorna Arnold, *Britain and the H-Bomb* (Basingstoke: Palgrave, 2001), p. 238.

2. Herbert York, *Race to Oblivion* (New York: Simon and Schuster, 1971), p. 111.
3. CRO/Canberra tel 1426 of 18/9/1956, AB 16/1433.
4. Note by DAWRE and DGAW, 20 November 1956, AVIA 65/1114.
5. Brundrett to CoS, 12 December 1956, AVIA 65/1114.
6. Mancroft to PM, 31 January 1957, AVIA 65/1195.
7. Note, 13 December 1956, E 1/752.
8. Cable UK High Commission to Commonwealth Relations Office, 10 January 1957.
9. Tomblin 1/1/1957 on file ES 1/753.
10. PM's minute, 29 January 1957, AVIA 65/854.
11. Minute by US/SAW, 30 January 1957, AVIA 65/854.
12. Mancroft/PM DS/4/57 of 31/1/1957 on file 'Tube Alloys (Testing) – Testing A weapons – series of KT trials in autumn of 1957 – Operation *Antler*' in PREM 11/2844.
13. Foreign Secretary/PM 30/1/1957, PREM 11/2844.
14. PM/Mancroft M26/27 of 1/2/1957 PREM 11/2844.
15. EXMAR 722 Wheeler/Lloyd 20/3/1957 on file ES 1/743.
16. Martin/Penney 2/4/1957 on file ES 1/756; Penney/Jackson 15/4/1957 on file ES 1/756.
17. These names originate in the early British concepts for an H-bomb design which used three stages, known to the weaponeers as Tom, Dick and Harry.
18. Arnold, *Britain and the H-Bomb*.
19. Ian Clarke, *Nuclear Diplomacy and the Special Relationship: Britain's Deterrent and America* (Oxford: Oxford University Press, 1994) p. 190.
20. Quoted in Clarke, *Nuclear Diplomacy and the Special Relationship*, pp. 195–6.
21. Harold Macmillan, *Riding the Storm* (London: Macmillan, 1971).
22. One of the *Grapple* shots, *Orange Herald*, was reported in the press as being an H-bomb when in fact it was a boosted fission weapon, and a theory that the genuine H-bomb tests had been a bluff to fool the US into recommencing nuclear collaboration circulated decades after the tests were concluded.
23. Quoted in Arnold, *Britain and the H-Bomb*, p. 89.
24. Arnold, *Britain and the H-Bomb*, p. 147.
25. *The Times*, 1 June 1957
26. Richard Moore, 'The Real Meaning of the Words: A Pedantic Glossary of British Nuclear Weapons', *Prospero* (Spring 2004).
27. The disappointing results of *Orange Herald* are set out Arnold, *Britain and the H-Bomb*, p. 147. Cook compares the possible and likely yields of a boosted *Blue Fox* in light of this in Note by Corner, 18 June 1957, ES 1/758.
28. Moore, 'The Real Meaning of the Words'.
29. Richard Moore, 'British Nuclear Warhead Design: How Much American Help?', *Defence Studies* Vol. 4 (2) (2004), p. 204. See also Arnold, *Britain and the H-Bomb*, pp. 176–7.
30. Brundrett noted in January 1957 that the new *Green Granite II* design 'was designed after we knew of Project R1 effect because it was then realised that other designs of megaton weapons were 10 times more vulnerable than *Green Granite* type weapons'. Notes for letter to Minister, 17 January 1957, DEFE 7/986.
31. Moore, 'British Nuclear Warhead Design'.

32. Meeting of Defence Research Policy Committee (Sub-Committee on Atomic Energy), 30 July 1957, AVIA 65/1116.

33. Letter to Brundrett, 28 June 1957, AVIA 65/854.

34. See letter to Brundrett, 28 June 1957, *ibid.*

35. Meeting of DPRC Sub-Committee, 30 July 1957, AVIA 65/1116.

36. Notes of meeting to discuss *Antler* firing programme, 26 August 1957, AVIA 65/1116.

37. Meeting of Defence Research Policy Committee (Sub-Committee on Atomic Energy), 26 August 1957, AVIA 65/1116. This had previously been recognized: Jackson Noted to Brundrett in June that, 'If we could ignore disarmament considerations there would be good reasons for not testing *Pixie* this year'. Letter to Brundrett, 28 June 1957, AVIA 65/854.

38. Note by Corner on yields expected at *Antler*, 18 June 1957, ES1/758.

39. Meeting of DPRC Sub-Committee, 30 July 1957, AVIA 65/1116.

10 *Antler* and After

1. The following is a selection from some 30 reports issued on Operation *Antler*:

T4/58 Operation *Antler*: Theoretical predictions (R. A. Siddons and D. Sams). See ES 5/208 in PRO.

T24/58 Operation *Antler*: Airborne sampling of radioactivity (Wing Commander A. W. Eyre). See ES 5/228 in PRO.

T38/58 Operation *Antler*: Meteorological services (H. R. Phillpot). See ES 5/242 for volume 1 (text), ES 5/243 for volume 2 (tables and figures).

T40/58 Operation *Antler*: Aerial survey of radioactivity deposited on the ground (Squadron Leader R. L. Carter). See ES 5/245 PRO.

T44/58 Operation *Antler*: Radiological survey operations in the Alice Road area (P. F. Beaver). See ES 5/249 PRO.

T45/58 Operation *Antler*: Health physics services (Major W. G. McDougall *et al.*). See ES 5/250 in PRO.

T7/60 Operation *Antler*: Decontamination Group report (H. Wells *et al.*). See ES 5/281 in PRO.

2. J. L. Symonds, *A History of British Atomic Tests in Australia* (Australian Government Publishing Service Canberra, 1985), pp. 421–44, 465–7.

3. *The Times*, 30 August 1957.

4. Note of meeting 6/6/1957, telex (u/d) Maralinga/AWRE, Powell/Bishop 31/7/1957, on file AVIA 65/856.

5. Note on memo Bishop/PM 1/8/1957 and D(57)7th Conclusion 2/8/1957, on file 'Tube Alloys (Testing) … Operation *Antler*' PREM 11/2844.

6. Note of meeting 30/10/1956 on file AVIA 65/857.

7. Report 4/9/1957 to Air Task Group Commander, *Antler*, on loss of balloons, on file ES 1/749.

8. File ES 1/749ES 5/208.

9. *Report of the Royal Commission into British Nuclear Tests in Australia* (Canberra: Australian Government Publishing Service, 1985), p. 392.

10. *AWTSC, Journal of Science* (September 1959).

11. Keith N. Wise and John R. Moroney: *Public Health Impact of Fallout from British Nuclear Weapons Tests in Australia 1952–1957* (July 1985).

12. *Australian Journal of Biological Sciences*, Vol. 11:3 (August 1958).
13. L. Van Middlesworth, *Nucleonics* Vol. 12, p. 56, 1954; *Science* Vol. 123 (1956), p. 982.
14. Note of meeting 18–19 October 1956 on file ES 1/320.
15. J. L. Symonds, *Chronology of Events 1950–1968* (Canberra: Australian Government Publishing Service, 1985), p. 63. We have found no indication of what Sir Macfarlane Bumet's comments were.
16. F. J. Bryant *et al.*, 'Strontium-90 in Fallout and in Man in Australia January 1959–January 1960', *Nature* (27 May 1961).
17. Lorna Arnold, *Britain and the H-Bomb* (Basingstoke: Palgrave, 2002), p. 152.
18. For a dramatic description of the 'vicious physics' in *Grapple* X, see Arnold, *Britain and the H-Bomb*, p. 160.
19. The words are those of Edwin Plowden, chairman of the UKAEA, cited in Ian Clarke, *Nuclear Diplomacy and the Special Relationship: Britain's Deterrent and America* (Oxford: Oxford University Press, 1994), p. 78.
20. Clarke, *Nuclear Diplomacy and the Special Relationship*, p. 77.
21. Cited in Clarke, *Nuclear Diplomacy and the Special Relationship*, p. 200
22. Clarke, *Nuclear Diplomacy and the Special Relationship*, p. 80
23. Dwight D. Eisenhower, *The White House Years: Waging Peace 1956–61* (London: Heinemann, 1960), p. 219.
24. Richard Moore, 'British Nuclear Warhead Design: How Much American Help?', *Defence Studies* Vol. 4 (2) (2004), p. 212.
25. A note by John Corner, probably submitted to the bilateral for this purpose, is printed in Lorna Arnold, *Britain and the H-Bomb* (Basingstoke: Palgrave, 2002).
26. Moore, 'British Nuclear Warhead Design', p. 213.

11   *Kittens, Rats* and *Vixens*

1. Relevant reports include the following:

   T51/57 Health Physics Report. *Tim* Series 2 (R. E. Holmes). See ES 5/187 in PRO.
   T15/58 Fallout measurements during Operation *Kittens* 1955 (K. G. Mayhew). See ES 5/219 in PRO.
   T21/58 Minor trials – the particle size distribution in certain *Tim* clouds (P. F. Beaver). See ES 5/225 in PRO.
   T39/58 Minor trials – health physics report, *Tim* series 3 (R. F. Carter). See ES 5/244 in PRO.
   T15/60 *Vixen* A trials: experiments to study the release of particulate material during the combustion of plutonium, uranium and beryllium in a petrol fire (K. Stewart). See ES 5/289 and ES 5/290 in PRO.
   T12/63 Maralinga Experimental Programme June 1961 – Vixen B: Decontamination Group Report (Wing Commander D. C. Beal). See ES 5/323 in PRO.
   T27/63 Experiments *Vixen* A with implosion assemblies – dispersal of berllium and uranium (K. Stewart). See ES 5/335 in PRO.

2. H L Deb, 7 April 1954, Vol. 186, cols 1134–5.
3. Penney/Cockcroft 5/1/1954 on file AB 16/1444.

4. Penney/Cockcroft 14/1/1954 on file AB 16/1444.
5. Penney/Plowden 9/2/1954 on file AB 16/1444.
6. AEX(54)5th meeting 9/3/1954; Forward/How 19/3/1954 and CRO/Canberra tel 77 SAVING 14/5/1954, on file AB 16/1444.
7. Penney/Perrott August 1954 on file AB 16/1444.
8. Canberra/CRO tel 251 of 23/12/1954 on file AB 16/1444.
9. Cmnd 537 (HMSO, July 1958).
10. Tomblin/Pilgrim 5/6/1957 on file ES 1/954.
11. Glen T. Seaborg, *Kennedy, Khrushchev and the Test Ban* (Berkeley: University of California Press, 1981), p. 12.
12. Circular 1/10/1958 on file ES 1/957.
13. Penney/Dean 1/10/1958 on file ES 1/957.
14. Signal AWRE/Maralinga 2/10/1958 on file ES 1/957.
15. Johnston/Hainsworth 19/11/1958 on file ES 1/957.
16. ADD/408/12/59 d. 17/12/1959 on file ES 1/960.
17. Halliday SRHP/IGH/2 of 16/10/1958 on file ES 1/957.
18. SSWA/1958/248 of 15/12/1958 on file ES 1/957.
19. Penney/Dean 1/10/1958 on file ES 1/957.
20. Pilgrim (u/d) on file ES 1/958 (1959).
21. CRO/Canberra tel 41 of 15/1/1959 on file AB 16/2966.
22. Levin/Jackson 19/5/1959 on file ES 1/959.
23. CRO/Canberra tel 671 of 30/7/1959 on file AB 16/2966.
24. The names *Vixen A* and *Vixen B* were adopted in March 1960. Previously, *Vixen A* was simply *Vixen*, and *Vixen B* went under the names *Salt Cellar* and *Hamster*.
25. CRO/Canberra tel 1005 of 29/10/1959 on file ES 1/960.
26. Titterton/Levin 9/8/1960, ES 1/960.
27. CRO/Canberra tel 77 of 2/6/1960 on file ES 1/1450.

12 The Maralinga Range after 1963

1. *Operation Ayres* in February/March 1960, *Operation Ayres 2* in 1962, *Operation Clean-Up* in 1963, and *Operation Hercules*.
2. *The Submission of the Government of the United Kingdom to the Royal Commission into British Nuclear Tests in Australia 1952–64*, September 1985, p. 688.
3. *Submission of the Government of the United Kingdom*, pp. 703–4.
4. *The Report of the Royal Commission into British Nuclear Tests in Australia: Conclusions and Recommendations* (Canberra: Australian Government Publishing Service, 1985).
5. Report by the Maralinga Rehabilitation Technical Advisory Committee (MARTAC), *Rehabilitation of Former Nuclear Test Sites at Emu and Maralinga* (Commonwealth of Australia, 2003), p. 42.
6. MARTAC Report, p. 28.
7. MARTAC Report, p. 45. MARTAC's figures are all metric, and are cited in that form in this chapter. However, as the rest of this book deals in imperial measurements, we have included the latter in brackets.
8. MARTAC Report, p. 27.

9. MARTAC Report, p. 27. See p.18 for a diagram of the plumes and the differing levels on contamination.
10. MARTAC Report, p. 126.
11. See MARTAC Report p. 128 for a description of these difficulties.
12. MARTAC Report, p. 132. See pp. 129–30 for a breakdown of the differing estimates.
13. MARTAC Report, p. 239. This also has a breakdown of the amount of material in individual pits.
14. MARTAC Report, p. 236.
15. MARTAC Report, p. 26.
16. MARTAC Report, p. 28.
17. MARTAC Report, p. 110.
18. MARTAC REPORT, Executive Summary, p. xlviii.
19. MARTAC REPORT, Executive Summary, p. xliii.
20. MARTAC Report, p. 116.
21. MARTAC Report, pp. 179–80.
22. MARTAC Report, p. 45.
23. MARTAC Report, p. 192.
24. MARTAC Report, p. 364.
25. MARTAC Report, p. 120.
26. MARTAC Report, p. 116.
27. MARTAC Report, p. 369.
28. MARTAC Report, p. 376.
29. MARTAC Report, p. 375.
30. MARTAC Report, p. 144.
31. The explosion, or 'transient event' as it is referred to in the MARTAC Report, is discussed in the Report pp. 250–2.
32. MARTAC Report, p. 255.
33. MARTAC Report, p. 271.
34. MARTAC Report, p. xlv.
35. MARTAC Report, p. 135.
36. MARTAC Report, p. 138.
37. MARTAC Report, p. 144.
38. MARTAC Report, pp. 291–5.
39. Transcript of 'Maralinga – The Fallout Continues', Radio National's Background Briefing Program Transcript, 16 April 2000. Available at http://www.abc.net.au/rn/talks/bbing/stories/s120383.htm.
40. See MARTAC Report p. 387 for a breakdown of the Environmental Monitor's assessment.
41. MARTAC Report, p. 388.
42. MARTAC Report, p. 392.

13   Health and Safety and the National Radiological Protection Board Studies

1. Quoted in Lorna Arnold, *Britain and the H-Bomb* (Basingstoke: Palgrave, 2001), p. 240.
2. See information available from the Australian Department of Veterans' Affairs at www.dva.gov.au.

3. C. R. Muirhead *et al.*, *Mortality and Cancer Incidence 1952–1998 in UK Participants in the UK Atmospheric Nuclear Weapons Tests and Experimental Programmes* (Oxford: National Radiological Protection Board, 2003).
4. E. G. Knox, T. Sorahan and A. Stewart, 'Cancer Following Nuclear Weapons Tests', *The Lancet* (9 April 1983), p. 815.
5. J. W. Boang *et al.*, 'Cancer Following Nuclear Weapons Tests', *The Lancet* (9 April 1983), p. 815.
6. E. G. Knox, T. Sorahan and A. M. Stewart, 'Cancer Following Nuclear Weapons Tests', *The Lancet* (8 October 1983), pp. 856–7.
7. S. C. Darby *et al.*, 'A Summary of Mortality and Incidence of Cancer in Men from the United Kingdom who Participated in the United Kingdom's Atmospheric Nuclear Weapon Tests and Experimental Programmes', *British Medical Journal*, Vol. 296 (30 January 1988), pp. 332–8.
8. S. C. Darby *et al.*, 'Further Follow-up of Mortality and Incidence of Cancer in Men from the United Kingdom who Participated in the United Kingdom's Atmospheric Nuclear Weapon Tests and Experimental Programmes', *British Medical Journal*, Vol. 307, No. 6918 (11 December 1993), pp. 1530–6.
9. Sue Rabbitt Roff, 'A Long Time Coming', *New Scientist* (6 February 1999), p. 51.
10. The diseases are:

    * all leukaemias except chronic lymphatic leukaemia;
    * cancers of the thyroid, breast, lung, bone, liver, skin, oesophagus, stomach, colon, pancreas, kidney, urinary bladder, ovaries, salivary gland, rectum;
    * posterior subcapsular cataracts;
    * non-malignant thyroid nodular disease;
    * parathyroid adenoma;
    * tumours of the brain and central nervous system;
    * multiple myeloma;
    * lymphomas other than Hodgkin's disease.

11. Neil Pearce, Ian Prior, David Methven, Christine Culling, Stephen Marshall, Jackie Auld, Gail de Boer and Peter Bethwaite, 'Follow-up of New Zealand Participants in British Atmospheric Nuclear Weapons Tests in the Pacific', *British Medical Journal*, Vol. 300 (5 May 1990), p. 1166.
12. 'Health Outcomes for the Children of Operation *Grapple* Veterans', General Practice Department Working Paper No. 4, General Practice Department, Wellington School of Medicine and Health Sciences, University of Otago.

14   In Retrospect

1. The US test was *Mike*, the first shot in the *Ivy* series at Eniwetok, 31 October 1952. The Soviet test was on 2 August 1953.
2. M. Gowing, *Independence and Deterrence* (London: Macmillan, 1974), Vol. 1, p. 450.
3. J. Simpson, *The Independent Nuclear State* (London: Macmillan, 1984), p. 104.
4. These periods would be 14 and 11 years respectively, if the years of the moratorium (November 1958–September 1961) are excluded.
5. Gowing, *Independence and Deterrence*, Vol. 1, p. 450.

6. The United States Atomic Energy Act 1946 as amended in 1951 and 1954.
7. *Agreement for Cooperation in the Uses of Atomic Energy for Mutual Defence Purposes* (Cmnd 537, London: HMSO, 1958).
8. Cmnd 859.
9. H. Macmillan, *Riding the Storm* (London: Macmillan, 1971), p. 500.
10. Macmillan, *Riding the Storm*, p. 566.
11. *Hurricane* (1952) and *Mosaic* (1956) at *Monte Bello*; *Grapple* and *Grapple X* (1957) and *Grapple Y* and *Z* (1958) at Christmas and Maiden Islands.
12. Wise and Moroney use 'population dose' as a convenient shorthand term for the formal 'collective effective dose equivalent commitment'. Keith N. Wise and John R. Moroney, *Public Health Impact of Fallout from British Nuclear Weapon Tests in Australia 1952–1957* (Australian Radiation Laboratory, unpublished).

Series	Round	Collective dose equivalent (man-sieverts)	Stochastic effects	
			Cancer deaths	Serious hereditary consequences*
Hurricane	1	110	1	1
Totem	1	70	1	1
	2	60	1	1
Mosaic	1	10	<1	<1
	2	52	<1	<1
Buffalo	1	83	1	<1
	2	11	<1	<1
	3	56	<1	<1
	4	101	1	1
Antler	1	3	<1	<1
	2	28	<1	<1
	3	118	1	1
Total		700	7	7

* Expressed in the first two generations

13. H C Deb., Vol. 449, Col. 1658, 1 May 1952.
14. AIRAC 9 (1983).
15. *Ibid.*, p. 64.
16. Russel Ward, *The History of Australia in the Twentieth Century* (London: Heinemann Educational Books, 1978), pp. 319, 372.
17. Ward, *The History of Australia in the Twentieth Century*, pp. 132–3.
18. Ward, *The History of Australia in the Twentieth Century*, pp. 372, 397.
19. In particular from the transcripts of evidence given to the Australian Royal Commission on British Atomic Tests in Australia 1984–85.
20. D = 5 (N-18), where D is the accumulated dose in rem and N is the age in years. This worked out at an average of 5 rems a year over a working lifetime.

The present ICRP occupational limit is 5 rems a year (50 millisieverts) effective dose equivalent; and 50 rems per annum to individual organs other than the eyes, for which it is 15 rems per annum.

21. These figures are taken from SIPRI Year Books 1974–85 and the US publication *Announced Nuclear Tests July 1945 to December 1984* (US Department of Energy).

22. These figures are taken from the 1982 UNSCEAR Report. Atmospheric tests were discontinued by the United Kingdom in 1958, and by the United States and USSR in 1963, but were continued by France until 1974 and by China into the 1980s.

23. Southern hemisphere countries had much less than the world average. See UNSCEAR Report 1958, p. 100 and map 1. Figures for strontium-90 deposits up to 1980 still show the southern hemisphere levels to be one-third of those in the northern hemisphere (UNSCEAR Report, 1980).

24. *Second Report on Hazards to Man of Nuclear and Allied Radiation* (Cmnd 1225, London: HMSO, 1960), pp. 46–50.

25. Edward Pochin, *Nuclear Radiation: Risks and Benefits* (Oxford: Oxford University Press, 1983), p. 173.

26. 'Sir John Cockcroft: Gains from Nuclear Test Ban Treaty', *The Times*, 3 September 1963.

Bibliography

Arnold, Lorna, *Windscale 1957: Anatomy of a Nuclear Accident* (Basingstoke: Palgrave, 1995).

Arnold, Lorna, *Britain and the H-Bomb* (Basingstoke: Palgrave, 2001).

Australian Commonwealth Department of Health, *Health of Atomic Test Personnel* (November 1983).

Barker, Elizabeth, *The British Between the Superpowers 1949–50* (London: Macmillan, 1983).

Bartlett, C. J., *The Long Retreat: A Short History of British Defence Policy 1945–70* (London: Macmillan, 1972).

Baylis, John, *Ambiguity and Deterrence: British Nuclear Strategy 1945–64* (Oxford: Oxford University Press, 1995)

Beadell, Len, *Blast the Bush* (Adelaide: Rigby Ltd, 1967).

Bryant, F. J. *et al.*, 'Strontium-90 in Fallout and in Man in Australia January 1959–June 1960', *Nature*, 27 May 1961.

Butement, W. A. S. *et al.*, 'Radioactive Fallout in Australia from Operation Mosaic', *Australian Journal of Science*, December 1957.

Butement, W. A. S. *et al.*, 'Radioactive Fallout in Australia from Operation Buffalo', *Australian Journal of Science*, October 1958.

Carter, Melvin W. and Moghissi, A. Alan, 'Three Decades of Nuclear Testing'. *Health Physics*, 33, July 1977, pp. 55–71.

Cathcart, Brian, *Test of Greatness: Britain's Struggle for the Bomb* (London: Murray, 1994)

Clarke, Ian, *Nuclear Diplomacy and the Special Relationship: Britain's Deterrent and America* (Oxford: Oxford University Press, 1994).

Cockburn, Stewart and Ellyard, David, *Oliphant* (Adelaide, Brisbane, Perth, Darwin: Axion Books, 1981).

Divine, Robert A., *Blowing on the Wind: The Nuclear Test Ban Debate 1954–1960* (New York: Oxford University Press, 1978).

Driver, Christopher, *The Disarmers: A Study in Protest* (London: Hodder and Stoughton, 1964).

Dwyer, L. J. *et al.*, 'Radioactive Fallout in Australia from Operation Antler', *Australian Journal of Science*, September 1959.

Glasstone, Samuel (ed.), *The Effects of Atomic Weapons* (New York: McGraw-Hill Book Company Inc., 1950).

Gowing, Margaret, *Britain and Atomic Energy 1939–1945* (London: Macmillan, 1964).

Gowing, Margaret, *Independence and Deterrence: Britain and Atomic Energy 1945–1952*, 2 volumes (London: Macmillan, 1974).

Gowing, Margaret, 'Britain, America and the Bomb', in David Dilkes (ed.), *The Retreat from Power* (London: Macmillan, 1981).

Groom, A. J. R., *British Thinking about Nuclear Weapons* (London: Frances Pinter, 1974).

Keam, D. W. *et al.*, 'Experiments on the 'Sticky Paper' Method of Radioactive Fallout Sampling', *Australian Journal of Science*, November 1958.

Lapp, R., *The Voyage of the 'Lucky Dragon'* (London: Penguin, 1958).

McKay, Alwyn, *The Making of the Atomic Age* (Oxford: Oxford University Press, 1954).

Macmillan, Harold, *Tides of Fortune 1945–1955* (London: Macmillan, 1969).

Macmillan, Harold, *Riding the Storm 1956–1959* (London: Macmillan, 1971).

Marston, H. R., 'The Accumulation of Radioactive Iodine in the Thyroids of Grazing Animals Subsequent to Atomic Weapon Tests', *Australian Journal of Biological Science*, Vol. II(3), August 1958.

Menaul, Stewart, *Countdown: Britain's Strategic Nuclear Forces* (London: Robert Hale, 1980).

Moore, Richard, 'British Nuclear Warhead Design: How Much American Help?', *Defence Studies* Vol. 4 (2), 2004.

Pierre, Andrew J., *Nuclear Politics* (Oxford: Oxford University Press, 1972).

Pochin, Edward, *Nuclear Radiation: Risks and Benefits* (Oxford: Oxford University Press, 1983).

Reissiand, J. A. (ed.), *Protocol for a Study of the Health of UK Participants in the UK Atmospheric Nuclear Weapons Tests* (NRPB-R154, National Radiological Protection Board, September 1983).

Reynolds, W., *Australia's Bid for the Atomic Bomb* (Melbourne: Melbourne University Press, 2000).

Rhodes, Richard, *The Making of the Atomic Bomb* (London: Penguin, 1988)

Rhodes, Richard, *Dark Sun: The Making of the H-Bomb* (New York: Simon and Schuster, 1996)

Seaborg, Glen T., *Kennedy, Kruschev and the Test Ban* (Berkeley: University of California Press, 1981).

Sherwin, M. J., *A World Destroyed: The Origins or the Arms Race* (London: Vintage, 1987)

Simpson, John, *The Independent Nuclear State* (London: Macmillan, 1983).

Symonds, J. L., *A History of British Atomic Tests in Australia* (Canberra: Australian Government Publishing Service, 1985).

Symonds, J. L., *British Atomic Tests in Australia – Chronology of Events 1950–1968* (Canberra: AGPS, 1984).

Tame, Adrian and Robotham, F. P. J., *Maralinga – British A-bomb Australian Legacy* (Melbourne: Fontana Books, 1982).

United Nations, *Reports of the United Nations Scientific Committee on Effects of Atomic Radiation* (1959 and 1982 especially).

Ward, Russel, *The History of Australia – The Twentieth Century 1901–1975* (London: Heinemann Educational Books, 1978).

Wise, Keith N. and Moroney, John R., *Public Health Impact of Fallout from British Nuclear Weapons Tests in Australia, 1952–1957* (Australian Radiation Laboratory, unpublished).

York, Herbert, *Race to Oblivion* (New York: Simon and Schuster, 1971).

York, Herbert, *The Advisors* (San Francisco: W. H. Freeman and Company, 1976).

Official sources

Australian Government Publishing Service, *The Report of the Royal Commission into British Nuclear Tests in Australia: Conclusions and Recommendations* (Canberra: Australian Government Publishing Service, 1985).

Australian Ionizing Radiation Advisory Council, *Radiological Safety and Future Land Use at the Maralinga Atomic Weapons Test Range* (AIRAC No 4: Canberra: Australian Government Publishing Service, January 1979).

Australian Ionizing Radiation Advisory Council, *British Nuclear Tests in Australia – a Review of Operational Safety Measures and of Possible After-effects* (AIRAC No 9: Canberra: Australian Government Publishing Service, January 1983).

Australian Ionizing Radiation Advisory Council, *AIRAC Report 1983–84* (AIRAC No 10: Canberra: Australian Publishing Service, 1985).

Australian Radiation Laboratory, *Residual Radioactive Contamination at Maralinga and Emu 1985*, ed. Keith H. Lokan. ARL/TR070, April 1985.

Maralinga Rehabilitation Technical Advisory Committee (MARTAC), *Rehabilitation of Former Nuclear Test Sites at Emu and Maralinga* (Commonwealth of Australia, 2003).

Medical Research Council, *Hazards to Man of Nuclear and Allied Radiations* (Cmnd 9780, London: HMSO, June 1956).

Medical Research Council, *Second Report on Hazards to Man of Nuclear and Allied Radiations* (Cmnd 1225, London: HMSO, December 1960).

Ministry of Defence, *The Submission of the Government of the United Kingdom to the Royal Commission into British Nuclear Tests in Australia 1952–64* (London: HMSO, September 1985).

C. R. Muirhead *et al.*, *Mortality and Cancer Incidence 1952–1998 in UK Participants in the UK Atmospheric Nuclear Weapons Tests and Experimental Programmes* (Oxford: National Radiological Protection Board, 2003).

Index